RECORDS OF THE GRAND HISTORIAN:
HAN DYNASTY II

REVISED EDITION

This edition is published with the aid of the
C.C.K. Foundation for International Scholarly Exchange

NUMBER LXV OF THE RECORDS OF CIVILIZATION:
SOURCES AND STUDIES

RECORDS OF THE GRAND HISTORIAN: HAN DYNASTY II

REVISED EDITION

By Sima Qian

Translated by Burton Watson

A *Renditions* – Columbia University Press Book

Hong Kong New York

Published by
The Research Centre for Translation
The Chinese University of Hong Kong
and
Columbia University Press

This work has been accepted in the Chinese Translations Series of
the United Nations Educational, Scientific and Cultural Organization
(UNESCO)

p 10 9 8 7 6 5 4 3 2 1

CONTENTS

Part III: The Plotters of Revolt

Part IV: The Collective Biographies

Map

HAN DYNASTY

VOLUME II

INTRODUCTION

The chapters of the *Shi ji* translated in this volume deal principally with the reign of Emperor Wu, the period of Sima Qian's own lifetime. The historian is here no longer copying and systematizing the written accounts of ancient China, as he had done in the chapters on pre-Qin history, nor relating the somewhat romanticized tales of the founding and early days of the Han that had been handed down to him. He is writing about "the present emperor", the ruler at whose court he spent his adult life, about the nobles and ministers he knew there, about his friends, and about his enemies.

Sima Qian was in an excellent position to gather material for a history of his age. Undoubtedly he heard the speeches of many of the men he describes, listened to the deliberations of the courtiers, consulted files of official documents kept in the palace, and observed the effects of various government policies when he accompanied the emperor on tours through the provinces. He had personally visited some of the barbarian lands that were being brought under Han rule by Emperor Wu's foreign conquests, and in other cases he no doubt heard from the generals themselves the accounts of their wars and hardships. Even his description of penal conditions under Emperor Wu is based, we may be sure, upon personal experience, since he himself was imprisoned for a time.

Regarding this last it may be well to review here the facts of Sima Qian's melancholy brush with the law. In 108 BC Sima Qian succeeded his father, who had died two years earlier, in the post of grand historian at the court of Emperor Wu. During the years immediately following, he was engaged in revising and correcting the calendar. At the same time he seems to have been busily at work writing his history of China's past, a task which his father had begun and had charged him to complete. In 99 BC, however, his fortunes, like those of so many of the officials he describes, took an unexpected and disastrous turn.

This year a large force of Chinese cavalry and infantry was sent to attack the Xiongnu, one of a long series of expeditions launched by Emperor Wu in an attempt to break the power of these troublesome northern tribes. One of the commanders, Li Ling, won a brilliant initial success against the enemy, news of which was received with rejoicing at the court. Later, however, when reinforcements failed to arrive and his troops had been decimated by a running battle, he was surrounded by the enemy and persuaded to surrender. Emperor Wu expected his unsuccessful generals to die with their men, and when word of Li Ling's capitulation reached him he was sick with rage. The other courtiers united in condemning Li Ling's action, but Sima Qian, who had known Li Ling personally, attempted to speak on his behalf, pointing out the glory which the general had won before he was overwhelmed by superior numbers, and suggesting that he had surrendered only in hopes of finding some opportunity to escape and return to China.

But the emperor was in no mood to listen to palliative arguments and summarily had Sima Qian handed over to the law officials for "investigation". Knowing what was expected of them, they found him guilty of attempting "to deceive the emperor", a crime punishable by death. With a sufficient amount of money Sima Qian might have bought commutation of the sentence, but this he did not possess. No one raised a hand to help him. According to Han custom, a gentleman of honour was expected to commit suicide before allowing himself to be dragged off to prison for investigation — which meant torture until the victim confessed. But Sima Qian declined to take this drastic step because, as he himself states, he hoped at all cost to finish writing his history. In the end he was sentenced to undergo castration, the severest penalty next to death and one which carried with it a peculiar aura of shame. Whether the emperor considered him too learned and valuable a man to execute, or whether Sima Qian himself requested to undergo this disgrace in preference to death and the end of his hopes for literary fame, we do not know.

After his punishment the emperor made him a palace secretary, a position of great honour and trust that could be filled only by a eunuch, since it involved waiting upon the emperor when the latter was at leisure in the women's quarters. At this time Sima Qian seems to have completed his history. We do not know when he died, though it was probably around 90 BC, a few years before the death of his sovereign.[1]

Obviously a man who had suffered such a punishment would have every reason to hate the ruler who inflicted it and to despise his fellow courtiers who had been too timid or callous to come to his aid. For this reason many critics have eyed the sections of the *Shi ji* relating to Emperor Wu and his court with

---

[1] For a more detailed account of the Li Ling affair and Sima Qian's life, see Watson, *Ssu-ma Ch'ien: Grand Historian of China* (New York, Columbia University Press, 1958).

suspicion and have suggested that the historian may have deliberately distorted the facts out of motives of spite and revenge. In the Later Han Emperor Ming (AD 58-75), who did not like Sima Qian's unflattering portrait of his predecessor, accused the historian of "using veiled words to criticize and slander, attacking his own times".[2] From very early times all but the opening paragraph of "The Basic Annals of Emperor Wu" has been missing, either lost or never written. Some writers have asserted that the chapter as Sima Qian wrote it was so derogatory that when it was shown to the emperor he scraped the writing off the tablets.

Unfortunately we have almost no other accounts of Emperor Wu with which to check the fairness of Sima Qian's version. No reports by Sima Qian's contemporaries, if they were ever written, have survived, and posterity must forever view Emperor Wu and his age solely through the eyes of a man whom the emperor, in a fit of petty rage, condemned to the most humiliating punishment conceivable. It is difficult to imagine a more striking and ironical example of the awesome power wielded by historians.

Sima Qian's portrait of Emperor Wu is a complex one: in this respect at least we may be sure that it does justice to its original. The personality of the emperor impresses one first and foremost by its tremendous energy. That the energy was often misdirected, guided by stubbornness and severity, or led astray by blatant charlatanism, we cannot deny. Yet not since the First Emperor of the Qin, whom Emperor Wu at times disturbingly resembles, had China had such a vigorous and strong-willed ruler, nor was it to have another one for many centuries to come. Much that he did was of undeniable benefit to the nation. Abroad he drove back the Xiongnu in the north and brought the Han into contact with the states of Central Asia and the tribes of the southwest, southeast, and Korea. At home he greatly strengthened the authority of the central government, built roads, constructed canals, and controlled the ravages of the Yellow River. He brought to the Han a power and splendour it had never known before, a splendour perhaps most vividly conveyed in the rich and exuberant language of his court poet, Sima Xiangru.

But it was a costly glory. Though Sima Qian never attempts to belittle the military triumphs and material benefits of the emperor's reign, he carefully notes the fearful price of each, in loss of fighting men and animals, in expenditures of

---

[2]*Ibid.*, p. 150.

gold, in labour and hardship to the people. And besides these material losses he notes, more subtly but no less positively, the spiritual losses of the empire — the growing timidity and sycophancy of the court ministers, the increasing harshness of the provincial officials, the callousness of the generals, the wiliness and ugly sophistication that were spreading among the once simple and law-abiding commoners, the slow death of freedom in all areas of life. It is not a pretty picture.

But were things really this bad? Or is this merely the biased view of a disillusioned scholar, steeped in the idealized tales of antiquity and embittered by the experiences of his lifetime? All we can say is that no historian writing in the centuries immediately after Sima Qian's death, when there was still time to correct distortions if they existed, ever attempted to ameliorate this sombre portrayal of the reign of Emperor Wu.

Emperor Ming's assertion that the *Shi ji* is written in "veiled words" introduces another problem. In Han times it was widely believed that Confucius had used "veiled words" in composing the *Spring and Autumn Annals* in order to convey his judgments of contemporary events and persons. And at the end of his account of the Xiongnu, Sima Qian makes a seemingly irrelevant reference to this tradition, by which he evidently wishes to warn the reader that he too is obliged to use such veiled and indirect language when writing about his own times. In view of this we are presumably justified in looking for irony and covert criticism in the pages that follow. But where are we to draw the line? Is no utterance of the historian to be taken at face value? Are even his infrequent praises suspect?

Such are the problems which confront the reader in understanding and assessing Sima Qian's narrative. They are problems which have never been settled, and there is no prospect that they ever will be. If there is irony in Sima Qian's writing, it is in many cases so subtle as to defy positive identification. If there is prejudice, it is not the kind which betrays itself through gross distortion or stoops to caricature. No man can be expected to give a completely unbiased account of his own age. That Sima Qian's description of the era of Emperor Wu, for all its sombreness, never exceeds the bounds of verisimilitude is probably the best indication we have of his integrity as a historian.

Sima Qian begins his history with an account of the ancient sage rulers, the Yellow Emperor, Emperors Yao and Shun, and Emperor Yu, the founder of the Xia dynasty. He traces the rise and decline of the Xia, of its successor, the Shang or Yin dynasty, and of the Zhou whose glories are described so profusely in the

Confucian Classics. He surveys the decay of the Zhou court and the division of the empire into a number of rival feudal states engaged in a protracted struggle for supremacy. He describes the steady rise to power of the state of Qin, the changes brought about by the First Emperor of the Qin, and the sudden collapse of his regime shortly after his death. Finally, in the part of his history translated in these volumes, he relates the story of the founding of the Han and the fortunes of the dynasty under the succeeding rulers.

This is the entire span of Chinese history — indeed of all human history — as Sima Qian knew it. Writing in the cold light of "today" — for him, around 100 BC — reviewing such a past, comparing it with his own time, was he filled with exhilaration, one wonders, or with despair? Did he see human history as a process of evolution, of devolution, or of endlessly repeating cycles? And if as the last, had they any meaning in his eyes?

These questions, like those I have mentioned above, the reader should keep in mind when reading the *Shi ji*, though I cannot guarantee that he will find any answers. Sima Qian is not a philosopher but a historian. Like most Chinese historians, he indulges in a minimum of personal comment, and such scattered opinions as he states cannot be made to conform to any recognizable school of thought. Somewhere behind the vast, sprawling array of facts and anecdotes we sense the personality of the historian, manipulating the figures of his drama, aligning cause and effect as he would like us to see them. But the more we seek to discover and define that personality, the more it eludes us. Like Tacitus, the historian of Western antiquity whom he most resembles, his interests are so broad and his sympathies so complex that it is never possible to say with certainty, "This is the *real* Sima Qian".

Yet, elusive as it may be, the personality of Sima Qian lights up for us the period of human experience known as the early Han. As the Persian Wars live only through Herodotus, the Peloponnesian War through Thucydides, so the early Han, and more especially the era of Emperor Wu, is illumined almost entirely through the writing of this one man. Had he not lived there would probably be only darkness there.

SHI JI 28: THE TREATISE ON THE FENG AND SHAN SACRIFICES[1]

Among those who have received the mandate of Heaven and become rulers, few have been blessed with the auspicious omens telling them that they are worthy to perform the Feng and Shan sacrifices. When these are carried out, there is none among the countless spirits who does not enjoy pure offerings. Thus I have traced the origins of the religious rites appropriate to the various gods, the famous mountains, and the great rivers, and made "The Treatise on the Feng and Shan Sacrifices".

Among the emperors and kings who from ancient times have received the mandate of Heaven to rule, why are there some who did not perform the Feng and Shan sacrifices? For all who were blessed with the heavenly omens signifying their worthiness to perform these rites hastened without fail to Mt. Tai to carry them out, and even some who had not received such signs took it upon themselves to perform them. Yet others, though they enjoyed the mandate to rule, felt that their merit was not yet sufficient; or, though their merit was sufficient, they felt that their virtue had not been fully manifested to all creatures; or again, though their virtue had been fully manifested, they felt that they could not spare the time to carry them out. This is the reason that these rites have seldom been performed!

One of the ancient books says, "If for three years rites are not performed, they will fall into disuse. If for three years music is not played, it will become lost."[2] When each dynasty attains the height of its glory, then the Feng and Shan

---

[1] The Feng and Shan were sacrifices of the greatest solemnity, performed by the emperor at Mt. Tai and addressed to Heaven and Earth respectively. Though apparently of fairly late origin, the Han scholars maintained that they had been performed by all the great sage rulers of antiquity. The present chapter has traditionally been interpreted as a veiled attack by Sima Qian upon Emperor Wu, the first Han ruler to decide that he was worthy to perform these rites.

[2] The quotation is now found in *Analects* XVII, 21, though Sima Qian is perhaps quoting from some lost work on ritual.

are celebrated, but when it reaches a period of decline, they are no longer performed. Thus the performances of these have at times been separated by periods of as many as a thousand or more years, and at the least by several hundred years. This is the reason that the details of the ancient ceremony have been completely lost, and it is now impossible to discover with any exactitude just how it was carried out.

In the *Book of Documents* we read:

> Emperor Shun, holding the jewelled astronomical instruments, checked the movements of the Seven Ruling Bodies.[3] Then he performed a special sacrifice to the Lord on High, made pure offerings to the Six Honoured Ones,[4] sacrificed from afar to the mountains and rivers, and performed his obeisance to all the various spirits. Gathering together the jade tokens of enfeoffment from the five ranks of feudal lords, he selected an auspicious month and day and held audience with the barons of the four directions and the governors of the various provinces, at which time he returned the jade tokens. In the second month of the year he journeyed east on a tour of inspection and made a visit to Daizong. (Daizong is Mt. Tai.) There he made a burnt offering to Heaven and sacrificed from afar to the various mountains and rivers in succession. After that he met with the princes of the east. (The princes of the east are the feudal lords.) He harmonized the seasons and months, corrected the days of the week, and standardized the pitch pipes and the measures of length, capacity, and weight. He attended to the five rites and the five kinds of jewels and received the three kinds of silk, the two living offerings, and the one dead one.[5] In the fifth month he journeyed south on a tour of inspection and made a visit to the Southern Peak. (The Southern Peak is Mt. Heng.) In the eighth

---

[3] The sun, the moon, and the planets Jupiter, Mars, Saturn, Venus, and Mercury. The passage is quoted from the first section of the *Book of Documents*, the Canon of Yao and Shun. The phrases in parentheses are Sima Qian's own glosses on the text. He quotes the passage here no doubt to show that even in the most ancient of the Confucian Classics there is no detailed account of the Feng and Shan sacrifices.

[4] The seasons, cold and heat, the sun, the moon, the stars, and drought.

[5] The five rites are the rites appropriate to each of the five feudal ranks; the five jewels are the jewelled tokens of enfeoffment for each rank. The two live offerings are lambs, presented by the high ministers, and wild geese, presented by the lesser officials. The one dead offering is pheasants, presented by the *shi*, or lesser nobility.

month he journeyed west on a tour of inspection and made a visit to the Western Peak. (The Western Peak is Mt. Hua.) In the eleventh month he journeyed north on a tour of inspection and made a visit to the Northern Peak. (The Northern Peak is Mt. Hengg.)[6] At all of these, he performed the same rites that he had at Daizong. (The Central Peak is Mt. Songgao.) Once every five years he made these inspection journeys.

Emperor Yu, the founder of the Xia dynasty, who succeeded Emperor Shun, followed this same procedure. Later, however, the fourteenth ruler of the dynasty, Emperor Kongjia, who practised evil ways and was too fond of supernatural affairs, committed sacrilege before the spirits, and the two dragons, sent to his court from Heaven, took their departure.[7]

Three generations later, Tang, the founder of the Shang dynasty, attacked and overthrew Jie, the last ruler of the Xia. Tang's followers wished to move the altars of the Xia rulers to their own territory, but Tang made the "Altars of Xia", a declaration proclaiming to them the reasons why this was impossible.[8] Eight generations after Tang, when Emperor Taiwu came to the throne of the Shang dynasty, a mulberry and a paper mulberry sprang up together in the court of his palace and in the space of one night grew so large that a person could not reach around them with his arms. The emperor was frightened, but his minister Yi Zhi said, "Evil omens cannot prevail over virtue!" Then Emperor Taiwu strove for greater virtue in his rule and the two mulberries died. Yi Zhi praised the emperor to the shaman Xian. It was at this time that the shaman Xian came to power.

Fourteen generations later, Emperor Wuding succeeded in obtaining Fu Yue as his minister and the Shang dynasty was once more restored to glory. In recognition of this Emperor Wuding was given the posthumous title of Great Patriarch. Once a pheasant came and climbed up on the ear of the emperor's

---

[6]Though the two characters are pronounced alike in modern Chinese, this Mt. Heng is written with an entirely different character from the southern Mt. Heng above. To distinguish them I have written the second "Heng" with two *g*'s.

[7]According to the version of the legend in *Shi ji* 2, "The Basic Annals of the Xia Dynasty", Heaven sent a pair of dragons to the court of Emperor Kongjia, but the emperor, not knowing how to feed them, turned them over to one of his barons to take care of. When the female of the pair died, the dragon keeper gave the emperor its flesh to eat. But here Sima Qian seems to have some other version of the tale in mind.

[8]Said to have been a section of the *Book of Documents*, now lost.

sacrificial cauldron and crowed. Wuding was afraid, but his minister Zu Ji said, "Only strive for virtue!" Wuding, by following this advice, was able to occupy his throne during a long and peaceful reign.

Five generations later, Emperor Wuyi defied the spirits and as a result he was killed by thunder. Three generations later, Emperor Zhou gave himself up to licentiousness and evil, until King Wu of the Zhou dynasty attacked and overthrew him.

From this we may see that the rulers at the beginning of each new dynasty never failed to conduct themselves with awe and reverence, but that their descendants little by little sank into indolence and vain pride.

The *Offices of Zhou* says:[9] "At the winter solstice a sacrifice shall be made to Heaven in the southern suburbs in order to greet the arrival of lengthening days. At the summer solstice a sacrifice shall be made to the Earth God. At both ceremonies music and dances shall be performed. Thus one may pay respect to the spirits."

The Son of Heaven sacrifices to all the famous mountains and great rivers of the empire. He regards the Five Peaks as his high ministers and the four great watercourses as his feudal lords. The feudal lords sacrifice only to the famous mountains and great rivers that are within their respective domains. The four watercourses are the Yangtze, the Yellow River, the Huai, and the Ji. The halls of state of the Son of Heaven are called the Bright Hall and the Water-encircled Hall. Those of the feudal lords are called Proclamation Palaces.

After the duke of Zhou became minister to King Cheng, the third ruler of the Zhou dynasty, he sacrificed to his distant ancestor Hou Ji, the Lord of Grain, in the southern suburb, treating him as the equal of Heaven; and in the Bright Hall he sacrificed to the founder of the dynasty, his father King Wen, treating him as the equal of the Lord on High. From the time of Emperor Yu on, there had always been sacrifices performed to the altars of the soil and, since Hou Ji taught the people how to grow grain, there were also offerings made to him. Thus the sacrifices to Hou Ji in the southern suburb and the sacrifices to the altars of the soil date from very ancient times.

The Zhou kings overthrew the Shang and founded a new dynasty but, during the fourteen generations of rulers which followed, the power of the Zhou gradually waned, its rites and music fell into disuse, and the feudal lords

---

[9] Also known as *The Rites of Zhou*. But the present text of this work does not contain any passage exactly like this. Perhaps Sima Qian is summarizing rather than quoting.

conducted themselves in any way they pleased. Finally, after King You of the Zhou had been defeated by the Dog Rong barbarians, the dynasty moved its capital east to the city of Luo (yang). Duke Xiang of the state of Qin came to the rescue of the Zhou by attacking the barbarians and for the first time a ruler of Qin was made a feudal lord of the Zhou dynasty on an equal footing with the lords of the other states (771 BC).

After Duke Xiang of Qin had become a feudal lord, since his domain was on the western border of the empire, he adopted the spirit of Shaogao as his patron deity and set up the so-called Altar of the West where he offered sacrifices to the White Emperor.[10] For sacrifices he used a red colt with a black mane, a yellow ox, and a ram.

Sixteen years later, when Duke Wen of Qin went east to hunt between the Qian and Wei rivers, he consulted his diviners to find out whether he should make his home in the region and was given a favourable answer. Duke Wen dreamed that he saw a yellow serpent dangling down from heaven and touching the ground, and its mouth came to rest in the Vale of Fu. When he consulted the historian Dun about his dream, Dun replied, "This is a sign from the Lord on High. You should offer sacrifices here!" The duke thereupon constructed the Altar of Fu where he conducted the suburban sacrifice to the White Emperor, using the three animals mentioned above. (Before the Altar of Fu had been constructed, there already existed in the region of Yong a Wu Altar on the southern side of Mt. Wu and a Hao Altar east of Yong, but both had fallen into disuse and no sacrifices were offered there. Some people claimed that, because the province of Yong occupied a region of highlands and provided a suitable place for spiritual beings to make their home, these altars had from ancient times been established there and suburban sacrifices offered to the Lord on High. Thus the places of worship of all the spirits came to be concentrated in this area. Such sacrifices had been conducted in the time of the Yellow Emperor, people claimed, and therefore, although it was now the declining years of the Zhou dynasty, there was no reason why suburban sacrifices should not be carried out in the same places. No evidence for these assertions could be found in the

---

[10]Shaogao was one of the mythical rulers of antiquity and was regarded as the guardian deity of the White Emperor, the god of the west. Eventually five of these heavenly emperors were recognized: the Green Emperor of the east, the Red Emperor of the south, the White Emperor of the west, the Black Emperor of the north and the Yellow Emperor of the centre, associated with the elements wood, fire, metal, water, and earth respectively.

classical texts, however, and for this reason men of learning refused to lend them any credence.)

Nine years after the construction of the Altar of Fu, Duke Wen came into possession of some stone-like objects which he placed in a shrine on the northern slopes of Chencang and sacrificed to. The spirits of the objects sometimes would not appear for a whole year, while at other times they would come several times in the year. They always appeared at night, shedding a brilliant light like shooting stars, coming from the southeast, and gathering on the wall of the shrine. They looked like roosters and made a screeching sound so that the fowl in the fields about began to crow in answer, although it was the middle of the night. Duke Wen made an offering of one set of sacrificial animals[11] and called the objects "The Treasures of Chen".

Seventy-eight years after the construction of the Altar of Fu, Duke De came to the throne of Qin. Consulting the arts of divination as to whether he should go to live in the region of Yong, he was told that "in ages to come your sons and grandsons shall water their horses in the Yellow River".[12] He therefore transferred his capital to Yong, and the various places of worship in Yong began from this time to prosper. He offered 300 sets[13] of sacrificial animals at the Altar of Fu, instituted sacrifices to quell baneful influences, and had dogs sacrificed at the four gates of the capital to prevent the entrance of evil and disaster. Duke De died two years after he came to the throne. Six years later Duke Xuan of Qin set up the Mi Altar south of the Wei River, where he sacrificed to the Green Emperor.

Fourteen years later Duke Mu came to the throne of Qin. Falling ill one time, he lay unconscious for five days, and when he awoke he reported that he had seen the Lord on High in a dream. The Lord on High had ordered him to pacify the revolt in the state of Jin. The historians at his court made a record of the event and stored it away in the treasury. Thus later ages all say, "Duke Mu of Qin ascended to Heaven".

Nine years after Duke Mu came to the throne of Qin, Duke Huan of Qi made himself leader of the feudal states and summoned all the lords to a

---

[11] A set of sacrificial animals consisted of an ox, a sheep, and a pig.

[12] Yong was the region west of the Yellow River which became the site of the Qin dynasty capital, Xianyang, and later of the Han capital, Chang'an.

[13] Three hundred sets is a prodigious number of sacrificial animals and some commentators would amend the text to read "three sets of white animals [the characters for 'white' and 'hundred' are similar]," since the Altar of Fu was dedicated to the White Emperor.

conference at Sunflower Hill. At this time he proposed to carry out the Feng and Shan sacrifices, but his minister Guan Zhong said: "It is related that in the past the rulers of seventy-two houses performed the Feng sacrifice at Mt. Tai and the Shan sacrifice at Liangfu, though I can find the names of only twelve of these in the records. In the most ancient times, Wu Huai performed the Feng at Mt. Tai and the Shan at Yunyun, and the same was done by Fu Xi, Shen Nong, and the Fire Emperor. The Yellow Emperor performed the Feng at Mt. Tai and the Shan at Tingting. Emperors Zhuan Xu, Ku, Yao, and Shun all performed the Feng at Mt. Tai and the Shan at Yunyun, while Emperor Yu, the founder of the Xia, performed the Feng at Mt. Tai and the Shan at Kuaiji. Tang, the founder of the Shang, performed the Feng at Mt. Tai and the Shan at Yunyun, while King Cheng, the ruler of the Zhou, performed the Feng at Mt. Tai and the Shan at Sheshou. All of these had first to receive the mandate of Heaven to rule before they could perform these sacrifices."

Duke Huan replied, "I have marched north to attack the mountain barbarians, past the land of Guzhu. In the west I have attacked the Great Xia, crossing the drifting sands and, binding tight my horses and strapping together the carriages, have ascended Bi'er Mountain. In the south I have invaded as far as Shaoling, and climbed the Bear's Ear Mountain to gaze out over the Yangtze and the Han rivers. Three times I have met with the other lords in war conferences and six times I have met with them in times of peace. Nine times I have called together the other feudal lords to order the affairs of the empire. None of the others lords dares to disobey me. How then am I different from the rulers of the Three Dynasties of antiquity with their mandates of Heaven?"

Guan Zhong saw that he could not dissuade Duke Huan from his intentions by such arguments and so he brought forward the following stipulations: "In ancient times when the Feng and Shan were performed, millet from Huoshang and grain from Beili were used as offerings. A certain kind of reed which grows between the Huai and Yangtze rivers and has three ridges was used to spread the grain offerings on. Fish were brought from the eastern sea having two eyes on one side of their heads, and pairs of birds from the western sea whose wings were grown together. In addition there were fifteen kinds of strange creatures which appeared of their own accord without being summoned. Now the phoenix and the unicorn have not come to our court and the auspicious grain does not spring up, but instead only weeds and brambles, tares and darnel, while kites and owls appear in swarms. Is it not unthinkable at such a time to attempt to perform the Feng and Shan sacrifices?" With this Duke Huan abandoned his proposal.

This same year Duke Mu of Qin sent his soldiers to escort Prince Yiwu of Jin, who was in exile, back to his state and set him up as duke of Jin. By his support Duke Mu thus made it possible for Prince Yiwu, who became Duke Hui of Jin, as well as the two succeeding rulers, Duke Huai and Duke Wen, to secure the throne of Jin. In this way he brought an end to the internal troubles in the state of Jin. Duke Mu of Qin died in the thirty-ninth year of his rule.

Some hundred years later, when Confucius was teaching and transmitting the Six Classics, he is reported to have said something to the effect that there had been over seventy rulers in the past who, on assuming new surnames and becoming kings, had performed the Feng at Mt. Tai and the Shan at Liangfu. He added, however, that the details of the rituals which they followed were far from clear and that it was impossible to say much about them. When someone asked him the meaning of the Great Sacrifice to the ancestors of the ruler, Confucius replied, "I do not know. If anyone knew the meaning of the Great Sacrifice, he would find it as easy to govern the empire as to look at the palm of his hand!"[14]

While Emperor Zhou, the last ruler of the Shang dynasty, still occupied the throne, King Wen received the mandate of Heaven to found a new dynasty, but his rule did not extend as far as Mt. Tai. His son, King Wu, finally overthrew the Shang dynasty, but passed away two years later before the empire had been brought to peace. It was his son "King Cheng who first manifested the virtue of the house of Zhou to the world."[15] King Cheng was therefore quite correct in performing the Feng and Shan sacrifices. Later, when the ministerial families of the feudal states came to exercise the power of government in place of their lords, however, the Ji family of the state of Lu sacrificed to Mt. Tai; such impertinence was severely condemned by Confucius.

At about the same time as Confucius there lived a certain Chang Hong who served King Ling of the Zhou dynasty with his magical arts. By this time none of the feudal lords troubled to journey to the Zhou court to pay their respects and the power of the Zhou had waned sadly. Chang Hong therefore lectured the king on matters pertaining to the spirits and persuaded him to hang up the head of a wildcat and use it as a target for archery. The wildcat's head symbolized

---

[14] The quotation is from *Analects* III, II.

[15] The passage in quotation marks differs in style from the rest of the narrative and appears to be a quotation. The words "the *Book of Odes* says," which appear erroneously in the text shortly before this, perhaps belong here.

the fact that the feudal lords did not come to court, and Chang Hong thus hoped by the use of this strange object to induce the lords to appear.[16] The lords, however, were not persuaded by this device, and later the men of Jin captured Chang Hong and murdered him. Chang Hong was the first among the men of Zhou to expound the use of such magical arts.

Some hundred years later Duke Ling of Qin constructed on the southern side of Mt. Wu an Upper Altar, where he sacrificed to the Yellow Emperor, and a Lower Altar, where he sacrificed to the Fire Emperor. Forty-eight years later Dan, the grand historian of the Zhou court, while visiting Duke Xian of Qin, made the statement: "Qin was originally joined with Zhou, but later they separated. After 500 years, however, they shall be joined again, and seventeen years after they are joined, a dictator king shall come forth!"[17]

A rain of metal fell at Yueyang, and Duke Xian of Qin, deciding that this was an auspicious sign of the power of the element metal, set up the Garden Altar at Yueyang, where he offered sacrifices to the White Emperor.

One hundred and twenty years later the state of Qin wiped out the Zhou dynasty and the nine sacred cauldrons of the Zhou were carried off to Qin. Some people, however, claim that the cauldrons were sunk in the Si River where it flows past the city of Pengcheng and that this took place at the time of the destruction of the Song state's altars of the soil at Big Hill, 115 years before the time when Qin conquered the empire.

After the First Emperor of the Qin had united the world and proclaimed himself emperor, someone advised him, saying, "The Yellow Emperor ruled by the power of the element earth, and therefore a yellow dragon and a great earthworm appeared in his time. The Xia dynasty ruled by the power of wood, and so a green dragon came to rest in its court and the grasses and trees grew luxuriantly. The Shang dynasty ruled by metal, and silver flowed out of the mountains. The Zhou ruled by fire, and therefore it was given a sign in the form of a red bird. Now the Qin has replaced the Zhou, and the era of the power of water has come. In ancient times when Duke Wen of Qin went out hunting, he captured a black dragon. This is an auspicious omen indicating the power of the element water." For this reason the First Emperor of the Qin changed the name

---

[16] Commentators disagree as to just why the wildcat's head had this symbolic meaning; some claim it is because another name for the wildcat is *bulai*, literally "not-come". In any event there was some kind of sympathetic magic involved in the use of the wildcat's head.

[17] Interpretations of this prophecy vary, but it is obviously intended to refer to the First Emperor of the Qin dynasty.

of the Yellow River to "Powerful Water". He began his year with the tenth month, honoured the colour black, and used the number six, the number of the element water, as a standard for all his measurements. Among the musical tubes he selected *Dalü* for the greatest honour, and in all his government affairs he put laws before everything else.[18]

Three years after he assumed the imperial title the First Emperor made a tour of the eastern provinces and districts. He performed a sacrifice at Mt. Yi in Zou and there set up a stone marker lauding the achievements of the Qin. He then summoned seventy Confucian masters and scholars from Qi and Lu to meet with him at the foot of Mt. Tai, where the scholars began to debate the proper procedure for carrying out the Feng and Shan sacrifices. "In ancient times when the Feng and Shan were performed," said some of them, "the wheels of the carriages were wrapped in rushes so as not to do any injury to the earth and grass of the mountain. The ground was swept clean and sacrifices performed, using rushes and peeled stalks of grain for mats. The ceremony, it is said, was very easy to carry out." But as the First Emperor listened to the debates of the scholars, he found that each of them expressed a different opinion and their recommendations were difficult to carry out, and with this he dismissed the whole lot.

Eventually he had a carriage road opened up, ascending from the southern foot of the mountain to the summit, where he set up a stone marker praising his own virtue as First Emperor of the Qin. This he did to make clear to all that he had succeeded in performing the Feng sacrifice. From the summit he descended by a road leading down the northern slope and carried out the Shan sacrifice at Liangfu. In both of these ceremonies he followed on the whole the procedure used by the master of invocations in sacrificing to the Lord on High at Yong, but the directions for the ritual were sealed and stored away, being kept strictly secret, so that none of the men of the time were able to record any description of the ceremonies.

When the First Emperor was ascending Mt. Tai he encountered a violent wind and rain storm halfway up the slope and had to stop for a while under a large tree. The Confucian scholars, who had been dismissed and were not allowed to take part in the ritual of the Feng sacrifice, hearing of the emperor's

---

[18]Supposedly because water is associated with the dark power, *yin,* the force of punishment and death, though actually it was because he was a follower of the Legalist philosophy of government.

TRANSLATOR'S NOTE

As I have said, no text exists for "The Basic Annals of Emperor Wu". Most likely Sima Qian never wrote the chapter but merely prepared the summary and first paragraph (translated in Volume I), and laid the work aside while he waited to see how the reign of Emperor Wu would turn out. The tale that Emperor Wu read the chapter and angrily destroyed it seems very dubious. As Sima Qian drew nearer to his own time in his narrative, he tended to use the Basic Annals section of his history for mere summaries of the official acts of the emperors, quoting at length from memorials and imperial edicts. Emperor Wu could hardly have objected to such material. Moreover, it was always Sima Qian's practice to present the most favourable picture of a person in the chapter devoted to that person, revealing the man's less pleasant aspects in other chapters. This is the way, for example, that he treats Emperor Wen in the chapters translated in Volume I. If he actually wrote a "Basic Annals of Emperor Wu", therefore, it is unlikely that it contained anything as derogatory to the emperor's reputation as the information found in the chapters which follow and which have survived without damage.

The first large section of the *Shi ji*, the "Basic Annals", is therefore not represented in this volume.[1] The reader must construct the biography of Emperor Wu for himself from the information contained in other chapters.

The second section, the "Chronological Tables", is represented by the brief introduction to Chapter 20, "The Chronological Table of Marquises Enfeoffed from the *Jianyuan* Era on". The last two chronological tables, Chapters 21 and 22, have only the tersest headings and have therefore not been included.

Of the third section, the "Treatises", I have presented here the last three chapters. The other five treatises, dealing with rites, music, the pitch pipes, the calendar, and astronomy, are either in fragmentary condition or too specialized for inclusion here.

---

[1] For a complete list of the chapters translated and where they are to be found, see the Finding List of Chapters Translated in Volumes I and II at the end of this volume.

Of the fourth section, the "Hereditary Houses", those chapters dealing with Han times, namely, Chapters 48 to 59, have been translated in Volume I. Chapter 60, "The Hereditary Houses of the Three Kings", contains no narrative, but simply the texts of memorials and edicts dealing with the enfeoffment of three of Emperor Wu's sons. Apparently Sima Qian never got around to working up the material into biographical form, and the chapter has accordingly been omitted.

The last and longest section of the *Shi ji*, comprising Chapters 61 to 130, consists of biographies of famous men and accounts of foreign peoples. In Volume I, I have translated or summarized all those dealing with the early Han, namely Chapter 84, Chapter 89 to 104, and Chapter 106. Chapter 105, the biographies of famous doctors, contains a great deal of specialized information on early Chinese medical lore. Unfortunately, it would require an expert in such matters to interpret and translate it adequately, and I have therefore omitted this chapter.

Volume II therefore begins with Chapter 107 and continues to the end with the following omissions. Chapter 126, "The Biographies of Wits and Humourists", deals with courtiers who were famous for their witty reprimands and retorts. Regrettably, they all belong to pre-Qin or Qin times and hence fall outside the scope of this translation. Chapter 128, "On Divination by the Tortoise Shell and Milfoil Stalks", is a fragment of doubtful authenticity and did not seem to merit inclusion. Chapter 130, "The Postface of the Grand Historian", containing the biographies of Sima Qian and his father, has already been translated in my study, *Ssu-ma Ch'ien: Grand Historian of China*. I have rearranged the order of the chapters slightly to facilitate reading.

In preparing the material in this part I have been aided by a new Japanese translation of the *Shi ji* by Noguchi Sadao and others, entitled *Shiki*, in the Chûgoku koten bungaku zenshû series (Tokyo: Heibonsha, 1958-59); and by *Food and Money in Ancient China*, by Nancy Lee Swann (Princeton: Princeton University Press, 1950), as well as by the works listed in the textual note in Volume I.

PART I

HEAVEN, EARTH, AND MAN

encounter with the storm, promptly used it as a basis to speak ill of him.

The First Emperor then proceeded east on his journey as far as the borders of the sea, stopping along the way to perform rituals and sacrifices to the various famous mountains and great rivers and to the Eight Spirits, and searching for immortal spirits such as Xianmen and his companions.

The Eight Spirits appear to have existed from ancient times. Some people say that their worship was begun at the time of the Grand Duke, the first lord of the state of Qi at the beginning of the Zhou dynasty.[19] But since the sacrifices were later discontinued, no one knows exactly when they originated.

Of the Eight Spirits, the first was called the Lord of Heaven; sacrifices to him were offered at the Navel of Heaven. The Navel of Heaven, or *Tianqi*, is the name of a spring situated at the foot of a mountain in the southern suburbs of the city of Linzi. It is said that the state of Qi takes its name from this place.

The second was called Lord of the Land and was sacrificed to at Liangfu near Mt. Tai. It appears that since Heaven loves the *yin*, the principle of darkness, it must be worshipped at the foot of a high mountain or on top of a small hill, at a place called an "Altar"; while because Earth honours the *yang*, the principle of light, the sacrifices to it must always be conducted on a round hill in the midst of a lowland.[20]

The third spirit was called Lord of Arms and was worshipped by offering sacrifices to Chi You.[21] The grave of Chi You is situated in the Lujian district in the province of Dongping, on the western border of the state of Qi.

The fourth was called Lord of the *Yin* and was worshipped at Three Mountains. The fifth was called Lord of the *Yang* and was worshipped at Zhifu. The sixth was called Lord of the Moon and was worshipped at Mt. Lai. All these places mentioned above are in the northern part of Qi along the Gulf of Bohai.

The seventh spirit was called Lord of the Sun and was worshipped at Mt. Cheng. Mt. Cheng juts out into the ocean like the handle of a dipper and is situated in the farthest corner of northeastern Qi. The sacrifices were thus held here in order to greet the sun as it rose from the sea. The eighth was called Lord of the Four Seasons and was worshipped at Langya. Langya is in the eastern part of Qi. It is said that at the beginning of each year sacrifices were offered at

---

[19] The sentence which follows this in the original belongs a little farther on in the text.

[20] That is, Heaven, representing the *yang,* the principle of light, fire, the male, loves its opposite, the *yin,* the principle of darkness, water, the female; while Earth, like a good wife, "honours" its opposite, the *yang.*

[21] A legendary warrior of antiquity.

all of these places consisting of one set of sacrificial animals, though the jade and silk offerings presented by the shamans and invocators who directed the ceremonies were of various kinds and number.

From the time of Kings Wei and Xuan of Qi, the disciples of the philosopher Zou Yan were very active in propounding their master's theory of the succession of the five elements. When the ruler of Qin took the title of emperor, the men of Qi accordingly explained to him this theory, and hence it was that the First Emperor selected water as the patron element of his reign.

Song Wuji, Zhengbo Qiao, Chong Shang, Xianmen Gao, and Zui Hou were all men of Yan who practised magic and followed the way of the immortals, discarding their mortal forms and changing into spiritual beings by means of supernatural aid. Zou Yan won fame among the feudal lords for his theories of the *yin* and *yang* and the succession of the five elements, but the magicians who lived along the seacoast of Qi and Yan, though they claimed to transmit his teachings, were unable to understand them. Thus from this time there appeared a host of men, too numerous to mention, who expounded all sorts of weird and fantastic theories and went to any lengths to flatter the rulers of the day and to ingratiate themselves with them.

From the age of Kings Wei and Xuan of Qi and King Zhao of Yan, men were sent from time to time to set out to sea and search for the islands of Penglai, Fangzhang, and Yingzhou. These were three spirit mountains which were supposed to exist in the Gulf of Bohai. They were not very far from the land of men, it was said, but the difficulty was that, whenever a boat was about to touch their shores, a wind would always spring up and drive it away. In the past, people said, there had been men who succeeded in reaching them, and found them peopled by fairy spirits who possessed the elixir of immortality. All the plants and birds and animals of the islands were white, and the palaces and gates were made of gold and silver. Seen from afar, the three spirit mountains looked like clouds but, as one drew closer, they seemed instead to be down under the water. In any event, as soon as anyone got near to them, the wind would suddenly come and drag the boat away, so that in the end no one could ever reach them.

The rulers of the time were all roused to envy by such tales, and when the First Emperor of the Qin united the empire under his sway and journeyed to the sea, a countless throng of magicians appeared to tell him of these wonders. The First Emperor decided that, even though he were to set out in person on the sea, he would most likely be unable to reach the islands, and so he ordered his men to gather together a number of youths and maidens and send them to sea to search in his stead. The sea was soon full of boats, crisscrossing this way and that, and when the parties returned without success they all used the wind as an excuse. "We were unable to reach the islands," they reported, "but we could see them in the distance!"

The following year the First Emperor again journeyed to the sea, going as far as Langya; then, passing by Mt. Hengg, he returned to the capital by way of Shangdang. Three years later he made a trip to Jieshi on the coast, at which time he cross-examined the magicians who were supposed to have gone to sea to look for the islands. He returned to the capital by way of Shang Province.

Five years after this he made a trip south to Mt. Xiang and from there went to climb Mt. Kuaiji. He followed along the sea coast on his way back, hoping to acquire some of the wonderful medicine of immortality brought from the three spirit mountains in the sea. But his hopes were in vain. When he had gone as far as Sandy Hill, he passed away.

The Second Emperor of the Qin made a tour east to Jieshi in the first year of his reign (209 BC) and from there followed the sea coast south past Mt. Tai as far as Kuaiji. At all these places he performed ceremonies and sacrifices, and had new inscriptions carved on the sides of the stones set up by his father, the First Emperor, in which he lauded his father's glorious achievements. This same autumn the feudal lords rose in revolt against the Qin, and in his third year the Second Emperor was assassinated. Thus the Qin dynasty fell just twelve years after the First Emperor performed the Feng and Shan sacrifices. The Confucian scholars loathed the Qin for having burned the *Book of Odes* and the *Book of Documents* and mercilessly put to death the scholars who expounded them, while the common people hated its harsh laws, so that the whole world rose up in rebellion. At this time everyone began to speak ill of the Qin, saying, "When the First Emperor ascended Mt. Tai, he was attacked by violent wind and rain and thus was never really able to carry out the Feng and Shan sacrifices!" This is an example, is it not, of a ruler who, though he did not possess the virtue necessary to perform the sacrifices, yet proceeded to carry them out?

The rulers of the Three Dynasties of antiquity all resided in the region between the Luo and Yellow rivers. Thus Mt. Song, which was nearby, was called the Central Peak, while the other four peaks of North, South, East, and West were situated in those directions respectively. The four watercourses were all east of the mountains. When the Qin ruler assumed the title of emperor and fixed his capital at Xianyang, however, it meant that all the five peaks and the four watercourses were east of the capital.

From the time of the ancient Five Emperors down to the Qin dynasty, periods of strong central government alternated with periods of decay, and the famous mountains and great rivers were sometimes in the possession of the feudal lords and sometimes in the possession of the Son of Heaven. The rituals employed in the worship of these places, therefore, were often changed and varied from age to age. It is consequently impossible to give a detailed description of them all here.

When the First Emperor united the world, he instructed the officials in charge of sacrifices to put into order the worship of Heaven and Earth, the famous mountains, the great rivers, and the other spirits that had customarily been honoured in the past. According to this new arrangement, there were five mountains and two rivers east of Yao designated for sacrifice. The mountains were the Great Hall (that is, Mt. Song), Mt. Hengg, Mt. Tai, Kuaiji, and Mt. Xiang. The two rivers were the Ji and the Huai. In the spring offerings of dried meat and wine were made to insure the fruitfulness of the year, and at the same time prayers were offered for the melting of the ice. In the autumn prayers were made for the freezing of the ice, and in the winter prayers and sacrifices were offered to recompense the gods for their favour during the year. A cow and a calf were invariably used as sacrifices, but the sacrificial implements and the offerings of jade and silk differed with the time and place.

From Mt. Hua west, seven mountains and four rivers were designated. The former were Mt. Hua, Mt. Bo (that is, Mt. Shuai), Mt. Yue, Mt. Qi, Wu Peak, Crane Mound, and Mt. Du (that is, Mt. Wen in Shu). The rivers were the Yellow River, which was worshipped at Linjin; the Mian, worshipped at Hanzhong; the Jiao Deep, worshipped at Chaona; and the Yangtze, worshipped at Shu. Sacrifices were offered in the spring and autumn for the thawing and freezing of the rivers, and in winter prayers of recompense the same as those for the mountains and rivers of the east were made; a cow and calf were used as sacrifices, but the implements and other offerings all differed. In addition the four great peaks of Crane Mound, Qi, Wu, and Yue all received offerings of new grain. The Treasures of Chen were worshipped at the season when they appeared. The Yellow River was given an additional offering of thick wine. All of these, being in the region of Yong near the capital of the emperor, were also given an offering of a carriage and four red horses with black manes.

The Ba, Chan, Changshui, Feng, Lao, Jing, and Wei are all small rivers but, since they are in the vicinity of Xianyang, they were all accorded the same worship as the great rivers, though without the additions mentioned above.

Rivers such as the Qian, Luo, Two Deeps, and Mingze, and Mt. Pu and Mt. Yuexu, though small in comparison to the other mountains and rivers, were also accorded ceremonies of recompense, thawing, and freezing each year, though the rituals used were not necessarily the same in all places.

In addition there were over 100 shrines dedicated to the worship of the sun, the moon, Orion, Antares, the Northern and Southern Dippers, Mars, Venus, Jupiter, Saturn, the twenty-eight constellations, the Lord of the Wind, the Master of the Rain, the Four Seas, the Nine Ministers, the Fourteen Ministers, the Displayers, the Majestic Ones, the Transmitters, etc., at Yong.[22]

To the west of the capital there were also some twenty or thirty places of worship. In the region of Hu sacrifices were offered to the Son of Heaven of the Zhou dynasty; in Xiagui to the Heavenly Spirit; and on the Feng and Hao rivers to the Radiant One and the Round Lake of the Son of Heaven. At Bo in Du there were three places of worship to the Lords of the Soil and the Stars of Long Life, and in the Thatch Shrine of Yong there was also a place for the worship of Lord Du. Lord Du was a leading general of the Zhou dynasty in ancient times. Even the most insignificant spirits of the region of Qin, if they displayed divine powers, were worshipped with offerings at the appropriate seasons of the year, but the Lords on High worshipped at the four Altars of Yong were regarded as the most honourable of the gods. The Treasures of Chen were also noteworthy because their gleaming lights had the power to move the common people.

At the four Altars of Yong prayers were offered in the spring for a successful crop and for the thawing of the waters; in the fall for the freezing of the waters; and in the winter to thank the deities for their aid. In the fifth month colts were sacrificed, and in the second month of each of the four seasons a "month" sacrifice was held, similar to that offered at the season when the Treasures of Chen appeared.[23] For this sacrifice red colts were used in spring and summer and red colts with black manes for fall and winter. The colts sacrificed at the Altars were always four in number, along with a belled chariot drawn by four dragons and a regular chariot drawn by four horses, these last two both modelled out of wood and painted the colour appropriate to the deity being sacrificed to. Four yellow calves and four lambs were also sacrificed along with a specified

---

[22]The Majestic Ones and Transmitters were apparently deities of the roads and fields, though their identity is uncertain, as is that of the Ministers. Mercury has probably dropped out of the list of planets and should be included.

[23]Following the reading in *Han shu* 25A.

number of jades and silks. All the sacrifices were buried alive in the ground and no sacrificial implements such as stands or platters were used.

The suburban sacrifice was performed once every three years. Since the Qin dynasty had designated the tenth month as the beginning of its year, it was always in the tenth month that the emperor fasted and journeyed to the suburbs to visit the deity. Beacon fires were raised at the place of worship, and the ruler went to pay his respects outside the city of Xianyang. White was used for the vestments, and the procedure followed was the same as that for ordinary sacrifices.

The sacrifices at the Altar of the West and the Garden Altar continued to be observed as before, though the emperor did not go in person to perform them. All of these places of worship were customarily under the jurisdiction of the master of invocations, who saw to it that offerings and sacrifices were made at the appropriate seasons of the year. As for the other famous mountains, great rivers, gods and deities such as the Eight Spirits, if the emperor happened to be passing by their places of worship, he performed sacrifices; otherwise, no ceremonies were carried out. The spirits and holy places of the various provinces and other distant regions were worshipped by the people of their respective localities and were not under the control of the emperor's religious officials. Among the religious officials of the court was one called the private invocator. If any disaster or evil omen appeared, it was his duty to offer sacrifices with all speed and pray that the blame for the mishap might be transferred from the ruler to the officials or the people.

At the time of the founding of the Han, when Gaozu was still a commoner, he once killed a great snake, whereupon a spirit appeared and announced, "This snake was the son of the White Emperor and he who killed him is the son of the Red Emperor!" When Gaozu first began his uprising, he offered prayers at the altar of the soil at White Elm in the city of Feng, and after he had won control of the district of Pei and become its governor he sacrificed to the warrior god Chi You and anointed his drums and flags with the blood of the sacrifice.

Eventually, in the tenth month of the year, he reached Bashang, where he joined with the other feudal lords in bringing order to the capital city of Xianyang and was made king of Han. He therefore designated the tenth month as the first month of the year and chose red as his patron colour.

In the second year of his reign (205 BC) he marched east to attack Xiang Yu and then returned once more to the area within the Pass. There he inquired what deities the Qin rulers had worshipped in their sacrifices to the Lords on

High and was told that there had been sacrifices to four deities, the White, the Green, the Yellow, and the Red Emperors.

"But I have heard that there are Five Emperors in Heaven," said Gaozu. "Why is it that the Qin rulers worshipped only four?"

When no one was able to offer an explanation, Gaozu replied, "I know the reason. They were waiting for me to come and complete the five!" He accordingly set up a place of worship for the Black Emperor, called the Altar of the North, with officials appointed to carry out its sacrifices; Gaozu did not go in person to perform sacrifices. He then summoned all of the former religious officials of the Qin dynasty and restored the posts of master of invocations and grand supervisor, ordering these officials to carry out the rites and ceremonies as they had in the past. He also gave instructions for altars of the dynasty to be erected in all the provinces and issued an edict saying, "I hold the places of worship in highest regard and deeply respect the sacrifices. Whenever the time comes for sacrifices to the Lord on High or for the worship of the mountains, rivers, or other spirits, let the ceremonies be performed in due season as they were in the past!"

Four years later, after peace had been restored to the empire, Gaozu issued an edict to the imperial secretary instructing the officials of the city of Feng to tend the altar of the soil at White Elm, performing ceremonies each season, with a sacrifice of a sheep and a pig each spring. He also ordered the religious officials to set up a place of worship to Chi You in the capital, Chang'an.

He appointed various officials for sacrifice and invocation in Chang'an, as well as women shamans. The shamans from the region of Liang worshipped such deities as Heaven and Earth, the Heavenly Altar, Heavenly Water, Within the House, and In the Hall. Those from the region of Jin worshipped the Five Emperors, the Lord of the East, the Lord in the Clouds, the Arbiter of Fate, the Altar of the Shamans, the Kinsman of the Shamans, the Bringer of Fire, etc. Those from Qin worshipped the Lord of the Altar, the Protector of Shamans, the Family Imprisoned, etc. The shamans of Jing worshipped the deities Below the Hall, Ancestor of Shamans, Arbiter of Fate, and Giver of Gruel.[24] Other shamans appointed especially for that purpose worshipped the Nine Heavens. All of these performed their sacrifices at the appropriate seasons during the year in the palace. The shamans of the Yellow River, however, performed their

---

[24] The nature of most of these deities is obscure and the translations of their names in many places only tentative.

sacrifices at Linjin, while those of the Southern Mountains performed sacrifices to these mountains and to Qinzhong. (Qinzhong is the spirit of the Second Emperor of the Qin.) All these sacrifices were performed at specified months and seasons.

Two years later someone advised the emperor, "At the beginning of the Zhou dynasty, in the city of Tai, a place of worship was set up for Hou Ji, the ancestor of the Zhou and god of agriculture, and from that time until today the blood and flesh of the sacrifices have continued to be offered for the benefit of the world." Gaozu accordingly issued an edict to the imperial secretary ordering places of worship set up in all the provinces, districts, and feudal kingdoms, called Shrines of the Sacred Star, and dedicated to Hou Ji, where oxen should be sacrificed at the appropriate seasons each year.

In the spring of the tenth year of Gaozu's reign (197 BC) the officials requested that the emperor order the districts to make offerings of a sheep and a pig to the altars of the soil and grain in the third and twelfth months of each year, the people in each district to raise the money for the sacrifices at their respective local shrines. The emperor gave his approval.

Eighteen years later Emperor Wen came to the throne. In the thirteenth year of his reign (167 BC) Emperor Wen issued an edict saying, "At the present time the private invocator is delegated to pray that the blame for any faults committed by me be transferred to himself or the lower officials. I find this practice wholly unacceptable. From now on, let the post of private invocator be abolished!"

Originally it had been left to the religious officials of the feudal lords to perform sacrifices and offerings to any of the famous mountains or great rivers that happened to be within their domains; the officials of the emperor had no jurisdiction over such affairs. When the kingdoms of Qi and Huainan were temporarily abolished, however, Emperor Wen ordered his master of invocations to see to it that all the proper ceremonies were carried out in these regions at the proper times as they had been in the past.

In this year the emperor issued a proclamation saying:

It has now been thirteen years since I came to the throne.[25] By the aid of the spirits of the ancestral temples and the blessing of the altars of the soil and grain, the land within the borders is at peace and my

---

[25] In "The Basic Annals of Emperor Wen" this proclamation is dated in the fourteenth year and reads, "It has now been fourteen years, etc".

people are without distress. Moreover, for the past several years the empire has enjoyed good harvests. How could I, who am of no virtue, be deserving of such fortune? Rather are these gifts, all of them, from the Lord on High and the other spirits.

I have heard that in ancient times when a ruler enjoyed reward for his virtue he invariably returned recompense to the gods for the merits they had bestowed. Therefore I would increase the sacrifices to the spirits. Let the officials open deliberations to increase the offerings at the Five Altars of Yong by the addition of a great chariot for each altar, fitted out with full trappings; and for the Western and Garden altars, one chariot each modelled in wood, with four wooden horses and full trappings. Let the Yellow, Qiao, and Han rivers be granted an addition of two pieces of jade each, and at all the various places of worship let the altars and altar grounds be broadened and the jades, silks, and other sacrificial implements be increased as may be proper to each place.

At present when prayers are offered for blessing, it is asked that all good fortune may come to me in person, while no mention is made of my people. From now on let the invocations be carried out with all reverence, but let there be no more such prayers for myself alone.

A man of Lu name Gongsun Chen submitted a letter to the throne stating, "Formerly the Qin dynasty ruled by the power of the element water. Now that the Han has succeeded the Qin it is obvious that it must rule by the power of the element earth, since the cycle of the five elements revolves, going back to the beginning when it has once ended. To confirm this, an omen of the power of earth will appear in the form of a yellow dragon. It is proper, then, that the month on which the year begins should be changed and the colour of the court vestments altered to pay honour to the colour yellow."

The chancellor at this time was Zhang Cang, who was very fond of matters of the pitch pipes and the calendar, and it was his contention that the Han belonged to a period in which the power of water was in ascendancy. Proof of this, he said, was to be found in the fact that the Yellow River had burst its dikes at a place called Metal Embankment (i.e., water ascendant over metal). The Han year should therefore begin with the tenth month, the first month of winter, and the vestments should be black on the outside and red within, thus corresponding to the element water. He declared that Gongsun Chen's opinion was completely false and the matter was allowed to drop.

Three years later[26] a yellow dragon appeared at Chengji. Emperor Wen thereupon summoned Gongsun Chen to court, made him an erudite, and set him to work with the other court scholars drawing up plans to change the calendar and the colour of the court vestments. In the summer the emperor issued an edict saying, "A supernatural being in the form of a strange creature has appeared at Chengji, but no harm will come to the people and the year will be a plentiful one. I wish to perform the suburban sacrifice and offer prayers to the Lord on High and the other spirits. Let the officials in charge of rites deliberate on the matter and let them not hesitate in their recommendations for fear of putting me to too much trouble."

The officials all replied, "In ancient times the Son of Heaven went in summer to the suburbs to sacrifice in person to the Lord on High. Hence this was called the suburban sacrifice."

In the summer of this year, in the fourth month, Emperor Wen for the first time performed the suburban sacrifice, visiting the Five Altars of Yong and worshipping there. His robes were all designed to honour the colour red.

A man of Zhao named Xinyuan Ping, appearing before the emperor to report an unusual cloud formation he had seen, asserted that in the sky northeast of Chang'an a supernatural emanation had appeared, made of five colours and shaped like a man's hat.

"The northeast is the dwelling place of the spirits," suggested someone else, "and the western region is where they have their graves. Now, since Heaven has sent down this auspicious sign, it is right that places of worship should be set up to offer sacrifices to the Lord on High in answer to this omen."

Accordingly the Temples of the Five Emperors were constructed north of the Wei River. They were housed under a single roof, but each emperor had his own hall of worship. Each of the five halls was fitted with a separate gate, painted in the colour appropriate to the deity worshipped there. The animals sacrificed and the ceremonies conducted were the same as those at the Five Altars of Yong.

In the summer, the fourth month, Emperor Wen went in person to pay his respects to the confluence of the Ba and Wei rivers, and at the same time performed the suburban sacrifice to the Five Emperors north of the Wei. The temples of the Five Emperors overlooked the Wei River on the south, and to the north channels had been cut to bring water into the Lake of Rushes. Beacon fires

---

[26]But "The Basic Annals of Emperor Wen" dates this in the fifteenth year, only one year later.

were raised while the sacrifices were performed, their light pouring forth and their flames seeming to reach to the heavens.

The emperor honoured Xinyuan Ping with the rank of superior lord and presented him with several thousand pieces of gold. He also ordered the erudites and court scholars to select material from the Six Classics and compose a work on the institutes of the rulers, as well as to begin plans for an inspection tour of the provinces and the performance of the Feng and Shan sacrifices.

As Emperor Wen was leaving the place called Long Gate he saw something that looked like five men standing to the north of the road. Because of this he had an altar to the Five Emperors set up on the spot, where he offered five sets of sacrificial animals.

The following year Xinyuan Ping had a man bring a jade cup and present it at the gate of the palace, along with a letter to the throne. Xinyuan Ping then remarked to the emperor, "There are emanations in the sky which indicate that someone has come to the palace gate with a precious object!" When a man was sent to verify this announcement, it was found that a jade cup bearing the inscription "Long Life to the Lord of Men" had in fact been presented at the gate.

Another time Xinyuan Ping announced that, according to his observations, the setting sun would stop in its course and ascend again to the centre of the sky. After a little while the sun began to move backward until it had returned to the meridian. Thereupon the emperor began to number the years of his reign over again, making the seventeenth year the first year of a new period, and ordered great feasting throughout the empire.

Next Xinyuan Ping announced, "The cauldrons of the Zhou dynasty were lost in the Si River. Now the Yellow River has overflowed and runs into the Si. Observing the sky in the northeast, I note that there are certain emanations right over Fenyin which indicate the presence of precious metal objects. That, I believe, is where the cauldrons will be found. When such an omen appears, however, unless some action is taken in response, nothing will ever come of it!"

The emperor therefore sent envoys to build a temple at Fenyin, overlooking the Yellow River to the south, and offer sacrifices, hoping to bring the cauldrons to light. At this time someone sent a letter revealing to the emperor that all of the emanations and supernatural occurrences described by Xinyuan Ping were frauds. Xinyuan Ping was handed over to the law officials for trial and was executed, along with his three sets of relatives.

After this Emperor Wen lost interest in changing the calendar and the colour of the vestments and in matters concerning the spirits. He ordered his sacrificial officials to see to the upkeep of the temples and altars of the Five Emperors north of the Wei River and at Long Gate and to perform ceremonies at the proper seasons, but he himself no longer visited them.

The following year the Xiongnu several times invaded the border and troops were raised to guard against further incursions. During the last years of his reign the harvests were not very plentiful.

A few years later Emperor Jing ascended the throne. During the sixteen years of his reign the officials in charge of sacrifices continued to perform their various duties at the appropriate seasons of the year, but no new forms of worship were instituted. And so things continued to the reign of the present emperor.

When the present emperor first came to the throne, he showed the greatest reverence in carrying out the sacrifices to the various spirits and gods. In the first year of his reign (140 BC), because it had been over sixty years since the founding of the Han, and the empire was at peace, the gentlemen of the court all hoped that the emperor would perform the Feng and Shan sacrifices and change the calendar and other regulations of the dynasty. The emperor favoured the teachings of the Confucians and summoned to court a number of men who were noted for their wisdom and good character. Among these were Zhao Wan, Wang Zang, and others of their group, who were made officials because of their literary accomplishments. These men wished to begin discussions on the establishment of a Bright Hall south of the capital, where the ruler would receive the feudal lords in audience, as had been done in ancient times. They also drew up rough plans for an imperial tour of inspection, the performance of the Feng and Shan, alterations of the calendar and the colour of court vestments, etc. Before any of these plans had been put into effect, however, the emperor's grandmother, Empress Dowager Dou, who was a follower of Taoist teachings and had no use for Confucianism, sent men in secret to spy on Zhao Wan and the rest and gather evidence to show that they were deriving illegal profit from their posts. Zhao Wan and Wang Zang were summoned to answer these charges, but both men committed suicide and all the projects which they had sponsored were abandoned.

Six years later (135 BC) Empress Dowager Dou passed away and the following year the emperor summoned to court a number of literary men such as Gongsun Hong. The next year (133 BC) the emperor journeyed to Yong for the first time to perform the suburban sacrifice at the Five Altars. From this time on he invariably performed the suburban sacrifice once every three years.

At this time the emperor also sought out the Spirit Mistress and housed her in the Tishi Tower in the Shanglin Park. The Spirit Mistress was originally a woman of Changling who died in childbirth. Later her spirit appeared and took possession of her brother's wife, Wanruo. Wanruo offered sacrifices to the spirit in her house, and many people came to join in the worship. Lady Pingyuan, the maternal grandmother of the present emperor, was among those who sacrificed to the spirit, and later her sons and grandsons all became famous and honoured. Thus when the present emperor came to the throne he treated the Spirit Mistress with great reverence and transferred her place of worship to his own palace in the Shanglin Park. It was said that one could hear the words spoken by the spirit but could not see her form.

It was at this time also that Li Shaojun appeared before the emperor to expound the worship of the god of the fireplace and explain his theories on how to achieve immortality through dietary restrictions. The emperor treated him with great respect. Li Shaojun had formerly been a retainer of the marquis of Shenze and specialized in magical arts. He kept his real age and place of birth a secret, always telling people that he was seventy years old. Claiming that he could make the spirits serve him and prevent old age, he travelled about to the courts of the various feudal lords, expounding his magic. He had no wife or children. When people heard of his power to command the spirits and drive away death they showered him with a constant stream of presents, so that he always had more than enough food and clothing and money. Impressed that he seemed to enjoy such affluence without engaging in any business, and also not knowing where he was from, people put even greater faith in his claims and vied with each other in waiting on him. He relied wholly on his ability to work magic and was clever at making pronouncements that were later found to have been curiously apt.

Once when he was staying with Tian Fen, the marquis of Wuan, and was drinking with the marquis and his friends, he told one of the guests, an old man of over ninety, that he had gone with the man's grandfather to such and such a place to practise archery. The old man had in fact, when he was a child, accompanied his grandfather, and remembered visiting the place that Li Shaojun mentioned. With this the whole party was struck with amazement.

When Li Shaojun appeared before the emperor, the latter questioned him about an ancient bronze vessel which the emperor had in his possession. "This vessel," replied Li Shaojun, "was presented at the Cypress Chamber in the tenth year of the reign of Duke Huan of Qi (676 BC)." When the inscription on the vessel was deciphered, it was found that it had in fact belonged to Duke Huan of Qi. Everyone in the place was filled with astonishment and decided that Li Shaojun must be a spirit who had lived hundreds of years.

Li Shaojun then advised the emperor, "If you sacrifice to the fireplace you can call the spirits to you, and if the spirits come you can transform cinnabar into gold. Using this gold, you may make drinking and eating vessels, which will prolong the years of your life. With prolonged life you may visit the immortals who live on the island of Penglai in the middle of the sea. If you visit them and perform the Feng and Shan sacrifices, you will never die. This is what the Yellow Emperor did. Once I wandered by the sea and visited Master Anqi, and he fed me jujubes as big as melons.[27] Master Anqi is an immortal who roams about Penglai. If he takes a liking to someone he will come to meet him, but if not he will hide."

As a result, the emperor for the first time began to sacrifice in person to the fireplace. He dispatched magicians to set out on the sea in search of Master Anqi and the immortals of Penglai, and attempted to make gold out of cinnabar sand and various kinds of medicinal ingredients.

After some time, Li Shaojun fell ill and died. The emperor, however, believed that he was not really dead but had transformed himself into a spirit, and he ordered Kuan Shu, a clerk from Huangchui, to carry on the magical arts which Li Shaojun had taught. None of the group sent out to search for Master Anqi in the island of Penglai succeeded in finding anything.

After this, any number of strange and dubious magicians from the seacoast of Yan and Qi appeared at court to speak to the emperor about supernatural affairs. Among them was a man from Bo named Miu Ji who instructed the emperor on how to sacrifice to the Great Unity. "The Great Unity," he explained, "is the most honoured of the spirits of Heaven and his helpers are the Five Emperors. In ancient times the Son of Heaven sacrificed to the Great Unity each spring and autumn in the southeastern suburbs, offering one set of sacrificial animals each day for seven days. An altar was constructed for the purpose which was open to the spirit roads of the eight directions."

The emperor accordingly ordered the master of invocations to set up such a place of worship southeast of Chang'an where sacrifices were conducted regularly according to the method described by Miu Ji.

---

[27]Following the reading in *Han shu* 25A.

Later someone submitted a letter to the throne stating that in ancient times the Son of Heaven had offered a set of sacrificial beasts once every three years to the spirits called the Three Unities. These were the Heavenly Unity, the Earthly Unity, and the Great Unity. The emperor gave his consent to the ritual and ordered the master of invocations to see to it that such sacrifices were carried out at Miu Ji's altar of the Great Unity in the manner recommended.

Later someone again sent a letter to the throne advising that in ancient times the Son of Heaven had always performed in the spring a ceremony to drive away evil in which he sacrificed an owl and a broken mirror[28] to the Yellow Emperor; a sheep to the god called Dark Ram; a blue stallion to the god Horse Traveller; an ox to the Great Unity, the Lord of Mt. Ze, and the Earth Elder; a dried fish to the lords of Wuyi; and an ox to the Messenger of the *Yin* and *Yang*. The emperor gave orders to the religious officials to see that such sacrifices were performed in the recommended manner at the side of Miu Ji's altar to the Great Unity.

Some time afterwards white deer appeared in the emperor's park. He had their hides made into a type of currency which he issued in order to make known this auspicious omen, and also had currency minted out of white metal.

The following year (122 BC) when the emperor went to Yong to perform the suburban sacrifice he captured a beast with one horn which looked like a unicorn. The officials announced, "Since Your Majesty has performed the suburban sacrifice with such reverence and care, the Lord on High has seen fit to reward you by presenting this one-horned beast. Is this not what is called a unicorn?"

The emperor thereupon visited the Five Altars and presented an additional burnt offering of an ox at each one. He presented the white metal coins, symbolic of the auspicious white deer, to the various feudal lords as a hint to them that he had by now received the necessary omens proving that he had found favour with Heaven.

The king of Jibei, assuming from these moves that the emperor was about to perform the Feng and Shan sacrifices, sent a letter to the throne in which he presented to the emperor Mt. Tai and the surrounding cities, which were situated in his domains. The emperor accepted the gift and conferred upon the king a

---

[28]According to some commentators "broken mirror" is the name of a beast which eats its own father. The owl is infamous in Chinese lore for eating its mother, and these two creatures were therefore offered in order to prevent unfilial behaviour.

district elsewhere by way of compensation. The king of Changshan was accused of some crime and transferred to another region. The emperor enfeoffed the king's younger brother in the region of Zhending so that he might carry on there the sacrifices to the former kings of Changshan, and made the region of Changshan, where Mt. Hengg is situated, into a province. Thus it was that, after these two events, all the regions in which the Five Peaks were situated came under the direct jurisdiction of the emperor.

The following year a man of Qi named Shaoweng gained the emperor's ear with his tales of ghosts and spirits. The emperor had formerly had a favourite concubine named Madam Wang who had died. It is said that Shaoweng by his magical arts succeeded in summoning forth at night the apparitions of Madam Wang and the god of the fireplace, while the emperor stood within a curtained enclosure and gazed at them from afar. The emperor accordingly honoured Shaoweng with the title of General of Peaceful Accomplishment and rewarded him with lavish gifts, treating him with the courtesy due to an imperial guest.

Shaoweng then said to the emperor, "I perceive that Your Majesty wishes to commune with the spirits. But unless your palaces and robes are patterned after the shapes of the spirits, they will not consent to come to you." He fashioned five chariots, symbolizing the five elements and painted with cloud designs, and on the days when each of the five elements was in ascendancy, he would mount the appropriate chariot and ride about, driving away evil demons. He also directed the emperor to build the Palace of Sweet Springs, in which was a terrace chamber painted with pictures of Heaven, Earth, the Great Unity, and all the other gods and spirits. Here Shaoweng set forth sacrificial vessels in an effort to summon the spirits of Heaven.

A year or so passed, however, and Shaoweng's magical arts seemed to grow less and less effective, for no spirits appeared to answer his summons. He then wrote a message on a piece of silk and fed it to an ox and, pretending to know nothing of the mater, announced to the emperor, "There appears to be some strange object in this ox's belly!" The ox was slaughtered and its belly opened, revealing the piece of silk, and the words written on it were exceedingly strange. The emperor, however, recognized the handwriting and, when he cross-examined Shaoweng, discovered that the message was in fact a fraud. He had Shaoweng executed but kept the matter a secret. Following this he built the Terrace of Cypress Beams with the Bronze Pillars, and atop them the Immortals holding in their palms the Pans for Receiving Dew, and similar structures.

The year after Shaoweng's execution (118 BC) the emperor was taken gravely ill at Cauldron Lake and, though all the doctors and shamans were summoned to attend him, none could cure his sickness. Earlier, a man of Youshui named Fa Gen had advised the emperor that in the province of Shang there lived a shamaness who, when ill, became possessed by spirits. The emperor had accordingly summoned the shamaness to the Palace of Sweet Springs and set up a place of worship for her. When the emperor later fell ill at Cauldron Lake he sent someone to consult the Spirit Mistress through the shamaness, who returned this answer: "The Son of Heaven need not worry about his illness. When he is a little better he should make an effort to come and meet with me at Sweet Springs!"

After this the emperor's illness improved somewhat until he was able to rise from his bed and journey to Sweet Springs. There he recovered completely and proclaimed a general amnesty to the empire. He set up the Temple of Long Life dedicated to the Spirit Mistress. The Spirit Mistress was accorded honour equal to that of the Great Unity.[29] Her helpers were called the Great Forbidden Ones, and it was said that the other deities such as the Arbiter of Fate were all her attendants. It was impossible to catch a glimpse of her form, but her words could be heard, sounding the same as a human voice. At times she went away and at other times returned, and when she came, the wind made a sighing sound. She dwelt within the curtains of the chamber and spoke sometimes during the day, though usually at night. The emperor would always perform rites of ablution before entering her presence and there, through the offices of the shamaness, he would eat and drink with the deity as though she were his host. Whatever the spirit wished to say to him she would relay by way of the shamaness. The emperor also set up another temple north of the Temple of Long Life, where he hung feathered banners and set out the implements of sacrifice to perform ceremonies in honour of the Spirit Mistress. Whenever the Spirit Mistress spoke, the emperor ordered his secretaries to take down the words, calling these messages his "Planning Laws". There was nothing the least bit extraordinary about the words of the deity, which were the sort of thing that anyone at all could say, but the emperor alone took great delight in them. The whole affair, however, was kept secret so that most people at the time knew nothing about it.

Three years later (114 BC) the officials advised the emperor, saying, "When

---

[29] The text at this point seems to be corrupt and the translation is highly tentative.

a ruler begins the numbering of the years of his reign over again, he should not call the periods merely 'first', 'second', etc., but should select names from the auspicious omens that have appeared at the time. Thus the first period of Your Majesty's reign should be called *jianyuan* or 'Establishment Period'; the second, when the comet appeared, should be called *yuanguang*, or 'Period of Light'; and the third, when the one-horned beast was captured at the time of the suburban sacrifice, should be called *yuanshou*, or 'Hunting Period'."[30]

In the winter of the following year (113 BC) the emperor performed the suburban sacrifice at Yong. He called his officials into conference and said, "I have now performed the suburban sacrifice in person to the Lord on High. But unless I also sacrifice to the Earth Lord, I fear these ceremonies will have no effect."

The officials debated with the grand historian[31] and the minister in charge of sacrifices, Kuan Shu, and made the following announcement: "In the past, at the sacrifices to Heaven and Earth, oxen with horns as small as silk cocoons or chestnuts were used. Now if Your Majesty wishes to sacrifice in person to the Earth Lord, it is necessary to set up five altars on a round hill in the middle of a swamp. At each altar a yellow calf and a set of three sacrificial animals should be offered, and when the ceremony is completed these should all be buried in the earth. All persons attending the ceremony should wear vestments honouring the colour yellow."

The emperor then journeyed east and for the first time set up the altar to the Earth Lord on top of Rump Hill in Fenyin as Kuan Shu and the others had recommended. There he personally performed worship ceremonies, following the same ritual as that used for the Lord on High. When the ceremony was completed the emperor proceeded to Xingyang and from there returned to the capital.

When he passed through Luoyang the emperor issued an edict which read: "The Three dynasties of antiquity are far removed in time and it is difficult at this day to make provisions for the preservation of their lines. Since Luoyang

---

[30] Emperors Wen and Jing had both begun the numbering of the years of their reigns over again several times, but no particular titles had been given to the periods of numbering. This was the first time that *nianhao* or "era names" were used. The practice was continued throughout later Chinese history and was imitated in Japan and Annam.

[31] Sima Tan, the father of Sima Qian.

was the capital of the Zhou dynasty, let thirty *li* of land here be set aside as a fief for the descendant of the Zhou rulers so that, with the title of Lord Zinan of Zhou, he may carry out sacrifices to his ancestors."

This year the emperor for the first time made a tour of the provinces and districts and visited Mt. Tai.

In the spring the marquis of Lecheng sent a letter to the throne recommending a man named Luan Da. Luan Da was a palace attendant of the king of Jiaodong. Originally he had studied under the same teacher as Shaoweng, the magician whom the emperor had executed, and later he became the master of magical arts to King Kang, the king of Jiaodong. King Kang's queen was the elder sister of the marquis of Lecheng. She had no children, however, and when King Kang died, one of his sons by a concubine was made king to succeed him. The queen was a woman of loose conduct and was on very poor terms with the new king; the two of them were constantly searching for some legal excuse to trip each other up. When the queen heard that the magician Shaoweng had been executed, she hoped to ingratiate herself with the emperor by dispatching Luan Da to the capital. She therefore enlisted the aid of her brother, the marquis of Lecheng, to help Luan Da gain an audience with the emperor so that he could expound his magic. The emperor, after having executed Shaoweng, began to regret that he had been so hasty with the death sentence and had not given the magician an opportunity to finish displaying his powers. He was therefore extremely delighted to see Luan Da.

Luan Da was tall and handsome and full of magical schemes and stratagems. He did not hesitate to come out with the most grandiose pronouncements and never betrayed any sign that he doubted the truth of what he was saying. "I once travelled far and wide over the sea," he informed the emperor, "and visited Anqi, Xianmen, and the other immortals. But they all considered me a man of humble station and would not confide in me. Also, because I served King Kang, who was only one of the feudal lords, they considered that I was not worthy to receive their teachings. I often spoke to King Kang about the matter, but he would not listen to my suggestions. My teacher had told me that gold could definitely be made from cinnabar, that the break in the dikes of the Yellow River could be repaired, the elixir of immortal life made, and the immortals persuaded to appear. But I was afraid that if I mentioned these things, I would meet the same fate as Shaoweng. This is the reason I and all the other magicians have kept our mouths closed. How could I dare under the circumstances to discuss my magic?"

"As for Shaoweng," said the emperor, "he happened to eat some horse liver and died, that was all.[32] But if you can really carry on his magic arts, what will I not give you?"

Luan Da replied, "My teacher has no reason to seek for men. It is men who seek for him. If Your Majesty really wishes to summon him, then you must first honour the envoys that you send to him, making them members of the imperial family,[33] and treating them as guests rather than subjects, doing nothing that would humiliate them. If you grant each of the envoys the imperial seals, they may go and speak to the spirit man. Whether or not he will consent to give ear, I do not know, but I believe that if you confer sufficient honours upon the envoys you send, then he may be persuaded to come."

In order to test Luan Da, the emperor instructed him to give a minor display of his magical powers by making some chessmen fight. When the board was set up, the chessmen were seen to rush against each other of their own accord.

At this time the emperor was very worried about the break in the dikes of the Yellow River and concerned that he had not been able to change cinnabar into gold. He therefore honoured Luan Da with the title of General of the Five Profits. After a few months, Luan Da was able to wear four seals at his girdle, those of General of the Heavenly Man, General of the Earthly Man, and General of the Great Way having been granted to him in addition to the previous one.

The emperor issued an edict to the imperial secretary which read: "In ancient times Emperor Yu opened up the nine rivers and fixed the courses of the four waterways. In recent years, however, the Yellow River has flowed out over the land and the labourers working on its dikes have been able to find no rest. For twenty-eight years I have watched over the empire, and now it is as though Heaven has sent me this man to open up the great way for me. In the *Book of Changes* we read of 'the flying dragon' and 'the wild swan advancing to the great rock'.[34] Do these oracles not apply to this great man whom Heaven has sent to me? Therefore let a fief of 2,000 households be granted to General

---

[32] Horse liver was believed to be poison.

[33] By seeking to become a member of the imperial family, presumably through a marriage alliance, Luan Da hoped to preclude the possibility of meeting the same fate as Shaoweng.

[34] From the *Book of Changes*, the oracles of the hexagrams *qian* and *jian*. Both refer to the finding of a worthy minister by the ruler.

Luan Da and let him be given the title of marquis of Letong."

In addition the emperor presented Luan Da with one of the finest mansions of the marquises, 1,000 servants, carriages for use on ordinary and special occasions, and hangings, draperies, and vessels of every kind to adorn his house. He also bestowed his daughter Princess Wei, the eldest daughter of Empress Wei, upon Luan Da to be his wife, along with 10,000 catties of gold, and changed the name of the princess's fief to "Princess Dangli". The emperor in person went to visit the home of Luan Da and in addition sent a constant stream of envoys to inquire how he was and supply him with anything he needed. From the emperor's aunt and the highest officials of the government on down, people invited him to their homes to dine and showered him with gifts.

The emperor then had another jade seal carved with the title "General of the Heavenly Way" and sent his envoy to present it to Luan Da. The presentation ceremony was performed at night, the envoy being dressed in a feather cloak and standing on a spread of white rushes, while Luan Da, similarly dressed and standing on the rushes, received the seal. This was done to indicate that Luan Da was not being treated as a subject of the emperor. The words "Heavenly Way" on the seal meant that Luan Da should open up a way to the heavenly spirits for the emperor.

After this Luan Da spent every evening offering sacrifices at his home, hoping that he would be able to call down the spirits. No spirits appeared, however, but only a multitude of ghosts who gathered around. These he was able to command. Sometime later he began to make preparations for a journey, announcing that he would travel east and set out upon the sea to search for his teacher.

In no more than a few months from the time he was granted an audience with the emperor, Luan Da bore at his girdle six seals, those of his five generalships and his marquisate, and his honour awed the empire. After this there was hardly a soul living on the seacoast of Yan and Qi who did not begin waving his arms about excitedly and proclaiming that he possessed secret arts and could command the spirits and immortals.

In the summer, during the sixth month of this year (113 BC), the shaman Jin of Fenyin was performing a sacrifice for the sake of the common people to the Earth Lord at the Rump Hill altar in the region of Wei, when he noticed an object shaped like a hook sticking up out of the ground at the side of the altar. Digging up the soil around it, he unearthed a cauldron. It was much larger than any ordinary cauldron and had a pattern incised on it, but no inscription.[35] Much struck by his find, he reported it to the officials, who in turn informed Sheng, the governor of Hedong Province. The governor having relayed intelligence of the affair to the throne, the emperor dispatched an envoy to question the shaman on how he had come into possession of the cauldron. The envoy, finding no evidence of fraud or deceit, sacrificed with full ceremony at the altar and bore the cauldron back with him to the Palace of Sweet Springs, where the emperor determined to take it along with him on one of this journeys and offer it to the spirits of Heaven. For this purpose he made a trip to the mountains, whereupon the sun shone forth with a bright, warm glow and a yellow cloud came and stood over the place where the cauldron was. Just then a large deer passed by the imperial party, which the emperor shot down in person and used as a sacrifice.

When the emperor and his party returned to Chang'an, the ministers and high officials all gathered in conference and requested that due honour be shown to the precious cauldron. The emperor announced, "Recently the Yellow River overflowed its banks and for several years the harvests were poor. Therefore I journeyed about the empire and performed sacrifices to the Earth Lord, praying for the sake of the common people that the grain might grow well. This year, though the harvest has been rich and plentiful, I have not yet returned thanks for this blessing. Why then should this cauldron appear?"

To this the officials all replied, "We have heard that in ancient times the Great Emperor Fu Xi made a single sacred cauldron. The number one symbolizes the unification of heaven and earth, showing that all things of creation were brought together. The Yellow Emperor made three precious cauldrons, symbolizing heaven, earth, and man, while Emperor Yu collected metal from the nine ancient provinces and cast nine cauldrons. All of them used the cauldrons to boil offerings and present them to the Lord on High and the other spirits. Only when a sage ruler appeared on the throne were these cauldrons made. The cauldrons were handed down during the successive dynasties of the Xia and Shang, but later, when the virtue of the Zhou rulers declined and the altars of the soil of the state of Song, ruled by the descendants of the Shang kings, were

---

[35] It will be recalled that in the reign of Emperor Wen the charlatan Xinyuan Ping had predicted that the lost cauldrons of Zhou would come to light at Fenyin. As commentators have suggested, Xinyuan Ping had probably had this cauldron buried at Fenyin so that it could be "discovered" to fulfil his prediction, but death cut short his career before the plan could be carried to completion.

destroyed, the cauldrons sank into the waters and disappeared from sight. The temple hymn in the *Book of Odes* reads:

> From hall to gatehouse,
> From ram to bull he moves,
> With great cauldron and small; ...
> Neither contentious nor proud,
> Beautiful shall be the blessing of long life for him![36]

"Now this cauldron was brought to the Palace of Sweet Springs and a radiance burst forth, shimmering like a dragon. Boundless beauty was received from on high when it was carried among the mountains. A cloud of yellow and white descended to cover it and an omen in the form of a beast appeared. With the great bow and a set of four arrows, the beast was captured and placed at the foot of the altar, a sacrifice of thanksgiving accepted with great favour on high. Only an emperor who has received the mandate of Heaven can understand the meaning of these signs, and he alone possesses the virtue needed to answer them. The cauldron should therefore be presented in the temple of the ancestors and stored away in the imperial court in accordance with these bright omens!"

The emperor gave his consent to this.

The men who had been sent to sea in search of the island of Penglai reported that it was not far away, but that they had as yet been unable to reach it because they could barely make out the emanations which indicated its location. The emperor therefore dispatched more men whose duty, it was said, was to watch the sky from afar and aid the magicians in locating the emanations.

In the autumn the emperor journeyed to Yong and was preparing to perform the suburban sacrifice when someone advised him, saying "The Five Emperors are no more than the helpers of the Great Unity. It would be well if Your Majesty were to set up an altar to the Great Unity and perform the suburban sacrifice in person to this spirit." The emperor, however, was in doubt about what to do and came to no decision.

At this point a man of Qi named Gongsun Qing appeared with a letter which he wished to present to the throne, reading as follows:

> This year the precious cauldron was found, and this winter the first
> day of the month, *xinsi*, corresponds with the winter solstice. This is

---

[36] From the *Book of Odes*, "Temple Hymns of the Zhou", "Siyi".

the same conjunction of circumstances that occurred in the time of the Yellow Emperor. I have in my possession a document on wood which states: "When the Yellow Emperor obtained the precious cauldron at Wangou he questioned Guiyu Qu, who replied, 'The Yellow Emperor has obtained the precious cauldron and the sacred calculations. This year the first day of the month, *jiyou*, corresponds to the winter solstice, which indicates that the heavenly reckonings are in order. When the cycles of heaven have come to an end, they shall begin again.' The Yellow Emperor then proceeded to reckon ahead and found that after approximately twenty years the first day of the month would once more fall on the winter solstice. After about twenty such cycles had passed, or 380 years, the Yellow Emperor became an immortal and ascended to heaven."

Gongsun Qing asked one of the officials named Suo Zhong to present this letter to the throne. But when Suo Zhong read over the letter, he saw that it made no sense and, suspecting that Gongsun Qing had concocted the whole thing out of his own head, he declined, saying, "The matter of the precious cauldron has already been disposed of. Nothing further can be done about it at this time."

Gongsun Qing then got one of the emperor's favourites to present his letter and the emperor was exceedingly pleased. He immediately summoned Gongsun Qing and questioned him, whereupon the latter replied, "I was given this letter by Master Shen, but he is dead."

"And who was Master Shen?" asked the emperor.

"Master Shen was a man of Qi who was friendly with the immortal, Master Anqi, and from him received the words of the Yellow Emperor. He possessed no writings, but only a cauldron inscription which said: 'When the Han dynasty comes to power, the months and days shall fall the same as they did at the time of the Yellow Emperor.' It further said: 'The sage of the Han shall be the grandson or great-grandson of Gaozu. A precious cauldron shall appear and he shall commune with the spirits at the Feng and Shan sacrifices. Of all the seventy-two rulers who attempted the Feng and Shan, only the Yellow Emperor was able to ascend Mt. Tai and perform the Feng!' Master Shen told me, 'The ruler of the Han shall also ascend the mountain and perform the Feng, and when he has done this, then he will become an immortal and will climb up to heaven!'

"In the time of the Yellow Emperor there were 10,000 feudal lords, and among these 7,000 lived in fiefs containing the places of worship of the gods. In the world there are eight famous mountains, three of them in the lands of the barbarians and five of them within China. The five in China are Mt. Hua, Mt. Shou, The Great Room, Mt. Tai, and Mt. Donglai. The Yellow Emperor often visited these five mountains and met there with the spirits. At times the Yellow Emperor made war, and at times he studied the arts of becoming an immortal, but he was distressed that the common people criticized his ways and so he beheaded anyone who spoke ill of the spirits. After 100 years or so he was able to commune with the spirits.

"The Yellow Emperor performed the suburban sacrifice to the Lord on High at Yong, camping there for three months. Guiyu Qu's other name was Great Crane, and when he died he was buried in Yong. Therefore the mountain is now called Crane Mound. Later the Yellow Emperor communed with the myriad spiritual beings in the Bright Court. The Bright Court was located at Sweet Springs, and Cold Gate was the name for the mouth of the valley.

"The Yellow Emperor collected copper from Mt. Shou and had it melted and cast into a cauldron at the foot of Mt. Jing. When the cauldron was completed, a dragon with whiskers hanging from its chin came down from the sky to fetch him. The Yellow Emperor mounted on the dragon's back, followed by his ministers and palace ladies, making a company of over seventy persons. When they had all mounted, the dragon rose from the ground and departed. The lesser ministers, unable to mount the dragon, clung to its whiskers until the whiskers came out and fell to the ground, along with the bow of the Yellow Emperor. The common people gazed up into the sky till the Yellow Emperor had reached heaven and then they clasped the whiskers and the bow and began to wail. Therefore in later ages the spot where all of this took place was named Cauldron Lake and the bow was called The Cry of Sorrow."

When the emperor heard this, he gave a great sigh and said, "Ah! If I could only become like the Yellow Emperor, I would think no more of my wife and children than of a castoff slipper!" He then honoured Gongsun Qing with the position of palace attendant and sent him east to wait upon the spirits at the Great Room, Mt. Song.

The emperor proceeded to carry out the suburban sacrifice at Yong, after which he travelled west as far as Longxi, climbed Mt. Kongtong in the west, and then returned to the Palace of Sweet Springs. There he gave orders to Kuan Shu and the other officials in charge of sacrifices to fit out an altar to the Great Unity. It was modelled after Miu Ji's altar to the Great Unity and had three levels. Surrounding the base of it were the altars of the Five Emperors, each disposed in the direction appropriate to the particular deity, except that the altar to the Yellow Emperor, the deity of the centre, was placed on the southwest side. Thus the eight roads by which demons approach were blocked. For the worship of the Great Unity the same offerings were used as at the altars of Yong, with the addition of such things as thick wine, jujubes, and dried meat. A yak was also slaughtered and offered with the appropriate dishes and other sacrificial implements. The Five Emperors were given only offerings of rich wine in the appropriate sacrificial vessels. Wine was poured on the ground at the four corners of the altar for the purpose, it was said, of giving sustenance to the lesser spirits and attendants and to the Big Dipper. When the offerings were completed, the beasts that had been sacrificed were all burned. The ox was white, and inside it was placed a deer, and inside the deer a pig; water was then sprinkled over them while they burned. An ox was offered to the sun and a ram or a pig to the moon. The priest who presented the offerings to the Great Unity wore robes of purple with brocade; those for the Five Emperors wore the colour appropriate to the particular deity. The robes of those who performed the sacrifice to the sun were red, and those for the moon white.

On the first day of the eleventh month, the day *xinsi* (24 Dec. 113 BC), which corresponded to the winter solstice, just before daylight, the emperor for the first time performed the suburban sacrifice in honour of the Great Unity. In the morning he made the morning bows to the sun, and in the evening the evening bows to the moon. The ritual used for the Great Unity was the same as that for the suburban sacrifice at Yong. The words of praise employed in the sacrifice read: "Heaven has for the first time granted to the Supreme Emperor the precious cauldron and the sacred calculations. The first day of the month corresponds to the winter solstice: when the cycles have come to an end, they shall begin again. The Supreme Emperor, reverently bowing, appears here."

The vestments used in the ceremony honoured the colour yellow. At the time of the sacrifice, the altar was covered with rows of torches, and at the side of the altar were set the vessels for boiling and roasting the sacrifices. "During the sacrifices," the officials concerned with the ceremony reported, "a light appeared in the sky over the offerings." The high ministers of the court announced, "The Supreme Emperor has for the first time performed the suburban sacrifice to the Great Unity at Yunyang. The officials presented large circlets of jade and offerings of the finest sacrificial animals. On the night of the sacrifice a beautiful light appeared, and the following day yellow exhalations rose from the altar and reached to heaven."

The grand historian and Kuan Shu and the other officials in charge of sacrifices advised the emperor, saying, "The spiritual beings in their beauty have come to aid Your Majesty with blessings and show forth auspicious omens. It is right that an Altar of the Great Unity should be permanently established in this region where the light shone, in clear answer to these portents." The emperor ordered the Altar to be placed under the jurisdiction of the master of invocations. The emperor performed the suburban sacrifice here in person once every three years, and during these intervals sacrifices were performed by the officials in the autumn and the last month of the year.

In the autumn, in preparation for the attack on the state of Southern Yue, an announcement was made to the Great Unity, along with prayers for success. A banner was made, fixed to a handle of thorn wood, and painted with representations of the sun, the moon, the Big Dipper, and an ascending dragon. These represented the Spear of the Great Unity (that is, the three stars in the mouth of the Big Dipper). It was called the "spirit banner" and when the announcement and prayers for the soldiers were offered, the grand historian took it in his hand and pointed it at the country that was about to be attacked.

Meanwhile the magician Luan Da, who had supposedly set off as the emperor's envoy to search for his teacher, had not ventured to set out to sea but had instead gone to Mt. Tai, where he was performing sacrifices. The emperor dispatched men to trail Luan Da and see whether there were any evidences of his magical powers. They reported that Luan Da had in fact met with no spiritual beings at all, and that the story of his going to visit his teacher was all nonsense. Since it seemed that Luan Da's magical powers were exhausted, and since his claims in most cases were not borne out by the facts, the emperor had him executed.

In the winter Gongsun Qing went to observe the spirits in the region of Henan and reported that he had seen the footprints of an immortal being on top of the city wall of Goushi, where a creature like a pheasant had flown back and forth over the wall. The emperor went in person to Goushi to examine the footprints. "Are you sure you are not trying the same sort of trick as Shaoweng and Luan Da?" the emperor asked.

"The immortals do not seek for the ruler of men," replied Gongsun Qing. "It is the ruler who must seek for them! Unless one sets about the task with a liberal and open-minded attitude, I am afraid that the spirits will never appear. When men discuss spiritual matters, their words are apt to sound wild and irrational, but if these matters are pursued for a sufficient number of years, the spirits can eventually be persuaded to come forth!"

After this all the provinces and feudal kingdoms set about busily cleaning their roads, and repairing their palaces and towers and the places of worship of the spirits and the famous mountains, anticipating a visit from the emperor.

In the spring, after the kingdom of southern Yue had been wiped out, Li Yannian, who became one of the emperor's favourite ministers, attracted the ruler's attention because of his knowledge of music. The emperor was much impressed with his views and ordered the high ministers to open discussions on the following question: "At the places of worship among the common people, musical instruments and dances are still in use, yet at present no such music is employed at the suburban sacrifice. How can this be right?"

"In ancient times," replied the ministers, "music was used at all the sacrifices to Heaven and Earth, and thus the deities of those two realms were treated with the highest degree of propriety." Others said, "The Great Emperor Fu Xi ordered the White Maiden to play upon a fifty-stringed zither. The music was exceedingly sad and the Great Emperor tried to stop her from playing, but she would not cease. Therefore he broke the zither in two, making an instrument of only twenty-five strings."

As a result of their deliberations, sacrifices and prayers of thanksgiving for the success of the expedition to Southern Yue were offered to the Great Unity and the Earth Lord, and at these music and dances were used for the first time. A number of boys were summoned to sing at the services and twenty-five stringed zithers and harps of the kind called *konghou* were made. It was at this time that zithers and harps first came into use for religious ceremonies.

In the winter of the following year (110 BC) the emperor held discussions with his ministers and announced, "In ancient times the troops were brought back from their posts and temporarily disbanded before the Feng and Shan sacrifices were performed." He proceeded to make a tour of the northern border, calling up a force of over a 100,000 troops to accompany him. He returned and sacrificed at the grave of the Yellow Emperor at Bridge Mountain and then disbanded the troops at Xuru. "I have been told that the Yellow Emperor did not die," said the emperor. "Why is it that we now find his grave here?" To this question someone replied, "After the Yellow Emperor had been transformed into an immortal and had ascended to Heaven, his ministers made a grave here for his robes and hat!"

After the emperor had returned to the Palace of Sweet Springs he began making preparations to perform the sacrifices at Mt. Tai, first offering a special sacrifice to the Great Unity. From the time the precious cauldron was discovered, the emperor had ordered his high ministers and court scholars to discuss the question of the Feng and Shan, but since these sacrifices were so seldom performed and since the last performance had been so long ago, no one knew the proper ceremony to be followed. The Confucian scholars selected material from the *Book of Documents*, the *Offices of Zhou*, and the *Institutes of a King* to show that it was a mountain sacrifice in which the ruler in person shot the sacrificial bull with an arrow. However, a certain Master Ding of Qi, who was over ninety years old, stated, "The word *feng* indicates the concept of immortality. The First Emperor of the Qin did not succeed in ascending the mountain and performing the Feng sacrifice. If Your Majesty wishes to make the ascent, you should do so in gradual stages, and when it is apparent that there is no wind or rain, you may proceed to the top and carry out the sacrifice."

The emperor therefore ordered the Confucian scholars to practise shooting bulls and to draw up rough plans for the performance of the Feng and Shan. Several years had passed since that time, and the emperor felt that the moment had come to perform the sacrifices. He had been told by Gongsun Qing and the other magicians, however, that when the Yellow Emperor and the rulers before him had performed the Feng and Shan, they had all succeeded in summoning forth supernatural beings and communing with the spirits. He therefore wished to imitate the example of these rulers by getting into touch with the spirits and the immortals of Penglai and achieving fame in the world so that his virtue might be compared to that of the Nine Bright Ones of antiquity. At the same time he wished to follow as much as possible the doctrines of the Confucians in order to lend elegance to the proceedings. The Confucian scholars for their part had been unable to produce any detailed information on the Feng and Shan ceremonies. Furthermore, they insisted upon confining themselves to what was written in the *Odes* and *Documents* and other old works and seemed incapable of coming forward with any worthwhile suggestions. When the emperor had sacrificial vessels made for use in the Feng and Shan and showed them to the Confucian scholars, some of them objected, saying, "These are not the same as the ones used in ancient times!" In addition an erudite named Xu Yan informed the emperor, "The scholars who are charged with the conducting of ceremonies under the master of ritual are not as skilful as those of Lu!" Another named Zhou Ba called all the scholars together and began making his own plans for the ceremony. With this the emperor demoted Xu Yan and Zhou Ba and called a halt to the discussions of the Confucian scholars, making no further use of their suggestions.

In the first month[37] the emperor journeyed east and visited Goushi. He stopped at Mt. Song, the Central Peak, and ascended the crest called The Great Room to pay his respects. The attendants who were waiting for him at the foot of the mountain reported that they had heard a voice that seemed to say "Long Life!" The emperor questioned the men who had ascended the mountain with him, but they replied that they had not spoken any such words, and the men at the foot of the mountain gave the same answer. The emperor then set aside a fief of 300 households to support the sacrifices to The Great Room, calling it The City Which Honours Mt. Song.

He then proceeded east and ascended Mt. Tai. At this time the grass and leaves of the trees had not yet come out and so, without fear of injuring them, he was able to order his men to drag a stone up the mountain and erect it on the summit of Mt. Tai.

From there the emperor journeyed along the seacoast, paying his respects and sacrificing to the Eight Spirits on the way. The men of Qi who came to the emperor with tales of supernatural beings and magical powers numbered in the tens of thousands, but none of them were able to offer any proofs. The emperor then dispatched a number of boats, ordering several thousand of the men who had brought him tales of the mountain of the gods in the middle of the sea to set out in search of the spiritual beings of Penglai.

Gongsun Qing in the meantime had been proceeding in advance of the emperor, bearing the seals of an imperial envoy and looking for signs of the spirits at the various famous mountains. When he reached Mt. Donglai, he reported that he had encountered a giant man at night who measured several *zhang* in height.[38] When he approached to speak to the being, it disappeared, but its footprints were still visible, he said, being very large and like those of an animal. One of the emperor's ministers also reported that he had seen an old man leading a dog. The man had said, "I am looking for the Great Lord!" and had then abruptly disappeared. The emperor had in the meantime gone to see the large footprints reported by Gongsun Qing, but was not yet persuaded that they were genuine. When his ministers told him about the old man with the dog, however, he became firmly convinced that it had actually been an immortal being. He therefore lingered for a while on the seacoast, providing his magicians with post carriages so that they could get about quickly and sending out several

---

[37] Following the reading in *Han shu* 6.

[38] A *zhang* was equal to about 7'7". One *zhang* is made up of ten *chi*.

thousand men to search in secret for immortal beings.

In the fourth month the emperor started back west, arriving at Fenggao. He had thought over the various recommendations which the Confucian scholars and the magicians had made concerning the Feng and Shan sacrifices, but he was troubled by the fact that each said something different and that many of their recommendations were absurd or almost impossible to put into practice. When he reached Liangfu, he sacrificed to the Lord of the Land. On the day *yimao* (17 May 110 BC) he ordered the Confucians who attended him to don leather caps and wide sashes and to carry out the shooting of the ox, performing the ceremony used at the suburban sacrifices to the Great Unity. The *feng* or altar mound was one *zhang* and two *chi* in breadth and nine *chi* high. Buried beneath it was a jade tablet inscribed with a message, but the contents were kept secret. After this ceremony was completed, the emperor alone, accompanied by only one attendant, the carriage server Zihou,[39] ascended Mt. Tai and again performed the Feng sacrifice. This latter ceremony was carried out entirely in secret. The following day the emperor descended the mountain by the northern road.

On the day *bingchen* (18 May) the emperor performed the Shan sacrifice at Mt. Suran in the northeast foothills of Mt. Tai, following the ceremony used for the sacrifices to the Earth Lord. At all of these ceremonies the emperor made his obeisance and presented himself in person, wearing garments honouring the colour yellow, and music was employed throughout. A type of rush having three ridges on one stalk, which grows between the Yangtze and Huai rivers, was used to make the sacred mats for the offerings, and earth of five colours was heaped on top of the sacrificial mound. In addition to the offerings all sorts of strange beasts, flying creatures, white pheasants, and other animals brought from distant regions were set free so that the ritual would be complete. Rhinoceroses, elephants, and such creatures, however, were not set free, but were brought to Mt. Tai and then taken away again. While the Feng and Shan were being performed, something like a light appeared in the sky at night, and during the day white clouds rose from the mounds.

Returning from the Shan sacrifice, the emperor took his seat in the Bright Hall, where all his ministers in turn offered him their congratulations. The emperor issued an edict to the imperial secretary which read:

---

[39] Huo Shan, the son of the famous general Huo Qubing.

I, in my humble and insignificant person, have been accorded the position of highest honour; constantly I tremble with fear that I shall not be worthy of it, for my virtue is poor and slight and I have no understanding of rites and music. When I performed the sacrifice to the Great Unity, something which looked like a beam of light was seen faintly from afar. I was filled with awe at this strange occurrence and would have proceeded no further, but I did not dare to halt. Thus I ascended Mt. Tai to perform the Feng sacrifice, journeyed to Liangfu, and later performed the Shan sacrifice at Mt. Suran, thus renewing myself. In recognition of this new beginning which I and my ministers have made, I grant to every hundred households of the common people one ox and ten piculs of wine, and in addition, to all those over eighty and to orphans and widows, two bolts of silk cloth. Bo, Fenggao, Yiqiu, and Licheng shall be exempted from *corvée* labour and need pay no taxes this year. In addition, let a general amnesty be granted to the empire of the same kind as that ordered in the year *yimao* (120 BC). None of the places which I have passed through in my visit shall be required to send labour forces, and no criminal charges dating from more than two years in the past shall be tried.

He also issued an edict saying,

In ancient times the Son of Heaven journeyed about on an inspection tour once every five years, and at that time he performed sacrifices to Mt. Tai. The feudal lords who came to pay court to him constructed their lodgings there. Let an order therefore be given to the feudal lords to build their own lodges at the foot of Mt. Tai.

The emperor had succeeded in performing the Feng and Shan and had not been troubled by wind or rain, and the magicians now came forward one after the other to assure him that the time had surely come when he would make contact with the spirits of Penglai. The emperor was overjoyed and, convinced that his meeting with the gods was near, he returned east once more to the seacoast, gazing from afar in hopes of sighting the island of Penglai. Instead, however, his carriage server Zihou, who had accompanied him to the top of Mt. Tai, was stricken with a violent sickness and died the same day. The emperor departed and, following the coast, journeyed north as far as Jieshi. From there he travelled through Liaoxi, passed along the northern border to Jiuyuan, and in the fifth month returned to the Palace of Sweet Springs.

The officials suggested that the era when the precious cauldron was found should be called *yuanding* or "Cauldron Period", and that the present year should be designated as the first year of a new era, to be called *yuanfeng*, the "Feng Period".

In the autumn a comet appeared in the constellation of the Eastern Well and some ten or twelve days later it appeared in the constellation of the Three Tai. Wang Shuo, a man versed in the observation of the skies, reported that he had seen the star[40] swell forth until it was as large as a melon, and after a while disappear again. The officials all assured the emperor, "Since Your Majesty has instituted the Feng and Shan sacrifices for the house of Han, Heaven has sent forth in response this star of virtue!" In the winter of the following year the emperor performed the suburban sacrifice to the Five Emperors at Yong and on his return he worshipped and sacrificed to the Great Unity. The following words of praise were used in the ceremony: "The star of virtue, large and brilliant, has shown us this auspicious omen. The Star of Long Life shines forth as before; deep and glowing is its great light.[41] The starry signs have appeared for all to see. The Supreme Emperor bows in reverence before the offerings of the master of invocation."

In the spring of this year Gongsun Qing reported that he had met a spiritual being at Mt. Donglai who seemed to be saying that he wished to see the Son of Heaven. The emperor therefore paid a visit to Goushi, where he honoured Gongsun Qing with the rank of palace counsellor, and then proceeded to Donglai. He lodged there for several days but did not succeed in meeting the spirit, though he did see what were said to be the footprints of a giant man. He once more dispatched a group of several thousand magicians to search for the spirits and gather the herbs of immortality.

This year there was a drought, and since the emperor had had no official business which could be used as an excuse for a trip to the east, he took this opportunity to journey to the altar of the Ten Thousand Mile Sands and offer prayers for rain. On his way back he sacrificed at Mt. Tai and then returned to Huzi, where he inspected the work which was being done to close the break in the dikes of the Yellow River there. He remained for two days and then, casting offerings into the Yellow River as a sacrifice, departed. He left orders for two

---

[40] Following the reading in *Shi ji* 12.

[41] The "star of virtue" is the comet; the Star of Long Life is Canopus, (Alpha Argus), whose shining was said to portend peace and order.

of his ministers to bring a force of soldiers and complete the closing of the breach, leading the waters off in two channels so that the river might be restored to the course it had followed in the time of Emperor Yu.

By this time the emperor had completed the conquest of the two barbarian kingdoms of Yue. A man of Yue named Yong Zhi informed the emperor that the spirits of the dead were highly honoured among the people of Yue and that at their sacrifices these spirits invariably appeared, often giving proofs of their power. In former times, he said, the king of Eastern Ou had honoured the spirits and had consequently lived to the age of 160, but later generations had grown careless and indifferent and therefore the power of Yue had declined. The emperor then ordered the shamans of Yue to set up a place for Yue sacrifices in the capital. It had a terrace but no altar. Here sacrifices were also offered to the spirits of Heaven, the Lord on High, and the various spirits of the dead, and a type of divination using chicken bones was employed which the emperor put great faith in. Thus the Yue sacrifices and chicken divination began from this time.

Gongsun Qing advised the emperor, saying, "It is quite possible to meet with the immortals. It is only that Your Majesty always rushes off in great haste to see them and therefore never succeeds. Now if you would only build some turrets like those on the city wall of Goushi and set out dried meat and jujubes, I believe the spirits could be induced to come, for they like to live in towers!"

Therefore the emperor gave orders for the construction of the Flying Eaves and Cassia Towers in Chang'an and the Increased Life and Long Life Towers at the Palace of Sweet Springs. He presented Gongsun Qing with the seals of an imperial envoy and ordered him to set out the necessary offerings and watch for the arrival of the spirits. He also built the Terrace that Reaches to Heaven and had the sacrificial utensils laid out at the foot, hoping to induce the spirits and immortals to visit it. In addition he constructed a Front Hall at the Palace of Sweet Springs and for the first time enlarged the various rooms of the palace.

In the summer the fungus of immortality sprang up in one of the rooms of the palace, and when the Terrace that Reaches to Heaven, which the emperor had built in honour of the closing of the breach in the dikes of the Yellow River, was completed, something that looked like a light in the sky was said to have appeared. The emperor therefore issued an edict saying, "In a room of the Palace of Sweet Springs the fungus of immortality, with its nine stalks, has sprung up.

A general amnesty shall be granted to the empire and no more construction labour shall be required."

The following year (108 BC) the army attacked Korea. In the summer there was a drought. Gongsun Qing informed the emperor, "In the time of the Yellow Emperor, whenever the Feng sacrifice was performed, Heaven sent a drought for three years in order to dry out the earth of the *feng* or altar mound." The emperor then issued an edict saying, "Heaven has sent this drought for the purpose of drying out the earth of the *feng*. Let all the empire be ordered to pay honour and sacrifice to the Sacred Star."

The following year the emperor performed the suburban sacrifice at Yong. He opened up a road through Huizhong and, passing through the region, reached Mingze in the spring, from whence he returned to the capital by way of Xihe.

In the winter of the following year (106 BC) the emperor visited Nan Province, travelling to Jiangling and the east, where he ascended and paid his respects to the Mountain of the Heavenly Pillar in Qian, which he designated the Southern Peak. He embarked on the Yangtze and travelled from Xunyang to Congyang, passing through Lake Pengli and paying his respects to the famous mountains and rivers along the way. From there he proceeded north to Langya, following the seacoast, and in the fourth month reached Fenggao, where he renewed the Feng sacrifice.

When the emperor first performed the Feng sacrifice at Mt. Tai a spot was pointed out to him at the northeast foot of the mountain which was said to be the site of the Bright Hall in ancient times. The place was steep and narrow, however, and the emperor wished to build his own Bright Hall in the vicinity of Fenggao, but he did not know what sort of plan to follow for the building. Then a man of Jinan named Gongyu Dai presented to the emperor a plan of the Bright Hall used in the time of the Yellow Emperor. According to this design, there was a hall in the centre, wall-less on all four sides and roofed with rushes. Streams flowed beside the fence which surrounded the building, and a two-storey walk, topped by towers, led into it from the southwest. The Son of Heaven entered by the walk, which was called Kunlun, and performed sacrifices here to the Lord on High. The emperor accordingly gave orders for a Bright Hall to be constructed beside the Wen River at Fenggao following the plan submitted by Gongyu Dai.

In the fifth year of *yuanfeng* (106 BC) when the emperor renewed the Feng sacrifice, he sacrificed to the Great Unity and the Five Emperors at the Bright Hall, placing them in the highest seats and placing the seat of Emperor Gaozu facing them. In the lower room he sacrificed to the Earth Lord. Twenty sets of animals were used for these sacrifices. The emperor entered from the Kunlun Walk and for the first time paid his respects at the Bright Hall, following the ceremony used at the suburban sacrifice. When the ceremony was completed the sacrifices were burned outside the hall.

The emperor then once more ascended Mt. Tai and performed a secret sacrifice at the summit, while at the foot of the mountain the officials performed sacrifices to the Five Emperors, each place of sacrifice being situated in the appropriate direction, except that that for the Yellow Emperor, the ruler of the centre, was combined with that for the Red Emperor of the south. When torches were lit on top of the mountain the officials at the foot all lit their torches in answer.

Two years later those who were in charge of reforming the calendar announced that it would be appropriate to carry out their changes on the day *jiazi* of the eleventh month (25 Dec. 105 BC), on which the first day of the month would correspond with the winter solstice. The emperor therefore went in person to Mt. Tai and on that day sacrificed in the Bright Hall to the Lord on High, but he did not renew the Feng and Shan. The words of praise used in the ceremony were as follows: "Heaven has once more granted to the Supreme Emperor the sacred calculations of the Great Beginning. When the cycles of the heavens have been completed, they shall in this way begin again. The Supreme Emperor respectfully bows to the Great Unity."

The emperor then proceeded east to the sea, where he examined those who had gone to sea and the magicians he had dispatched to seek for the gods, but none of them were able to report any success. He sent a large party of them out again, however, still hoping to accomplish some meeting with the spirits.

In the eleventh month, the day *yiyou* (15 Jan. 104 BC), a fire broke out at the Terrace of Cypress Beams.

On the first day of the twelfth month, the day *jiawu* (24 Jan.), the emperor in person performed the Shan sacrifice at Mt. Gaoli and offered sacrifices to the Earth Lord. He then went on to the Gulf of Bohai, where he performed sacrifices from afar to the island of Penglai and such places, hoping always to reach their wonderful halls.

The emperor then returned to the capital area and, because the Terrace of Cypress Beams had been destroyed by fire, held his court at the Palace of Sweet Springs and received the yearly accounts from the provinces and kingdoms there. Gongsun Qing informed him, "The Yellow Emperor constructed the Blue Spirit Terrace, but twelve days later it burned down. He then built the Bright Court, which was located at the site of the present Palace of Sweet Springs." Many of the other magicians likewise assured the emperor that there had been rulers in ancient times who had had their capital at Sweet Springs. The emperor therefore decided that in the future he would also hold court with the feudal lords at Sweet Springs, where mansions would be built to house the lords during their visits.

Yong Zhi of Yue informed the emperor, "According to the custom of Yue, when there has been a fire and the buildings are rebuilt, they must always be larger than before in order to overcome the evil influences." The emperor then constructed the Jianzhang Palace or Palace for Establishing the Statutes. It had a countless number of gates and doors, and the front hall was larger than that of the Eternal Palace. On the east side was the Phoenix Tower, measuring over twenty *zhang* in height. On the west were the walks, with a garden measuring twenty or thirty *li* in which tigers were kept. North of the palace was built a large lake called the Great Fluid, with the Terrace of the Lapping Water rising over twenty *zhang* from it. In the middle of the lake were Penglai, Fangzhang, Yingzhou, and Huliang, islands built to represent the spirit isles of the sea or such things as turtles and fish. On the south were the Jewelled Hall, the Jade Gate, the Great Bird, and similar constructions, as well as the Terrace of the Spirits and the Railing Tower, measuring fifty *zhang*, all connected by walks for the imperial palanquin.

In the summer the calendar of the Han dynasty was changed so that the official year began with the first month. Yellow, the colour of earth, was chosen as the colour of the dynasty, and the titles of the officials were recarved on seals so that they all consisted of five characters, five being the number appropriate to the element earth. This year was designated as the first year of the era *taichu* or "Great Beginning".

This year the armies marched west to attack Ferghana. Swarms of locusts appeared. Ding Furen, Yu Chu of Luoyang, and others used their magical arts and sacrifices to put a curse upon the leaders of the Xiongnu and Ferghana.

The following year the officials informed the emperor that there were no proper vessels for use in boiling the sacrificial animals at the Five Altars of Yong, and for this reason the fragrance of the offerings was not being properly presented. The emperor therefore ordered the sacrificial officials to present vessels to the altars for use in the calf offerings. The colour of the sacrificial animals was to be that appropriate to whichever of the Five Emperors was being sacrificed to. He ordered, however, that wooden models of horses be substituted for the former offerings of colts.[42] Real colts were to be used only when the emperor in person performed the suburban sacrifice. Likewise all of the sacrifices to famous mountains and rivers which had previously used colts were to substitute wooden horses except when the emperor visited the region to perform the sacrifice himself. In all other respects the ceremonies were to be carried out in the same way as before.

The following year (102 BC) the emperor journeyed east to the sea to examine the men who had been sent to search for the immortals, but none of them had any success to report. The magicians then informed him that in the time of the Yellow Emperor there had been five city walls and twelve towers at Zhiqi from which the spirits were observed, which were called "Prolonged Life". The emperor gave permission for the construction of similar walls and towers according to the directions of the magicians, to be called "Bright Life". The emperor sacrificed there in person to the Lord on High.

Gongyu Dai advised the emperor, saying, "When the Yellow Emperor was alive, although he performed the Feng sacrifice at Mt. Tai, his ministers Fenghou, Fengju, and Qibo instructed him to perform the Feng at the Eastern Mt. Tai and the Shan at Mt. Fan as well. Only when he had thus obeyed the omens sent from Heaven was he able to obtain immortal life!"

The emperor accordingly ordered the sacrificial utensils prepared and journeyed to the Eastern Mt. Tai, but he found it to be a small hill of no great height, in no way measuring up to the exalted name it bore. He therefore ordered the sacrificial officials to conduct ceremonies there, but he did not perform the Feng or Shan sacrifices. He later ordered Gongyu Dai to perform sacrifices and watch for spiritual beings.

In the summer the emperor proceeded to Mt. Tai to renew the Feng sacrifice, as was appropriate every five years, using the same ceremony he had used before except that he also performed the Shan sacrifice at Stone Gate. Stone Gate is located at the southern foot of Mt. Tai. According to a number of the magicians, it is the gateway to the village of the immortals and for this reason

---

[42] The Han was chronically short of horses, and particularly at this time when large armies were needed for the campaigns against Ferghana and the Xiongnu. The five characters which follow this in the text appear to be a later addition and have not been translated.

the emperor performed the Shan in person there.

Five years later (98 BC) he once more went to Mt. Tai to renew the Feng sacrifice, and on his way back to the capital he sacrificed at Mt. Hengg.

The sacrifices instituted by the present emperor, then, are those to the Great Unity and the Earth Lord, as well as the suburban sacrifices performed by the ruler in person every three years. He has established the Feng and Shan sacrifices for the Han dynasty, which are renewed every five years, as well as the five sacrifices to the Great Unity recommended by Miu Ji, the Three Unities, the Dark Ram, the Horse Traveller, the Red Star, and those at the altars recommended by Kuan Shu, with officials to perform the ceremonies to them at the appropriate seasons. All of the last six groups of sacrifices are under the jurisdiction of the master of invocations.

As for the Eight Spirits and the other deities, Bright Life, Mt. Fan, and similar sacrificial places mentioned, if the emperor happens to be passing by, then sacrifices are performed to them, and when he has departed, they are discontinued. Any places of sacrifice instituted by the magicians themselves are left to their own charge; they continue as long as the particular man is living, and are discontinued at his death, the sacrificial officials of the government having nothing to do with them. All other sacrifices are carried on as they were in previous reigns.

The present emperor, after performing the Feng and Shan, made another tour twelve years later (98 BC), visiting all the Five Peaks and the Four Watercourses. The magicians who had been instructed to watch for spirit beings, and those who had been sent to search for the island of Penglai in the sea, failed completely during that time to produce any evidence of success. Gongsun Qing was supposed to be observing the spirits, but he too had nothing to show for his efforts and could only make excuses by pointing out the footprints of giant men. Thus the emperor grew increasingly weary and disgusted with the inane tales of the magicians, and yet he was bound and snared by them and could not free himself, for always he hoped to find one who spoke the truth. From this time on, the magicians who came to him recommending sacrifices to this or that deity grew even more numerous, but the results of all this are as one can see.

The Grand Historian remarks: I accompanied the emperor when he journeyed about to sacrifice to Heaven and Earth, the other deities, and the famous mountains and rivers, and when he went to perform the Feng and Shan. I entered the Temple of Long Life and assisted at the sacrifices there when the deity spoke, and I thus had an opportunity to study and examine the ways of the magicians and the sacrificial officials. Later I retired and wrote down in order all that I knew about the worship of the spirits from ancient times on, setting forth both the outside and the inside stories of these affairs. Gentlemen in later ages will thus be able to peruse what I have written. As for the details of sacrificial plates and utensils, the types of jades and silks offered, or the exact ritual to be followed in presenting them — these I have left to the officials who handle such matters.

SHI JI 29: THE TREATISE ON THE YELLOW RIVER AND CANALS

In ancient times Emperor Yu deepened the rivers and saved the empire from flood, bringing relief and security to the nine provinces. Concerning the waterways that were opened or diked, the river courses that were fixed, and the canals that were constructed, I made "The Treatise on the Yellow River and Canals".

The documents on the Xia dynasty tell us that Emperor Yu spent thirteen years controlling and bringing an end to the floods, and during that period, though he passed by the very gate of his own house, he did not take the time to enter. On land he travelled in a cart and on water in a boat; he rode a sledge to cross the mud and wore cleated shoes in climbing the mountains. In this way he marked out the nine provinces, led the rivers along the bases of the mountains, decided what tribute was appropriate for each region in accordance with the quality of its soil, opened up the nine roads, built embankments around the nine marshes, and made a survey of the nine mountains.

Of all the rivers, the Yellow River caused the greatest damage to China by overflowing its banks and inundating the land, and therefore he turned all his attention to controlling it. Thus he led the Yellow River in a course from Jishi past Longmen and south to the northern side of Mt. Hua; from there eastward along the foot of Dizhu Mountain, past the Meng Ford and the confluence of the Luo River to Dapei. At this point Emperor Yu decided that, since the river was descending from high ground and the flow of the water was rapid and fierce, it would be difficult to guide it over level ground without danger of frequent disastrous break-throughs. He therefore divided the flow into two channels, leading it along the higher ground to the north, past the Jiang River and so to Dalu. There he spread it out to form the Nine Rivers, brought it together again to make the Backward-flowing River (i.e., tidal river), and thence led it into the Gulf of Bohai.[1] When he had thus opened up the rivers of the nine provinces

---

[1] Needless to say, this is simply a description of the course of the Yellow River in ancient times. The passage, though not a direct quotation, is based upon the "Tribute of Yu" section of the *Book of Documents*.

and fixed the outlets of the nine marshes, peace and order were brought to the lands of the Xia and his achievements continued to benefit the Three Dynasties which followed.

Sometime later the Hong Canal was constructed, leading off from the lower reaches of the Yellow River at Xingyang, passing through the states of Song, Zheng, Chen, Cai, Cao, and Wey, and joining up with the Ji, Ru, Huai, and Si rivers. In Chu two canals were built, one in the west from the Han River through the plains of Yunmeng, and one in the east to connect the Yangtze and Huai rivers.[2] In Wu a canal was dug to connect the three mouths of the Yangtze and the Five Lakes, and in Qi one between the Zi and Ji rivers. In Shu, Li Bing, the governor of Shu, cut back the Li Escarpment to control the ravages of the Mo River and also opened up channels for the Two Rivers through the region of Chengdu.

All of these canals were navigable by boat, and whenever there was an overflow of water it was used for irrigation purposes, so that the people gained great benefit from them. In addition there were literally millions of smaller canals which led off from the larger ones at numerous points along their courses and were employed to irrigate an increasingly large area of land, but none of these are worth mentioning here.

Ximen Bao built a canal to lead off the waters of the Zhang River and irrigate Ye, and as a result the region of Henei in the state of Wei became rich.

Another time the state of Hann, learning that the state of Qin was fond of undertaking large projects, dispatched a water engineer named Zheng Guo to go to Qin and persuade the ruler to construct a canal from a point on the Jing River west of Mt. Zhong to the pass at Hukou, and from there along the Northern Mountains east into the Luo River, a distance of over 300 *li*. Ostensibly the purpose of the project was to provide irrigation for the fields, though in fact Zheng Guo and the rulers of Hann hoped thereby to wear out the energies of the state of Qin so that it would not march east to attack Hann. Zheng Guo succeeded in getting the project started, but halfway through the real nature of his mission came to light. The Qin ruler was about to kill him, but Zheng Guo said, "It is true that I came here originally with underhanded intentions. But if the canal is completed, it will profit the state of Qin as well!"

The Qin ruler, deciding that this was sensible, in the end allowed him to go ahead with the canal. When it was finished, it was used to spread muddy,

---

[2]Following the reading in *Han shu* 29.

silt-laden water over more than 40,000 *qing* of land in the area which up until this time had been very brackish, bringing the yield of the land up to one *zhong* per acre (*mu*).[3] As a result the area within the Pass was converted into fertile fields and no longer suffered from lean years; Qin became rich and powerful and eventually was able to conquer all the other feudal lords and unite the empire. In honour of its builder the canal was named Zheng Guo Canal.

Thirty-nine years after the founding of the Han (168 BC), in the reign of Emperor Wen, the Yellow River overflowed its banks at Suanzao and destroyed the Metal Embankment east of there. Accordingly a large force of labourers was called up in Dong Province to repair the break.

Some forty years later,[4] during the era *yuanguang* (134-129 BC) of the present emperor, the Yellow River broke its banks at Huzi, flowing southeast into the marsh of Juye and joining up with the Huai and Si rivers. The emperor accordingly ordered Ji An and Zheng Dangshi to raise a force of labourers and repair the breach, but no sooner had they done so than the river broke through again. At this time Tian Fen, the marquis of Wuan, was serving as chancellor and his income came from an estate in Shu. Shu is located north of the Yellow River, and since the break was on the southern side, suffered no damage from floods; on the contrary the revenue from the estate actually increased. Tian Fen said to the emperor, "Breaks in the banks of the Yangtze and the Yellow River are all the work of Heaven. It is no easy task to stop up such breaks forcibly by human labour, and indeed to do so would hardly be in accord with the will of Heaven!" The numerologists and those who interpret the emanations in the sky supported him in this view and the emperor therefore hesitated and for a long time made no further attempts to repair the break.

At this time Zheng Dangshi, who was serving as minister of agriculture, said to the emperor, "Up to now grain from east of the Pass has been brought to the capital by being transported up the Wei River. The operation requires six months to complete and the course is over 900 *li* and beset with dangerous places. Now if we were to dig a canal from the Wei River, beginning at Chang'an and following along the Southern Mountains to the Yellow River, the distance could be reduced to something over 300 *li*. We would have a much easier route

---

[3] One *qing* was equal to about fifty-seven English acres, and there were 500 *mu* in a *qing*. One *zhong* was equal to ten *hu*, or about five-and-a-half bushels.

[4] Sima Qian's figure is misleading; the break took place in 132 BC, only thirty-six years after the earlier break.

for transporting grain, and the trip could be accomplished in three months. Moreover, the people living along the canal could utilize the water to irrigate over 10,000 *qing* of farmland. Thus we could reduce the time and labour required to haul grain and at the same time increase the fertility of the lands within the Pass and obtain a higher yield."

Approving the plan, the emperor ordered Xu Bo, a water engineer from Qi, to plot the course of the transport canal and called up a force of 20,000 or 30,000 labourers to do the digging. After three years of labour, it was opened for use in hauling grain and proved extremely beneficial. From this time on grain transport to the capital gradually increased, while the people living along the canal were able to make considerable use of the water to irrigate their fields.

After this, Pan Xi, the governor of Hedong, said to the emperor, "Every year over 1,000,000 piculs of grain are transported to the capital from the area east of the mountains. Since it is brought up the Yellow River, it must be shipped through the dangerous narrows at Dizhu Mountain, where much of it is lost, and in addition the cost of transportation is very high. Now if we were to dig canals from the Fen River to irrigate the region of Pishi and parts of Fenyin, and other canals from the Yellow River to irrigate Puban and the rest of Fenyin, I believe we could bring 5,000 *qing* of land under cultivation. At present this region is nothing more than a strip of uncultivated land along the Yellow River where the people graze their flocks but, if it were turned into irrigated fields, I think it could be made to yield over 2,000,000 piculs of grain. This could be transported up the Wei River to the capital and would be no more expensive than grain produced in the area within the Pass. It would then no longer be necessary to haul grain from the east past the dangerous part of the river at Dizhu."

The emperor considered this a sound idea and called up a force of 20,000 or 30,000 labourers who worked for several years diging canals and opening up the fields. But the Yellow River changed its course so that the water did not flow into the canals properly and the farmers who worked the newly opened fields were unable to produce enough to repay the cost of planting. After some time, therefore, the newly opened canals and fields in Hedong were abandoned and the area was turned over to settlers from the state of Yue. What little revenue it produced was allotted to the privy treasury.

Following this, someone sent a letter to the throne proposing that a road be opened up between the Bao and Ye rivers, and that they be used to transport grain. The emperor referred the proposal to the imperial secretary Zhang Tang who, after conducting an inquiry, reported as follows: "At present anyone wishing to travel to the province of Shu must go over the Old Road, a very long and roundabout route beset with steep places. Now if the Bao and Ye rivers were dredged and a road opened between them, it would provide a much more level route and the distance could be reduced to 400 *li*. The Bao River runs into the Mian River and the Ye River runs into the Wei, both of which can be used to transport grain. Therefore grain could be brought from Nanyang up the Mian River and into the Bao, and where the Bao ends it could be transported overland by carts for a distance of 100 *li* or so to where the Ye begins, and from there down the Wei to Chang'an. Thus grain from Hanzhong could be brought to the capital. At the same time, by making use of the Mian River, grain could be transported from east of the mountains in unlimited quantities and the route would be much more convenient than the present one up the Yellow River and through the narrows at Dizhu. Moreover, the region of the Bao and Ye is as rich in timber and bamboo as the provinces of Ba and Shu."

The emperor approved the proposal and appointed Zhang Tang's son Zhang Ang as governor of Hanzhong, calling up a force of 20,000 or 30,000 labourers and setting them to work constructing the Bao and Ye road and waterway which extended more than 500 *li*. When the road was finished it did in fact prove to be much shorter and more convenient than the old route, but the rivers were too full of rapids and boulders to be used for transporting grain.

Following this, a man named Zhuang Xiongpi reported to the emperor that the people of Linjin wished to dig a canal from the Luo River to be used to irrigate some 10,000 *qing* of land east of Chongquan. The land in this area was brackish, but the people believed that if it could be irrigated with water led in from the Luo River, it could be made to produce ten piculs per acre. The emperor therefore called up a labour force of over 10,000 men and set them to work digging a canal leading off from the Luo River at Zheng and extending to the foot of Mt. Shangyan. There, however, it was found that the banks of the canal kept collapsing, so the men dug wells, some of them over forty *zhang* deep, at various points along the course and induced the water to flow from one well to another. Thus the water disappeared from sight at Mt. Shangyan and flowed underground to the eastern side of the mountain, a distance of over ten *li*. This was the beginning of the so-called well-canals. In the course of the digging a dragon bone was discovered and the canal was therefore named Dragon Head Canal. It has been over ten years now since it was constructed but, although the water flows through it fairly well, the land has not yet shown much improvement.

More than twenty years had passed since the Yellow River broke through its banks at Huzi. The break had not been repaired and the harvests were frequently poor, the damage being particularly severe in Liang and Chu. The emperor, having gone east to perform the Feng and Shan sacrifices (110 BC), made a tour through the empire, sacrificing to various mountains and rivers. The following year (109 BC) there was a drought (the purpose of which, it was said, was to dry out the earth of the altar mound constructed for the Feng sacrifice), and very little rain fell. The emperor ordered Ji Ren and Guo Chang to raise a force of 20,000 or 30,000 men and close the break in the banks of the Yellow River at Huzi, while he himself went east to pray for rain at the Altar of the Ten Thousand Mile Sands. On his way back to the capital he stopped to inspect the break in person and cast offerings of jade and a white horse into the river. He ordered all the courtiers and ministers who were accompanying him, from the generals on down, to carry bundles of brushwood and help close the break in the embankment. As it happened, the people of Dong Province had just burned off all their grasslands, so there was very little brushwood to be found in the area. The workmen were therefore obliged to sink lengths of bamboo from the Qi Park to form a weir across the opening. As the emperor surveyed the break, he was filled with despair at the difficulty of the task and composed this song:

> The river broke through at Huzi;
> What could we do?
> Beneath its rushing waves,
> Villages all became rivers.
> The villages have all become rivers
> And there is no safety for the land.
> Our labours know no rest,
> Our mountains crumble.
> Our mountains crumble
> And the marsh of Juye overflows.
> Even the fish lament
> As the winter days press near.
> The river raged from its boundaries,
> It has left its constant course.
> Dragons and water monsters leap forth,
> Free to wander afar.
> Let it return to the old channel
> And we will truly bless the gods.

> But for my journey to the Feng and Shan,
> How would I have known what it was like?
> Ask the Lord of the River for me,
> "Why are you so cruel?
> Your surging inundations will not cease;
> You grieve my people!
> The city of Niesang is awash;
> The Huai and Si brim over,
> So long, and yet you will not return —
> You overstep the watery bounds!"
>
> The river rages on,
> Its wild waters tossing.
> It swirls back to the north,
> A swift and dangerous torrent.
> We bring the long stakes
> And cast the precious jade.
> The Lord of the River hears our plea
> But there is not enough brushwood.
> There is not enough brushwood —
> The fault of the people of Wey.
> They have wasted the land with fire —
> What can we use to check the waters?
> We sink the forest bamboo
> And ballast the weir with stones.
> We will stem the break at Xuanfang
> And bring ten thousand blessings!

Thus they finally succeeded in closing the gap at Huzi and built a temple on top of the embankment called the Temple of Xuanfang. They led the waters of the river off to the north in two channels so that it returned to the course it had followed in the time of Emperor Yu. Safety was restored to the regions of Liang and Chu, and they no longer suffered any damage from flood waters.

After this the men who were concerned with such affairs all rushed to the emperor with proposals for utilizing the rivers to greater advantage. As a result canals were dug in Shuofang, Xihe, Hexi, and Jiuquan to draw off water from the Yellow River or smaller rivers in the valleys and use it to irrigate the fields. Within the Pass the Fu and Lingzhi canals were constructed, making use of the water of various rivers in the region; in Ru'nan and Jiujiang water was drawn off from the Huai River; the Donghai from the marsh of Juding; and at the foot of Mt. Tai from the Wen River. In all these places canals were dug to water the fields, providing irrigation for over 10,000 *qing* of land in each area. In addition many other small canals and waterways through the mountains were opened up, but they are too numerous to describe here. Of all these exploits, however, the most outstanding was the closing of the break in the Yellow River at Xuanfang.

The Grand Historian remarks: I have climbed Mt. Lu in the south to observe the courses which Emperor Yu opened up for the nine tributaries of the Yangtze. From there I journeyed to Kuaiji and Taihuang and, ascending the heights of Gusu, looked out over the Five Lakes. In the east I have visited the confluence of the Yellow and Luo rivers, Dapei, and the Backward-flowing River, and have travelled along the waterways of the Huai, Si, Ji, Ta, and Luo rivers. In the west I have seen Mt. Min and the Li Escarpment in the province of Shu, and I have journeyed through the north from Longmen to Shuofang. How tremendous are the benefits brought by these bodies of water, and how terrible the damages! I was among those who carried bundles of brushwood on their backs to stem the break at Xuanfang and, deeply moved by the song of Huzi, I made this treatise on the Yellow River and the Canals.

SHI JI 30: THE TREATISE ON
THE BALANCED STANDARD

The purpose of currency is to provide a medium of exchange between farmers and merchants, but in extreme cases it is subject to all kinds of clever manipulation. As a result, the great landholders increase their power and men compete for the opportunity to turn a neat profit, abandoning the pursuit of agriculture, which is basic, to follow the secondary occupations of commerce. Thus I made "The Treatise on the Balanced Standard", showing how these changes come about.

When the Han dynasty came to power, it inherited the evils left by the Qin. The able-bodied men were all away with the army, while the old and underaged busily transported supplies for them. There was much hard work and little wealth. The Son of Heaven himself could not find four horses of the same colour to draw his carriage, many of his generals and ministers were reduced to riding about in ox carts, and the common people had nothing to lay away in their storehouses.

Because the currency of the Qin was heavy and cumbersome to use, the Han ordered the people to mint new coins. The unit for gold was one catty. The laws and prohibitions of the Qin having been simplified or done away with, people who were intent upon making a profit by underhanded means began to hoard their wealth, buying up the commodities on the market, so that the price of goods shot up. Grain put up for sale brought as much as 10,000 cash[1] a picul, and a horse fetched 100 catties of gold.

After peace had been restored to the empire, Gaozu issued an order forbidding merchants to wear silk or ride in carriages, and increased the taxes that they were obliged to pay in order to hamper and humiliate them.[2] During the reigns of Emperor Hui and Empress Lü, because the empire had only just

---

[1] Ten thousand copper cash were equal in value to one catty of gold.

[2] The traditional Chinese practice of making life difficult for the merchants in order to encourage agriculture.

begun to recover from the period of war and confusion, the laws concerning the merchants were relaxed, though the sons and grandsons of merchant families were prohibited from holding government office.

The salaries of officials and the costs of the administration were estimated, and the necessary funds collected from the people in the form of a poll tax. Revenues from the natural resources of mountains, rivers, parks, and lakes, as well as those from the government market places and from other kinds of taxes, were all used for the private maintenance of the Son of Heaven or the feudal lords and princesses from whose lands they were collected, and were not entered in the budget for the empire as a whole. The amount of grain transported from east of the mountains each year to supply the officials of the capital did not exceed 200,000 or 300,000 piculs.

In the time of Emperor Wen, because the "elm-pod" coins, minted earlier, had grown too numerous and light in weight, new coins were cast weighing four *shu* and inscribed with the words *banliang* or "half-tael". The people were allowed to mint them at will.[3] As a result the king of Wu, though only a feudal lord, was able, by extracting ore from the mountains in his domain and minting coins, to rival the wealth of the Son of Heaven. It was this wealth which he eventually used to start his revolt. Similarly, Deng Tong, who was only a high official, succeeded in becoming richer than a vassal king by minting coins. The coins of the king of Wu and Deng Tong were soon circulating all over the empire, and as a result the private minting of coinage was finally prohibited.

At this time the Xiongnu were making frequent raids across the northern border, and farming garrisons had to be set up along the frontier to stop them. The grain produced by these garrisons alone, however, was not sufficient to feed all the border troops. The government then called upon the people to supply grain, offering honourary ranks to those who were prepared to send grain to the frontier. The ranks varied with the amount of grain but reached as high as the eighteenth rank, called *dashuzhang*. Later, during Emperor Jing's reign, because of the drought which prevailed in Shang Province and the west, the order concerning the sale of ranks was revived, but the price of the ranks was reduced in order to attract more people. In addition men who had been condemned to duty on the frontier for a year, together with the women of their families who were sentenced to menial service in the government workshops, were permitted

---

[3] Though Gaozu had allowed the people to mint the "elm-pod" shaped coins, there is evidence that Empress Lü put a stop to the practice of private minting.

to buy off their sentences by transporting grain to the government. More pastures for raising horses were opened up in order to supply the needs of the nation, and the number of palaces and pleasure towers, carriages and horses at the disposal of the emperor was increased.

By the time the present emperor had been on the throne a few years, a period of over seventy years had passed since the founding of the Han. During that time the nation had met with no major disturbances so that, except in times of flood or drought, every person was well supplied and every family had enough to get along on. The granaries in the cities and the countryside were full and the government treasuries were running over with wealth. In the capital the strings of cash had been stacked up by the hundreds of millions until the cords that bound them had rotted away and they could no longer be counted. In the central granary of the government, new grain was heaped on top of the old until the building was full and the grain overflowed and piled up outside, where it spoiled and became unfit to eat. Horses were to be seen even in the streets and lanes of the common people or plodding in great numbers along the paths between the fields, and anyone so poor as to have to ride a mare was disdained by his neighbours and not allowed to join the gatherings of the villagers. Even the keepers of the community gates ate fine grain and meat. The local officials remained at the same posts long enough to see their sons and grandsons grow to manhood, and the higher officials occupied the same positions so long that they adopted their official titles as surnames. As a result, men had a sense of self-respect and regarded it as a serious matter to break the law. Their first concern was to act in accordance with what was right and to avoid shame and dishonour.

At this time, however, because the net of the law was slack and the people were rich, it was possible for men to use their wealth to exploit others and to accumulate huge fortunes. Some, such as the great landowners and powerful families, were able to do anything they pleased in the countryside, while the members of the imperial house and the nobility, the high officials and the lesser government officers, strove to outdo each other in luxurious living; there was no limit to how far each would go in aping the houses, carriages, and dress of his social superiors.

But it has ever been the law of change that when things reach their period of greatest flourishing, they must begin to decay. Shortly after this time Zhuang Zhu, Zhu Maichen, and others invited the people of the region of Eastern Ou to move to China, intervening in the war between the two kingdoms of Yue, and the area between the Huai and Yangtze rivers, to which they were transferred, was put to great trouble and expense. Tang Meng and Sima Xiangru opened up a road to the land of the barbarians in the southwest, cutting a passage over 1,000 *li* long through the mountains in order to broaden the provinces of Ba and Shu, but the undertaking exhausted the people of these regions. Peng Wu established relations with the peoples of Weimo and Chaoxian and set up the province of Canghai on the Korean Peninsula, but the move caused great unrest among the inhabitants of the neighbouring states of Yan and Qi.[4]

After Wang Hui made his unsuccessful attempt to ambush the Xiongnu at Mayi, peaceful relations with the Xiongnu came to an end and they began to invade and plunder the northern border. Armies had to be dispatched time and again and could not be disbanded, causing extreme hardship to the empire. As the conflicts became fiercer day by day, men set off to war carrying their packs of provisions, while those left behind at home had to send more and more goods to keep them supplied. Those at home and those on the frontier were kept busy guarding the empire and supplying rations until the common people were exhausted and began to look for some clever way to evade the laws. The funds of the government were soon used up and, in order to supply the deficiencies, it was agreed that men who presented goods would be appointed to official positions, and those who made appropriate contributions would be pardoned for their crimes. The old system of selecting officials on the basis of merit fell into disuse, and modesty and a sense of shame became rare qualities. Military achievement was now the key to advancement. The law were made stricter and more detailed, and officials whose main job was to make a profit for the government for the first time appeared in office.

After this the Han generals every year led forces of 20,000 or 30,000 cavalry in attacks on the barbarians and the general of carriage and cavalry Wei Qing seized the region south of the bend of the Yellow River from the Xiongnu and fortified Shuofang.

At the same time the Han government was building the road through the region of the southwestern barbarians, employing a force of 20,000 or 30,000 labourers. Provisions for them had to be carried for a distance of 1,000 *li*, and of ten or more *zhong* sent out, only one picul, or less than one tenth of the original amount, reached its destination. In addition gifts of money were distributed to

---

[4]Following the reading in *Han shu* 24B. Detailed accounts of these events will be found in the chapters dealing with foreign peoples later on in this volume.

the inhabitants of Qiong and Po in order to win their support. Several years passed, however, and the road was still not completed. In the meantime, the barbarians several times attacked the labourers, and the Han officials were forced to call out troops to control them. All the taxes from the region of Ba and Shu were insufficient to cover the expenses of the road, and it was decided to invite wealthy families to open up farms in the region of the southern barbarians; for any grain which they turned over to the government, they would be reimbursed in cash by the financial officers of the ministry of agriculture in the capital. Again, when the road was opened up to the province of Canghai in the east, the expenditures for labourers were just as great. In addition, a force of over 100,000 men was conscripted to build the fortifications at Shuofang and guard them. Provisions for all these undertakings had to be transported great distances over land and water, and the burden fell upon all the regions east of the mountains. Expenditures ran from two to three to ten billions of cash and the government treasuries became emptier then ever. An order was issued allowing those who presented male or female slaves to the government to be exempted from military and labour services for lifetime or, if the donor was already a palace attendant and therefore exempt, to receive an advancement in rank. It even reached the point where men were made palace attendants because of donations of sheep!

Four years later (124 BC) the general in chief Wei Qing, commanding six generals and an army of over 100,000, attacked the Xiongnu leader known as the Wise King of the Right, beheading or capturing 15,000 of the enemy. The following year Wei Qing again led six generals in another attack on the barbarians, beheading or capturing 19,000 men. Those who had beheaded or captured enemy soldiers were presented with gifts totalling over 200,000 catties of gold. Generous gifts were also given to the tens of thousands of enemy captives, and food and clothing were supplied to them by the government. The men and horses killed on the Han side amounted to over 100,000. In addition, there were the expenses for weapons and the cost of provisions transported to the armies.

By this time the reserves of cash stored up by the ministry of agriculture from earlier years had been exhausted and the revenue from taxes had likewise been used up, so that there was not enough money left to support the troops. When the officials reported this fact to the emperor, he replied, "I have been told that the Five Emperors of antiquity did not necessarily follow the same policies, and yet they all achieved good government; that the rulers Yu and Tang did not necessarily use the same kind of laws, though they were both worthy kings. The roads they followed were different, but all led to the same ultimate goal of establishing virtue. Now peace has not yet been restored to the northern frontier, a fact which grieves me deeply. Recently the general in chief attacked the Xiongnu and beheaded or captured 19,000 of the enemy, and yet the rewards and supplies due him and his men are held back and they have not yet received them. Let deliberations begin on a law to allow the people to purchase honourary ranks and to buy mitigations of punishments or freedom from prohibitions against holding office."

The officials responded by requesting the establishment of honourary official positions, to be known as "ranks of military merit". One grade of the rank was to be priced at 170,000 cash, the total value of the sale amounting to over 300,000 catties of gold.[5] Among the purchasers of "ranks of military merit", those of the *guanshou* or fifth grade or above were to be accorded the same privileges as regular government officials of the fifth lord class. Those guilty of some crime were to have two grades deducted from the ranks they purchased, but were to be allowed to purchase as high as *leqing*, the eighth grade. The purpose of this was to honour military achievements, but where such achievements were particularly numerous, the awards exceeded the limits set for the various grades, so that those with the most distinguished records were enfeoffed as marquises or appointed as high government officials. As a result, so many avenues to official position were opened and such confusion reigned that the whole system of government offices broke down in chaos.

After Gongsun Hong secured the post of chancellor because of his recommendations for correcting the conduct of ministers according to the principles of the *Spring and Autumn Annals*, and after Zhang Tang was made commandant of justice because of his enforcement of decisions on the basis of severe laws, the legal principle that anyone who allows a criminal act to go unreported is as guilty as the criminal himself came into being, and the law officials were busily engaged in conducting investigations of officials who ignored, impeded, or criticized the orders of the government.

The following year (122 BC) the plans for revolt laid by the kings of Huainan, Hengshan, and Jiangdu came to light. The high ministers conducted a thorough investigation of everyone connected with the affair and ferreted out all the conspirators. Twenty or thirty thousand persons were tried and executed.

---

[5] The sentence is obscure, and commentators differ widely in their interpretations.

The government authorities became increasingly cruel and exacting and the laws more precise and detailed than ever.

At this time the emperor had sent out a call for men of unusual character and learning to take positions in the government, and some of them had reached the highest offices. Among them Gongsun Hong, who became chancellor, made a point of using coarse bedding and refusing to eat highly spiced food, hoping to set an example for the empire. His efforts, however, had no effect upon the customs of the time and men only devoted themselves with greater energy to the pursuit of reward and gain.

The following year the general of swift cavalry Huo Qubing led another attack on the Xiongnu, returning with 40,000 enemy heads. In the fall the Hunye king, leading 30,000 or 40,000 of his barbarian subjects, came to surrender to the Han. The Han dispatched 20,000 carriages to fetch them, and when they arrived in the capital, gifts and rewards were bestowed upon them, as well as upon the Han soldiers who had distinguished themselves. This year the total expenditures amounted to over ten billion cash.

Some ten or more years previous to this the Yellow River had broken its banks in the region of Guan, and during the years that followed, the regions of Liang and Chu suffered repeatedly from floods. The provinces bordering the river would no sooner repair the embankments then the water would break through again, so that an incalculable amount of money was spent in vain.

Some time after this Pan Xi, hoping to avoid the difficulties involved in transporting grain past Mt. Dizhu, on the Yellow River, began work on irrigation canals from the Yellow and Fen rivers which were intended to open up the region between the two rivers for farming, a project requiring a labour force of 20,000 or 30,000 men. Zheng Dangshi, considering the transport of grain via the Wei River to be too lengthy and circuitous, began work on a canal running directly from Chang'an to Huayin, a project which required a similar number of labourers. Still other canals were under construction at Shuofang, requiring the same number of labourers. Each of these projects had been in progress for two or three years without reaching completion and each necessitated expenditures ranging into billions of cash.

The emperor also turned his attention to the large-scale raising of horses for use in campaigns against the barbarians. Twenty or thirty thousand horses were brought to the region of Chang'an to be pastured, but as there were not enough conscripts in the area within the Pass to train and take care of them, more men were recruited from the neighbouring provinces. The Xiongnu barbarians who had surrendered were all supposed to be fed and clothed by the government, but funds in the government offices proved insufficient, and the emperor was obliged to reduce the expenses of his own table, dispense with his carriage drawn by four horses of matched colour, and pay out money from his private reserves in order to make up the deficiency.

The next year (120 BC) the lands east of the mountains were troubled by floods and many of the people were reduced to starvation. The emperor dispatched envoys to the provinces and kingdoms to empty the granaries and relieve the sufferings of the poor, but there was not enough food to go around. He then called upon wealthy families to make loans to the needy, but even this did not remedy the situation. At last he ordered some 700,000 of the poor to emigrate and resettle in the lands west of the Pass and the region of New Qin south of Shuofang. Food and clothing were to be supplied to them for the first few years by the government officials, who were also instructed to lend them what they needed to start a livelihood. Envoys sent to supervise the various groups of emigrants poured out of the capital in such numbers that their carts and carriage covers were constantly in sight of each other on the roads. The expenses of the move were estimated in the billions, the final sum reaching incalculable proportions.

By this time the funds of the government officials were completely exhausted. The rich merchants and big traders, however, were busy accumulating wealth and forcing the poor into their hire, transporting goods back and forth in hundreds of carts, buying up surplus commodities and hoarding them in the villages; even the feudal lords were forced to go to them with bowed heads and beg for what they needed. Others who were engaged in smelting iron and extracting salt from sea water accumulated fortunes amounting to tens of thousands of catties of gold, and yet they did nothing to help the distress of the nation, and the common people were plunged deeper and deeper into misery.

With this the emperor consulted his high ministers on plans to change the coinage and issue a new currency in order to provide for the expenses of the state and to suppress the idle and unscrupulous landlords who were acquiring such huge estates. At this time there were white deer in the imperial park, while the privy treasury was in possession of a considerable amount of silver and tin. It had been over forty years since Emperor Wen changed over to the four-*shu* copper coins. From the beginning of Emperor Wu's reign, because revenue in coin had been rather scarce, the government officials had from time to time extracted copper from the mountains in their areas and minted new coins, while among the common people there was a good deal of illegal minting of coins, until the number in circulation had grown beyond estimate. As the coins became more numerous and of poorer quality, goods became scarcer and higher in price. The officials therefore advised the emperor, saying, "In ancient times, currency made of hides was used by the feudal lords for gifts and presentations. At present there are three types of metal in use: gold, which is the most precious; silver, which ranks second; and copper, which is third. The 'half-tael' coins now in use are supposed by law to weigh four *shu*, but people have tampered with them to such an extent, illegally filing off bits of copper from the reverse side, that they have become increasingly light and thin and the price of goods has accordingly risen. Such currency is extremely troublesome and expensive to use, especially in distant regions."

The white deer in the imperial park were accordingly killed and their hides cut into one-foot squares, embroidered at the borders with silk thread of different colours, and made into hide currency. Each square was valued at 400,000 cash. When members of the imperial house and the nobility appeared at court in the spring and autumn and offered their gifts to the throne, they were required to present their jade insignia upon one of these deerskin squares before they were allowed to proceed with the ceremony.

In addition, "white metal" coins were made from an alloy of silver and tin. Since the dragon is most useful in the heavens, the horse most useful on earth, and the tortoise most useful to mankind,[6] the coins were made in three grades. The first was inscribed "weight eight taels" and was round, with a picture of a dragon on it. It was called a "white *xuan*" and was valued at 3,000 cash. The second was inscribed "less in weight", was square, and bore a picture of a horse. It was worth 500 cash. The third was inscribed "still less in weight", was oval in shape, and bore a picture of a tortoise. It was valued at 300 cash. Orders were sent to the government officials to melt down the old "half-tael" coins and mint new three-*shu* coins, inscribed with their weight. Orders were also given that all persons found guilty of illegally minting any of the new silver or copper coins should be put to death. In spite of this, however, any number of persons in the government and among the people were apprehended for illegally minting silver coins.

At this time Dongguo Xianyang and Kong Jin were appointed assistants to

---

[6]Because its shell may be used for divination.

the ministry of agriculture and put in charge of the control of salt and iron, while Sang Hongyang, because of his experience in money matters, was given a post in the palace. Dongguo Xianyang was a leading salt manufacturer of Qi, and Kong Jin a great iron smelter of Nanyang; both of them had accumulated fortunes amounting to 100,000 catties of gold and for that reason had been recommended for office by Zheng Dangshi. Sang Hongyang was the son of a merchant of Luoyang who, because of his ability to work sums in his head, had been made a palace attendant at the age of thirteen. When it came to a question of how to make a profit, therefore, the three of them knew their business down to the smallest detail.

By this time the laws had been made much stricter, and many of the lesser officials had been dismissed from office as a result. Military expeditions were frequent, but since many people had bought exemption from military service, purchasing ranks as high as the equivalent of fifth lord, there were fewer and fewer men left who could be called into service. The government therefore decided to demote men of the *qianfu* or fifth lord rank to the level of petty officials, making them subject to conscription; anyone who wished to avoid service was then obliged to present a horse to the government. The petty officials who had been dismissed were punished by being made to cut underbrush in the Shanglin Park or work on the construction of the Kunming Lake.[7]

The following year (119 BC) the general in chief Wei Qing and the general of swift cavalry Huo Qubing marched in great force to attack the Xiongnu, capturing or killing 80,000 or 90,000 of the barbarians. Rewards handed out for the expedition amounted to 500,000 catties of gold. The Han armies lost over 100,000 horses. In addition, there were the usual costs for transporting provisions and for carriages and weapons. At this time the government treasuries were so depleted that the fighting men received hardly any of their pay.

The officials, complaining that the three-*shu* coins were too light and easy to tamper with, proposed that the provinces and feudal kingdoms be ordered to mint five-*shu* coins with rims around the edge of the reverse side so that it would be impossible to file them down without detection.

The minister of agriculture also brought to the emperor's attention a proposal of his assistants in charge of salt and iron, Kong Jin and Dongguo Xianyang, which read:

---

[7]The lake was used to practise naval tactics in preparation for an attack on the region of southwest China known at this time as Kunming; hence its name.

Mountains and seas are the storehouses of heaven and earth, and it is proper that any revenue from them should go to the privy treasury of the Son of Heaven. Your Majesty, however, being of an unselfish nature, has turned over the control of these natural resources to the ministry of agriculture to supplement the income from taxes. We propose, therefore, that the manufacture of salt be permitted to any of the common people who are willing to supply their own capital and agree to use implements furnished by the government. Evaporating pans will be rented to them by the officials. At present there are people with no fixed residence or occupation who attempt without authority to gain control of the resources of the mountains and seas, accumulating enormous fortunes and exploiting the poor. Countless proposals have already been made on ways to prevent this situation. We suggest that anyone who dares to cast his own iron vessels and engage in the evaporation of salt be condemned to wear fetters on his left foot, and that his vessels and other equipment be confiscated by the government. In provinces which do not produce iron, suboffices for the control of iron goods should be set up, subject for convenience's sake to the jurisdiction of the district in which they are located.

As a result of this proposal, Kong Jin and Dongguo Xianyang were sent by post carriage to travel about the empire and put into effect their scheme for salt and iron monopolies, establishing the necessary government bureaus. Wealthy men who had previously been engaged in the salt and iron industries were appointed as officials in the bureaus so that the way to official position became even more confused, depending less and less upon the older methods of selection, and many merchants actually got to be government officials.

The merchants, taking advantage of the frequent changes in currency, had been hoarding goods in order to make a profit. The high officials therefore announced to the emperor:

The provinces and kingdoms have suffered from repeated disasters and many of the poorest people who had no means of livelihood have been moved to broader and more fertile lands. To effect this, Your Majesty has economized on food and other expenses and paid out funds from the privy treasury to relieve the sufferings of your subjects, liberalizing the terms of loans and taxes. And yet there are still some who do not turn to the work of the fields, while merchants grow more numerous than ever. The poor have no stores of provisions left and must look to the government for support.

Formerly graded taxes were levied on small carts and on the strings of cash in the possession of merchants. We request that these taxes be levied again in the same way as before. All merchants and those engaged in secondary occupations, all those who lend money for interest, who buy up goods and hoard them in the villages, and who travel about in search of profit, although their names are not listed on the market registers, should be required to make a declaration of their possessions and should be taxed at the rate of one *suan* (120 cash) on each 2,000 cash. For all craftsmen and founders who have already paid a tax to carry on their occupation, the rate should be one *suan* on each 4,000 cash. All those who are not equal in rank to petty officials, or who are not "elders"[8] or soldiers engaged in the defence of the northern frontier, should be required to pay one *suan* for each cart; but for merchants the rate should be two *suan* per cart. Boats five *zhang* or more in length should be taxed one *suan*. Anyone hiding his possessions and failing to report them, or failing to make a complete report, should be sent to a frontier post to serve for a year and his wealth should be confiscated. Anyone who can produce evidence that a false report has been made should receive half of the wealth confiscated as a result. Merchants who are enrolled in the market registers, as well as the members of their families, should be forbidden to register any farm lands in their names. The purpose of this would be to benefit the farmers. Anyone found guilty of violating this law should have his lands and field labourers confiscated.[9]

The emperor, impressed by the words of a man named Bu Shi, summoned him to court and made him a palace attendant, giving him the honourary rank of *zuoshuzhang* and presenting him with ten *qing* of land. These rewards were announced throughout the empire so that everyone might know of Bu Shi's example.

---

[8] Distinguished men over fifty chosen from among the common people to act as consultants to government officials.

[9] As in the case of the proposal above for the minting of three-*shu* coins, the text gives only the suggestion of the officials and does not say what action was taken on it. In both cases, however, the proposals were put into effect.

Bu Shi was a native of Henan, where his family made a living by farming and animal raising. When his parents died, Bu Shi left home, handing over the house, the lands, and all the family wealth to his younger brother, who by this time was full grown. For his own share he took only 100 or so of the sheep they had been raising, which he led off into the mountains to pasture. In the course of ten years or so, Bu Shi's sheep had increased to over 1,000 and he had bought his own house and fields. His younger brother in the meantime had failed completely in the management of the farm, but Bu Shi promptly handed over to him a share of his own wealth. This happened several times. Just at that time the Han was sending its generals at frequent intervals to attack the Xiongnu. Bu Shi journeyed to the capital and submitted a letter to the throne, offering to turn over half of his wealth to the government to help in the defence of the border. The emperor dispatched an envoy to ask if Bu Shi wanted a post in the government.

"From the time I was a child," Bu Shi replied, "I have been an animal raiser. I have had no experience at government service and would certainly not want such a position."

"Perhaps then your family has suffered some injustice that you would like to report?" inquired the envoy.

But Bu Shi answered, "I have never in my life had a quarrel with anyone. If there are poor men in my village, I lend them what they need, and if there are men who do not behave properly, I guide and counsel them. Where I live, everyone does as I say. Why should I suffer any injustice from others? There is nothing I want to report!"

"If that is the case," said the envoy, "then what *is* your objective in making this offer?"

Bu Shi replied, "The Son of Heaven has set out to punish the Xiongnu. In my humble opinion, every worthy man should be willing to fight to the death to defend the borders, and every person with wealth ought to contribute to the expense. If this were done, then the Xiongnu could be wiped out!"

The envoy made a complete record of Bu Shi's words and reported them to the emperor. The emperor discussed the matter with the chancellor Gongsun Hong, but the latter said, "The proposal is simply not in accord with human nature! Such eccentric people are of no use in guiding the populace, but only throw the laws into confusion. I beg Your Majesty not to accept his offer!"

For this reason the emperor put off answering Bu Shi for a long time, and finally, after several years had passed, turned down the offer, whereupon Bu Shi went back to his fields and pastures.

A year or so later the armies marched off on several more expeditions, and the Hunye king and his people surrendered to the Han. As a result the expenditures of the government increased greatly and the granaries and treasuries were soon empty. The following year a number of poor people were transferred to other regions, all of them depending upon the government for their support, and there were not enough supplies to go around. At this point Bu Shi took 200,000 cash of his own and turned the sum over to the governor of Henan to assist the people who were emigrating to other regions. A list of the wealthy men of Henan who had contributed to the aid of the poor was sent to the emperor and he recognized Bu Shi's name. "This is the same man who once offered half his wealth to aid in the defence of the border!" he exclaimed, and presented Bu Shi with a sum of money equivalent to the amount necessary to buy off 400 men from military duty.[10] Bu Shi once more turned the entire sum over to the government. At this time the rich families were all scrambling to hide their wealth; only Bu Shi, unlike the others, had offered to contribute to the expenses of the government. The emperor decided that Bu Shi was really a man of exceptional worth after all, and therefore bestowed upon him the honours mentioned above in order to hint to the people that they might well follow his example.

At first Bu Shi was unwilling to become a palace attendant, but the emperor told him, "I have some sheep in the Shanglin Park which I would like you to take care of." Bu Shi then accepted the post of palace attendant and, wearing a coarse robe and straw sandals, went off to tend the sheep. After a year or so, the sheep had grown fat and were reproducing at a fine rate. The emperor, when he visited the park and saw the flocks, commended Bu Shi on his work. "It is not only with sheep," Bu Shi commented. "Governing people is the same way. Get them up at the right time, let them rest at the right time, and if there are any bad ones, pull them out at once before they have a chance to spoil the flock!"

The emperor, struck by his words, decided to give him a trial as magistrate of the district of Goushi. When his administration proved beneficial to the people of Goushi, the emperor transferred him to the post of magistrate of Chenggao and put him in charge of the transportation of supplies, where his

---

[10] Men were allowed to purchase exemption from military service on the border for 300 cash. According to the interpretation I have followed, therefore, the emperor returned to Bu Shi the sum of 120,000 cash, though there are other interpretations of the sentence.

record was also outstanding. Because of his simple, unspoiled ways and his deep loyalty, the emperor finally appointed him grand tutor to his son Liu Hong, the king of Qi.

Meanwhile Kong Jin had been sent throughout the empire to establish the government monopoly on the casting of iron vessels, and in the course of three years had reached the position of minister of agriculture, ranking as one of the nine highest officers in the government. Sang Hongyang acted as his assistant and had charge of all affairs pertaining to accounts. Little by little they set up the offices for equalization of goods through transportation,[11] by which they hoped to achieve an equal distribution of goods. For the first time an order was issued allowing the petty officials to purchase promotion to higher offices by the presentation of grain; in the case of palace attendants they were allowed to advance as high as posts paying 600 piculs of grain.

Five years after the minting of the silver coins and the five-*shu* cash some 200,000 or 300,000 officials and commoners who had been condemned to death for illegal minting of coins were pardoned by a general amnesty, while the number whose crimes were hushed up and never came to light is beyond computing. At the time of the amnesty (in 115 BC) over 1,000,000 persons came forward to confess their crimes, but this can hardly be half of the number who were actually guilty.[12] In effect, the whole empire was engaged in minting silver and copper coins. Those guilty of violations of the laws were so numerous that the officials could not get around to punishing them all. The emperor therefore dispatched the erudites Chu Da, Xu Yan and others to journey in groups to the various provinces and feudal kingdoms and apprehend the great landholders and governors or prime ministers who were conniving for their own profit.

At this time the imperial secretary Zhang Tang was at the height of his power, with Jian Xuan and Du Zhou as his assistants. Men such as Yi Zong, Yin Qi, and Wang Wenshu were winning high ministerial posts because of their harsh and stern administration, and the imperial inquisitors such as Xia Lan appeared for the first time.

Shortly before this, the minister of agriculture Yan Yi had been put to death. Yan Yi had originally been a village head in Ji'nan. Because of his honesty and

---

[11] These were government offices which bought up goods that were cheap in one part of the country and transported them to regions where they were scarce for resale. The purpose was ostensibly to provide better distribution of goods throughout the nation, though it would seem that the actual object was to make money for the government.

[12] The text of this passage appears to be corrupt and the translation is highly tentative.

integrity, he was gradually promoted in office until he became one of the nine highest ministers. After the emperor and Zhang Tang had made the "deer money" out of the hides of the white deer, the emperor questioned Yan Yi on his opinion of the move. Yan Yi replied, "When the kings and marquises come to court to offer their congratulations, they are expected to present their insignia of green jade, which are worth several thousand cash apiece. Now, however, they will be required to present the insignia on deer hides worth 400,000 cash. There seems to be a certain lack of balance between the basic elements of the ceremony and those that are only secondary." The emperor was not at all pleased by these words.

In addition, Yan Yi was on bad terms with Zhang Tang. When someone brought an accusation against Yan Yi for some other affair, the matter was referred to Zhang Tang for investigation. Earlier Yan Yi had been talking with one of his guests, when the guest remarked that some new law that had just been put into effect did not seem very practical. Yan Yi had made no answer, but given only a subtle wry twist of his lips. Zhang Tang sent a memorial to the throne relating this affair and stating, "Yan Yi, one of the nine highest ministers, having seen that the law was impractical, did not state his opinion to the emperor, but nevertheless disapproved of it in his heart. For this offence he is deserving of death!" From this time on, the crime known as "disapproval at heart" became a part of the law, and most of the high ministers and officials resorted to gross flattery in order to stay in the good graces of the emperor.

The emperor had already issued the order for levies on strings of cash and had also heaped honours on Bu Shi, but it was soon found that no other private citizens were willing to imitate Bu Shi's example by donating wealth to the government officials. The emperor therefore began to listen to as many accusations as could be brought forward against persons attempting to hide their wealth in order to avoid the levy.

In the provinces and kingdoms there was so much illegal minting going on that the cash had become extremely numerous and light in weight. The high officials therefore asked that the officials in the capital who were in charge of casting metal be ordered to mint coins with red rims, each of which would be worth five of the five-*shu* cash presently in circulation. No taxes or other payments to the government were to be accepted unless made in these coins. The silver coins had likewise little by little become debased in value until the people no longer regarded them as worth using. The government attempted to halt this tendency by laws, but these had no effect and by the time a year or so had passed, the silver coins had gone completely out of circulation.

This same year (116 BC) Zhang Tang died, an occurrence which grieved the common people not at all.

Two years later, the red-rimmed coins had become worthless, the people having managed to use them while cleverly evading the intention of the law. They were declared impractical and withdrawn from circulation.

With this an order was issued forbidding any further minting of coins in the provinces and feudal kingdoms. All minting was to be done by three offices set up in the Shanglin Park. Since there were already a number of coins in circulation, it was ordered that no cash other than those minted by the three offices should be accepted as legal tender anywhere in the empire. All copper coins previously minted in the provinces and kingdoms were withdrawn from circulation and melted down, the copper being turned over to the three offices. After this there were fewer and fewer people who attempted to mint their own cash, since the cost of making a passable imitation did not repay the effort. Only highly skilled professional criminals continued to produce counterfeit coins.

Bu Shi was transferred to the post of prime minister of Qi. At the instigation of Yang Ke, charges were brought forward all over the empire against men who attempted to conceal their wealth from the levy; practically every family of middling means or over found itself under accusation. Du Zhou was put in charge of the investigations and, of those brought to trial, very few got off with a light sentence. The emperor dispatched parties of assistants under the imperial secretary and the commandant of justice to go to the various provinces and kingdoms and examine the charges of concealed wealth. The wealth confiscated from the people as a result of their investigations was calculated in the billions of cash, with male and female slaves numbering in the thousands; the confiscated fields amounted to several hundred *qing* in the larger districts, and over 100 *qing* in the smaller ones, with a proportionate number of houses. Practically all the merchants of middling or better means were ruined and the people, deciding that they had better indulge in tasty food and fine clothing while they still had the opportunity, made no effort to lay away any wealth for the future. The government officials for their part found themselves with more and more funds at their disposal, due to the salt and iron monopolies and the confiscations of wealth.

The customs barrier at the Hangu Pass was moved east to enlarge the area within the Pass, and the left and right districts of the capital were established.

Originally the minister of agriculture had charge of the salt and iron monopolies, but the number of government offices and the expenses involved proved so large that an official called the director of waterworks was set up to take charge of the salt and iron monopolies. Later, when the confiscation of concealed wealth was initiated by Yang Ke, the goods and funds stored in the Shanglin Park became so numerous that the director of waterworks was ordered to take charge of the park. The treasuries of the park were already full by this time and had to be continually enlarged.

At this time the kingdom of Southern Yue was preparing to use its ships to attack and drive out the Han forces in its territory. For this reason extensive alterations were made on the Kunming Lake, rows of observation towers built along its borders, and ships constructed with superstructures rising ten *zhang* or more and topped with banners and flags, forming a most impressive spectacle. The emperor was so stirred by the sight that he ordered the construction of the Terrace of Cypress Beams, which measured twenty or thirty *zhang* in height. From this time on the building of imperial palaces proceeded on a more lavish scale day by day.

The wealth confiscated as a result of the accusations was divided among the director of waterworks, the privy treasurer, the minister of agriculture, and the master of carriage. Each of these appointed agricultural officials who travelled from time to time about the provinces and directed the cultivation of the confiscated fields as soon as they were taken over from their former owners. The male and female slaves who had been seized were assigned to the imperial parks to raise dogs, horses, other animals, and birds, or were sent to the various government offices for employment. The government offices became increasingly confused in function and were set up in greater and greater number, while the number of slaves moved from the provinces to the capital was so large that only by transporting 4,000,000 piculs of grain up from the lower reaches of the Yellow River, and adding it to the grain bought up by the officials, was the capital able to keep itself adequately supplied.

When Suo Zhong informed the emperor that among the sons of the old established families and the rich merchants there were many who engaged in cock fighting, horse racing, hunting, and gambling, thereby setting a bad example for the common people, the emperor ordered the officials to arrest such persons for violation of the laws and regulations. By getting one suspect to implicate his associates as well, they managed to drag in several thousand persons, who were called "rooted-out convicts". If those arrested were willing to pay a sufficient price to the government, however, they were pardoned and even appointed as palace attendants. This marked the ruin of the old system of selecting palace attendants on the basis of merit.

At this time the lands east of the mountains were suffering from floods caused by the Yellow River, and for several years the harvests had been poor. Within an area of 1,000 or 2,000 *li* square the distress was so great that people were reduced at times to cannibalism. The emperor, taking pity upon the plight of the people, issued an edict which read: "In the region of the Yangtze they burn their fields before ploughing and flood them before hoeing. Let the famine victims now be permitted to leave their homes and emigrate to the area between the Huai and the Yangtze rivers in search of food, and if they wish to settle there, let them do so." He dispatched a veritable stream of officials along the roads to look out for the people and had grain sent down from Ba and Shu to relieve the crisis.

The following year (114 BC) the emperor for the first time made a tour of the provinces and kingdoms, travelling east across the Yellow River. The governor of Hedong Province east of the river, not expecting the emperor to visit his territory, had made no preparations. He committed suicide. (In the following year) the emperor travelled west, crossing the Long Mountains. The imperial entourage arrived so suddenly that the governor of Longxi was unable to provide food for all of the emperor's attendants, and he too committed suicide. The emperor then journeyed north through the Xiao Pass and, accompanied by 20,000 or 30,000 cavalry, hunted in the region of New Qin, where he inspected the disposition of the troops along the border before returning to the capital. He discovered that in New Qin stretches of land measuring as much as 1,000 *li* or more were being left wide open without guards or patrol posts. To remedy the situation he executed the governor of Beidi and his subordinates, who were responsible for this state of affairs, and gave orders that the people were to be allowed to raise horses in the districts along the border. Mares were lent out by the government officials for a period of three years, after which they were to be returned with an interest of one foal for every ten mares. The people of the region were also exempted from the reports and levies on wealth, so that the region of New Qin was soon filled with immigrants.

By this time the precious cauldron had been found and altars set up to the Earth Lord and the Great Unity, and the high officials were debating on plans for the performance of the Feng and Shan sacrifices. Throughout the empire the provinces and feudal kingdoms were all busy repairing roads and bridges and putting the old palaces in order, while in the various districts along the imperial highway the district officials laid in provisions and prepared their tableware in anticipation of the imperial visit.

The next year (112 BC) the kingdom of Southern Yue rebelled and the Qiang barbarians of the west invaded the border, pillaging and murdering. Because the region east of the mountains was still suffering from a lack of food, the emperor declared a general amnesty to the empire. With the prisoners thereby released, and the men trained in the south for service on the towered ships — a force of over 200,000 in all — an attack was launched on Southern Yue. At the same time 20,000 or 30,000 cavalry men from the provinces of Henei, Hedong, and Henan were sent west to attack the Qiang barbarians. Another 20,000 or 30,000 were sent across the Yellow River to fortify the western border at Lingju. The provinces of Zhangye and Jiuquan were set up, and in the provinces of Shang, Shuofang, Xihe, and Hexi, officials in charge of the opening of new lands, as well as soldiers designated to garrison the lands along the border, numbering 600,000 men, were set to working the lands in garrison farms. Roads were repaired and provisions sent to the forces from the central part of the empire. All of the men were dependent upon the ministry of agriculture for their supplies, although the distance over which supplies had to be transported was anywhere from 1,000 to 3,000 *li*.

Since there were not enough arms to supply the men on the border, weapons were dispatched from the imperial armoury and workshops to make up the deficiency. There was also a serious lack of horses for carriages and cavalry and, since the government officials had so little money, they found it difficult to buy up enough to keep the troops supplied. The government therefore issued an order to everyone, from the feudal lords down to officials of the 300 picul class, commanding them to donate a specified number of stallions to the government, depending upon their rank. At village posts throughout the empire men were set to breeding colts, for which they received a certain interest each year.

Bu Shi, at this time the prime minister of Qi, sent a letter to the throne saying, "I have always heard that the distresses of the sovereign are a source of shame to his subjects. Now that the kingdom of Southern Yue has revolted, I beg that my sons and I be allowed to join the men of Qi who are skilled in naval warfare to go and die in battle!"

The emperor responded with an edict saying, "Although Bu Shi in person ploughed the fields and pastured his animals, he did not work for private gain. If he had any surplus, he immediately turned it over to the government officials to aid in the expenses of government. Now unhappily the empire faces this threat from abroad, and Bu Shi, roused to action, has volunteered to go with his sons to die in battle. Although he has not actually taken part in combat, it is obvious that he bears in his heart a true sense of duty!" The emperor therefore presented Bu Shi with the rank of marquis in the area within the Pass, along with sixty catties of gold and ten *qing* of farmland. He had the action widely publicized throughout the empire, but no one responded to the hint. Among all the hundreds of marquises, there was not one who volunteered to join the armies in attacking the Qiang and Yue barbarians.

In the eighth month, when the feudal lords came to present new wine in the ancestral temples of the dynasty, the officials of the privy treasury made a close examination of the tributes of gold which they brought with them. As a result, over 100 marquises were tried on charges of having presented insufficient or faulty gold and were deprived of their titles.

Following this, Bu Shi was appointed to the post of imperial secretary. After he took over this position, he discovered that in the provinces and kingdoms the system of government salt and iron monopolies was working to great disadvantage. The utensils supplied by the government were poor in quality and high in price, and yet at times the people were actually being forced by the officials to buy them. In addition, because of the tax on boats, traders had diminished in number and the price of goods gone up. He therefore asked Kong Jin to speak on his behalf to the emperor, recommending the abolition of the boat tax. From this time on the emperor began to dislike Bu Shi.

After three years of continuous fighting, the Han forces managed to suppress the Qiang barbarians and wipe out the kingdom of Southern Yue. On the southern border, from Panyu[13] on the coast to the south of Shu, seventeen new provinces were set up. These were governed in accordance with the old customs of the inhabitants and were not required to pay taxes. The provinces of Nanyang, Hanzhong, and those further on, were ordered to supply food and money to the officials and soldiers of the new provinces which adjoined their respective borders, as well as horses and equipment for the relay service. From time to time, however, there were minor uprisings in the new provinces in which Han officials were murdered, so that the central government was obliged to dispatch troops recruited from the south to punish the rebels. In the space of a

---

[13] The region of the present city of Canton. The line of new provinces ran from here west to present-day Sichuan Province.

year over 10,000 men had been dispatched and the expenses for all of this had
to be borne by the ministry of agriculture. Because of its system of equitable
transport and its levies on salt and iron, which it used to supplement the revenue
from taxes, the ministry of agriculture was able to meet these expenses. In the
districts through which the troops passed, however, the officials, concerned only
that they should have enough funds to supply the armies without running short,
did not dare to complain of the inordinate tax burden placed upon them.

The following year, the first year of the era *yuanfeng* (110 BC), Bu Shi was
degraded to the post of grand tutor to the heir apparent. Sang Hongyang was
made secretary in charge of grain and put in control of the ministry of agriculture, as well as taking over from Kong Jin complete supervision of the salt and
iron monopolies throughout the empire. Sang Hongyang believed that the
reason prices had risen so sharply was that the various government officials were
engaging in trade and competing against each other. Furthermore, when goods
were transported to the capital as payment for taxes from various parts of the
empire, their value often did not equal the cost of transportation. He therefore
proposed that some twenty or thirty assistants be appointed to the ministry of
agriculture who would be sent out to supervise the various provinces and
kingdoms, where they would travel about and set up the necessary transport
offices for equalizing prices, as well as salt and iron offices. In the case of distant
regions, orders were to be given that local products commanding a high price,
such as would ordinarily be carted away and sold by the traders in other regions,
should be transported to the capital in lieu of taxes. In the capital a balanced
standard office was to be set up which would receive and store these goods
brought in from various parts of the empire. The government artisans were to
be ordered to make carts and other equipment needed to put the system into
effect. All expenses would be borne by the ministry of agriculture, whose
officials would then have complete control over all the goods in the empire,
selling when prices were high and buying when they were low. In this way the
wealthy merchants and large-scale traders, deprived of any prospect of making
big profits, would go back to farming, and it would become impossible for any
commodity to rise sharply in price. Because the price of goods would thereby
be controlled throughout the empire, the system was to be called the "balanced
standard".

The emperor agreed with this idea and gave permission for it to be put into
effect. Following this, the emperor travelled north as far as Shuofang; from there
he proceeded to Mt. Tai, journeyed along the seacoast and the northern border,

and returned to the capital. He handed out gifts and awards to the places he visited along the way, doling out over 1,000,000 rolls of silk as well as cash and gold in the hundreds of millions, all of which the ministry of agriculture was able to supply.

Sang Hongyang proposed that petty officials be allowed to buy office by presenting grain to the government, and that men accused of crimes be permitted to purchase their ransom in the same way. He also suggested that the common people be allowed to present varying quantities of grain to the granary at Sweet Springs in exchange for lifetime exemption from military service and guarantees that they would not be subject to accusations leading to confiscation of their wealth.

Areas that were in need were immediately supplied by shipments of grain from other provinces, and the various officials of the ministry of agriculture all drew grain from east of the mountains, so that the amount transported to the capital increased to 6,000,000 piculs annually. Within a year the granary at Taicang in the capital and that at Sweet Springs had been filled, the frontiers enjoyed a surplus of grain and other goods, and the transportation offices had 5,000,000 rolls of silk. Though taxes on the people had not been increased, there was now more than enough to cover the expenditures of the empire. As a result Sang Hongyang was rewarded with the rank of *zuoshuzhang* and once more presented with 100 catties of gold.

This year there was a minor drought and the emperor ordered the officials to pray for rain. Bu Shi remarked to the emperor, "The government officials are supposed to collect what taxes they need for their food and clothing, and that is all! Now Sang Hongyang has them sitting in the market stalls buying and selling goods and scrambling for a profit. If Your Majesty were to boil Sang Hongyang alive, then I think Heaven might send us rain!"

The Grand Historian remarks: When the farmers, the artisans, and the merchants first began to exchange articles among themselves, that was when currency came into being — tortoise shells and sea shells, gold and copper coins, knife-shaped money and spade-shaped money. Thus its origin is very old. Concerning the time of Emperor Ku[14] and the ages before him we can say nothing, for they are too far away. The *Book of Documents*, however, tells us

---

[14] The third of the legendary "Five Emperors" of antiquity.

something about the reigns of Emperors Yao and Shun, while the *Book of Odes* describes the Shang and Zhou dynasties. Thus we know that in times of peace and security, stress was laid upon the system of schools; agricultural pursuits, which are the basis of the nation, were honoured; secondary occupations such as trade were disparaged, and the people were taught a sense of propriety and duty in order to discourage them from the search for profit. In periods of war and unrest, however, the opposite situation prevailed. When a thing has reached its height it must begin to decay, and when an age has gone to one extreme it must turn again in the opposite direction; therefore we find periods of rude simplicity and periods of refinement alternating with each other endlessly.

From the description of the nine provinces in the "Tribute of Yu"[15] we learn that, in the time of that ruler, each region submitted as its tribute to the throne whatever goods it was best fitted to produce and whatever the people had the most of. King Tang, the founder of the Shang dynasty, and King Wu, the founder of the Zhou dynasty, both heirs to the chaos of the dynasties which preceded them, worked to put the empire into order, causing the people to be unflagging in their efforts, and both of them, by their diligence and circumspection, succeeded in establishing firm rule. And yet little by little the ages after them sank into weakness and decay.

Duke Huan of Qi, following the advice of his minister Guan Zhong, initiated the system of buying up goods when the price was low and selling when it was high, and of exploiting the resources of the mountains and seas, until he had the other feudal lords paying court to him and, with what had up until then been the little and out-of-the-way state of Qi, had won for himself the title of dictator. Similarly the king of Wei, by following the theories of Li Ke, was able to secure the maximum yield from his lands and become a powerful ruler.

From the time of these men on, the empire was torn by the strife of the warring kingdoms. Men honoured deceit and power and scoffed at benevolence and righteousness; they put wealth and possession first and courtesy and humility last. Thus it happened that commoners grew so rich that their wealth was counted in the hundreds of millions, while among the poor there were those who could not even get enough dregs and chaff to fill their bellies. The more powerful rulers annexed the smaller fiefs and made subjects of their lords, while in the weaker states the ruling families were wiped out and the sacrifices to their ancestors cut off forever. So it continued until the Qin finally united all the land

---

[15] A section of the *Book of Documents*. Emperor Yu was the founder of the Xia dynasty.

within the four seas under a single rule.

The currency of the times of Emperor Shun and the Xia dynasty consisted of three types of metal: gold, silver, and copper; while in Zhou times there was copper cash, knife-shaped money, cloth-shaped money, and money made of tortoise shells or sea shells. When the Qin united the world, only two[16] kinds of currency were used throughout the nation. The more valuable was that made of gold in denominations of twenty taels. The less valuable was the copper cash, inscribed with the words "half-tael" and weighing that amount. (Pearls, jade, tortoise shells, sea shells, silver, tin, and similar materials, though used for utensils or ornaments or stored away as treasures, were not employed as currency.) The currency, however, fluctuated according to the times, having no fixed value. At that time the ruler was busy driving back the barbarians from the borders of the empire, while within the empire he was carrying out various construction works and projects, so that although the men who remained at home worked the fields, they could not supply enough to eat, and though the women wove and spun, they could not produce enough clothing. And so we see that in antiquity there was once a time when the entire wealth and resources of the nation were exhausted in the service of the ruler, and yet he found them insufficient. There was but one reason for this: the stream of circumstances flowed so violently at that time that it made such a situation inevitable. Surely there is nothing strange about this![17]

---

[16] Most texts erroneously read "three".

[17] This last is of course a veiled attack on Emperor Wu, whose foreign wars and various other expensive undertakings — "stream of circumstances", as Sima Qian euphemistically calls them — brought the empire to the same state of exhaustion as that which prevailed under the First Emperor of the Qin.

PART II

STATESMEN, GENERALS, AND FOREIGN PEOPLES

SHI JI 107: THE BIOGRAPHIES OF
THE MARQUISES OF WEIQI AND WUAN

When Wu and Chu rose in revolt, Dou Ying, the marquis of Weiqi, proved to be the wisest leader among the families related to the imperial house by marriage. He appreciated the worth of other men and as a result they all flocked to him. He led his army to Xingyang east of the mountains and there blocked the advance of the rebel armies. Thus I made "The Biographies of the Marquises of Weiqi and Wuan".

Dou Ying, the marquis of Weiqi, was the son of a cousin of Empress Dou, the consort of Emperor Wen and mother of Emperor Jing. Up until his father's time, his family had been residents of Guanjin.[1] He himself was very fond of supporting guests and retainers in his home.

In the reign of Emperor Wen, Dou Ying was appointed prime minister of Wu, but later retired on grounds of ill health. When Emperor Jing first came to the throne, Dou Ying was made steward of the household of the empress and the heir apparent.

King Xiao of Liang was the younger brother of Emperor Jing and the favourite son of Empress Dowager Dou. Whenever he came to court Emperor Jing would hold a banquet for him, treating him as a brother rather than a vassal. On one such occasion, before Emperor Jing had formally announced his choice for heir apparent, he remarked casually at the height of the drinking, "After my thousand years of life are over, I shall pass the rule of the empire along to the king of Liang!"

Empress Dowager Dou was delighted at this announcement, but Dou Ying, seizing a goblet of wine and hastening forward to offer it to the emperor, said, "The empire is the empire of the founder, Gaozu, and it is a law of the Han dynasty that the rule must pass from father to son! How could Your Majesty

---

[1] The old home of Empress Dou. After she became empress, she summoned her relatives to the capital.

arbitrarily hand it over to the king of Liang?"

Because of this affair Empress Dowager Dou grew to hate Dou Ying, while he in turn came to despise his post of steward and resigned on grounds of illness. The empress dowager then had his name removed from the roster of officials that was kept at the palace gate so that he could no longer come and go at court as he had in the past.

In the third year of Emperor Jing's reign, when the kings of Wu and Chu revolted, the emperor began to cast about among the members of the imperial house and the Dou family for able leaders and found that no one could match the wisdom of Dou Ying. He accordingly summoned Dou Ying to an audience, but when the later appeared before the emperor he adamantly declined to accept any appointment, insisting that he was unfit because of illness to take on the responsibilities of leadership. Empress Dowager Dou likewise was embarrassed by the emperor's proposal to appoint Dou Ying. But the emperor refused to listen. "At a time when the empire is faced with crisis, how can you think of making polite excuses?" he demanded, and proceeded to appoint Dou Ying as general in chief, presenting him with a gift of 1,000 catties of gold. Dou Ying in turn recommended Yuan Ang, Luan Bu, and other distinguished military men and worthy gentlemen who were not at the time employed in the government and succeeded in having them appointed to various posts. The money presented to him by the emperor he stored along the corridors and in the gatehouse of his home, where his junior officers, if they needed any for military expenditures, could help themselves to it without further ado. Not a cent of it went into his own coffers.

Dou Ying marched east to guard Xingyang and observe the movements of the troops of Qi and Zhao. After the armies of the seven rebellious kingdoms had been defeated, he was enfeoffed as marquis of Weiqi, and all sorts of gentlemen with no fixed place of employment, guests and retainers, vied with each other in offering him their services. During the reign of Emperor Jing, whenever there was some important matter to be discussed at court, none of the marquises dared to try to stand on an equal footing with Zhou Yafu, the marquis of Tiao, and Dou Ying, the marquis of Weiqi.

In the fourth year of his reign, when Emperor Jing set up his son Prince Li as heir apparent, he appointed Dou Ying as the boy's tutor. In the seventh year, however, the emperor decided to dismiss Prince Li from the position of heir apparent, and though Dou Ying several times remonstrated with him, he was unable to prevent the move. Pleading illness once more, he retired to Lantian in the foothills of the Southern Mountains, where he lived in seclusion for several months. Although a number of his retainers and rhetoricians attempted to make him change his mind, he refused to return to the capital. Among them was a man from Liang named Gao Sui who advised him in these words: "The emperor has the power to make you rich and honoured and the empress dowager, your relative, can offer you intimate friendship. Now you have been appointed to tutor the heir apparent and, in spite of your protests, he has been dismissed from his position. Yet, though you were unable to argue your case successfully, you have also proved yourself unable to die for your cause. Instead you have taken yourself off on the excuse of illness and sit here, living a life of ease and retirement, dallying with beautiful women and, with your band of followers, passing judgement on the rest of the world. By such conduct you are deliberately attempting, it would seem, to broadcast to everyone the faults of the ruler! But if you should thereby incur the anger of both the emperor and the empress dowager, I fear, General, it would mean extinction for you and your whole family!"

Dou Ying, realizing that what he said was true, eventually returned to the capital and attended court as before.

At this time Liu She, the marquis of Tao, retired from the post of chancellor, and Empress Dowager Dou several times suggested to Emperor Jing that Dou Ying be appointed as his successor, but the emperor replied, "I hope you do not think, Mother, that I begrudge him the post. It is only that Dou Ying tends to be somewhat self-righteous and fond of having his own way. On numerous occasions he has acted rather thoughtlessly, and I am afraid that it would be difficult to entrust him with the heavy responsibilities of chancellor." In the end Dou Ying did not get the post; instead Wei Wan, the marquis of Jianling, was appointed chancellor.

Tian Fen, the marquis of Wuan, was a younger brother of Empress Wang, the consort of Emperor Jing and mother of Emperor Wu; he was born after his mother, Zang Er, had remarried into the Tian family and was living in Changling. When Dou Ying had already become general in chief and was at the height of his power, Tian Fen still held a rather humble post as palace attendant. He used to go to Dou Ying's house from time to time to wait on him and serve him his wine, bowing politely and treating Dou Ying with great courtesy as though he himself were one of Dou Ying's sons. Toward the end of Emperor Jing's reign Tian Fen began to enjoy increasing favour at court until he had risen to the post of palace counsellor.

Tian Fen was a very skilful talker and studied the "Cauldron Inscriptions"[2] and similar works on statecraft. His sister, Empress Wang, had great respect for his wisdom. When Emperor Jing passed away and the heir apparent, Empress Wang's son, was proclaimed emperor, the empress for a while issued edicts in her son's name, and many of the measures which she took to insure order and stability in the government during the period of change were suggested to her by Tian Fen's retainers. In the same year, the third year of the latter part of Emperor Jing's reign (141 BC), Tian Fen and his younger brother Tian Sheng were both enfeoffed, Tian Fen as marquis of Wuan and Tian Sheng as marquis of Zhouyang. This was done because they were both younger brothers of Empress Dowager Wang.[3]

Tian Fen found himself in a position of new importance at court and decided that he would like to become chancellor. He therefore conducted himself with great humility before his guests and retainers and worked to advance eminent gentlemen who were living in retirement and secure them honourable positions, hoping thereby to outshine Dou Ying and the elder statesmen of the time.

In the first year of the era *jianyuan* (140 BC) Wei Wan retired from the post of chancellor because of ill health, and the emperor began deliberations with the court to decide who should be appointed to fill this position, as well as that of grand commandant. Ji Fu, one of Tian Fen's retainers, advised him, saying, "Dou Ying has held a position of great honour for a long time and many of the most worthy men of the empire were originally members of his group. Now, although you have begun to come up in the world, you still cannot rival Dou Ying. If the emperor offers to make you chancellor, you should therefore yield the post to Dou Ying. If Dou Ying is made chancellor, you will surely be made grand commandant, a position which is just as distinguished as that of chancellor. In addition you will thereby gain a reputation for humility and wisdom!"

Impressed by this advice, Tian Fen mentioned the matter in secret to his sister, Empress Dowager Wang, asking her to drop a hint with the emperor to this effect. As a result the emperor appointed Dou Ying as chancellor and Tian Fen as grand commandant.

Ji Fu went to congratulate Dou Ying on his new appointment but took the

---

[2] A work in 26 sections, no longer extant, supposedly compiled by Kong Jia, the official historian at the court of the Yellow Emperor.

[3] Although the year is designated as the third year of the latter period of Emperor Jing's reign, the enfeoffments took place two months after the death of Emperor Jing when Empress Dowager Wang was managing the government for her son, Emperor Wu.

opportunity to deliver a grave warning: "It is Your Lordship's nature, I know, to delight in good men and hate evil ones. At the present time it happens that the good men have joined together in praising you and you have thereby been able to reach the position of chancellor. And yet you hate evil, and evil men are numerous. It will not be long before they too join together — to slander you! If you could find some way to get along with both groups, then I believe you could enjoy your present high position for a long time. But if not, their slanders will drive you right out of office!" Dou Ying paid no attention to this advice.

Dou Ying and Tian Fen were both admirers of Confucian teachings, and they combined their efforts in boosting Zhao Wan into the post of imperial secretary and Wang Zang into that of chief of palace attendants and in bringing the eminent Confucian scholar Master Shen of Lu to court. They also worked for the establishment of a Bright Hall like the great audience halls of antiquity, ordered the marquises to proceed to their territories, abolished the customs barriers, and changed the funeral ceremonies to conform with correct ritual practice, striving to bring about an era of peace and prosperity. In addition, they conducted an inquiry into the members of the various branches of the imperial family and the Dou family and expunged the names of anyone found guilty of misconduct. At this time many of the male members of the families related to the throne by marriage had become marquises and, since a number of them were married to princesses of the blood, they had no desire to leave the capital and proceed to their own territories. They were unanimously opposed to the new order directing them to leave the capital and their criticisms of the law day after day came to the ears of the emperor's grandmother, Empress Dowager Dou.

Empress Dowager Dou was very fond of the teachings of the Yellow Emperor and Lao Zi, while Dou Ying, Tian Fen, Zhao Wan, Wang Zang, and the others of their group all did their best to advance the influence of Confucian doctrines and disparage the teachings of the Taoist school. As a result Empress Dowager Dou grew more and more displeased with Dou Ying and his party.

Eventually, in the second year of *jianyuan* (139 BC), when the imperial secretary Zhao Wan asked the emperor for permission to dispose of state affairs himself without consulting Empress Dowager Dou, the empress dowager flew into a rage and proceeded to expel Zhao Wan, Wang Zang, and the others from office and to force the resignation of the chancellor Dou Ying and the grand commandant Tian Fen. She then had Xu Chang, the marquis of Bozhi, appointed as the new chancellor, and Zhuang Qingdi, the marquis of Wuqiang, as imperial secretary.

As a result of this affair Dou Ying and Tian Fen were both obliged to retire to their homes to live the life of ordinary marquises. Tian Fen, however, although holding no position in the government, still enjoyed his usual favour and intimacy with his sister, Empress Dowager Wang, and was therefore able on occasion to express his opinion concerning affairs of state with considerable effect. The officers and gentlemen of the empire and all who sought after profit and position thereupon abandoned Dou Ying and flocked about Tian Fen, who grew more arrogant in his ways with each passing day.

In the sixth year of the era *jianyuan* (135 BC) Empress Dowager Dou passed away. The chancellor Xu Chang and the imperial secretary Zhuang Qingdi were accused of delay in arranging the funeral ceremonies and were dismissed from office. Tian Fen was then appointed chancellor and Han Anguo, the former minister of agriculture, was made imperial secretary. The gentlemen of the empire, the officials of the provinces, and the other marquises hastened in even greater numbers to ally themselves with Tian Fen.

Tian Fen was rather short and unimposing in appearance but, because he was related by birth to the emperor, he conducted himself with a very lordly air. He believed that, since many of the marquises and kings were men of mature years, while the emperor, who had just ascended the throne, was still very young, it was up to him as a close relative of the ruler and chancellor of the central government to force others to submit to his will and treat him with the proper courtesy. Otherwise, he felt, the world would have no respect for the imperial house.

At this time, whenever he would enter the palace to report on some affair connected with his duties as chancellor, he would sit for hours, and sometimes for days, in conference with the emperor, and whatever suggestions he made were always followed. In recommending people for office he succeeded on occasion in having men promoted in one leap from private citizen to official of the 2,000 picul rank. His authority in fact outweighed that of the emperor himself, who remarked to him one day, "Have you quite finished making your appointments and dismissals of officials? Because if you have, I think I might like to make a few appointments too!" Another time Tian Fen asked the emperor for the land used by the government artisans so that he could increase the grounds of his estate, to which the emperor replied angrily, "Why yes! And while you're about it why don't you go ahead and take over the imperial arsenal as well!" After this last remark, Tian Fen conducted himself with somewhat more discretion in the emperor's presence.

Once when he had invited some guests to his home to drink, he seated his older brother, Wang Xin, the marquis of Gai, in a place facing south, while he himself took the place of honour facing east. He explained that this arrangement was necessary because of the honour due to himself as chancellor of the Han, which could not be disregarded for the sake of a private family relationship such as that of older and younger brother.

From this time on Tian Fen lived a life of increasing arrogance and ostentation, building for himself the finest mansions in the capital, laid out with sumptuous grounds and gardens; the merchants with their wares from the distant provinces stood in lines before his door. In his front hall he hung bells and drums, with pennants on curved flagstaffs, while the women's quarters at the back housed wives and maidens in the hundreds. The other nobles flocked about with gifts of gold and jewels, dogs, horses, and trinkets for his amusement, in quantities too great to be reckoned. Dou Ying for his part had grown more and more estranged from the emperor since the death of Empress Dowager Dou. His advice was no longer heeded, his power was gone, and his friends and retainers one by one drifted away, treating him with scorn and indifference. Only General Guan continued to respect him as before. He spent his days in silent frustration and despair, lavishing his generosity on his one remaining friend, General Guan.

General Guan Fu was a native of Yingyin. His father, whose name was Zhang Meng, had originally been a servant of Guan Ying, the marquis of Yingyin, and had enjoyed great favour. Eventually, on the strength of the marquis's recommendation he advanced to a post paying 2,000 piculs, and out of gratitude he adopted the family name of his patron, being known thereafter as Guan Meng. At the time of the revolt of Wu and Chu, Guan He, who had succeeded to the marquisate after the death of his father, Guan Ying, was made a general in the command of the grand commandant Zhou Yafu. He requested that Guan Meng be made a subordinate commander and his son Guan Fu be allowed to accompany his father as head of a battalion of 1,000 men. Guan Meng was actually too old for such a post, but the marquis pressed his request until he succeeded in getting permission. Guan Meng was profoundly embittered by the reluctance with which his appointment had been granted and decided that he would never be allowed to exercise his authority with any freedom; therefore, whenever a battle took place he always plunged into the midst of the enemy's fortifications. Eventually he died a prisoner in the Wu camp.

According to the rules of warfare, when a father and son are both taking part in a campaign and one of them is killed, the other is permitted to accompany the body home for burial. But Guan Fu refused to take his father's body back home, declaring passionately, "I would far rather seize the head of the king of Wu or one of his generals and thereby avenge my father's death!" Donning his armour and taking up his halberd, he went about the camp, gathering together twenty or thirty stalwart young friends of his who were willing to accompany him. When the group emerged from the gate of the Han camp, however, none of the men dared advance any further. In the end Guan Fu, with only two companions and ten or twelve mounted attendants, galloped off to the encampment of the Wu army, fighting his way right up to the headquarters of the Wu general and killing or wounding twenty or thirty of the enemy. When he found that he could advance no further, he wheeled about and galloped back to the Han fortifications. His companions had lost almost all of their attendants, only one returning with the party, and Guan Fu himself bore over ten serious wounds. Fortunately he happened to have some excellent medicine which he applied to his injuries and thus saved his life.

When his wounds had healed a little, he again spoke to his commanding officer, General Guan He. "Now that I know a little more about the ins and outs of the Wu camp, I beg you to let me make another try!" The general admired his bravery and sympathized with his desire, but he was afraid that this time he would surely lose Guan Fu. He therefore took the matter up with the grand commandant, but the latter absolutely forbade another such foray.

After the armies of Wu had been defeated, the story of Guan Fu's daring exploit spread all over the empire. General Guan He recommended him to Emperor Jing, who appointed him as a general of palace attendants, but after a few months he was accused of some violation of the law and dismissed. After this he made his home in Chang'an, where he was known and praised by all the gentlemen of the capital. He was later recalled to government service and during the reign of Emperor Jing reached the post of prime minister of the kingdom of Dai.

When Emperor Jing passed away and the present emperor first came to the throne, he was afraid that the province of Huaiyang, being one of the main crossroads of the empire and noted for its military strength, might become a source of trouble and he therefore shifted Guan Fu to the position of governor of Huaiyang. In the first year of the *jianyuan* era (140 BC) he summoned Guan Fu to court to take over the post of master of carriage.

In the second year of the same era Guan Fu was one time drinking with Dou Fu, the colonel of the guard of the Palace of Lasting Joy, when the two men got into an argument over some question of etiquette. Guan Fu, who was drunk at the time, ended by striking Dou Fu. Dou Fu, it happened, was a close relative of Empress Dowager Dou, and the emperor, fearful that the empress dowager would demand Guan Fu's life for the insult, hastily transferred him to the post of prime minister of Yan. Several years later Guan Fu was accused of some violation of the law and removed from office, after which he returned to private life in Chang'an.

Guan Fu was a very stubborn and outspoken man, especially when he had had something to drink, and despised any kind of flattery. When he was in the company of members of the aristocracy, influential statesmen, or anyone who was socially his superior, he showed great reluctance to treat them with the proper politeness, and indeed was actually insulting; but when it came to men who were socially inferior, the poorer and more humble they were the greater respect he showed them, behaving as though they were his equals. When he was with a large group, he made a point of recommending and showing favour to his inferiors, a trait for which he was much admired by people.

He had no taste for literature but loved feats of honour and daring and was absolutely true to his word. All his friends were rich or influential citizens, local bosses, or gangster leaders. His wealth amounted to almost 10,000 cash in gold, and every day he had from twenty or thirty to 100 men eating at his house. He owned a number of lakes and farm lands in Yingchuan Province from which his relatives and the retainers of the family derived great profit, and this permitted the Guan family to run the affairs of the province in any way they pleased. The children of Yingchuan made up a song about this which went:

> While the waters of the Ying run bright
> It means the Guans are still all right;
> But when the waters run polluted
> We'll know they've all been executed!

When Guan Fu returned to private life in Chang'an, although he was still very wealthy, his political influence was gone, and he soon found the ministers and courtiers, the guests and retainers who had frequented his home in the past gradually drifting away. When Dou Ying likewise lost his political power, he was happy to make friends with Guan Fu and rid himself once and for all of those acquaintances who had avidly sought his company in the old days but later turned their backs upon him. Guan Fu in turn profited from his friendship with Dou Ying, which allowed him to mingle with the nobles and members of the imperial family and increase his fame. Thus the two men aided and respected each other and their friendship was like that of father and son. They never tired of the pleasures they shared and their only regret was that they had come to know each other so late in life.

Once, while Guan Fu was in mourning for one of his relatives, he happened to pay a call on the chancellor Tian Fen. In the course of the visit Tian Fen remarked casually, "I was thinking that I would like to go with you some time to call on Dou Ying, but of course at the moment you are in mourning."[4]

"If you would really be so kind as to go with me to visit Dou Ying, I would certainly not let the matter of my mourning stand in the way!" replied Guan Fu. "If I may have your permission, I will speak to Dou Ying about it at once so that he may make preparations to entertain you. I trust he may expect the honour of your presence early tomorrow morning."

Tian Fen gave his consent, whereupon Guan Fu went to tell Dou Ying, repeating to him what Tian Fen had said. Dou Ying and his wife hastily laid in a large supply of beef and wine and spent the night sweeping and cleaning the house, working until dawn to set up the curtains and lay out the dishes. When daybreak came Dou Ying sent his servants to escort Tian Fen to his house, but noon came and the chancellor had still not appeared.

"You don't think the chancellor has forgotten, do you?" Dou Ying asked Guan Fu, who replied uneasily, "I was the one who invited him to come, in spite of the fact that I am in mourning. I had better go and see what has happened."

Guan Fu then rode off in his carriage to fetch the chancellor in person. As it turned out, however, Tian Fen had only been joking the day before when he consented to the visit and had not the slightest intention of going. When Guan Fu reached Tian Fen's house, he found that the chancellor was still in bed. He marched straight into the room and confronted Tian Fen. "Yesterday you were kind enough to agree to visit Dou Ying, and that gentleman and his wife have made all the preparations! They have been waiting from dawn until now without daring to take a bite to eat!"

Tian Fen was very startled and began to apologize, saying, "I was a little drunk yesterday and I completely forgot about our conversation." He finally got up and set off in his carriage, but on the way he insisted upon driving very slowly, which made Guan Fu angrier than ever.

---

[4] And therefore ought not, according to custom, pay social calls.

When the party finally got started and the drinking had reached its height, Guan Fu stood up and performed a dance, requesting the chancellor to follow with a dance of his own, but Tian Fen merely sat where he was and refused to move. Guan Fu then began to make insulting remarks from his seat until Dou Ying pulled him to his feet and hurried him out of the room, apologizing to the chancellor for his behaviour. Tian Fen stayed and drank until evening when, having enjoyed himself thoroughly, he took his leave.

Some time later, Tian Fen set his retainer Ji Fu to ask Dou Ying if he would mind turning over to him some farm land south of the city which Dou Ying owned. Dou Ying was furious when he heard the request. "Though I am only an old man who has been abandoned by his friends and though the chancellor is a high official, he has absolutely no right to try to seize my possessions from me like this! I refuse to give up the land!"

When Guan Fu heard of the incident he cursed Ji Fu roundly. Ji Fu for his part was sorry to see enmity develop between Dou Ying and Tian Fen and so he did his best to smooth over the affair, returning to Tian Fen with excuses which he himself had invented. "After all, Dou Ying is an old man and will die soon. Surely you can do without the land for a while. You had better wait a bit," he said.

Later on, however, Tian Fen chanced to hear that Dou Ying and Guan Fu had in fact been greatly angered at his request and had refused to hand over the land, whereupon he too became incensed. "Once in the past Dou Ying's son killed a man but I managed to save him from punishment. I have always treated Dou Ying with respect and done everything he has asked me to. Why should he begrudge me a few acres of land? As for Guan Fu, what does he have to say in the matter? If that is the way they act, I will make no further requests for land!" Because of this Tian Fen came to bear a deep grudge against Guan Fu and Dou Ying.

In the spring of the fourth year of *yuanguang* (131 BC) Tian Fen reported to the emperor that Guan Fu's family in Yingchuan were behaving with complete disregard for the law and causing great hardship to the common people. He requested that their conduct be investigated. "It is up to you as chancellor to settle such matters," replied the emperor. "Why ask me about it?" Meanwhile Guan Fu happened to learn about certain secret dealings of the chancellor involving illegal profits, bribes received from the king of Huainan, and agreements made between the king and the chancellor. The retainers of Tian Fen and Guan Fu undertook to mediate between the two men and eventually persuaded them to cease their attacks and let each other alone.

In the summer of the same year Tian Fen married the daughter of Liu Jia, the king of Yan. Empress Dowager Wang issued an edict inviting all of the nobles and members of the imperial family to visit Tian Fen and offer their congratulations. Dou Ying called on Guan Fu and asked him to go with him to Tian Fen's house, but Guan Fu declined. "I have already been in trouble with the chancellor on several occasions by trying to drink with him. And anyway at the moment he and I are not on good terms."

"But that matter has been all settled!" said Dou Ying, and kept insisting until Guan Fu finally agreed to join him. When the drinking had reached its height, Tian Fen arose and proposed a toast, whereupon all the guests moved off their mats and bowed.[5] This over, Dou Ying proposed a toast, but only his old friends moved off their mats, the rest of the company simply kneeling where they were.

Guan Fu, highly displeased at the way things were going, got up with a container of wine and went over to pour a drink for Tian Fen. "I can't drink a whole cup!" Tian Fen protested, rising to his knees on the mat.

Guan Fu was angrier than ever, but he gave a forced laugh and said, "Come, sir, surely a man of your eminence .... I insist!" But Tian Fen refused to drink.

Guan Fu went next with the wine container to the marquis of Linru. The marquis was at the moment busy whispering in the ear of Cheng Bushi, and he too failed to get off his mat. Guan Fu, unable to find any other outlet for his rage, began to curse the marquis. "On ordinary days you go around speaking ill of Cheng Bushi and telling people he isn't worth a cent, and yet today all of a sudden when one of your elders comes and offers you a drink, you start cooing in Cheng Bushi's ear like a love-sick maiden!"

Tian Fen called Guan Fu aside and said, "Cheng Bushi and Li Guang are the commanders of the guards at the Eastern and Western Palaces, you know.[6] If you start insulting General Cheng in front of everyone, won't you be casting aspersions on your friend General Li as well?"

"Let them cut off my head or rip open my breast right now!" said Guan Fu.

---

[5] As in Japan today, the highest degree of courtesy was expressed by sliding all the way off one's mat and kneeling on the floor. A lesser degree of courtesy was expressed by straightening up on the mat and coming to a kneeling position.

[6] The Eastern Palace, of which Cheng Bushi was the commander of the guard, was the residence of the empress dowager; the Western Palace was another name for the emperor's palace.

"What do I care about Cheng or Li?"

With this the guests began to excuse themselves and go out to the toilet, one by one drifting away from the party. When Dou Ying was about to leave, he motioned to Guan Fu to go out with him, but Tian Fen exclaimed angrily, "I was at fault for ever letting Guan Fu behave in such an arrogant manner!" and ordered his horsemen to detain Guan Fu. Thus when Guan Fu tried to leave the house he found he could not get out. Ji Fu jumped up and came forward to apologize, pushing Guan Fu by the neck and trying to make him kneel down and apologize too, but Guan Fu only grew angrier than ever and refused to offer any apology.

Tian Fen then signalled to his horsemen to bind Guan Fu and take him to the post station. After this he sent for his chief secretary and, explaining that he had invited the members of the imperial family to his house in accordance with an edict from the empress dowager, instructed him to draw up charges against Guan Fu for insulting the guests and failing to show the proper respect, and to have him put into chains in the Inquiry Room. He then proceeded to investigate the earlier rumours of the misconduct of Guan Fu's relatives and sent his officers out in parties to arrest all the branches of the Guan family and charge them with crimes punishable by public execution.

Dou Ying was greatly distressed by this turn of events and, laying out funds from his own resources, sent his retainers to plead on Guan Fu's behalf, but they were unable to obtain his release. Tian Fen's officers did their best to carry out their orders but the other members of the Guan family all succeeded in escaping into hiding. Since Guan Fu was bound and imprisoned, he had no opportunity to report to the emperor what he knew about Tian Fen's secret dealings.

Dou Ying tried everything he could to save Guan Fu. His wife warned him, saying, "Guan Fu has offended the chancellor and gotten into trouble with Empress Dowager Wang and her whole family. How can you possibly save him?" But Dou Ying replied, "I won the title of marquis by my own efforts and if necessary I will give it up of my own accord and have no regrets. In any event I could not think of leaving Guan Fu to die while I am still alive!"

Then, without informing his family, he slipped out of the house and sent a letter to the emperor. He was immediately summoned to an audience at which he explained in detail that Guan Fu's misconduct had been due simply to an excess of wine and did not deserve the death penalty. The emperor expressed his agreement and even invited Dou Ying to dine in the palace. "However," he added, "you will have to go to the Eastern Palace and explain things to the empress dowager."

Proceeding to the court of the empress dowager, Dou Ying began to point out with zeal all of Guan Fu's good points. He explained that Guan Fu had behaved rudely when he was in his cups, but that the chancellor was trying to use other charges to build a false case against him. The chancellor, however, who was also present, set out with equal zeal to accuse Guan Fu of arrogant and unlawful conduct, claiming that he was guilty of rebellion and treason. Dou Ying, judging that no other course would be of any avail, finally began to speak ill of the chancellor himself.

Tian Fen replied to these charges as follows: "Today the world is blessed with peace and harmony, and I have the special fortune to belong to a family which is related to the imperial house by marriage. I am the sort of man who delights in music, in dogs and horses, gardens and houses; I have a fondness for singers, actors, and clever craftsmen. In this respect I am different from Dou Ying and Guan Fu, who summon to their homes all the powerful bosses and daring young men of the empire and sit day and night talking with them; whose hearts are set on slander and whose minds are full of deceit; who, when they are not searching the heavens for omens of change, are scanning the earth to plot their campaigns, always with a crafty eye fixed upon the relations between the emperor and the empress dowager, praying that the empire may be convulsed by some strife and that they may thereby win great merit for themselves! To what lengths men like Dou Ying and his party will go, I would not venture to guess!"

The emperor then assembled the ministers of his court and asked them which of the two contestants, Dou Ying or Tian Fen, they believed was in the right. The imperial secretary Han Anguo gave his opinion as follows: "As Dou Ying has pointed out, Guan Fu's father died in the service of the dynasty, while Guan Fu himself seized his spear and galloped into the midst of the rebel camp of Wu, facing untold danger. He bore on his body a dozen wounds and his fame outshone that of every other soldier in the three armies. Truly he is one of the bravest men of the empire. Now he has committed no serious offence, but only become involved in a petty argument over a cup of wine. There is therefore no reason, as Dou Ying says, to drag in other charges and condemn him to execution. In this respect Dou Ying's opinion is correct.

"On the other hand the chancellor has charged Guan Fu with associating with evil and lawless men, oppressing the poor, amassing a fortune that runs into millions, running his affairs in Yingchuan in an arbitrary and tyrannical manner, insulting the dignity of the imperial house, and molesting men who are flesh and blood of that family. As the proverb says, 'When the branches grow bigger than the roots, then something must break; when the shins grow mightier than the thighs, then something must give.' Thus the opinion of the chancellor is also correct. It remains only for our enlightened sovereign to decide in the case."

The master of titles chief commandant Ji An expressed himself in agreement with Dou Ying, and the prefect of the capital Zheng Dangshi also said he thought Dou Ying was right, though in the course of the deliberations he became frightened and did not dare to defend his assertion. (None of the other officials ventured to offer any opinion at all.) The emperor was furious with Zheng Dangshi and said, "All the time you go around discoursing on the relative merits and faults of Dou Ying and Tian Fen, and yet today when I summon you to court to give your opinion, you cringe and hang your head like a pony in the shafts! I ought to cut off your head as well!"

With this the emperor dismissed the court and, rising from his seat, retired to the inner palace to wait on his mother, Empress Dowager Wang, while she took her meal. The empress dowager had sent her observers to court and they had already reported to her in detail the discussions which had taken place. She was in a rage and refused to eat. "Even while I am alive, people go about insulting my brother Tian Fen! After I have passed on, I have no doubt that they will gobble him up like so much fish and meat! And you — you are no man of stone! You are mortal the same as everyone else! Can't you see that these men are only biding their time and pretending to be docile while you are still alive? After your days are ended, do you think there is one of them who can be trusted?"

The emperor apologized, saying, "It is only because Tian Fen and Dou Ying are both related to the imperial family by marriage that I brought the matter before the court for discussion. If it were not for that, the affair could be left for any law officer to settle."

At this time the chief of palace attendants Shi Jian drew up for the emperor a list of the opinions presented for and against the two contestants. When the court session was over Tian Fen left the palace and went to the gate where the carriages were drawn up. Calling to the imperial secretary Han Anguo to join him in his carriage, he began to berate him angrily. "You and I together are pitted against a single, bald-headed old man, Dou Ying! Why did you have to be so timid in expressing your opinion, like a rat trying to look both ways at once?"

After considering for some time, Han Anguo replied, "You ought to think a little more highly of yourself. If Dou Ying abuses you, you should remove your cap, undo your seals of office and, handing them over to the emperor, say, 'Because of my family connections I have graciously been permitted to serve Your Majesty, but I am basically unfit for the position. Everything that Dou Ying has said about me is quite correct!' In that case the emperor would be sure to admire your humility and would refuse to accept your resignation. As for Dou Ying, he would be so ashamed of himself that he would retire to his home and, biting his tongue with remorse, take his own life. Instead of that, when someone abuses you, you begin abusing him back until the two of you end up quarrelling like a pair of fishwives! This is surely not a very dignified way to behave!"

"I am sorry," said Tian Fen, acknowledging his fault. "In the heat of the argument I became so carried away that it never occurred to me to do such a thing."

Shortly after, the emperor ordered the imperial secretary Han Anguo to draw up charges against Dou Ying, accusing him of making statements in Guan Fu's defence that were wholly false and irresponsible. Dou Ying was impeached and imprisoned in the custody of the head of criminal affairs for the imperial family.

Previously, at the end of Emperor Jing's reign, Dou Ying had received a testamentary edict from the emperor stating, "If you ever find yourself in any difficulty, you should appeal your case directly to the throne." Now Guan Fu had been arrested and accused of a crime punishable by death for himself and his whole family, and the situation grew more serious each day. Moreover, none of the officials dared make any further attempt to explain Dou Ying's position to the emperor. Dou Ying therefore directed his brother's son to write a letter on his behalf to the emperor requesting that he be granted another audience. The letter was submitted to the throne, but when the master of documents searched the files, he could find no such testamentary edict among the papers dating from the time of Emperor Jing's decease. The only copy of the edict in existence, it appeared, was the one preserved in Dou Ying's house, bearing the seal of Dou Ying's private secretary. Hence Dou Ying was charged with having forged an edict of the former emperor, a crime punishable by execution in the market place.

In the tenth month of the fifth year of *yuanguang* (130 BC) Guan Fu and all the members of his family were condemned to execution. After some time, news of this reached Dou Ying in jail. He was deeply embittered and, being afflicted with a swelling in his joints, refused to eat anything in hopes that he would soon die. Someone assured him, however, that the emperor had no intention of executing him, and with this he took heart and began to eat again so that his illness improved. The emperor and his ministers had in fact decided not to sentence Dou Ying to death, but just then rumours began to reach the emperor's ears that Dou Ying was speaking evilly of him, and so on the last day of the twelfth month the emperor ordered the death sentence.[7] Dou Ying was executed in the market place of Weicheng.

The following spring, Tian Fen, the marquis of Wuan, fell ill; he spent all his time crying out "I was at fault!" and begging forgiveness for his crimes. When he summoned sorcerers with the power to discern ghosts and asked them what they saw, they reported that they could see Dou Ying and Guan Fu standing watch together by his bedside and preparing to kill him. Before long Tian Fen died and his son Tian Tian succeeded to the marquisate. In the third year of the era *yuanshuo* (126 BC) Tian Tian was tried on charges of disrespect for the throne because he came to the palace dressed in short robes, and was deprived of his territory.

Sometime afterwards it was discovered that Liu An, the king of Huainan, had been plotting a revolt. Liu An and his conspirators were brought to justice, and in the course of the investigations it was found that once in the past, when the king paid a visit to court, Tian Fen, then grand commandant, had driven out as far as Bashang to greet him. "The emperor has not yet designated an heir apparent," Tian Fen was reported to have said, "while Your Highness is the most worthy among the kings, being a grandson of the founder of the dynasty, Gaozu. If there should be a funeral in the imperial palace, I cannot think of anyone but you who would be suitable to succeed to the throne!" The king of Huainan, it was said, was greatly pleased with these words and presented Tian Fen with generous gifts of money and goods.

From the time of the Dou Ying affair the emperor no longer put any trust in Tian Fen, but merely tolerated him because he was a brother of the empress dowager. When he heard these reports of money presented to Tian Fen by the king of Huainan, he declared, "If Tian Fen were still around today I would have him and his whole family executed!"

---

[7]Since spring is the time when life returns to the earth, it was considered unlucky to perform executions in the spring, and the beginning of spring (the first month) was often accompanied by an amnesty. Tian Fen therefore had to work quickly to spread his rumours in order to dispose of his enemy before the end of the twelfth month.

The Grand Historian remarks: Dou Ying and Tian Fen both commanded great respect because they belonged to families related to the throne by marriage. Guan Fu became famous as a result of a daring exploit made on the spur of the moment; Dou Ying won promotion in the Wu and Chu rebellion; but Tian Fen's position of honour was more a matter of time and fortunate circumstance.[8]

Dou Ying, however, did not know how to change with the times, and Guan Fu, though a man of no learning, refused to be humble. Both men tried to help each other, but they succeeded only in bringing disaster upon themselves.

Tian Fen enjoyed great honour and loved the feel of power, but because of the resentment occasioned by a single cup of wine, he set about to destroy two men. How pitiful! Those who attempt to vent their anger on innocent persons can never hope to live for long. Those who fail to win the commendation of the mass of lesser men will end by suffering their slanders. Alas, alas! No misfortune ever comes without due cause!

---

[8] I.e., that Emperor Jing died young and Tian Fen's sister, Empress Dowager Wang, was able to exercise great power.

SHI JI 108: THE BIOGRAPHY OF HAN CHANGRU[1]

His wisdom was such that he could respond to the changes of the present age; his kindness enabled him to win over others. Thus I made "The Biography of Han Changru".

The imperial secretary Han Anguo was born in Cheng'an in Liang; later he moved to Suiyang, the capital of Liang. In his youth he studied the theories of the Legalist philosopher Han Fei Zi and those of the other philosophical schools with Master Tian of Zou and served as a palace counsellor to King Xiao of Liang.

When the states of Wu and Chu began their rebellion, King Xiao dispatched Han Anguo and Zhang Yu as generals to block the advance of the Wu army on the eastern border. Zhang Yu fell upon the rebels outright, while Han Anguo proceeded with caution and foresight, and between them they kept the army of Wu from advancing beyond Liang. After the rebellion was put down, both Han Anguo and Zhang Yu became well known for the part they had played in its suppression.

King Xiao of Liang was a younger brother of Emperor Jing. Their mother, Empress Dowager Dou, loved him dearly and persuaded Emperor Jing to allow him to appoint his own prime minister and officials of the 2,000 picul class, though this was contrary to Han custom. In his travels, his hunting expeditions, and his whole way of life, King Xiao imitated the Son of Heaven, a fact which secretly displeased Emperor Jing when he learned of it. The empress dowager, well aware of the emperor's displeasure, vented her annoyance on the envoys from Liang, refusing to receive them in audience and presenting them with a list of the king's misdemeanours.

Han Anguo, who came to court as an envoy from Liang, visited Emperor

---

[1] Changru is the polite name of Han Anguo; Sima Qian uses it in the title of the biography but in the biography itself refers to him throughout by his familiar name, Han Anguo.

Jing's sister, the Elder Princess, and, weeping, said, "No one is a more filial son and a more loyal subject than the king of Liang. Why is it that the empress dowager will not recognize this? Some time ago, when Wu, Chu, Qi, Zhao, and the others of the Seven Kingdoms rebelled, all the lands east of the Pass joined together in alliance and began their march westward to the capital. Only Liang remained faithful and shouldered the burden of resistance. The king of Liang, thinking of the empress dowager and the emperor far away in the capital and observing the lawlessness of the other feudal lords, wept floods of tears with each word he spoke. Kneeling and bidding farewell to me and his other six generals, he sent us with a force of men to attack and drive back the armies of Wu and Chu. Therefore the rebels did not dare advance westward and were in the end defeated and wiped out. This was all due to the efforts of the king of Liang!

"Now, because of some petty scruple, some fine point of behaviour, the empress dowager has become angry with the king of Liang. One must remember, however, that the king's father was an emperor, and his older brother is emperor today; he has been accustomed from youth to the pomp of imperial life. Therefore he has his attendants cry 'Clear the way!' and 'Attention!' when he leaves or returns to his palace, in the manner of an emperor. As for the imperial flags which he flies from his carriage, they were all presented to him by the emperor. If he uses these when he rides about his kingdom, making a show before the country towns and putting on a boastful appearance in the eyes of the other feudal lords, it is because he wishes the whole empire to know that he enjoys the love of the empress dowager and the emperor. And yet now when the Liang envoys come to court they are summarily confronted with a list of the king's misdemeanours. The king is deeply afraid. Day and night he weeps, thinking fondly of his loved ones in the capital but not knowing what to do! How can the empress dowager be so cold-hearted toward one who is such a filial son and loyal subject?"

The Elder Princess reported to the empress dowager everything that Han Anguo had said. The empress dowager was pleased and said, "For the king's sake you had better tell the emperor about this." The Elder Princess repeated her story to the emperor, whose annoyance was somewhat appeased. When he went to pay his respects to his mother, the empress dowager, he removed his hat and apologized, saying, "I am afraid that, because my brother and I had some difference of opinion, we have caused our mother unnecessary anxiety!"

He then received all the Liang envoys in audience and rewarded them with generous gifts. From this time on the king of Liang enjoyed greater favour and intimacy with the emperor. The empress dowager and the Elder Princess also presented gifts to Han Anguo amounting to over 1,000 catties of gold. Because of this incident Han Anguo grew more famous than ever and came to be on close terms with the imperial family.

Sometime later Han Anguo was tried for an offence and condemned to punishment. Tian Something-or-other,[2] the prison official of Meng where Han Anguo was held for questioning, took the occasion to humiliate him.

"Do you think," said Han Anguo, referring to his present state of disgrace, "that because the fire has for the moment died out in these ashes, it will never come to life again?"

"If it does," replied Tian, "I will piss on it!"

Shortly afterwards the post of internal secretary of Liang fell vacant and an envoy was sent from the central government to appoint Han Anguo to the position. In one stroke he was raised from the status of a convict to that of a 2,000 picul official. The prison official Tian fled into hiding, but Han Anguo sent word to him: "If you do not return to your post, I will execute all the members of your family!" Tian finally appeared and, with his arms bared, apologized for his former behaviour. "Now is the time to piss on me!" said Han Anguo with a laugh. "I certainly can't be bothered punishing the likes of you!" In the end he treated Tian very well.

When the post of internal secretary fell vacant, King Xiao had just obtained the services of a rhetorician from Qi named Gongsun Gui and, finding him to his liking, was thinking of asking the emperor for permission to appoint this man as internal secretary. The empress dowager, hearing of his plans, ordered the king to appoint Han Anguo to the post. Gongsun Gui and another rhetorician named Yang Sheng had been urging the king to try to get himself designated as heir apparent to his brother, Emperor Jing, and to increase his lands, but they were afraid that the high officials of the Han court would never listen to such proposals. They therefore sent men in secret to assassinate the officials of the Han court who were opposing these measures, and succeeded in murdering Yuan Ang, the former prime minister of Wu. Emperor Jing, learning in time that Gongsun Gui and Yang Sheng were the authors of the assassination plot, dispatched envoys with orders to arrest the two men without fail. A group of ten

---

[2]Sima Qian has been unable to ascertain the personal name of the official and has substituted the word *jia*, or "A".

Han officials arrived at the court of Liang and, enlisting the services of everyone from the prime minister on down, began a search for the culprits throughout the kingdom, but over a month passed and they had still not succeeded in apprehending them.

Han Anguo, learning that King Xiao was concealing them in his own residence, went to the king and, with tears in his eyes, said, "The shame of the lord, it is said, must be paid for by the death of his ministers. It is because Your Highness has no worthy ministers that affairs have reached this wretched state. Now, since Gongsun Gui and Yang Sheng have not been arrested, I beg to be relieved of my post and sentenced to death!"

"But why go to this extreme?" the king protested.

Han Anguo, the tears coursing down his face, replied, "Your Highness is on intimate terms with the emperor. But, though you are his brother, are you as close to him as Emperor Gaozu was to his father, the Grand Supreme Emperor, or as the king of Linjiang was to the present emperor?"[3]

"Surely not," said the king.

"These men were linked by the closest bond possible — that of father and son. And yet Emperor Gaozu boasted that 'It was *I* who won the empire with my three-foot sword' and consequently his father, the Grand Supreme Emperor, never took any part in the governing of the empire but lived in retirement in Yueyang. Similarly the king of Linjiang, though the eldest son of the emperor and the rightful heir, was deprived of the title of heir apparent because of one little slip in speech committed by his mother, Lady Li.[4] Later he was accused of having torn down the wall of one of the ancestral temples, and finally he committed suicide in the office of the palace military commander. Why did Emperor Gaozu and the present emperor treat their closest kin in this way? Because in governing the empire one must never let private feelings interfere with the public welfare! There is a popular saying, 'Though he's your father, he may still turn out to be a tiger; though he's your older brother, he may still turn

---

[3] Liu Rong, the eldest son of Emperor Jing, was originally designated as heir apparent but later removed from that position and appointed king of Linjiang. See in Volume I his biography, in "Hereditary Houses of the Five Families", and that of his mother, Lady Li, in "Hereditary Houses of the Families Related to the Emperors by Marriage".

[4] In the biography of Lady Li we are told that, although Emperor Jing asked her to look after his sons in the event of his death, she "had refused to acknowledge his request, and when she did speak her words were lacking in humility". This is probably the "slip in speech" to which Han Anguo is referring.

out to be a wolf!'

"Now, although you are ranked among the feudal lords, you have been beguiled by the fatuous advice of evil ministers into violating the prohibitions of the emperor and perverting the enlightened laws of the land. For the sake of the empress dowager, the Son of Heaven has forborne to call you to account before the law. The empress dowager herself weeps day and night, praying that you will mend your ways of your own accord, and yet you have failed to wake to your error. But someday if the funeral carriages were to bear the empress dowager away to her final rest, whom would you have left to turn to?"

Before he had finished speaking, the tears began to stream down King Xiao's face and, apologizing to Han Anguo, he said, "I will expel Gongsun Gui and Yang Sheng from their hiding place!" Gongsun Gui and Yang Sheng committed suicide, and the Han envoys returned to the capital to report to the emperor. Thus the settlement of the affair was due solely to the efforts of Han Anguo. From this time on Emperor Jing and Empress Dowager Dou held Han Anguo in even higher esteem.

After King Xiao died and his son, Liu Mai, posthumously known as King Gong, came to the throne, Han Anguo was tried for some offence and removed from his post, after which he lived at home in retirement.

During the era *jianyuan* (140-135 BC) Tian Fen, the marquis of Wuan, was made grand commandant of the Han court and enjoyed great favour and honour in the exercise of his duties. Han Anguo presented him with a gift of 500 catties of gold, in exchange for which Tian Fen spoke on his behalf to his half-sister, Empress Dowager Wang, the mother of the present emperor. The emperor had also heard of Han Anguo's reputation for wisdom and summoned him to be chief commandant of Beidi. Shortly afterwards he was transferred to the post of minister of agriculture. When the state of Minyue attacked its neighbour, Southern Yue, Han Anguo and the grand messenger Wang Hui were dispatched with troops to put down the trouble. Before they had reached Minyue, however, the people of that state murdered their king and surrendered, whereupon the Han forces withdrew.

In the sixth year of *jianyuan* (135 BC) Tian Fen was made chancellor and Han Anguo was made imperial secretary. At this time the Xiongnu had come with offers of a peace alliance and the emperor had referred the question to his ministers for debate. The grand messenger Wang Hui, a native of Yan who had several times served as an official on the northern border and was familiar with the ways of the Xiongnu, stated his opinion: "Although the Han concludes peace treaties with the Xiongnu, it is never more than a couple of years before they violate the agreement. It would be better to refuse their offer and send troops to attack them!"

Han Anguo, however, replied, "No profit comes to an army that has to fight 1,000 miles from home. The Xiongnu move on the feet of swift war horses, and in their breasts beat the hearts of beasts. They shift from place to place as fast as a flock of birds, so that it is extremely difficult to corner them and bring them under control. Though we were to win possession of their land, it would be no great addition to the empire, and though we ruled their hosts of warriors, they would do little to strengthen our power. From the most ancient times the Xiongnu have never been regarded as a part of humanity. If we march thousands of miles away and try to fight with them, our men and horses will be worn out, and then the wretches will muster all their strength and fall upon us. An arrow from the most powerful crossbow, when it has reached the end of its flight, will not pierce the sheerest Lu gauze; the strongest wind, when its force is spent, will not lift a goose feather — not because both are not strong at the outset, but because their force in time is dispersed. It would not be expedient to attack the Xiongnu. Better to make peace with them!"

Many of the other ministers agreed with Han Anguo's opinion, and the emperor therefore consented to the peace alliance.

The following year, the first year of the era *guangyuan* (134 BC) Nie Wengyi, an influential man from the city of Mayi in Yanmen Province, conveyed word to the emperor via the grand messenger Wang Hui, saying, "Now that peaceful relations have been established with the Xiongnu and they are on good terms with us here on the border, it would be an ideal opportunity to entice them with prospects of gain." The emperor therefore ordered Nie Wengyi to cross the border in secret and, in the guise of a refugee, to enter the territory of the Xiongnu. Once there, he had an interview with the *Shanyu*, the Xiongnu leader, and said, "If you wish, I can murder the governor of Mayi and his officials and turn the city over to you so you can seize all the wealth there!"

The *Shanyu*, trusting Nie Wengyi, was attracted by his offer and agreed to cooperate. Nie Wengyi returned to Mayi and, putting to death some condemned criminals instead, hung their heads on the city wall as a sign to the *Shanyu*'s envoys that he had carried out his part of the agreement, telling them at the same time, "The high officials of Mayi have all been killed. Now is the time to attack with all speed!" The *Shanyu* then broke through the border defences and, with a force of over 100,000 cavalry, invaded the empire through the barrier at

Wuzhou.

At this time the Han had a force of over 300,000 infantry, cavalry, and bowmen concealed in the valley around Mayi, lying in wait for the Xiongnu. The colonel of the guard Li Guang commanded the cavalry; the master of carriage Gongsun He commanded the light carriages; the grand messenger Wang Hui was the garrison commander; the palace counsellor Li Xi was commander of the bowmen; and the imperial secretary Han Anguo was in command of the supporting army. All the other leaders were under Han Anguo's command. An agreement was made that as soon as the *Shanyu* had entered the city of Mayi, the Han troops would pour out of hiding to attack him. Wang Hui, Li Xi, and Li Guang were to lead a separate force across from the direction of Dai and concentrate on attacking the baggage trains of the enemy.

As already stated, the *Shanyu* broke through the Great Wall at the Wuzhou barrier and began to march toward Mayi, plundering as he went along. He was still some 100 *li* from the city when, noticing that there were large numbers of domestic animals in the fields but no people anywhere insight, he began to grow suspicious. He attacked a beacon warning station and captured one of the defence officials of Wuzhou. He was about to run the official through with his sword, but instead began to question him, whereupon the official told him, "There are 20,000 or 30,000 Han troops lying in ambush at Mayi!"

The *Shanyu*, turning to those around him, said, "It appears that we have been tricked by the Han!" and began to lead his forces back toward the border. After he got beyond the pass, he said, "Heaven was on my side when I captured this defence official!" and he awarded the man the title of "Heavenly King".

When word came from the border that the *Shanyu* had turned around and was leading his troops back out of the country, the Han forces set out in pursuit. They followed him as far as the border but, realizing that they could not overtake him, abandoned the pursuit. Meanwhile Wang Hui and the others of his group of 30,000, hearing that the *Shanyu* had not made contact with the Han armies, and considering that if they tried to attack the baggage trains they would be pitted against the finest soldiers of the *Shanyu* and would surely suffer defeat, likewise abandoned any idea of attack. Thus none of the generals achieved any distinction.

The emperor was furious at Wang Hui for failing to cross the border to attack the *Shanyu*'s baggage train, but instead leading his troops back to the capital in defiance of orders. Defending himself, Wang Hui said, "If the wretches had gotten as far as Mayi and the other Han troops had made contact with the *Shanyu* according to the agreement, then I could have attacked his baggage train with good prospects of success. But when the *Shanyu* discovered the plot and turned back before reaching the city, I knew that my 30,000 men could never stand up to his hordes and that we would win nothing but disgrace. I was perfectly aware, of course, that I would be executed as soon as I returned to the capital, but I wished to save the lives of those 30,000 men of Your Majesty's."

Wang Hui was handed over to the commandant of justice, who recommended that he be executed for cowardly shirking of duty. Wang Hui secretly sent 1,000 pieces of gold to the chancellor Tian Fen to speak on his behalf, but Tian Fen did not dare to say anything directly to the emperor. Instead he spoke to Empress Dowager Wang: "Wang Hui was the one who engineered the plot to attack the *Shanyu* at Mayi. Now if he is to be executed for its failure, this is simply doing the Xiongnu the favour of satisfying their anger!"

When the emperor came to pay his morning visit to his mother, Empress Dowager Wang, she repeated to him what Tian Fen had said, but the emperor replied, "Wang Hui was indeed the one who engineered the Mayi plot. It was because of him that I called out several hundred thousand troops and disposed them as he recommended. Even if it was impossible to capture the *Shanyu*, Wang Hui and his group of men could at least have attacked his baggage train and won some sort of gain to repay the soldiers for all their labour. Now if I fail to execute him, I will have no way to apologize to the empire for this failure!"

When Wang Hui heard what the emperor had said, he committed suicide.

Han Anguo was the sort of man who is full of grand schemes. He was wise enough to know how to get along in the world, but at the same time his actions all sprang from a deep sense of loyalty. Although he himself was greedy in matters of money, those whom he recommended for office were all men of scrupulous integrity and worthier than himself. He worked for the promotion of such men as Hu Sui, Zang Gu, and Zhi Tuo from his own state of Liang, all of whom became famous throughout the empire. Everyone admired him for his efforts to promote others and the emperor himself considered him an invaluable asset to the nation.

Han Anguo had been imperial secretary for some four years when the chancellor Tian Fen died. Han Anguo temporarily took over the duties of chancellor but one day, when he was leading the imperial procession, he fell from his carriage and injured his foot. The emperor had begun discussions on a replacement for the post of chancellor and was anxious to appoint Han Anguo, but when he sent someone to see how Han Anguo was, the man reported that he was still limping badly as a result of his fall. The emperor therefore appointed Xue Ze, the marquis of Pingji, as chancellor instead of Han Anguo, who declined the post on grounds of his illness.

After a few months Han Anguo's limp went away and the emperor made him palace military commander; a year or so later he was transferred to the post of colonel of the guard. At this time the carriage and cavalry general Wei Qing attacked the Xiongnu, riding north from Shanggu Province and defeating the barbarians at Longcheng. General Li Guang, who took part in the expedition, was captured by the Xiongnu but managed to escape, while another of the generals, Gongsun Ao, lost a large number of his men. Both were condemned to die but were allowed to buy off the death sentence and become commoners instead.

The following year the Xiongnu crossed the border in great numbers and murdered the governor of Liaoxi. From Liaoxi they advanced to Yanmen, killing and carrying off several thousand men. The carriage and cavalry general Wei Qing marched out of Yanmen to attack them, leaving the colonel of the guard Han Anguo in command of a force of bowmen to garrison Yuyang. One of the Xiongnu whom Han Anguo had taken prisoner informed him that the Xiongnu hordes had by this time moved on far away from the area, and Han Anguo therefore sent a letter to the throne requesting that, since it was time for the work in the fields to begin, he be allowed to disband the army at the garrison for a while. Permission was granted, but the garrison army had not been disbanded for more than a month or so when the Xiongnu invaded Shanggu and Yuyang in great numbers. Han Anguo had no more than 700 some men in the fort where he was stationed and, though they marched out and engaged the enemy, they could win no advantage and were forced to retire into the fort again. The Xiongnu meanwhile plundered the region, seizing over 1,000 prisoners and all the domestic animals before they left the area.

When word of this reached the emperor he was furious and sent a messenger to reprimand Han Anguo. He then transferred Han Anguo far to the east, putting him in charge of the garrison at Youbeiping, because one of the Xiongnu prisoners had said that the Xiongnu were preparing to invade in the east.

Han Anguo had been imperial secretary early in his career and had commanded the armies at Mayi, but later he incurred the displeasure of the emperor and was demoted to lesser posts, while the emperor's new favourite, the young general Wei Qing, continued to pile up achievements and rise in importance.

Han Anguo suffered this increasing estrangement from the emperor in gloomy silence. After he was made garrison commander and was tricked by the Xiongnu into losing so many of his men, he was filled with the deepest humiliation and requested permission to resign his post and return home. Instead of this, however, he was transferred further east to command another garrison, where he continued to grow more depressed and melancholy than ever. A few months after his transfer, he fell ill and spat blood and died. His death occurred during the second year of the era *yuanshuo* (127 BC).

The Grand Historian remarks: I worked on the establishment of the new calendar with Hu Sui, whom Han Anguo had recommended to office, and had an opportunity to observe Han Anguo's strict sense of duty and Hu Sui's deep and abiding loyalty. It is no wonder people these days say that Liang is rich in worthy men. Hu Sui advanced as high as the post of steward in the household of the empress dowager and the heir apparent. The emperor had great faith in him and was planning to make him chancellor when death ended his career. Had he lived, he would, with his integrity and fine conduct, have been one of the most conscientious and diligent men alive today.

SHI JI 109: THE BIOGRAPHY OF GENERAL LI GUANG

Valorous in the face of the enemy, good to his men, he gave no petty or vexatious orders, and for this reason his subordinates looked up to him with admiration. Thus I made "The Biography of General Li Guang".

General Li Guang was a native of Chengji in Longxi Province. Among his ancestors was Li Xin, a general of the state of Qin, who pursued and captured Dan, the crown prince of Yan.[1] The family originally lived in Huaili but later moved to Chengji. The art of archery had been handed down in the family for generations.

In the fourteenth year of Emperor Wen's reign (166 BC) the Xiongnu entered the Xiao Pass in great numbers. Li Guang, as the son of a distinguished family, was allowed to join the army in the attack on the barbarians. He proved himself a skilful horseman and archer, killing and capturing a number of the enemy, and was rewarded with the position of palace attendant at the Han court. His cousin Li Cai was also made a palace attendant. Both men served as mounted guards to the emperor and received a stipend of 800 piculs of grain. Li Guang always accompanied Emperor Wen on his hunting expeditions. The emperor, observing how he charged up to the animal pits, broke through the palisades, and struck down the most ferocious beasts, remarked, "What a pity you were not born at a better time! Had you lived in the age of Emperor Gaozu, you would have had no trouble in winning a marquisate of at least 10,000 households!"

When Emperor Jing came to the throne, Li Guang was made chief commandant of Longxi; later he was transferred to the post of general of palace horsemen. At the time of the revolt of Wu and Chu, he served as a cavalry commander under the grand commandant Zhou Yafu, joining in the attack on the armies of Wu and Chu, capturing the enemy pennants, and distinguishing

---

[1] He had sent a man to the Qin court in an unsuccessful attempt to assassinate the king who later became the First Emperor of the Qin. See *Records of the Grand Historian, Qin Dynasty*.

himself at the battle of Changyi. But because he had accepted the seals of a general from the king of Liang without authorization from the Han government, he was not rewarded for his achievements when he returned to the capital.

Following this he was transferred to the post of governor of Shanggu Province, where he engaged in almost daily skirmishes with the Xiongnu. The director of dependent states Gongsun Kunye went to the emperor and, with tears in his eyes, said, "There is no one in the empire to match Li Guang for skill and spirit and yet, trusting to his own ability, he repeatedly engages the enemy in battle. I am afraid one day we will lose him!" The emperor therefore transferred him to the post of governor of Shang Province.[2]

At this time the Xiongnu invaded Shang Province in great force. Emperor Jing sent one of his trusted eunuchs to join Li Guang, ordering him to train the troops and lead them in an attack on the Xiongnu. The eunuch, leading a group of twenty or thirty horsemen, was casually riding about the countryside one day when he caught sight of three Xiongnu riders and engaged them in a fight. The three Xiongnu, however, began circling the party and shooting as they went until they had wounded the eunuch and were near to killing all of his horsemen. The eunuch barely managed to flee back to the place where Li Guang was. "They must be out hunting eagles!" said Li Guang, and galloped off with 100 horsemen in pursuit of the three Xiongnu. The Xiongnu, having lost their horses, fled on foot. After they had journeyed twenty or thirty *li*, Li Guang caught up with them and, ordering his horsemen to fan out to the left and right of them, began to shoot at them. He killed two with his arrows and took the third one alive. As he had guessed, they were eagle hunters.

Li Guang had bound his prisoner and remounted his horse, when he spied several thousand Xiongnu horsemen in the distance. The Xiongnu, catching sight of Li Guang and his men, supposed that they were a decoy sent out from the main body of the Han forces to lure them into combat. They made for a nearby hill in alarm and drew up their ranks on its crest.

Li Guang's horsemen were thoroughly terrified and begged him to flee back to camp as quickly as possible, but he replied, "We are twenty or thirty *li* away from the main army. With only 100 of us, if we were to try to make a dash for it, the Xiongnu would be after us in no time and would shoot down every one

---

[2] The thirty-one characters which follow at this point in the text have been shifted in the translation to a point farther along in the narrative, following the reading in the parallel passage in *Han shu* 54.

of us. But it we stay where we are, they are bound to think we are a decoy from the main army and will not dare to attack!"

Instead of retreating, therefore, Li Guang gave the order to his men to advance. When they had reached a point some two *li* from the Xiongnu ranks, he told his men, "Dismount and undo your saddles!"

"But there are too many of them and they are almost on top of us!" his men protested. "What will we do if they attack?"

"They expect us to run away," said Li Guang. "But now if we all undo our saddles and show them we have no intention of fleeing, they will be more convinced than ever that there is something afoot."

The Xiongnu in fact did not venture to attack, but sent out one of their leaders on a white horse to reconnoitre. Li Guang mounted again and, with ten or so of his horsemen, galloped after the barbarian leader and shot him down. Then he returned to his group and, undoing his saddle, ordered his men to turn loose their horses and lie down on the ground. By this time night was falling and the Xiongnu, thoroughly suspicious of what they had seen, still had not ventured to attack. They concluded that the Han leaders must have concealed soldiers in the area and be planning to fall upon them in the dark, and so during the night the Xiongnu chiefs and their men all withdrew. When dawn came Li Guang finally managed to return with his group to the main army, which, having no idea where he had gone, had been unable to follow him.

After this Li Guang was assigned to the governorship of several other border provinces in succession, returning finally to Shang Province. In the course of these moves he served as governor of Longxi, Beidi, Yanmen, Dai, and Yunzhong Provinces and in each won fame for his fighting.

After some time, Emperor Jing passed away and the present emperor came to the throne. The emperor's advisers informed him of Li Guang's fame as a general, and he made Li Guang the colonel of the guard of the Eternal Palace, while allowing him to retain the governorship of Shang Province.

At this time Cheng Bushi was the colonel of the guard of the Palace of Lasting Joy. Cheng Bushi had been a governor in the border provinces and a garrison general at the same time as Li Guang. When Li Guang went out on expeditions to attack the Xiongnu, he never bothered to form his men into battalions and companies. He would make camp wherever he found water and grass, leaving his men to set up their quarters in any way they thought convenient. He never had sentries circling the camp at night and beating on cooking pots, as was the custom, and in his headquarters he kept records and other clerical work down to a minimum. He always sent out scouts some distance around the camp, however, and he had never met with any particular mishap.

Cheng Bushi, on the other hand, always kept his men in strict battalion and company formation. The sentries banged on the cooking pots, his officers worked over their records and reports until dawn, and no one in his army got any rest. He likewise had never had any mishaps. Cheng Bushi once expressed the opinion, "Although Li Guang runs his army in a very simple fashion, if the enemy should ever swoop down on him suddenly he would have no way to hold them off. His men enjoy plenty of idleness and pleasure, and for that reason they are all eager to fight to the death for him. Life in my army may be a good deal more irksome, but at least I know that the enemy will never catch me napping!"

Li Guang and Cheng Bushi were both famous generals at this time, but the Xiongnu were more afraid of Li Guang's strategies, while the Han soldiers for the most part preferred to serve under him and disliked being under Cheng Bushi's command. Cheng Bushi advanced to the position of palace counsellor under Emperor Jing because of the outspoken advice he gave the emperor on several occasions. He was a man of great integrity and very conscientious in matters of form and law.

Sometime later, the Han leaders attempted to entice the *Shanyu* into entering the city of Mayi, concealing a large force of men in the valley around the city to ambush the Xiongnu. At this time Li Guang was appointed as cavalry general under the command of Han Anguo, the leader of the supporting army. As it happened, however, the *Shanyu* discovered the plot and escaped in time, so that neither Li Guang nor any of the other generals connected with the plot achieved any merit.

Four years later (129 BC) Li Guang, because of his services as colonel of the guard, was made a general and sent north from Yanmen to attack the Xiongnu. But the Xiongnu force he was pitted against turned out to be too numerous and succeeded in defeating Li Guang's army and capturing him alive.

The *Shanyu* had for a long time heard of Li Guang's excellence as a fighter and had given orders, "If you get hold of Li Guang, take him alive and bring him to me!" As it turned out, the barbarian horsemen did manage to capture Li Guang and, since he was badly wounded, they strung a litter between two horses and, laying him on it, proceeded on their way about ten *li*. Li Guang pretended to be dead but managed to peer around him and noticed that close by this side was a young Xiongnu boy mounted on a fine horse. Suddenly he leaped out of the litter and onto the boy's horse, seizing his bow and pushing him off the horse.

Then, whipping the horse to full gallop, he dashed off to the south. After travelling twenty or thirty *li* he succeeded in catching up with what was left of his army and led the men back across the border into Han territory. While he was making his escape, several hundred horsemen from the party that had captured him came in pursuit, but he turned and shot at them with the bow he had snatched from the boy, killing his pursuers, and was thus able to escape.

When he got back to the capital, he was turned over to the law officials, who recommended that he be executed for losing so many of his men and being captured alive. He was allowed to ransom his life and was reduced to the status of commoner.

Following this, Li Guang lived in retirement for several years, spending his time hunting. His home was in Lantian, among the Southern Mountains, adjoining the estate of Guan Qiang, the grandson of Guan Ying, the former marquis of Yingyin.

One evening Li Guang, having spent the afternoon drinking with some people out in the fields, was on his way back home, accompanied by a rider attendant, when he passed the watch station at Baling. The watchman, who was drunk at the time, yelled at Li Guang to halt.

"This is the former General Li," said Li Guang's man.

"Even present generals are not allowed to go wandering around at night, much less former ones!" the watchman retorted, and made Li Guang halt and spend the night in the watch station.

Shortly after this, the Xiongnu invaded Liaoxi, murdered its governor, and defeated General Han Anguo. Han Anguo was transferred to Youbeiping, where he died, and the emperor forthwith summoned Li Guang to be the new governor of Youbeiping. When he accepted the post, Li Guang asked that the watchman of Baling be ordered to accompany him, and as soon as the man reported for duty Li Guang had him executed.[3]

After Li Guang took over in Youbeiping, the Xiongnu, who were familiar with his reputation and called him "The Flying General", stayed away from the region for several years and did not dare to invade Youbeiping.

Li Guang was out hunting one time when he spied a rock in the grass which he mistook for a tiger. He shot an arrow at the rock and hit it with such force

---

[3] The parallel text in *Han shu* 54 records that Li Guang wrote a letter to the emperor apologizing for this act of personal vengeance, but the emperor replied that he expected his generals to be merciless so that they would inspire awe in their men and terrify the enemy.

that the tip of the arrow embedded itself in the rock. Later, when he discovered that it was a rock, he tried shooting at it again, but he was unable to pierce it a second time.

Whatever province Li Guang had been in in the past, whenever he heard that there was a tiger in the vicinity he always went out to shoot it in person. When he got to Youbeiping he likewise went out one time to hunt a tiger. The beast sprang at him and wounded him, but he finally managed to shoot it dead.

Li Guang was completely free of avarice. Whenever he received a reward of some kind, he at once divided it among those in his command, and he was content to eat and drink the same things as his men. For over forty years he received a salary of 2,000 piculs, but when he died he left no fortune behind. He never discussed matters of family wealth. He was a tall man with long, ape-like arms. His skill at archery seems to have been an inborn talent, for none of his descendants or others who studied under him were ever able to equal his prowess. He was a very clumsy speaker and never had much to say. When he was with others he would draw diagrams on the ground to explain his military tactics or set up targets of various widths and shoot at them with his friends, the loser being forced to drink. In fact, archery remained to the end of his life his chief source of amusement.

When he was leading his troops through a barren region and they came upon some water, he would not got near it until all his men had finished drinking. Similarly he would not eat until every one of his men had been fed. He was very lenient with his men and did nothing to vex them, so that they all loved him and were happy to serve under him. Even when the enemy was attacking, it was his custom never to discharge his arrows unless his opponent was within twenty or thirty paces and he believed he could score a hit. When he did discharge an arrow, however, the bowstring had no sooner sounded than his victim would fall to the ground. Because of this peculiar habit he often found himself in considerable difficulty when he was leading his troops against an enemy, and this is also the reason, it is said, that he was occasionally wounded when he went out hunting wild beasts.

Sometime after Li Guang was made governor of Youbeiping, Shi Jian died, and Li Guang was summoned to take his place as chief of palace attendants.

In the sixth year of *yuanshuo* (123 BC) Li Guang was again made a general and sent with the general in chief Wei Qing to proceed north from Dingxiang and attack the Xiongnu. Most of the other generals who took part in the expedition killed or captured a sufficient number of the enemy to be rewarded for their achievements by being made marquises, but Li Guang's army won no distinction.

Three years later Li Guang, as chief of palace attendants, was sent to lead a force of 4,000 cavalry north from Youbeiping. Zhang Qian, the Bowang marquis, leading 10,000 cavalry, rode out with Li Guang but took a somewhat different route. When Li Guang had advanced several hundred *li* into enemy territory, the Xiongnu leader known as the Wise King of the Left appeared with 40,000 cavalry and surrounded Li Guang's army. His men were all terrified, but Li Guang ordered his son Li Gan to gallop out to meet the enemy. Li Gan, accompanied by only twenty or thirty riders, dashed straight through the Xiongnu horsemen, scattering them to left and right, and then returned to his father's side, saying, "These barbarians are easy enough to deal with!" After this Li Guang's men were somewhat reassured.

Li Guang ordered his men to draw up in a circle with their ranks facing outward. The enemy charged furiously down on them and the arrows fell like rain. Over half the Han soldiers were killed, and their arrows were almost gone. Li Guang then ordered the men to load their bows and hold them in readiness, but not to discharge them, while he himself, with his huge yellow crossbow, shot at the sub-commander of the enemy force and killed several of the barbarians. After this the enemy began to fall back a little.

By this time night had begun to fall. Every one of Li Guang's officers and men had turned white with fear, but Li Guang, as calm and confident as though nothing had happened, worked to get his ranks into better formation. After this the men knew that they could never match his bravery.

The following day Li Guang once more fought off the enemy, and in the meantime Zhang Qian at last arrived with his army. The Xiongnu forces withdrew and the Han armies likewise retreated, being in no condition to pursue them. By this time Li Guang's army had been practically wiped out. When the two leaders returned to the capital, they were called to account before the law. Zhang Qian was condemned to death for failing to keep his rendezvous with Li Guang at the appointed time, but on payment of a fine he was allowed to become a commoner. In the case of Li Guang it was decided that his achievements and his failures cancelled each other out and he was given no reward.

Li Guang's cousin Li Cai had begun his career along with Li Guang as an attendant at the court of Emperor Wen. During the reign of Emperor Jing, Li Cai managed to accumulate sufficient merit to advance to the position of a 2,000 picul official, and under the present emperor he became prime minister of Dai.

In the fifth year of *yuanshuo* (124 BC) he was appointed a general of light carriage and accompanied the general in chief Wei Qing in an attack on the Xiongnu Wise King of the Right. His achievements in this campaign placed him in the middle group of those who were to receive rewards and he was accordingly enfeoffed as marquis of Lean. In the second year of *yuanshou* (121 BC) he replaced Gongsun Hong as chancellor of the central court. In ability one would be obliged to rank Li Cai very close to the bottom, and his reputation came nowhere near to equalling that of Li Guang. And yet, although Li Guang never managed to obtain a fief and never rose higher than one of the nine lower offices of the government, that of colonel of the guard, his cousin Li Cai was enfeoffed as a marquis and eventually reached the position of chancellor, one of the three highest posts. Even some of Li Guang's own officers and men succeeded in becoming marquises.

Li Guang was once chatting with Wang Shuo, a diviner who told men's fortunes by the configurations of the sky, and remarked on this fact. "Ever since the Han started attacking the Xiongnu, I have never failed to be in the fight. I've had men in my command who were company commanders or even lower and who didn't even have the ability of average men, and yet twenty or thirty of them have won marquisates on the strength of their achievements in attacking the barbarian armies. I have never been behind anyone else in doing my duty. Why is it I have never won an ounce of distinction so that I could be enfeoffed like the others? Is it that I just don't have the kind of face to become a marquis? Or is it all a matter of fate?"

"Think carefully, general," replied Wang Shuo. "Isn't there something in the past that you regret having done?"

"Once, when I was governor of Longxi, the Qiang tribes in the west started a revolt. I tried to talk them into surrendering, and in fact persuaded over 800 of them to give themselves up. But then I went back on my word and killed them all the very same day. I have never ceased to regret what I did. But that's the only thing I can think of."

"Nothing brings greater misfortune than killing those who have already surrendered to you," said Wang Shuo. "This is the reason, general, that you have never become a marquis!"

Two years later the general in chief Wei Qing and the general of swift cavalry Huo Qubing set off with a large force to attack the Xiongnu. Li Guang several times asked to be allowed to join them, but the emperor considered that he was too old and would not permit him to go. After some time, however, the emperor changed his mind and gave his consent, appointing him as general of the vanguard. The time was the fourth year of *yuanshou* (119 BC).

Li Guang accordingly joined the general in chief Wei Qing and set off to attack the Xiongnu. After the group had crossed the border, Wei Qing captured one of the enemy and learned the whereabouts of the *Shanyu*. He therefore decided to take his own best troops and make a dash for the spot, ordering Li Guang to join forces with the general of the right Zhao Yiji and ride around by the eastern road. The eastern road was rather long and roundabout and, since there was little water or grass in the region, it presented a difficult route for a large army to pass over. Li Guang therefore asked Wei Qing to change the order. "I have been appointed as general of the vanguard," he said, "and yet now you have shifted my position and ordered me to go around by the east. I have been fighting the Xiongnu ever since I was old enough to wear my hair bound up, and now I would like to have just one chance to get at the *Shanyu*. I beg you to let me stay in the vanguard and advance and fight to the death with him!"

Wei Qing had been warned in private by the emperor that Li Guang was an old man and had already had a lot of bad luck in the past. "Don't let him try to get at the *Shanyu*, or he will probably make a mess of things!" the emperor had said. Also, at this time Gongsun Ao, who had recently been deprived of his marquisate, was serving as a general under Wei Qing, and Wei Qing wanted to take him along with him in his attack on the *Shanyu* so that Gongsun Ao would have a chance to win some distinction. For these reasons he removed Li Guang from his post of general of the vanguard.

Li Guang was aware of all this and tried his best to get out of obeying the order, but Wei Qing refused to listen to his arguments. Instead he sent one of his clerks with a sealed letter to Li Guang's tent and orders to "proceed to your division at once in accordance with the instructions herein!" Li Guang did not even bother to take leave of Wei Qing but got up and went straight to his division, burning with rage and indignation and, leading his troops to join those of the general of the right Zhao Yiji, set out by the eastern road. Lacking proper guides, however, they lost their way and failed to meet up with Wei Qing at the appointed time. Wei Qing in the meantime engaged the *Shanyu* in battle, but the latter fled and Wei Qing, being unable to capture him, was forced to turn back south again. After crossing the desert, he joined up with the forces of Li Guang and Zhao Yiji.

When Li Guang had finished making his report to Wei Qing and returned to his own camp, Wei Qing sent over his clerk with the customary gifts of dried rice and thick wine for Li Guang. While the clerk was there, he began to inquire how it happened that Li Guang and Zhao Yiji had lost their way, since Wei Qing had to make a detailed report to the emperor on what had happened to the armies. Li Guang, however, refused to answer his questions.

Wei Qing sent his clerk again to reprimand Li Guang in the strongest terms and order him to report to general headquarters at once and answer a list of charges that had been drawn up against him. Li Guang replied, "None of my commanders was at fault. I was the one who caused us to lose our way. I will send in a report myself."

Then he went in person to headquarters and, when he got there, said to his officers, "Since I was old enough to wear my hair bound up, I have fought over seventy engagements, large and small, with the Xiongnu. This time I was fortunate enough to join the general in chief in a campaign against the soldiers of the *Shanyu* himself, but he shifted me to another division and sent me riding around by the long way. On top of that, I lost my way. Heaven must have planned it this way! Now I am over sixty — much too old to stand up to a bunch of petty clerks and their list of charges!" Then he drew his sword and cut his throat.

All the officers and men in his army wept at the news of his death, and when word reached the common people, those who had known him and those who had not, old men and young boys alike, were all moved to tears by his fate. Zhao Yiji was handed over to the law officials and sentenced to death, but on payment of a fine he was allowed to become a commoner.

Li Guang had three sons, Danghu, Jiao, and Gan, all of whom were palace attendants. One day when the present emperor was amusing himself with his young favourite, Han Yan, the boy behaved so impertinently that Li Danghu struck him and drove him from the room. The emperor was much impressed with Danghu's courage. Li Danghu died young. Li Jiao was made governor of Dai Province. He and Danghu both died before their father. Danghu had a son named Li Ling who was born shortly after Danghu died. Li Gan was serving in the army under the general of light cavalry Huo Qubing when Li Guang committed suicide.

The year after Li Guang's death his cousin Li Cai, who was serving as chancellor at the time, was accused of appropriating land that belonged to the funerary park of Emperor Jing. He was to be handed over to the law officials for trial, but he too committed suicide rather than face being sent to prison, and his fief was abolished.

Li Gan served as a commander under Huo Qubing, taking part in an attack on the Xiongnu Wise King of the Left. He fought bravely in the attack, seizing the drums and pennants of the barbarian king and cutting off many heads. He was rewarded by being enfeoffed as a marquis in the area within the Pass, receiving the revenue from a city of 200 households. In addition he was appointed to replace his father, Li Guang, as chief of palace attendants.

Sometime afterwards, deeply resentful at the general in chief Wei Qing for having brought about his father's disgrace, he struck and wounded Wei Qing. Wei Qing, however, hushed up the incident and said nothing about it. Shortly afterwards, Li Gan accompanied the emperor on a trip to Yong. When the party reached the Palace of Sweet Springs, an imperial hunt was held. Huo Qubing, who was on very close terms with Wei Qing, took the opportunity to shoot and kill Li Gan. At this time Huo Qubing enjoyed great favour with the emperor, and the emperor therefore covered up for him, giving out the story that Li Gan had been gored and killed by a stag. A year or so later, Huo Qubing died.

Li Gan had a daughter who became a lady in waiting to the heir apparent and was much loved and favoured by him. Li Gan's son Li Yu also enjoyed favour with the heir apparent, but he was somewhat too fond of profit. So the fortunes of the Li family gradually waned.

(When Danghu's son Li Ling grew up, he was appointed as supervisor of the Jianzhang Palace, being in charge of the cavalry. He was skilful at archery and took good care of his soldiers. The emperor, considering that the Li family had been generals for generations, put Li Ling in charge of a force of 800 cavalry. Once he led an expedition that penetrated over 2,000 *li* into Xiongnu territory, passing Juyan and observing the lay of the land, but he returned without having caught sight of the enemy. On his return he was appointed a chief commandant of cavalry and put in command of 5,000 men from Danyang in the region of Chu, and for several years he taught archery and garrisoned the provinces of Jiuquan and Zhangye to protect them from the Xiongnu.

In the autumn of the second year of *tianhan* (99 BC) the Sutrishna General Li Guangli led a force of 30,000 cavalry in an attack on the Xiongnu Wise King of the Right at the Qilian or Heavenly Mountains. He ordered Li Ling to lead a force of 5,000 infantry and archers north from Juyan and advance about 1,000 *li* into enemy territory. In this way he hoped to split the Xiongnu forces so that they would not all race in his direction.

Li Ling had already reached the point he was ordered to proceed to and had begun the march back, when the *Shanyu* with a force of 80,000 men surrounded his army and began to attack. Li Ling and his army of 5,000 fought a running battle for eight days, retreating as they fought, until all their weapons and arrows were gone and half the men had been killed. In the course of the fighting they managed to kill or wound over 10,000 of the enemy.

When they reached a point only 100 *li* or so from Juyan, the Xiongnu cornered them in a narrow valley and cut off their avenue of escape. Li Ling's food supplies were exhausted and no rescue troops were in sight, while the enemy pressed their attack and called on Li Ling to surrender. "I could never face the emperor and report such a disaster," Li Ling told his men, and finally surrendered to the Xiongnu. Practically all his soldiers perished in the fight; only some 400 managed to escape and straggle back to Han territory. The *Shanyu* had already heard of the fame of Li Ling's family and observed his bravery in battle, and as a result he gave him his own daughter as a wife and treated him with honour. When the emperor received news of this, he executed Li Ling's mother and his wife and children. From this time on the name of the Li family was disgraced and all the retainers of the family in Longxi were ashamed to be associated with it.)[4]

The Grand Historian remarks: One of the old books says, "If he himself is upright, those under him will act without being ordered to; if he himself is not upright, they will not obey even when ordered."[5] It refers, no doubt, to men like General Li.

I myself have seen General Li — a man so plain and unassuming that you would take him for a peasant, and almost incapable of speaking a word. And yet the day he died all the people of the empire, whether they had known him or not, were moved to the profoundest grief, so deeply did men trust his sincerity of purpose. There is a proverb which says, "Though the peach tree does not speak, the world wears a path beneath it." It is a small saying, but one which is capable of conveying a great meaning.

---

[4] This last section in parentheses is most likely not by Sima Qian, but a later addition. It differs from the account of Li Ling's life in *Han shu* 54 and deals with events that are later than those described elsewhere in the *Shi ji*. It may be recalled that Sima Qian was condemned to castration for speaking out in defense of Li Ling to the emperor when the news of Li Ling's surrender reached the court. Sima Qian's own account of Li Ling's battle and surrender is found in his letter to Ren Shaoqing, translated in *Ssu-ma Ch'ien: Grand Historian of China*, pp. 57-67.

[5] *Analects* XIII, 6.

SHI JI 110: THE ACCOUNT OF THE XIONGNU

From the time of the Three Dynasties on, the Xiongnu have been a source of constant worry and harm to China. The Han has attempted to determine the Xiongnu's periods of strength and weakness so that it may adopt defensive measures or launch punitive expeditions as the circumstances allow. Thus I made "The Account of the Xiongnu".

The ancestor of the Xiongnu was a descendant of the rulers of the Xia dynasty by the name of Chunwei. As early as the time of Emperors Yao and Shun and before, we hear of these people, known as Mountain Barbarians, Xianyun, or Hunzhu, living in the region of the northern barbarians and wandering from place to place pasturing their animals. The animals they raise consist mainly of horses, cows, and sheep, but include such rare beasts as camels, asses, mules, and the wild horses known as *taotu* and *tuoji*. They move about in search of water and pasture and have no walled cities or fixed dwellings, nor do they engage in any kind of agriculture. Their lands, however, are divided into regions under the control of various leaders. They have no writing, and even promises and agreements are only verbal. The little boys start out by learning to ride sheep and shoot birds and rats with a bow and arrow, and when they get a little older they shoot foxes and hares, which are used for food. Thus all the young men are able to use a bow and act as armed cavalry in time of war. It is their custom to herd their flocks in times of peace and make their living by hunting, but in periods of crisis they take up arms and go off on plundering and marauding expeditions. This seems to be their inborn nature. For long-range weapons they use bows and arrows, and swords and spears at close range. If the battle is going well for them they will advance, but if not, they will retreat, for they do not consider it a disgrace to run away. Their only concern is self-advantage, and they know nothing of propriety or righteousness.

From the chiefs of the tribe on down, everyone eats the meat of the domestic animals and wears clothes of hide or wraps made of felt or fur. The young men eat the richest and best food, while the old get what is left over, since the tribe honours those who are young and strong and despises the weak and aged. On the death of his father, a son will marry his stepmother, and when brothers die, the remaining brothers will take the widows for their own wives. They have no polite names[1] but only personal names, and they observe no taboos in the use of personal names.

When the power of the Xia dynasty declined, Gong Liu, the ancestor of the Zhou dynasty, having lost his position as minister of grain, went to live among the Western Rong barbarians, adopting their ways and founding a city at Bin. Some 300 years later the Rong and Di tribes attacked Gong Liu's descendant, the Great Lord Danfu. Danfu fled to the foot of Mt. Qi and the whole population of Bin followed after him, founding a new city there. This was the beginning of the Zhou state.

A hundred and some years later Chang, the Zhou Earl of the West, attacked the Quanyishi tribe, and ten or twelve years later, his son, King Wu, overthrew Emperor Zhou, the last ruler of the Shang dynasty, and founded a new capital at Luo. He also occupied the regions of Feng and Hao, drove the barbarians north beyond the Jing and Luo rivers, and obliged them to bring tribute to his court at specified times. Their lands were known as "the submissive wastes".

Some 200 years later, when the power of the Zhou dynasty had declined, King Mu attacked the Dog Rong and brought back with him four white wolves and four white deer which he had seized. From this time on, the peoples of the "submissive wastes" no longer journeyed to court. (At this time the Zhou adopted the penal code of Marquis Fu.)[2]

Some 200 years after the time of King Mu, King You of the Zhou, egged on by his beloved concubine Baosi, quarrelled with Marquis Shen. In anger, Marquis Shen joined forces with the Dog Rong and attacked and killed King You at the foot of Mt. Li. Eventually the barbarians seized the region of Jiaohuo from the Zhou, occupied the area between the Jing and Wei rivers, and invaded and plundered the central region of China. Duke Xiang of Qin came to the rescue of the Zhou court, and King You's successor King Ping abandoned the regions of Feng and Hao and moved his capital east to the city of Luo. (At this time Duke Xiang of Qin attacked the barbarians and advanced as far as Mt. Qi; as a

---

[1] The text says "no family names or polite names", but the word "family names" is probably an error here. Polite names are names which are used in place of personal names to avoid the appearance of over-familiarity.

[2] The penal code now comprises a chapter of the *Book of Documents*, where it is known as the code of Marquis Lü.

result he was for the first time ranked among the feudal lords of the Zhou dynasty.)

Sixty-five years later (704 BC) the Mountain Barbarians crossed through the state of Yan and attacked Qi. Duke Li of Qi fought with them in the suburbs of his capital. Forty-four years later the Mountain Barbarians attacked Yan, but Yan reported its distress to Duke Huan of Qi, who rode north and attacked the barbarians, driving them off.

Some twenty years later the barbarians rode as far as the capital city of Luo and attacked King Xiang of the Zhou; King Xiang fled to the city of Fan in Zheng. Previously King Xiang had wanted to attack the state of Zheng and had therefore married a daughter of the barbarians and made her his queen; then, with the aid of the barbarian forces, he had made his attack on Zheng. Having accomplished his purpose, however, he cast aside his barbarian queen, much to her resentment. King Xiang's stepmother, Queen Hui, had a son named Zidai whom she wished to place on the throne, and therefore Queen Hui, her son, and the barbarian queen agreed to cooperate with the barbarian attackers from within the capital by opening the city to them. Thus the barbarians were able to enter, defeat and drive out King Xiang, and set up Zidai as Son of Heaven in his place.

After this the barbarians occupied the area of Luhun, roaming as far east as the state of Wey, ravaging and plundering the lands of central China with fearful cruelty. The empire was deeply troubled, and therefore the poets in the *Book of Odes* wrote:

> We smote the barbarians of the north.
> We struck the Xianyun
> And drove them to the great plain.
> We sent forth our chariots in majestic array
> And walled the northern regions.[3]

After King Xiang had been driven from his throne and had lived abroad for four years, he sent an envoy to the state of Jin to explain his plight. Duke Wen of Jin, having just come to power, wanted to make a name for himself as dictator and protector of the royal house, and therefore he raised an army and attacked and drove out the barbarians, executing Zidai and restoring King Xiang to his throne in Luo.

---

[3] Sima Qian quotes from three different poems: "Bigong" of the "Temple Odes of Lu", and "Liuyue" and "Chuju" of the "Lesser Odes".

At this time Qin and Jin were the most powerful states in China. Duke Wen of Jin expelled the Di barbarians and drove them into the region west of the Yellow River between the Yun and Luo rivers; there they were known as the Red Di and the White Di. Shortly afterwards, Duke Mu of Qin, having obtained the services of You Yu,[4] succeeded in getting the eight barbarian tribes of the west to submit to his authority.

Thus at this time there lived in the region west of Long the Mianzhu, the Hunrong, and the Diyuan tribes. North of Mts. Qi and Liang and the Jing and Qi rivers lived the Yiqu, Dali, Wuzhi, and Quyan tribes. North of Jin were the Forest Barbarians and the Loufan, while north of Yan lived the Eastern Barbarians and Mountain Barbarians. All of them were scattered about in their own little valleys, each with their own chieftains. From time to time they would have gatherings of a hundred or more men, but no one tribe was capable of unifying the others under a single rule.

Some 100 years later Duke Dao of Jin sent Wei Jiang to make peace with the barbarians, so that they came to pay their respects to the court of Jin. A hundred or so years after this, Viscount Xiang of the Zhao family of Jin crossed Mt. Juzhu, defeated the barbarians, and annexed the region of Dai, bringing his state into contact with the Huhe tribes. Shortly afterwards he joined with the viscounts of the Hann and Wei families in wiping out their rival, Zhi Bo, and dividing up the state of Jin among the three of them. Thus the Zhao family held possession of Dai and the lands north of Mt. Juzhu, while the Wei family held the provinces of Hexi (Ordos) and Shang, bordering the lands of the barbarians.

After this the Yiqu tribes began to build walls and fortifications to protect themselves, but the state of Qin gradually ate into their territory and, under King Hui, finally seized twenty-five of their forts. King Hui also attacked the state of Wei, forcing it to cede to him the provinces of Hexi and Shang.

During the reign of King Zhao of Qin the ruler of the Yiqu barbarians had illicit relations with King Zhao's mother, the Queen Dowager Xuan, by whom he had two sons. Later the queen dowager deceived and murdered him at the Palace of Sweet Springs and eventually raised an army and sent it to attack and

---

[4] You Yu's ancestors came from the state of Jin; he himself had been born among the barbarians but could speak the language of Jin. The barbarian king sent him to the court of Duke Mu of Qin, who questioned him closely on the customs, lands, and military strength of the barbarians. Duke Mu later succeeded in arousing enmity between the barbarian ruler and You Yu, and the latter finally fled to Qin and became the duke's adviser on barbarian affairs. The fuller account is found in *Shi ji* 5, "The Basic Annals of Qin", in vol. III.

ravage the lands of the Yiqu. Thus Qin came into possession of Longxi, Beidi, and Shang Provinces, where it built long walls to act as a defence against the barbarians.

At the same time King Wuling of Zhao changed the customs of his people, ordering them to adopt barbarian dress and to practise riding and shooting, and then led them north in a successful attack on the Forest Barbarians and the Loufan. He constructed a defensive wall stretching from Dai along the foot of the Yin Mountains to Gaoque, establishing the three provinces of Yunzhong, Yanmen, and Dai.

A little later a worthy general named Qin Kai appeared in the state of Yan. He had earlier been sent as a hostage to the barbarians and had won their deepest confidence; on returning to his state, he led an attack on the Eastern Barbarians, defeating and driving them over 1,000 *li* from the border of the state. (The Qin Wuyang who took part with Jing Ke in the attempted assassination of the king of Qin was this man's grandson.) Yan also constructed a long wall from Zaoyang to Xiangping and set up the provinces of Shanggu, Yuyang, Youbeiping, Liaoxi, and Liaodong to guard against the attacks of the barbarians.[5]

By this time China, the land of caps and girdles, was divided among seven states, three of which bordered the territory of the Xiongnu. Later, while the Zhao general Li Mu was living, the Xiongnu did not dare to cross the border of Zhao.

Finally Qin overthrew the other six states, and the First Emperor of the Qin dispatched Meng Tian to lead a force of 100,000 men north to attack the barbarians. He seized control of all the lands south of the Yellow River and established border defences along the river, constructing forty-four walled district cities overlooking the river and manning them with convict labourers transported to the border for garrison duty. He also built the Direct Road from Jiuyuan to Yunyang. Thus he utilized the natural mountain barriers to establish the border defences, scooping out the valleys and constructing ramparts and building installations at other points where they were needed. The whole line of defences stretched over 10,000 *li* from Lintao to Liaodong and even extended across the Yellow River and through Yangshan and Beijia.

---

[5] From this it may be seen that the First Emperor of the Qin, in building the Great Wall, did not have to begin from scratch, as is often implied, but simply repaired and linked up the older walls of these northern states.

At this time the Eastern Barbarians were very powerful and the Yuezhi were likewise flourishing. The *Shanyu* or chieftain of the Xiongnu was named Touman. Touman, unable to hold out against the Qin forces, had withdrawn to the far north, where he lived with his subjects for over ten years. After Meng Tian died and the feudal lords revolted against the Qin, plunging China into a period of strife and turmoil, the convicts which the Qin had sent to the northern border to garrison the area all returned to their homes. The Xiongnu, the pressure against them relaxed, once again began to infiltrate south of the bend of the Yellow River until they had established themselves along the old border of China.

Touman's oldest son, the heir apparent to his position, was named Maodun, but the *Shanyu* also had a younger son by another consort whom he had taken later and was very fond of. He decided that he wanted to get ride of Maodun and set up his younger son as heir instead, and he therefore sent Maodun as hostage to the Yuezhi nation. Then, after Maodun had arrived among the Yuezhi, Touman made a sudden attack on them. The Yuezhi were about to kill Maodun in retaliation, but he managed to steal one of their best horses and escape, eventually making his way back home. His father, struck by his bravery, put him in command of a force of 10,000 cavalry.

Maodun had some arrows made that whistled in flight and used them to drill his troops in shooting from horseback. "Shoot wherever you see my whistling arrow strike!" he ordered, "and anyone who fails to shoot will be cut down!" Then he went out hunting for birds and animals, and if any of his men failed to shoot at what he himself had shot at, he cut them down on the spot. After this, he shot a whistling arrow at one of his best horses. Some of his men hung back and did not dare shoot at the horse, whereupon Maodun at once executed them. A little later he took an arrow and shot at his favourite wife. Again some of his men shrank back in terror and failed to discharge their arrows, and again he executed them on the spot. Finally he went out hunting with his men and shot a whistling arrow at one of his father's finest horse. All his followers promptly discharged their arrows in the same direction, and Maodun knew that at last they could be trusted. Accompanying his father, the *Shanyu* Touman, on a hunting expedition, he shot a whistling arrow at his father and every one of his followers aimed their arrows in the same direction and shot the *Shanyu* dead. Then Maodun executed his stepmother, his younger brother, and all the high officials of the nation who refused to take orders from him, and set himself up as the new *Shanyu*.

At this time the Eastern Barbarians were very powerful and, hearing that Maodun had killed his father and made himself leader, they sent an envoy to ask if they could have Touman's famous horse that could run 1,000 *li* in one day. Maodun consulted his ministers, but they all replied, "The thousand-*li* horse is one of the treasures of the Xiongnu people. You should not give it away!"

"When a neighbouring country asks for it, why should I begrudge them one horse?" he said, and sent them the thousand-*li* horse.

After a while the Eastern Barbarians, supposing that Maodun was afraid of them, sent an envoy to ask for one of Maodun's consorts. Again Maodun questioned his ministers, and they replied in a rage, "The Eastern Barbarians are unreasoning beasts to come and request one of the *Shanyu*'s consorts. We beg to attack them!"

But Maodun replied, "If it is for a neighbouring country, why should I begrudge them one woman?" and he sent his favourite consort to the Eastern Barbarians.

With this the ruler of the Eastern Barbarians grew more and more bold and arrogant, invading the lands to the west. Between his territory and that of the Xiongnu was an area of over 1,000 *li* of uninhabited land; the two peoples made their homes on either side of this wasteland.[6] The ruler of the Eastern Barbarians sent an envoy to Maodun saying, "The Xiongnu have no way of using this stretch of wasteland which lies between my border and yours. I would like to take possession of it!"

When Maodun consulted his ministers, some of them said, "Since the land is of no use you might as well give it to him," while others said, "No, you must not give it away!"

Maodun flew into a rage. "Land is the basis of the nation!" he said. "Why should I give it away?" And he executed all the ministers who had advised him to do so.

Then he mounted his horse and set off to attack the Eastern Barbarians, circulating an order throughout his domain that anyone who was slow to follow would be executed. The Eastern Barbarians had up until this time despised Maodun and made no preparations for their defence; when Maodun and his soldiers arrived, they inflicted a crushing defeat, killing the ruler of the Eastern Barbarians, taking prisoner his subjects, and seizing their domestic animals. Then he returned and rode west, attacking and routing the Yuezhi, and annexed

---

[6] The Gobi Desert.

the lands of the ruler of Loufan and the ruler of Boyang south of the Yellow River. Thus he recovered possession of all the lands which the Qin general Meng Tian had taken away from the Xiongnu; the border between his territory and that of the Han empire now followed the old line of defences south of the Yellow River, and from there he marched into the Chaona and Fushi districts and then invaded Yan and Dai.

At this time the Han forces were stalemated in battle with the armies of Xiang Yu, and China was exhausted by warfare. Thus Maodun was able to strengthen his position, massing a force of over 300,000 skilled crossbowmen.

Over 1,000 years had elapsed from the time of Chunwei, the ancestor of the Xiongnu, to that of Maodun, a vast period during which the tribes split up and scattered into various groups, sometimes expanding, sometimes dwindling in size. Thus it is impossible to give any ordered account of the lineage of the Xiongnu rulers. When Maodun came to power, however, the Xiongnu reached their peak of strength and size, subjugating all of the other barbarian tribes of the north and turning south to confront China as a rival nation. As a result of this, it is possible to give an account here of the later Xiongnu rulers and of the offices and titles of the nation.

Under the *Shanyu* are the Wise Kings of the Left and Right, the left and right Luli kings, left and right generals, left and right commandants, left and right household administrators, and left and right Gudu marquises. The Xiongnu word for "wise" is "*tuqi*", so that the heir of the *Shanyu* is customarily called the "*Tuqi* King of the Left". Among the other leaders, from the wise kings on down to the household administrators, the more important ones command 10,000 horsemen and the lesser ones several thousand, numbering twenty-four leaders in all, though all are known by the title of "Ten Thousand Horsemen". The high ministerial offices are hereditary, being filled from generation to generation by the members of the Huyan and Lan families, and in more recent times by the Xubu family. These three families constitute the aristocracy of the nation. The kings and other leaders of the left live in the eastern sector, the region from Shanggu east to the lands of the Huimo and Chaoxian peoples. The kings and leaders of the right live in the west, the area from Shang Province west to the territories of the Yuezhi and Qiang tribes. The *Shanyu* has his court in the region north of Dai and Yunzhong. Each group has its own area, within which it moves about from place to place looking for water and pasture. The Left and Right Wise Kings and Luli kings are the most powerful, while the Gudu marquises assist the *Shanyu* in the administration of the nation. Each of the twenty-four leaders in turn appoints his own "chiefs of a thousand", "chiefs of a hundred", and "chiefs of ten", as well as his subordinate kings, prime ministers, chief commandants, household administrators, *juqu*[7] officials, and so forth.

In the first month of the year the various leaders come together in a small meeting at the *Shanyu*'s court to perform sacrifices, and in the fifth month a great meeting is held at Longcheng at which sacrifices are conducted to the Xiongnu ancestors, Heaven and Earth, and the gods and spirits. In the autumn, when the horses are fat, another great meeting is held at the Dai Forest when a reckoning is made of the number of persons and animals.

According to Xiongnu law, anyone who in ordinary times draws his sword a foot from the scabbard is condemned to death. Anyone convicted of theft has his property confiscated. Minor offences are punished by flogging and major ones by death. No one is kept in jail awaiting sentence longer than ten days, and the number of imprisoned men for the whole nation does not exceed a handful.[8]

At dawn the *Shanyu* leaves his camp and makes obeisance to the sun as it rises, and in the evening he makes a similar obeisance to the moon. In seating arrangements the left side or the seat facing north is considered the place of honour. The days *wu* and *ji* of the ten-day week are regarded as most auspicious.

In burials the Xiongnu use an inner and an outer coffin, with accessories of gold, silver, clothing, and fur, but they do not construct grave mounds or plant trees on the grave, nor do they use mourning garments. When a ruler dies, the ministers and concubines who were favoured by him and who are obliged to follow him in death often number in the hundreds or even thousands.

Whenever the Xiongnu begin some undertaking, they observe the stars and the moon. They attack when the moon is full and withdraw their troops when it wanes. After a battle those who have cut off the heads of the enemy or taken prisoners are presented with a cup of wine and allowed to keep the spoils they have captured. Any prisoners that are taken are made slaves. Therefore, when they fight, each man strives for his own gain. They are very skilful at using decoy troops to lure their opponents to destruction. When they catch sight of the enemy, they swoop down like a flock of birds, eager for booty, but when they find themselves hard pressed and beaten, they scatter and vanish like the mist.

---

[7] It is impossible to tell from the name alone what this title means. In later times, when these peoples invaded and conquered northern China, Juqu became a Chinese surname.

[8] Sima Qian is inviting a comparison with the situation in China in his own day, when the jails were full to overflowing with men awaiting sentence.

Anyone who succeeds in recovering the body of a comrade who has fallen in battle receives all of the dead man's property.

Shortly after the period described above, Maodun launched a series of campaigns to the north, conquering the tribes of Hunyu, Qushe, Dingling, Gekun, and Xinli. Thus the nobles and high ministers of the Xiongnu were all won over by Maodun, considering him a truly worthy leader.

At this time Gaozu, the founder of the Han, had just succeeded in winning control of the empire and had transferred Xin, the former king of Hann, to the rulership of Dai, with his capital at Mayi. The Xiongnu surrounded Mayi and attacked the city in great force, whereupon Hann Xin surrendered to them. With Hann Xin on their side, they then proceeded to lead their troops south across Mt. Juzhu and attack Taiyuan, marching as far as the city of Jinyang. Emperor Gaozu led an army in person to attack them, but it was winter and he encountered such cold and heavy snow that two or three out of every ten of his men lost their fingers from frostbite. Maodun feigned a retreat to lure the Han soldiers on to an attack. When they came after him in pursuit, he concealed all of his best troops and left only his weakest and puniest men to be observed by the Han scouts. With this the entire Han force, supplemented by 320,000 infantry, rushed north to pursue him; Gaozu led the way, advancing as far as the city of Pingcheng.

Before the infantry had had a chance to arrive, however, Maodun swooped down with 400,000 of his best cavalry, surrounded Gaozu on White Peak, and held him there for seven days. The Han forces within the encirclement had no way of receiving aid or provisions from their comrades outside, since the Xiongnu cavalry surrounded them on all sides, with white horses on the west side, greenish horses on the east, black horses on the north, and red ones on the south.[9]

Gaozu sent an envoy in secret to Maodun's consort, presenting her with generous gifts, whereupon she spoke to Maodun, saying, "Why should the rulers of these two nations make such trouble for each other? Even if you gained possession of the Han lands, you could never occupy them, and the ruler of the Han may have his guardian deities as well as you. I beg you to consider the matter well!"

----

[9] These four colours are symbolic of the four directions in Chinese belief and, if the narrative is correct, in Xiongnu belief as well.

Maodun had previously arranged for the troops of Wang Huang and Zhao Li, two of Hann Xin's generals, to meet with him, but though the appointed time had come, they failed to appear and he began to suspect that they were plotting with the Han forces. He therefore decided to listen to his consort's advice and withdrew his forces from one corner of the encirclement. Gaozu ordered his men to load their crossbows with arrows and hold them in readiness pointed toward the outside. These preparations completed, they marched straight out of the encirclement and finally joined up with the rest of the army.

Maodun eventually withdrew his men and went away, and Gaozu likewise retreated and abandoned the campaign, dispatching Liu Jing to conclude a peace treaty with the Xiongnu instead.

After this Hann Xin became a general for the Xiongnu, and Zhao Li and Wang Huang repeatedly violated the peace treaty by invading and plundering Dai and Yunzhong. Shortly afterwards, Chen Xi revolted and joined with Hann Xin in a plot to attack Dai. Gaozu dispatched Fan Kuai to go and attack them; he recovered possession of the provinces and districts of Dai, Yanmen, and Yunzhong, but did not venture beyond the frontier.

At this time a number of Han generals had gone over to the side of the Xiongnu, and for this reason Maodun was constantly plundering the region of Dai and causing the Han great worry. Gaozu therefore dispatched Liu Jing to present a princess of the imperial family to the *Shanyu* to be his consort. The Han agreed to send a gift of specified quantities of silk floss and cloth, grain, and other food stuffs each year, and the two nations were to live in peace and brotherhood. After this Maodun raided the frontier less often than before. Later Lu Wan, the king of Yan, revolted and led his party of several thousand followers across the border to surrender to the Xiongnu; they roamed back and forth in the region from Shanggu to the east, causing considerable disturbance.

After Emperor Gaozu passed away, Emperor Hui and Empress Lü in turn ruled the country. At this time the Han had just come to power and the Xiongnu, unimpressed by its strength, were behaving with great arrogance. Maodun even sent an insulting letter to Empress Lü.[10] She wanted to launch a campaign against him, but her generals reminded her that "even Emperor Gaozu, with all his wisdom and bravery, encountered great difficulty at Pingcheng", and she was

---

[10] In his letter Maodun suggested that, since both he and Empress Lü were old and lonely, they might get together and console each other.

finally persuaded to give up the idea and resume friendly relations with the Xiongnu.

When Emperor Wen came to the throne he renewed the peace treaty with the Xiongnu. In the fifth month of the third year of his reign (177 BC), however, the Xiongnu Wise King of the Right invaded the region south of the Yellow River, plundering the loyal barbarians of Shang Province who had been appointed by the Han to guard the frontier, and murdering and carrying off a number of the inhabitants. Emperor Wen ordered the chancellor Guan Ying to lead a force of 85,000 carriages and cavalry to Gaonu, where they attacked the Wise King of the Right. The latter fled beyond the frontier. The emperor in person visited Taiyuan, at which time the king of Jibei revolted. When the emperor returned to the capital he disbanded the army which Guan Ying had used in the attack on the barbarians.

The following year the *Shanyu* sent a letter to the Han court which read:

The great *Shanyu* whom Heaven has set up respectfully inquires of the emperor's health. Formerly the emperor broached the question of a peace alliance, and I was most happy to comply with the intentions expressed in his letter. Certain of the Han border officials, however, imposed upon and insulted the Wise King of the Right, and as a result he heeded the counsel of Houyi, Luhou, Nanzhi, and others of his generals and, without asking my permission, engaged in a skirmish with the Han officials, thus violating the pact between the rulers of our two nations and rupturing the bonds of brotherhood that joined us. The emperor has twice sent letters complaining of this situation and I have in turn dispatched an envoy with my answer, but my envoy has not been allowed to return, nor has any envoy come from the Han. As a result, the Han has broken off peaceful relations and our two neighbouring countries are no longer bound in alliance.

Because of the violation of the pact committed by the petty officials, and the subsequent events, I have punished the Wise King of the Right by sending him west to search out the Yuezhi people and attack them. Through the aid of Heaven, the excellence of his fighting men, and the strength of his horses, he has succeeded in wiping out the Yuezhi, slaughtering or forcing to submission every member of the tribe. In addition he has conquered the Loulan, Wusun, and Hujie tribes, as well as the twenty-six states nearby, so that all of them have become a part of the Xiongnu nation. All the people who live by drawing the bow are now united into one family and the entire region of the north is at peace.

Thus I wish now to lay down my weapons, rest my soldiers, and turn my horses to pasture; to forget the recent affair and restore our old pact, that the peoples of the border may have peace such as they enjoyed in former times, that the young may grow to manhood, the old live out their lives in security, and generation after generation enjoy peace and comfort.

However, I do not as yet know the intentions of the emperor. Therefore I have dispatched my palace attendant Xihuqian to bear this letter. At the same time I beg to present one camel, two riding horses, and eight carriage horses. If the emperor does not wish the Xiongnu to approach his frontier, then he should order the officials and people along the border to withdraw a good distance back from the frontier. When my envoy has arrived and delivered this, I trust that he will be sent back to me.

The envoy bearing the letter arrived in the region of Xinwang during the sixth month. When it was delivered to the emperor, he began deliberations with his ministers as to whether it was better to attack or make peace. The high officials all stated, "Since the *Shanyu* has just conquered the Yuezhi and is riding on a wave of victory, he cannot be attacked. Moreover, even if we were to seize the Xiongnu lands, they are all swamps and saline wastes, not fit for habitation. It would be far better to make peace."

The emperor agreed with their opinion and in the sixth year of the former part of his reign (174 BC) he sent an envoy to the Xiongnu with a letter which read as follows:

The emperor respectfully inquires about the health of the great *Shanyu*. Your palace attendant Xihuqian has brought us a letter which states: "The Wise King of the Right, without asking my permission, heeded the counsel of Houyi, Luhou, Nanzhi, and others of his generals, violating the pact between the rulers of our two nations and rupturing the bonds of brotherhood that joined us, and as a result the Han has broken off peaceful relations with me, and our two neighbouring countries are no longer bound in alliance. Because of the violation of the pact committed by the petty officials, I have punished the Wise King of the Right by sending him west to attack the Yuezhi. Having completed the conquest of the region, I wish to lay down my weapons, rest my soldiers, and turn my horses to pasture; to forget the recent affair and restore our old pact so that the peoples of the border may have peace, the young may grow to manhood, the old live out their lives in security, and generation after generation enjoy peace and comfort."

We heartily approve these words. This indeed is the way the sage rulers of antiquity would have spoken.

The Han has made a pact of brotherhood with the Xiongnu, and for this reason we have sent generous gifts to you. Any violations of the pact or ruptures of the bonds of brotherhood have been the work of the Xiongnu. However, as there has been an amnesty since the affair of the Wise King of the Right occurred,[11] you need not punish him too severely. If your intentions are really those expressed in your letter, and if you will make them clearly known to your various officials so that they will henceforth act in good faith and commit no more violations of the pact, then we are prepared to honour the terms of your letter.

Your envoy tells us that you have led your troops in person to attack the other barbarian nations and have won merit, suffering great hardship on the field of battle. We therefore send you from our own wardrobe an embroidered robe lined with patterned damask, an embroidered and lined underrobe, and a brocaded coat, one each; one comb; one sash with gold ornaments; one gold-ornamented leather belt; ten rolls of embroidery; thirty rolls of brocade; and forty rolls each of heavy red silk and light green silk, which shall be delivered to you by our palace counsellor Yi and master of guests Jian.

Shortly after this, Maodun died and his son Jizhu was set up with the title of Old *Shanyu*. When Jizhu became *Shanyu*, Emperor Wen sent a princess of the imperial family to be his consort, dispatching a eunuch from Yan named Zhonghang Yue to accompany her as her tutor. Zhonghang Yue did not wish to

---

[11] It is not clear what amnesty this refers to. The *Han shu* "Annals of Emperor Wen" records a general amnesty in the seventh year (173 BC), but none for the years between the Xiongnu attack and the date of this letter. Perhaps the letter should be dated in the seventh year. The whole statement about the amnesty is of course no more than a cleverly phrased assertion of the Han emperor's sovereignty over the Xiongnu.

undertake the mission, but the Han officials forced him to do so. "My going will bring nothing but trouble to the Han!" he warned them.

After Zhonghang Yue reached his destination, he went over to the side of the *Shanyu*, who treated him with the greatest favour.

The Xiongnu had always had a liking for Han silks and food stuffs, but Zhonghang Yue told them, "All the multitudes of the Xiongnu nation would not amount to one province in the Han empire. The strength of the Xiongnu lies in the very fact that their food and clothing are different from those of the Chinese, and they are therefore not dependent upon the Han for anything. Now the *Shanyu* has this fondness for Chinese things and is trying to change the Xiongnu customs. Thus, although the Han sends no more than a fifth of its goods here, it will in the end succeed in winning over the whole Xiongnu nation. From now on, when you get any of the Han silks, put them on and try riding around on your horses through the brush and brambles! In no time your robes and leggings will be torn to shreds and everyone will be able to see that silks are no match for the utility and excellence of felt or leather garments. Likewise, when you get any of the Han foodstuffs, throw them away so that the people can see that they are not as practical or as tasty as milk and kumiss!"

He also taught the *Shanyu*'s aides how to make an itemized accounting of the number of persons and domestic animals in the country.

The Han letters addressed to the *Shanyu* were always written on wooden tablets one foot and one inch in length and began, "The emperor respectfully inquires about the health of the great *Shanyu* of the Xiongnu. We send you the following articles, etc., etc." Zhonghang Yue, however, instructed the *Shanyu* to use in replying to the Han a tablet measuring one foot two inches, decorated with broad stamps and great long seals, and worded in the following extravagant manner: "The great *Shanyu* of the Xiongnu, born of Heaven and Earth and ordained by the sun and moon, respectfully inquires about the health of the Han emperor. We send you the following articles, etc., etc."

When one of the Han envoys to the Xiongnu remarked scornfully that Xiongnu custom showed no respect for the aged, Zhonghang Yue began to berate him. "According to Han custom," he said, "when the young men are called into military service and sent off with the army to garrison the frontier, do not their old parents at home voluntarily give up their warm clothing and tasty food so that there will be enough to provide for the troops?"

"Yes, they do," admitted the Han envoy.

"The Xiongnu make it clear that warfare is their business. And since the old and the weak are not capable of fighting, the best food and drink are naturally allotted to the young men in the prime of life. So the young men are willing to fight for the defence of the nation, and both fathers and sons are able to live out their lives in security. How can you say that the Xiongnu despise the aged?"

"But among the Xiongnu," the envoy continued, "fathers and sons sleep together in the same tent. And when a father dies, the sons marry their own stepmothers, and when brothers die, their remaining brothers marry their widows! These people know nothing of the elegance of hats and girdles, nor of the rituals of the court!"

"According to Xiongnu custom," replied Zhonghang Yue, "the people eat the flesh of their domestic animals, drink their milk, and wear their hides, while the animals graze from place to place, searching for pasture and water. Therefore, in wartime the men practise riding and shooting, while in times of peace they enjoy themselves and have nothing to do. Their laws are simple and easy to carry out; the relation between ruler and subject is relaxed and intimate, so that the governing of the whole nation is no more complicated than the governing of one person. The reason that sons marry their stepmothers and brothers marry their widowed sisters-in-law is simply that they hate to see the clan die out. Therefore, although the Xiongnu encounter times of turmoil, the ruling families always manage to stand firm. In China, on the other hand, though a man would never dream of marrying his stepmother or his brother's widow, yet the members of the same family drift so far apart that they end up murdering each other! This is precisely why so many changes of dynasty have come about in China! Moreover, among the Chinese, as etiquette and the sense of duty decay, enmity arises between the rulers and the ruled, while the excessive building of houses and dwellings exhausts the strength and resources of the nation. Men try to get their food and clothing by farming and raising silkworms and to insure their safety by building walls and fortifications. Therefore, although danger threatens, the Chinese people are given no training in aggressive warfare, while in times of stability they must still wear themselves out trying to make a living. Pooh! You people in your mud huts — you talk too much! Enough of this blubbering and mouthing! Just because you wear hats, what does that make you?"

After this, whenever the Han envoys would try to launch into any sermons or orations, Zhonghang Yue would cut them off at once. "Not so much talk from the Han envoys! Just make sure that the silks and grainstuffs you bring to the Xiongnu are of the right measure and quality, that's all. What's the need for talking? If the goods you deliver are up to measure and of good quality, all right. But if there is any deficiency or the quality is no good, then when the autumn harvest comes we will take our horses and trample all over your crops!"

Day and night he instructed the *Shanyu* on how to manoeuver into a more advantageous position.

In the fourteenth year of Emperor Wen's reign (166 BC) the *Shanyu* led a force of 140,000 horsemen through the Chaona and Xiao passes, killing Sun Ang, the chief commandant of Beidi Province, and carrying off large numbers of people and animals. Eventually he rode as far as Pengyang, sent a surprise force to break into and burn the Huizhong Palace, and dispatched scouts as far as the Palace of Sweet Springs in Yong.[12]

Emperor Wen appointed the palace military commander Zhou She and the chief of palace attendants Zhang Wu as generals and put them in command of a force of 1,000 chariots and 100,000 horsemen to garrison the vicinity of Chang'an and guard the capital from the barbarian invaders. He also appointed Lu Qing, the marquis of Chang, as general of Shang Province; Wei Su, the marquis of Ning, as general of Beidi; Zhou Zao, the marquis of Longlu, as general of Longxi; Zhang Xiangru, the marquis of Dongyang, as general in chief; and Dong Chi, the marquis of Cheng, as general of the vanguard, and sent them with a large force of chariots and cavalry to attack the barbarians. The *Shanyu* remained within the borders of the empire for a little over a month and then withdrew. The Han forces pursued him beyond the frontier but returned without having been able to kill any of the enemy.

The Xiongnu grew more arrogant day by day, crossing the border every year, killing many of the inhabitants, and stealing their animals. Yunzhong and Liaodong suffered most severely, while in Dai Province alone over 10,000 persons were killed. The Han court, greatly distressed, sent an envoy with a letter to the Xiongnu, and the *Shanyu* in turn dispatched one of his household administrators to apologize and request a renewal of the peace alliance.

In the second year of the latter part of his reign (162 BC) Emperor Wen sent an envoy to the Xiongnu with a letter that read:

> The emperor respectfully inquires about the health of the great *Shanyu*. Your envoys, the household administrator and *juqu* Diao

---

[12]Bringing them within sight of the capital.

Qunan and the palace attendant Han Liao, have delivered to us two horses, which we have respectfully accepted.

According to the decree of the former emperor, the land north of the Great Wall, where men wield the bow and arrow, was to receive its commands from the *Shanyu*, while that within the wall, whose inhabitants dwell in houses and wear hats and girdles, was to be ruled by us; thus might the countless inhabitants of these lands gain their food and clothing by agriculture, weaving, or hunting; father and son live side by side; ruler and minister enjoy mutual security; and all forsake violence and rebellion. Now we have heard that certain evil and deluded men, succumbing greedily to the lure of gain, have turned their backs upon righteousness and violated the peace alliance, forgetting the fate of the countless inhabitants and disrupting the concord which existed between the rulers of our two states.

This, however, is an affair of the past. In your letter, you say that "since our two countries have been joined again in peace and the two rulers are once more in concord," you desire "to rest your soldiers and turn your horses to pasture, in order that generation after generation may know prosperity and joy and we may make a new beginning in peace and harmony." We heartily approve these words. The sage, it is said, renews himself daily, reforming and making a new beginning in order that the old people may have rest and the young grow to manhood, that each may preserve his own life and fulfil the years which Heaven has granted him. So long as we and the *Shanyu* join in walking this road, following the will of Heaven and pitying the people, bestowing the blessing of peace on generation after generation without end, then there will be no one in the whole world who will not benefit.

Our two great nations, the Han and the Xiongnu, stand side by side. Since the Xiongnu dwell in the north, where the land is cold and the killing frosts come early, we have decreed that our officials shall send to the *Shanyu* each year a fixed quantity of millet, leaven, gold, silk cloth, thread, floss, and other articles.

Now the world enjoys profound peace and the people are at rest. We and the *Shanyu* must be as parents to them. When we consider past affairs, we realize that it is only because of petty matters and trifling reasons that the plans of our ministers have failed. No such matters are worthy to disrupt the harmony that exists between brothers.

We have heard it said that Heaven shows no partiality in sheltering mankind, and Earth no bias in bearing it up. Let us, then, with the *Shanyu*, cast aside these trifling matters of the past and walk the great road together, wiping out former evils and planning for the distant future, in order that the peoples of our two states may be joined together like the sons of a single family. Then, from the countless multitudes of the people down to the very fish and turtles, the birds which fly above, all creatures that walk or breathe or move, there will be none that fail to find peace and profit and relief from peril.

To allow men to come and go without hindrance is the way of Heaven. Let us both forget past affairs. We have pardoned those of our subjects who fled to the Xiongnu or were taken prisoner. Let the *Shanyu* likewise ask no further concerning Zhang Ni and the other Xiongnu leaders who surrendered to us.

We have heard that the rulers of ancient times made their promises clearly known and that, once they had given their consent, they did not go back on their words. The *Shanyu* should consider this well, so that all the world may enjoy profound peace. Once the peace alliance has been concluded, the Han shall not be the first to violate it! Let the *Shanyu* ponder these words!

When the *Shanyu* expressed his willingness to abide by the peace agreement, Emperor Wen issued an edict to the imperial secretary which read:

The great *Shanyu* of the Xiongnu has sent us a letter signifying that the peace alliance has been concluded. No action need be taken concerning those who have fled from one state to the other, since they are not sufficiently numerous to affect the population or size of our territories. The Xiongnu shall not enter within our borders, nor shall the Han forces venture beyond the frontier. Anyone who violates this agreement shall be executed. It is to the advantage of both nations that they should live in lasting friendship without further aggression. We have given our consent to this alliance, and now we wish to publish it abroad to the world so that all may clearly understand it.

Four years later the Old *Shanyu* Jizhu died and was succeeded by his son Junchen. After Junchen assumed the title of *Shanyu*, Emperor Wen once more renewed the former peace alliance. Zhonghang Yue continued to act as adviser to the new *Shanyu*.

A little over a year after Junchen became *Shanyu* (158 BC)[13] the Xiongnu again violated the peace alliance, invading Shang and Yunzhong provinces in great numbers; 30,000 horsemen attacked each province, killing and carrying off great numbers of the inhabitants before withdrawing. The emperor dispatched three generals with armies to garrison Beidi, the Juzhu Pass in Dai, and the Flying Fox Pass in Zhao, at the same time ordering the other garrisons along the border to guard their defences in order to hold off the barbarians. He also stationed three armies in the vicinity of Chang'an at Xiliu, at Jimen north of the Wei River, and at the Ba River, so as to be prepared for the barbarians in case they entered that area. The Xiongnu cavalry poured through the Juzhu Pass in Dai, and the signal fires along the border flashed the news of their invasion to Chang'an and the Palace of Sweet Springs. After several months the Han troops reached the border, but by that time the Xiongnu had already withdrawn far beyond and the Han troops were recalled.

A year or so later Emperor Wen passed away and Emperor Jing came to the throne. At this time Liu Sui, the king of Zhao, sent envoys in secret to negotiate with the Xiongnu. When Wu, Chu, Zhao, and the other states revolted, the Xiongnu planned to cooperate with Zhao and cross the border, but the Han forces besieged and defeated the king of Zhao, and the Xiongnu called off their plans for an invasion.

After this Emperor Jing once more renewed the peace alliance with the Xiongnu, allowing them to buy goods in the markets along the Han border and sending them supplies and a princess of the imperial family, as had been done under the earlier agreements. Thus, throughout Emperor Jing's reign, although the Xiongnu from time to time made small plundering raids across the border, they did not carry out any major invasion.

When the present emperor came to the throne he reaffirmed the peace alliance and treated the Xiongnu with generosity, allowing them to trade in the markets of the border stations and sending them lavish gifts. From the *Shanyu* on down, all the Xiongnu grew friendly with the Han, coming and going along the Great Wall.

The emperor then dispatched Nie Wengyi, a native of the city of Mayi, to carry contraband goods to the Xiongnu and begin trading with them. This done, Nie Wengyi deceived them by offering to hand over the city of Mayi to the

---

[13]Following the reading in *Han shu* 94A.

Shanyu, intending by this ruse to lure him into the area. The *Shanyu* trusted Nie Wengyi and, greedy for the wealth of Mayi, set out with a force of 100,000 cavalry and crossed the border at the barrier of Wuzhou. The Han in the meantime had concealed 300,000 troops in the vicinity of Mayi, headed by four generals under the imperial secretary Han Anguo, who was the leader of the expeditionary forces, ready to spring on the *Shanyu* when he arrived.

The *Shanyu* crossed the Han border but was still some 100 *li* from Mayi when he began to notice that, although the fields were full of animals, there was not a single person in sight. Growing suspicious, he attacked one of the beacon warning stations. A defence official of Yanmen who had been patrolling the area but had caught sight of the barbarian invaders had at this time taken refuge in the warning station, for he knew of the plan of the Han forces to ambush them. When the *Shanyu* attacked and captured the warning station, he was about to put the defence official to death when the latter informed him of the Han troops hiding in the valley. "I suspected as much!" exclaimed the *Shanyu* in great alarm, and proceeded to lead his forces back to the border. After they had safely crossed the border he remarked. "Heaven was on my side when I captured this defence official. In effect Heaven sent you to warn me!" and he awarded the defence official the title of "Heavenly King".

The Han forces had agreed to wait until the *Shanyu* had entered Mayi before launching their attack but, since he never proceeded that far, they had no opportunity to strike. Meanwhile another Han general, Wang Hui, had been ordered to lead a special force from Dai and attack the Xiongnu baggage train, but when he heard that the *Shanyu* had retreated and that his forces were extremely numerous, he did not dare to make an attack. When it was all over the Han officials condemned Wang Hui to execution on the grounds that, though he was the one who had engineered the entire plot, he had failed to advance when the time came.

After this the Xiongnu broke off friendly relations with the Han and began to attack the border defences wherever they happened to be. Time and again they crossed the frontier and carried out innumerable plundering raids. At the same time they continued to be as greedy as ever, delighting in the border markets and longing for Han goods, and the Han for its part continued to allow them to trade in the markets in order to sap their resources.

Five years after the Mayi campaign, in the autumn (129 BC), the Han government dispatched four generals, each with a force of 10,000 cavalry, to make a surprise attack on the barbarians at the border markets. General Wei

Qing rode out of Shanggu as far as Longcheng, killing or capturing 700 of the enemy. Gongsun He proceeded from Yunzhong, but took no captives. Gongsun Ao rode north from Dai Province, but was defeated by the barbarians and lost over 7,000 of his men. Li Guang advanced from Yanmen, but was defeated and captured, though he later managed to escape and return to the Han. On their return, Gongsun Ao and Li Guang were thrown into prison by the Han officials but were allowed to purchase a pardon for their offences and were reduced to the status of commoners.

In the winter the Xiongnu several times crossed the border on plundering expeditions, hitting hardest at Yuyang. The emperor dispatched General Han Anguo to garrison Yuyang and protect it from the barbarians. In the autumn of the following year 20,000 Xiongnu horsemen invaded the empire, murdered the governor of Liaoxi, and carried off over 2,000 prisoners. They also invaded Yuyang, defeated the army of over 1,000 under the command of the governor of Yuyang, and surrounded Han Anguo's camp. Han Anguo at this time had a force of over 1,000 horsemen under his command, but before long even these were on the point of being wiped out. Relief forces arrived from Yan just in time, and the Xiongnu withdrew. The Xiongnu also invaded Yanmen and killed or carried off over 1,000 persons.

The Han then dispatched General Wei Qing with a force of 30,000 cavalry to ride north from Yanmen, and Li Xi to ride out from Dai Province to attack the barbarians. They succeeded in killing or capturing several thousand of the enemy.

The following year Wei Qing again rode out of Yunzhong and proceeded west as far as Longxi, attacking the kings of the Loufan and Baiyang barbarians south of the Yellow River, capturing or killing several thousand of the enemy, and seizing over 1,000,000 cattle and sheep. Thus the Han regained control of the area south of the bend of the Yellow River and began to build fortifications at Shuofang, repairing the old system of defences that had been set up by Meng Tian during the Qin dynasty and strengthening the frontier along the Yellow River. The Han also abandoned claims to the district of Shibi and the region of Zaoyang that had formed the extreme northern part of the province of Shanggu, handing them over to the Xiongnu. This took place in the second year of the era *yuanshuo* (127 BC).

The following winter the *Shanyu* Junchen died and his younger brother, the Luli King of the Left, Yizhixie, set himself up as *Shanyu*. He attacked and defeated Junchen's heir, Yudan, who fled and surrendered to the Han. The Han enfeoffed Yudan as marquis of Shean, but he died several months later.

The summer after Yizhixie became *Shanyu* the Xiongnu invaded the province of Dai with 20,000 or 30,000 cavalry, murdering the governor, Gong You, and carrying off over 1,000 persons. In the fall the Xiongnu struck again, this time at Yanmen, killing or carrying off over 1,000 of the inhabitants. The following year they once more invaded Dai, Dingxiang, and Shang Provinces with 30,000 cavalry in each group, killing or carrying off several thousand persons. The Wise King of the Right, angry that the Han had seized the territory south of the Yellow River and built fortifications at Shuofang, several times crossed the border on plundering raids; he even went so far as to invade the region south of the river, ravaging Shuofang and killing or carrying off a large number of the officials and inhabitants.

In the spring of the following year (124 BC) the Han made Wei Qing a general in chief and sent him with an army of over 100,000 men and six generals to proceed north from Shuofang and Gaoque and strike at the barbarians. The Wise King of the Right, convinced that the Han forces could never penetrate far enough north to reach him, had drunk himself into a stupor when the Han army, marching 600 or 700 hundred *li* beyond the border, appeared and surrounded him in the night. The king, greatly alarmed, barely escaped with his life, and his best horsemen managed to break away in small groups and follow after him; the Han, however, succeeded in capturing 15,000 of his men and women, including over ten petty kings.

In the autumn a Xiongnu force of 10,000 cavalry invaded Dai Province, killed the chief commandant Zhu Ying, and carried off over 1,000 men.

In the spring of the following year (123 BC) the Han again dispatched the general in chief Wei Qing with six generals and a force of over 100,000 cavalry; they rode several hundred *li* north from Dingxiang and attacked the Xiongnu. All in all they succeeded in killing or capturing over 19,000 of the enemy, but in the engagements the Han side lost two generals and over 3,000 cavalry. Of the two generals one of them, Su Jian, the general of the right, managed to escape, but the other, Zhao Xin, the marquis of Xi, who was acting as general of the vanguard, surrendered to the Xiongnu when he saw that his men could not win a victory.

Zhao Xin was originally a petty king of the Xiongnu who later went over to the side of the Han. The Han enfeoffed him as marquis of Xi and made him general of the vanguard, sending him to accompany Su Jian, the general of the right, on a different line of advance from that of the rest of the expedition. Zhao

Xin and the forces under his command were alone, however, when they encountered the *Shanyu*'s men, and as a result his troops were wiped out. The *Shanyu*, having accepted Zhao Xin's surrender, appointed him to the rank of Zici king, gave him his own sister as a wife, and began to plot with him against the Han. Zhao Xin advised the *Shanyu* to withdraw farther north beyond the desert instead of manoeuvering near the Chinese border. In this way he would be able to lure the Han troops after him and, when they were thoroughly exhausted, take advantage of their weakness to wipe them out. The *Shanyu* agreed to follow this plan.

The following year 10,000 barbarian horsemen invaded Shanggu and killed several hundred inhabitants.

In the spring of the next year (121 BC) the Han dispatched the general of swift cavalry Huo Qubing to lead 10,000 cavalry out of Longxi. They rode more than 1,000 *li* beyond Mt. Yanzhi and attacked the Xiongnu, killing or capturing over 18,000 of the enemy cavalry, defeating the Xiutu king, and seizing the golden man which he used in worshipping Heaven.[14]

In the summer Huo Qubing, accompanied by Gongsun Ao, the Heqi marquis, led a force of 20,000 or 30,000 cavalry some 2,000 *li* out of Longxi and Beidi to attack the barbarians. They passed Juyan, attacked in the region of the Qilian Mountains, and captured or killed over 30,000 of the enemy, including seventy or more petty kings and their subordinates.

Meanwhile the Xiongnu invaded Yanmen in Dai Province, killing or carrying off several hundred persons. The Han dispatched Zhang Qian, the Bowang marquis, and General Li Guang to ride out of Youbeiping and attack the Xiongnu Wise King of the Left. The Wise King of the Left surrounded Li Guang's army and came near to wiping out his 4,000 men, though he managed to inflict extraordinary damage on the enemy. Zhang Qian's forces came to the rescue just in time and Li Guang was able to escape, but the Han losses amounted to several thousand men. When the armies returned to the capital, Gongsun Ao was accused of having arrived late at a rendezvous with Huo Qubing and was condemned to die along with Zhang Qian; both men purchased pardons and were reduced to the rank of commoners.

The *Shanyu* was angry at the Hunye and Xiutu kings who lived in the

---

[14]Scholars have long speculated whether the "golden man" might not have been a Buddhist image. If so, this passage would mark the earliest record of Chinese contact with the Buddhist religion.

western part of his domain because they had allowed the Han to capture or kill 20,000 or 30,000 of their men; in the autumn he sent them a summons, intending to execute them. The Hunye and Xiutu kings, terrified, sent word to the Han that they were willing to surrender. The Han dispatched Huo Qubing to go and meet them, but on the way the Hunye king murdered the Xiutu king and combined the latter's forces with his own. When he surrendered to the Han, he had a force of over 40,000 men, though it was commonly referred to as a force of 100,000. Having gained the allegiance of the Hunye king, the Han found itself far less troubled by barbarian invasions in the regions of Longxi, Beidi, and Hexi. It therefore moved a number of poor people from east of the Pass to the region south of the bend of the Yellow River known as New Qin, which had been seized from the Xiongnu, in order to populate the area, and reduced the number of garrison troops along the border west of Beidi to half.

The following year (120 BC) the Xiongnu invaded Youbeiping and Dingxiang with a force of 20,000 or 30,000 cavalry in each region, killing or carrying off over 1,000 persons before withdrawing.

In the spring of the following year (119 BC) the Han strategists plotted together, saying, "Zhao Xin, the marquis of Xi, who is acting as adviser to the *Shanyu*, is convinced that, since the Xiongnu are living north of the desert, the Han forces can never reach them." They agreed therefore to fatten the horses on grain and send out a force of 100,000 cavalry, along with 140,000 horses to carry baggage and other equipment (this in addition to the horses provided for transporting provisions). They ordered the force to split up into two groups commanded by the general in chief Wei Qing and the general of swift cavalry Huo Qubing. The former was to ride out of Dingxiang and the latter out of Dai; it was agreed that the entire force would cross the desert and attack the Xiongnu.

When the *Shanyu* received word of the approach of these armies, he ordered his baggage trains to withdraw to a distance and, with his finest soldiers, waited on the northern edge of the desert, where he closed in battle with the army of Wei Qing. The battle continued throughout the day and, as evening fell, a strong wind arose. With this the Han forces swooped out to the left and right and surrounded the *Shanyu*. The *Shanyu*, perceiving that he was no match for the Han forces, abandoned his army and, accompanied by only a few hundred of his finest horsemen, broke through the Han encirclement and fled to the northwest. The Han forces set out after him in the night and, though they did not succeed in capturing him, cut down or seized 19,000 of the enemy on the way. They proceeded north as far as Zhao Xin's fort at Mt. Tianyan before turning back.

After the *Shanyu* had fled, his soldiers, mingling with the Han forces in the confusion, little by little made their way after him. It was therefore a considerable time before the *Shanyu* was able to reassemble his army again. The Luli King of the Right, believing that the *Shanyu* had been killed in battle, declared himself the new *Shanyu*, but when the real *Shanyu* gathered his forces together again the Luli king renounced the title and resumed his former position.

Huo Qubing had meanwhile advanced some 2,000 *li* north from Dai and closed in battle with the Xiongnu Wise King of the Left. The Han forces killed or captured over 70,000 of the enemy and the Wise King and his generals all fled. Huo Qubing performed a Feng sacrifice at Mt. Langjuxu and a Shan sacrifice at Mt. Guyan, gazing out across the sea of sand before returning. After this the Xiongnu withdrew far from the Chinese border, and their leaders no longer established their courts south of the desert.

In the territory beyond the Yellow River from Shuofang west to Lingju the Han established irrigation works and set up garrison farms here and there, sending 50,000 or 60,000 officials and soldiers to man them. Gradually the farms ate up more and more territory until they bordered the lands of the Xiongnu to the north.

In the campaign just concluded, when the two Han generals advanced north in great force and surrounded the *Shanyu*, the Han had succeeded in killing or capturing 80,000 or 90,000 of the enemy. At the same time, however, 20,000 or 30,000 Han soldiers lost their lives in the expedition and over 100,000 horses were killed. Thus, although the Xiongnu had withdraw far to the north to nurse their wounds, the Han, being short of horses, was unable to strike at them again. Following the advice of Zhao Xin, the Xiongnu dispatched an envoy to the Han court to use soft words and request a peace alliance. When the emperor referred the proposal to his ministers for deliberation, some of them spoke in favour of a peace pact, while others urged that the Han pursue the Xiongnu and force them to submission. Ren Chang, the chief secretary to the chancellor, announced his opinion, "Since the Xiongnu have just recently been defeated and their spirits broken, they should be treated as foreign vassals and required to come to the border in the spring and autumn to pay their respects to the Han."

The emperor accordingly sent Ren Chang to the *Shanyu* with this counter-proposal. When the *Shanyu* heard Ren Chang's suggestion, he flew into a rage and detained him in his camp, refusing to send him back to China. (Earlier, one of the Xiongnu envoys had gone over to the side of the Han and remained in

China and the *Shanyu* therefore detained Ren Chang by way of retaliation.)

The Han then began to gather together a force of men and horses in preparation for another campaign, but just at that time the general of swift cavalry Huo Qubing died and so for several years the Han made no further attacks on the Xiongnu.

The *Shanyu* Yizhixie, after having ruled for thirteen years, died and was succeeded by his son Wuwei. This occurred in the third year of the *yuanding* era (114 BC). At the time that Wuwei became *Shanyu*, the Son of Heaven made his first imperial tour of the various provinces, and after that the Han armies were busy in the south putting down the rebellion in the two kingdoms of Southern and Eastern Yue, so no attacks were made on the Xiongnu. The Xiongnu for their part likewise made no raids across the border.

Three years after Wuwei became *Shanyu* the Han, having wiped out the kingdom of Southern Yue, dispatched the former master of carriage Gongsun He at the head of a force of 15,000 cavalry; they rode more than 2,000 *li* north from Jiuyuan, advancing as far as Fujujing before turning back, but they did not catch sight of a single Xiongnu. The Han also dispatched Zhao Ponu, the former Congpiao marquis, with over 10,000 cavalry to ride out of Lingju; Zhao Ponu proceeded several thousand *li*, reaching the Xionghe River before turning back, but he too failed to see a single Xiongnu.

At this time the emperor was making a tour of the border. When he reached Shuofang, he held an inspection of 180,000 cavalry soldiers in order to make a display of military might, at the same time dispatching a man named Guo Ji to the *Shanyu* to make sure that the Xiongnu were fully informed of the event.

When Guo Ji reached the Xiongnu, the Xiongnu master of guests asked him what his business was. Replying in very polite and humble terms, Guo Ji said, "I would like to wait until I am granted an audience with the *Shanyu* before stating my business."

When he was shown before the *Shanyu* he said, "The head of the king of Southern Yue hangs above the northern gate of the Han capital. Now, if you are able, advance and engage the Han forces in battle! The Son of Heaven has led his troops in person and is waiting on the border. But if you are not able, then turn your face to the south and acknowledge yourself a subject of the Han! Why this useless running away and hiding far off north of the desert in a cold and bitter land where there is no water or pasture? It will get you nowhere!"

When he had finished speaking, the *Shanyu*, livid with rage, ordered the master of guests who had ushered him in to be cut down on the spot. He detained

Guo Ji and would not let him return to China; later he moved him to the shore of the Northern Sea (Lake Baikal). In the end, however, the *Shanyu* refused to be provoked into invading the Han border but turned his horses to pasture, rested his troops, and practised archery and hunting instead, sending envoys to the Han from time to time to speak with soft words and honeyed phrases and request a peace alliance.

The Han in turn sent Wang Wu and others as envoys to observe the Xiongnu. According to Xiongnu law, unless an envoy from the Han surrendered his credentials and allowed his face to be tattooed in black, he would not be admitted to the *Shanyu*'s tent. Wang Wu had been born in the north and was familiar with the barbarian customs, and therefore he readily gave up his credentials, submitted to the tattooing, and was able to gain admittance to the *Shanyu*'s tent. The *Shanyu* showed a great liking for him and pretended to agree amiably with whatever he said, even with the suggestion that he send his son, the heir apparent to the position of *Shanyu*, as a hostage to the Han in order to secure a peace alliance. The Han then dispatched Yang Xin as envoy to the Xiongnu.

At this time the Han forces in the east had conquered the barbarian states of Huimo and Chaoxian and made provinces out of them, while in the west the Han had created the province of Jiuquan in order to drive a wedge between the Xiongnu and the Qiang barbarians and cut off communications between them. It had also established relations with the Yuezhi people and Daxia (Bactria) farther west and had sent an imperial princess to marry the ruler of the Wusun people, all in an effort to create a split between the Xiongnu and the states to the west which had up to this time aided and supported them. In addition, the Han continued to expand its agricultural lands in the north until the frontier had been pushed out as far as Xuanlei. In spite of all these moves, however, the Xiongnu did not dare to voice any objections. This year Zhao Xin, the marquis of Xi, who had been acting as adviser to the *Shanyu*, died.

The Han administrators believed that the Xiongnu had already been sufficiently weakened and could now be made to acknowledge themselves subjects of the Han and submit to Chinese rule, and therefore they had dispatched Yang Xin as envoy to the *Shanyu*. But Yang Xin was by nature very outspoken and unyielding and had never been high in the Han bureaucracy; the *Shanyu* showed no liking for him. When summoned for an interview in the *Shanyu*'s tent, he refused to surrender his credentials, and so the *Shanyu* had mats spread outside his tent and received Yang Xin there. "If you wish to conclude a peace alliance,"

Yang Xin announced when he had been shown into the *Shanyu*'s presence, "you must send your heir to the Han court as a hostage!"

"That is not the way things were done under the old alliance!" the *Shanyu* objected. "Under the old alliance the Han always sent us an imperial princess, as well as allotments of silks, foodstuffs, and other goods, in order to secure peace, while we for our part refrained from making trouble on the border. Now you want to go against the old ways and make me send my son as a hostage. I have no use for such proposals!"

It is the way with the Xiongnu that, whenever an envoy from the Han comes who is not a high court official, if he is the scholarly Confucian type, they assume that he has come to lecture them and they do all they can to squelch his rhetoric, while if he is a young man, they assume he has come with assassination in mind and concentrate on destroying his nerve. Every time a Han envoy arrives among the Xiongnu, they send an envoy of their own to the Han in exchange. If the Han detains the Xiongnu envoy, then the Xiongnu detain the Han envoy and will not release him until they have received what they consider just treatment.

After Yang Xin returned from his mission to the Xiongnu, the Han dispatched Wang Wu again, and once more the *Shanyu* began to talk in a mild and conciliatory way, hoping to be given a sizable grant of Han goods. As part of the deception he told Wang Wu, "I would like to make a trip to the Han and visit the Son of Heaven so that face to face we may swear a pact of brotherhood!"

When Wang Wu returned and reported on his mission, the Han built a residence for the *Shanyu* in Chang'an. The *Shanyu*, however, sent word that "unless some important member of the Han government is sent as envoy, I cannot discuss the matter seriously."

Meanwhile the Xiongnu dispatched one of their important men as envoy to the Han. When the man reached China, however, he fell ill and, although the Han doctors gave him medicine and tried to cure him, he unfortunately died. The Han then sent Lu Chongguo to act as envoy and to accompany the body of the dead Xiongnu back to his country, spending several thousand gold pieces on a lavish funeral for him. Lu Chongguo was given the seals of a 2,000 picul official to wear at his belt and bore assurances to the Xiongnu that "this man is an important official of the Han". The *Shanyu*, however, was convinced that the Han had murdered the Xiongnu envoy and therefore detained Lu Chongguo and refused to let him return to China. By this time everyone on the Han side was of the opinion that the *Shanyu* had only been deceiving Wang Wu with empty talk and in fact had no intention of coming to China or sending his son as a hostage. After this the Xiongnu several times sent surprise parties of troops to raid the border, and the Han for its part conferred on Guo Chang the title of "Barbarian Quelling General" and sent Zhao Ponu, the marquis of Zhuoye, to garrison the area from Shuofang to the east and defend it against the Xiongnu.

Lu Chongguo had been detained by the Xiongnu for three years when the *Shanyu* Wuwei died, having ruled for ten years. He was succeeded by his son, Wushilu. Wushilu was still young and was therefore called the Boy *Shanyu*. The change took place in the sixth year of the *yuanfeng* era (105 BC).

After this the *Shanyu* gradually moved farther to the northwest, so that the soldiers of his left or eastern wing occupied the area north of Yunzhong, while those of his right wing were in the area around Jiuquan and Dunhuang provinces.

When the Boy *Shanyu* came to power the Han dispatched two envoys, one to the new *Shanyu* to convey condolences on the death of his father, and the other to convey condolences to the Wise King of the Right, hoping in this way to cause dissension between the two leaders. When the envoys entered Xiongnu territory, however, the Xiongnu guides led them both to the *Shanyu*. The *Shanyu*, discovering what they were up to, was furious and detained them both. The Xiongnu had already detained over ten Han envoys in the past, while the Han had likewise detained a proportionate number of Xiongnu envoys. This same year the Han sent the Sutrishna General Li Guangli west to attack Dayuan (Ferghana) and ordered the Yinyu General Gongsun Ao to build a fortified city called Shouxiangcheng, the "City for Receiving Surrender".

In the winter the Xiongnu were afflicted by heavy snowfalls, and many of their animals died of starvation and cold. The *Shanyu*, still a young boy, had a great fondness for warfare and slaughter, and many of his subjects were restless under his leadership. The Xiongnu chief commandant of the left wanted to assassinate the *Shanyu* and sent a messenger in secret to report to the Han, "I wish to assassinate the *Shanyu* and surrender to the Han, but the Han is too far away. If the Han will send a party of troops to meet me, however, I will at once carry out the plot."

It was in fact because of this report that the Han had built the fortified City for Receiving Surrender. But the Han still considered that the chief commandant of the left was too far away to carry out his plot successfully.

In the spring of the following year the Han sent Zhao Ponu, the marquis of Zhuoye to lead a force of over 20,000 cavalry some 2,000 *li* northwest from Shuofang and make contact with the chief commandant of the left at Mt. Junji before returning. Zhao Ponu arrived at the point of rendezvous but, before the chief commandant of the left could carry out the assassination, his plot was discovered. The *Shanyu* had him executed and dispatched the forces from his left wing to attack Zhao Ponu. Zhao Ponu had by this time begun to withdraw, taking prisoners and killing several thousand Xiongnu soldiers on the way. When he was still 400 *li* from the City for Receiving Surrender, however, 80,000 Xiongnu cavalry swooped down and surrounded him. Zhao Ponu slipped out of the encirclement during the night and went by himself to look for water, but was captured alive by Xiongnu scouts. The main body of the Xiongnu then pressed their attack on Zhao Ponu's army. Guo Zong and Wei Wang, two of the high officers in the Han army, plotted together, saying, "All of us, down to the company commanders, are afraid that, having lost our commanding general, we will be executed under military law. Therefore no one is anxious to return home." Eventually the whole army surrendered to the Xiongnu. The Boy *Shanyu* was delighted with his catch and sent a raiding party to attack the City for Receiving Surrender, but the city held fast. The party then plundered the border area and withdrew.

The following year the *Shanyu* again set out to attack the City for Receiving Surrender, this time in person, but before he reached his destination he fell ill and died. He had been *Shanyu* only three years. Since his son was still very small, the Xiongnu appointed his uncle Goulihu, the former Wise King of the Right and younger brother of the *Shanyu* Wuwei, as the new *Shanyu*. This took place in the third year of the era *taichu* (102 BC).

After Goulihu had become *Shanyu* the Han sent the superintendent of the imperial household Xu Ziwei to ride out of the barrier at Wuyuan and range through the area from several hundred to 1,000 *li* or more north of the border, building forts and watch stations as far as Mt. Luqu. The Han also dispatched the scouting and attacking general Han Yue and the marquis of Changping, Wei Kang, to garrison the region, at the same time sending the chief commandant of strong crossbowmen Lu Bode to build fortifications along the swamp at Juyan.

In the autumn the Xiongnu invaded Dingxiang and Yunzhong in great force, murdering or carrying off several thousand persons. They also defeated several officials of the 2,000 picul rank before withdrawing, and destroyed the forts and watch stations that Xu Ziwei had built as they went along. At the same time the Wise King of the Right invaded Jiuquan and Zhangye provinces and carried off several thousand persons. The Han general Ren Wen, however, came to the rescue, attacking the Xiongnu and forcing them to give up all the spoils and prisoners they had taken.

This year the Sutrishna General Li Guangli defeated the kingdom of Dayuan, cut off the head of its ruler, and returned. The Xiongnu tried to block his return but could not reach him in time. In the winter they planned an attack on the City for Receiving Surrender, but just at that time the *Shanyu* died. The *Shanyu* Goulihu had ruled for only a year when he died. The Xiongnu set up his younger brother, Judihou, the former chief commandant of the left, as *Shanyu*.

At this time the Han had just conquered the kingdom of Dayuan, and its might filled the neighbouring states with terror. The emperor had hopes of carrying out the final suppression of the Xiongnu and issued an edict which read:

> Emperor Gaozu has left us the task of avenging the difficulties which he suffered at Pingcheng. Furthermore, during the reign of Empress Lü the *Shanyu* sent to the court a most treasonable and insulting letter. In ancient times when Duke Xiang of Qi avenged an insult which one of his ancestors nine generations earlier had suffered, Confucius praised his conduct in the *Spring and Autumn Annals*.

This year was the fourth year of the era *taichu* (101 BC).[15]

After Judihou became *Shanyu* he returned all of the Han envoys who had not gone over to his side. Thus Lu Chongguo and the others were able to come home. When the new *Shanyu* assumed the rule, he was afraid that the Han would attack him and so he said, "I consider that I am but a little child. How could I hope to equal the Han Son of Heaven? The Son of Heaven is like a father to me."

The Han dispatched the general of palace attendants Su Wu to present generous gifts to the *Shanyu*. With this the *Shanyu* grew increasingly arrogant and behaved with great rudeness, betraying the hopes of the Han.

The following year Zhao Ponu managed to escape from the Xiongnu and return home. The year after, the Han sent Li Guangli with 30,000 cavalry north from Jiuquan to attack the Wise King of the Right in the Heavenly Mountains. He killed or captured over 10,000 of the enemy before returning. The Xiongnu,

---

[15] Sima Qian's narrative probably ends somewhere around this point; the remainder of the chapter down to the closing remarks, a series of rather choppy notes, is most likely the work of Chu Shaosun or one of the other writers who undertook to make additions to the *Shi ji*.

however, surrounded him in great force and he was barely able to escape; six or seven out of every ten of his men were killed.

The Han also sent Gongsun Ao north from Xihe; at Mt. Zhuotu he joined forces with Lu Bode, but neither of them succeeded in killing or capturing any of the enemy. The Han also sent the cavalry commandant Li Ling with a force of 5,000 infantry and cavalry to march north from Juyan. After they had proceeded over 1,000 *li* they engaged the *Shanyu* in battle. Li Ling killed or wounded over 10,000 of the enemy, but his provisions soon gave out and his men began to scatter and flee for home. The Xiongnu then surrounded Li Ling, who surrendered to them. Most of his men were wiped out, only 400 of them managing to return to safety. The *Shanyu* treated Li Ling with great honour and gave him his own daughter for a wife.

Two years later the Han again dispatched Li Guangli with 60,000 cavalry and 100,000 infantry to march north from Shuofang. Lu Bode led some 10,000 men to join them, while Han Yue advanced with 30,000 infantry and cavalry from Wuyuan. Gongsun Ao proceeded from Yanmen with 10,000 cavalry and 30,000 infantry. When the *Shanyu* received word of their advance, he moved all his family and wealth far to the north beyond the Yuwu River. He himself, with 10,000 cavalry, waited south of the river and engaged Li Guangli in battle. Li Guangli's lines broke and he began to retreat, fighting a running battle with the *Shanyu* for over ten days. But when word reached him that his entire family had been wiped out as a result of the witchcraft affair,[16] he and all his men surrendered to the Xiongnu. Only one or two out of every 1,000 men who set out with him managed to return to China. Han Yue did not succeed in killing or capturing any of the enemy, while Gongsun Ao, though he fought with the Wise King of the Left, was unable to win any advantage and likewise retreated. From all the parties that went out to attack the Xiongnu this year, among those who returned there were none to testify as to what degree of success the various generals had achieved and therefore no honours were awarded. An imperial edict had been issued ordering the arrest of the grand physician Sui Dan. He in turn gave out the news that Li Guangli's family had been exterminated and thereby caused Li Guangli to surrender to the Xiongnu.

---

[16] In 91 BC the heir apparent, Prince Li, and his mother, Empress Wei, were accused of attempting to kill the emperor by black magic. Many high officials of the dynasty were implicated in the investigations that followed, among them Li Guangli. But the battle referred to above took place in 99 BC, so the text is obviously out of order.

The Grand Historian remarks: When Confucius wrote the *Spring and Autumn Annals*, he was very open in treating the reigns of Yin and Huan, the early dukes of Lu; but when he came to the later period of Dukes Ding and Ai, his writing was much more covert. Because in the latter case he was writing about his own times, he did not express his judgments frankly, but used subtle and guarded language.[17]

The trouble with the ordinary run of men these days who discuss Xiongnu affairs is that they seek only for some temporary advantage, resorting to any kind of flattery in order to have their own views accepted, without considering what the effect may be on all parties concerned. At the same time the generals and military leaders, relying upon the vastness and might of China, grow increasingly bold, and the ruler follows their advice in making his decisions. Thus no profound achievement is ever reached.

Emperor Yao in ancient times, as wise as he was, was not completely successful as a ruler; the nine provinces of China had to wait until the reign of Emperor Yu before they knew real peace. If one would establish a truly worthy dynasty such as those of old, therefore, nothing is more important than selecting the right generals and ministers! Nothing is more important than selecting the right generals and ministers!

---

[17]Sima Qian's purpose in making these seemingly irrelevant remarks about Confucius and the *Spring and Autumn Annals* is of course to warn the reader that he too is obliged to use "guarded language" in his discussion of the Xiongnu problem.

SHI JI 111: THE BIOGRAPHIES OF GENERAL WEI QING AND THE SWIFT CAVALRY GENERAL HUO QUBING

They patrolled the winding frontier, broadened our lands south of the bend of the Yellow River, defeated the enemy at Qilian, opened up contact with the western states, and overpowered the northern barbarians. Thus I made "The Biographies of General Wei Qing and the Swift Cavalry General Huo Qubing".

The general in chief Wei Qing was a native of Pingyang. His father, Zheng Ji, was a clerk in the household of the marquis of Pingyang, where he had illicit relations with Dame Wei, a concubine of the marquis. From this union Wei Qing was born. Before this Dame Wei had already given birth to a boy, Wei Changzi, and a girl, Wei Zifu. The latter, because she was employed in the household of the princess of Pingyang, the wife of the marquis of Pingyang and older sister of Emperor Wu, later managed to obtain favour with the emperor. For this reason Wei Qing also adopted the family name Wei and the polite name Zhongqing, and his brother Zhangzi changed his name to Changjun. The oldest daughter of their mother was named Wei Ru, her second daughter Wei Shaoer, and her third daughter Wei Zifu. Later she had another son named Buguang. All her children adopted the surname Wei.[1] Wei Qing became a servant in the household of the marquis of Pingyang.

When he was young Wei Qing went to live with his father, but his father set him to herding sheep and all his half-brothers, sons of his father's legitimate wife, treated him like a slave and refused to recognize him as a brother.

Once, while Wei Qing was a servant, he had occasion to visit the prison at the Palace of Sweet Springs. There one of the convicts in chains examined his

---

[1] The narrative is remarkably confused. Was Zheng Ji the father of all Dame Wei's children, and was Wei her own family name? Or did she have a husband named Wei? Apparently Sima Qian was not certain of the facts when he wrote the passage.

face and said, "You will become a great man and will rise to the position of marquis!"

Wei Qing laughed and said, "I was born a slave and if I can get by without being beaten and scolded that will be good enough. How would *I* ever get to be a marquis?"

When he grew to manhood he became a rider in the marquis's household and attended the princess of Pingyang.

In the second year of *jianyuan* (139 BC) Wei Qing's elder sister Wei Zifu went to live in the palace and won favour with Emperor Wu. The emperor's consort at this time was Empress Chen, the daughter of the Elder Princess of Tangyi, the older sister of Emperor Jing. Empress Chen had no children and was of a very jealous nature. When the Elder Princess heard that Wei Zifu had won favour with the emperor and was pregnant, she was very envious and sent men to arrest Wei Qing. Wei Qing at this time was serving in the Jianzhang Palace and was little known, so that the Elder Princess was able to have him seized without difficulty. She was about to put him to death when Wei Qing's friend Gongsun Ao, a palace horseman, went with a band of young men to the place where he was being held and managed to snatch Wei Qing up and carry him off to safety. Thus his life was saved.

When the emperor heard of the incident, he summoned Wei Qing and made him superintendent of the guards at the Jianzhang Palace. He also summoned Wei Qing's brothers, the other sons of Dame Wei, and appointed them to high positions, in the course of a few days showering them with gifts amounting to 1,000 pieces of gold. Wei Qing's eldest sister Wei Ru was given as a wife to the master of carriage Gongsun He. His next eldest sister, Wei Shaoer, had previously had an affair with Chen Zhang and the emperor therefore summoned Chen Zhang and gave him a high post. Gongsun Ao won fame because of his part in saving Wei Qing's life, Wei Zifu became a lady of the palace, and Wei Qing was advanced to the rank of palace counsellor.

In the fifth year of the *yuanguang* era (129 BC) Wei Qing was appointed general of carriage and cavalry and sent out of Shanggu to attack the Xiongnu; the master of carriage Gongsun He was made general of light carriage and sent out of Yunzhong; the palace counsellor Gongsun Ao was made cavalry general and sent out of Dai Province; and the colonel of the guard Li Guang was made general of resolute cavalry and sent out of Yanmen. Each commander had a force of 10,000 horsemen. Wei Qing reached Longcheng and killed or captured several hundred of the enemy. Gongsun Ao lost several thousand of his horseman, and Li Guang was taken prisoner by the enemy, though he managed to escape. Both Gongsun Ao and Li Guang were condemned to execution for their failures, but were allowed to ransom their lives and become commoners. Gongsun He likewise failed to win any distinction in the campaign.

In the spring of the first year of *yuanshuo* (128 BC) Wei Zifu gave birth to a son and was designated as the new empress. In the autumn Wei Qing as general of carriage and cavalry rode out of Yanmen with a force of 30,000 horsemen and attacked the Xiongnu, killing or capturing several thousand of the enemy.

The following year the Xiongnu crossed the border and killed the governor of Liaoxi, carrying off over 2,000 of the inhabitants of Yuyang and defeating the army of General Han Anguo. The emperor ordered General Li Xi to attack them from Dai and Wei Qing to attack from Yunzhong. Wei Qing proceeded west to Gaoque and from there invaded the region south of the bend of the Yellow River as far as Longxi. He captured or killed several thousand of the enemy, seized 20,000 or 30,000 of their domestic animals, and put to flight the kings of the Baiyang and Loufan tribes, thus making it possible to establish the province of Shuofang south of the bend of the river. Because of this Wei Qing was enfeoffed as marquis of Changping with 3,800 households. His subordinate commander Su Jian, who had also won distinction in the campaign, was enfeoffed as marquis of Pingling with 1,100 households and sent to build fortifications in Shuofang. Another subordinate commander, Zhang Cigong, was enfeoffed as marquis of Antou because of his achievements.

The imperial edict issued on the occasion read:

> The Xiongnu have turned their backs on the principles of Heaven and brought disorder to human relations, assaulting and maltreating the aged and dedicating themselves to rapine and plunder. They have tricked the other barbarians into joining their plots and lending them their soldiers, and have repeatedly violated our borders. Therefore we have called out the armies and dispatched the generals to punish their offences. Does it not say in the *Book of Odes*:
>
> We struck the Xianyun
> And drove them to the great plain.
>
> We sent forth our chariots in majestic array
> And walled the northern regions.[2]

---

[2] From the poems entitled "Liuyue" and "Chuju" of the "Lesser Odes".

Now the general of carriage and cavalry Wei Qing has crossed the upper reaches of the Yellow River and marched as far as Gaoque, capturing and killing 2,300 of the enemy and seizing all of their baggage and animals. For this he has been enfeoffed as a ranking marquis. After this he proceeded west to win control of the land south of the bend of the Yellow River as far as the old frontier at Elm Valley; he has crossed the Catalpa Ridge, built a bridge across the North River, struck the enemy at Puni, defeated them at Fuli, and cut down their swiftest soldiers, capturing 3,071 of their scouts. By questioning the captives, he was able to discover and seize the main body of their force. Then, with over 1,000,000 horses, oxen, and sheep, and with his entire army still intact, he returned. Therefore we have increased his fief by 3,000 households.

The following year the Xiongnu invaded Dai Province and killed the governor, Gong You; they also crossed into Yanmen and carried off over 1,000 of the inhabitants. The year after, they invaded Dai, Dingxiang, and Shang Provinces in great force, killing and carrying off several thousand Chinese.

In the spring of the following year, the fifth year of *yuanshuo* (124 BC), the Han ordered the general of carriage and cavalry Wei Qing to proceed from Gaoque with a force of 30,000 cavalry; the colonel of the guard Su Jian was appointed scouting and attacking general; the left prefect of the capital Li Ju was made general of strong bowmen; the master of carriage Gongsun He was made cavalry general; and the prime minister of Dai, Li Cai, was made general of light carriage. All were under the command of Wei Qing and rode north from Shuofang. The grand messenger Li Xi and the marquis of Antou, Zhang Cigong, were appointed as generals and ordered to proceed from Youbeiping and join the others in attacking the Xiongnu.

The Xiongnu Wise King of the Right, whose forces were matched against those of Wei Qing, considered that the Han soldiers would never be able to reach his headquarters and had drunk himself into a stupor. During the night Wei Qing and his men reached the Xiongnu encampment and surrounded the Wise King of the Right. He woke in great astonishment and fled in the night, accompanied only by his favourite concubine and a few hundred of his best horsemen, galloping through the Han encirclement and making off to the north. The light cavalry colonel Guo Cheng and several others pursued him for 200 or 300 *li*, but were unable to overtake him. In the action, however, Wei Qing managed to capture ten or more petty chiefs under the Wise King of the Right, as well as over 15,000 of his men and women and between 100,000 and 1,000,000 domestic animals. Wei Qing then led his forces back to the frontier.

The emperor sent a messenger to meet him and present him with the seals of general in chief, conferring this title upon him. From this time on, all the troops of the other generals were under his command. After assuming his new title, Wei Qing returned to the capital.

The emperor issued an edict saying:

> The general in chief Wei Qing has led the troops in person and won a great victory in battle, capturing over ten of the petty chiefs of the Xiongnu. Therefore let his fief be increased by 6,000 households and let his son Wei Kang be enfeoffed as marquis of Yichun, his son Wei Buyi as marquis of Yin'an, and his son Wei Deng as marquis of Fagan.

Wei Qing firmly declined to accept the honours accorded to his sons, saying, "Unworthy as I am, I have been granted the privilege of riding into battle. Through the divine wisdom of Your Majesty, the army has won a great victory, but the merit is due wholly to the fighting ability of my officers. Your Majesty has graciously increased my own fief, but my sons are still in swaddling clothes and have performed no service. Though Your Majesty kindly wishes to set aside lands and enfeoff them as well, I fear it would do little to encourage the men who have fought under me. How could I dare to accept fiefs for Kang and my other sons?"

But the emperor replied, "I have not forgotten the achievements of your officers. At this very moment I am considering how to reward them."

Then he issued an edict to the imperial secretary which read:

> The chief commandant of the supporting army Gongsun Ao has three times served under the general in chief in attacking the Xiongnu, providing constant protection for the army and joining with the other divisions in capturing a number of the Xiongnu leaders. Let him be enfeoffed as Heqi or "Combined Cavalry" marquis with 1,500 households. The chief commandant Han Yue followed the general in chief in riding out of Yuhun, proceeding to the court of the Wise King of the Right, and fighting under the general in chief's command in the capture of the Xiongnu leaders. Let him be enfeoffed as marquis of Longwo with 1,300 households. The cavalry general Gongsun He accompanied the general in chief in capturing the Xiongnu leaders, for which he shall

be enfeoffed as marquis of Nanpao with 1,300 households. The general of light carriage Li Cai twice accompanied the general in chief in capturing groups of Xiongnu leaders, for which he shall be enfeoffed as marquis of Lean with 1,600 households. The subordinate commanders Li Shuo, Zhao Buyu, and Gongsun Rongnu all served three times under the general in chief and took part in the capture of the enemy leaders, for which Li Shuo shall be enfeoffed as marquis of Shezhi with 1,300 households, Zhao Buyu as marquis of Suicheng with 1,300 households, and Gongsun Rongnu as marquis of Congping with the same number. Since the generals Li Ju and Li Xi and the subordinate commander Dou Ruyi have also won distinction, they shall be awarded the rank of marquis within the Pass and granted the revenue from towns of 300 households each.

In the fall the Xiongnu invaded Dai, killing the chief commandant Zhu Ying.

In the spring of the following year the general in chief Wei Qing rode out of Dingxiang. The Heqi marquis Gongsun Ao acted as his general of the centre; the master of carriage Gongsun He as general of the left; the marquis of Xi, Zhao Xin, as general of the vanguard; the colonel of the guard Su Jian as general of the right; the chief of palace attendants Li Guang as general of the rear; and the left prefect of the capital Li Ju as general of strong bowmen, all of them under the command of the general in chief. They succeeded in killing or capturing several thousand of the enemy before returning.

A month or so later they rode out of Dingxiang again to attack the Xiongnu, capturing or killing over 10,000 of the enemy.

The general of the right Su Jian and the general of the vanguard Zhao Xin, with a combined force of 3,000 or more cavalry, being separated from the main body of the army, faced the soldiers of the *Shanyu* alone and fought with them for over a day until most of their own men had been wiped out. Zhao Xin was actually a Xiongnu himself, who had later gone over to the Chinese side and been enfeoffed as marquis of Xi. When his situation became critical, the Xiongnu tempted him with promises until he finally fled with the 800 or so cavalry that remained of his army and surrendered to the *Shanyu*. Su Jian lost his entire army and barely managed to escape alone and make his way back to the headquarters of the general in chief.

The general in chief questioned his expert on military law, Hong, his chief secretary An, his adviser Zhou Ba, and others as to what punishment they thought Su Jian deserved for his defeat. Zhou Ba replied, "Since you took the field as a military commander, you have never had occasion to execute any of your subordinate generals. Now that Su Jian has abandoned his army, it would be well to execute him in order to give a clear demonstration of your might!"

Hong and An objected, however, saying, "That would not be right! According to the laws of military science, a small force that attempts to hold its ground at all cost will end up as the prisoners of a larger force. Now Su Jian, with only a few thousand men, has had to face 20,000 or 30,000 of the *Shanyu*'s soldiers. He fought them for over a day until his men were wiped out and then, not daring to be disloyal, he made his way back of his own accord. If you execute men who return of their own volition, you will only succeed in demonstrating that from now on it does not pay to return! He should not be executed!"

Wei Qing then spoke, saying, "Because I am related to the empress, I have graciously been allowed to serve in the field. I am not worried about my might, and Zhou Ba's suggestion that I do something to demonstrate it is wholly at variance with my wishes. Moreover, though it might be proper and within my power to execute a general, considering the confidence and favour the emperor has shown me I would hardly dare to carry out the punishment arbitrarily and on my own authority here beyond the frontier. Would it not be better to return, report to the emperor in full, and allow him to make the decision himself? In this way I can show that I do not venture to abuse my authority."

His officers all agreed that this would be the best course and Su Jian was consequently made a prisoner and sent to the place where the emperor was residing. Wei Qing then led his forces back across the border and disbanded them.

This year Huo Qubing, the eighteen-year-old son of Wei Qing's elder sister Shaoer,[3] was favoured by being made an attendant of the emperor. He was skilful at riding and shooting, and accompanied his uncle Wei Qing on two campaigns. Wei Qing, acting on imperial order, granted him a force of young fighting men and gave him the title of swift commander. Huo Qubing, with 800 of the fastest and most daring riders, promptly broke away from the main army and ranged ahead several hundred *li* in search of gain, killing and capturing a disproportionately large number of the enemy. The emperor accordingly issued an edict, saying:

---

[3] His father, Huo Zhongru, had had an affair with Wei Shaoer before her marriage to Chen Zhang.

The swift commander Huo Qubing has killed and captured 2,028 of the enemy, including a prime minister and a household administrator; he has cut down Chan, the marquis of Jiruo, one of the *Shanyu*'s elder relatives, has captured alive the *Shanyu*'s uncle Luogubi, and has in both campaigns won the highest distinction in the army. He shall therefore be enfeoffed with 1,600 households and the title of Guanjun or "Highest in the Army" marquis. In addition, Hao Xian, the governor of Shanggu Province, who has served in four campaigns under the general in chief and has killed or captured over 2,000 of the enemy, shall be enfeoffed with 1,100 households and the title of Zhongli or "Manifold Gain" marquis.

In the campaigns this year two armies, those of Su Jian and Zhao Xin, were lost (Zhao Xin deserting to the enemy), and the armies failed to achieve any outstanding accomplishments. Therefore Wei Qing's fief was not increased. When Su Jian was brought back to the capital, the emperor did not execute him but pardoned his offences and allowed him to ransom his life and become a commoner. After Wei Qing returned, the emperor awarded him 1,000 pieces of gold.

At this time Lady Wang had begun to enjoy favour with the emperor. A certain Ning Cheng accordingly advised Wei Qing, saying, "Although you have not yet won any extraordinary amount of distinction, you enjoy the revenue from 10,000 households and all three of your sons have become marquises. All this is due merely to the fact that you are a brother of the empress. Now Lady Wang enjoys the emperor's favour, but the members of her family have not yet acquired wealth and honour. I would suggest, general, that you take the thousand gold pieces which you have received and give them to Lady Wang's mother as a birthday present."

Wei Qing followed this advice and presented 500 of the gold pieces to Lady Wang's mother. When the emperor heard about it, he questioned Wei Qing, who told him exactly how he had come to make the presentation. The emperor then honoured Ning Cheng with the post of chief commandant of Donghai Province.

Zhang Qian also served under Wei Qing in the army. Formerly he had been sent as envoy to Daxia (Bactria) and had been detained for a long time by the Xiongnu. He therefore knew where the best pastures and watering places in the barbarian territory were situated and guided the army to them; in this way he saved the army from hunger and thirst. Because of the merit he had won on his earlier mission to the distant lands of the west, he was enfeoffed with the title of Bowang or "Broad Vision" marquis.

After Huo Qubing had been a marquis for three years he was appointed general of swift cavalry and sent with a force of 10,000 horsemen out of Longxi in the spring of the second year of the era *yuanshou* (121 BC). In recognition of his achievements on this campaign the emperor announced:

> The general of swift cavalry Huo Qubing has led his fighting men across Mt. Wuli and struck at the tribes of Supu; he has crossed the Hunu River and marched through the lands of five barbarian rulers with his baggage trains and hosts of followers, sparing only those who submitted in fear before him. Hoping to capture the son of the *Shanyu*, he fought a running battle for six days, riding 1,000 *li* or more beyond Mt. Yanzhi, meeting the enemy in close combat, killing the ruler of Lan, slaying the barbarian King Lu, wiping out the entire enemy force and capturing the son of the Hunye king and his ministers and chief commandants. He has killed and captured over 8,000 of the enemy and seized the golden man which the Xiutu king uses in worshipping Heaven. Therefore let his fief be increased by 2,000 households.

In the summer Huo Qubing and the Heqi marquis Gongsun Ao proceeded north from Beidi, taking different routes, while the Bowang marquis Zhang Qian and the chief of palace attendants Li Guang rode north from Youbeiping, also by different routes, all with the objective of attacking the Xiongnu. Li Guang, with a force of 4,000 cavalry, made contact with the enemy first, while Zhang Qian and his 10,000 horsemen were still on the way. The Xiongnu Wise King of the Left, commanding a force of 20,000 or 30,000 horsemen, surrounded Li Guang's army. Li Guang fought with him for two days until over half of his own men had been killed and a far larger number of the enemy had perished. When Zhang Qian arrived with reinforcements, the Xiongnu soldiers finally withdrew. On his return to the capital Zhang Qian was tried for having been late in arriving and was condemned to execution, but was allowed to ransom his life and become a commoner.

Meanwhile Huo Qubing had proceeded north from Beidi and penetrated deep into enemy territory, but Gongsun Ao lost his way and failed to make contact with Huo Qubing's army as planned. Huo Qubing crossed through Juyan and reached the Qilian Mountains, killing and capturing many of the enemy.

The imperial edict read:

The swift cavalry general Huo Qubing has crossed through Juyan, passed the land of the Lesser Yuezhi, and attacked the enemy at the Qilian Mountains, capturing the Qiutu king and receiving the surrender of 2,500 of his men. He has killed or taken prisoner 3,200 of the enemy, captured five kings and their mothers, as well as the consort of the *Shanyu*, fifty-nine princes and sixty-three high ministers, generals, and chief commandants. Yet only three tenths of his own men were lost in the campaign. Therefore his fief shall be increased by 5,000 households. Moreover, the subordinate commanders who followed him to the land of the Lesser Yuezhi shall be awarded the rank of junior chiefs of the multitude.

The hawklike attacking marshal Zhao Ponu has twice accompanied Huo Qubing, executing the king of Supu, capturing the king of Jiju and his general of a thousand cavalry, seizing a king, the mother of a king, and forty-one princes and lesser leaders, and taking prisoner 3,330 of the enemy; then, advancing ahead of the rest of the army, he captured another 1,400 prisoners. Therefore he shall be granted a fief of 1,500 households and the title of Congpiao or "Follower of the Swift Cavalry General" marquis.

The subordinate commander Gouwang Gao Buzhi accompanied Huo Qubing on his campaign and captured the Huyutu king, eleven princes and minor leaders, and 7,768 of the enemy, for which he shall be enfeoffed with 1,100 households and the title of Yiguan or "Worthy of His Command" marquis. The subordinate commander Pu Duo has also won distinction and shall be enfeoffed as marquis of Huiqu.

The Heqi marquis Gongsun Ao was tried for having proceeded at too slow a pace and failing to meet with Huo Qubing's army at the scheduled rendezvous. He was condemned to execution but on payment of a fine was reduced to the status of commoner.

The soldiers and horses under the command of the older generals were no match for the exploits of Huo Qubing. For one thing, Huo Qubing always saw to it that he had a select group of soldiers, and in addition he was daring enough to penetrate deep into enemy territory, time and again riding off ahead of the main body of the army with the best cavalry. Moreover, his men seemed to enjoy the favour of Heaven, for they had never encountered any serious difficulties. The older generals, on the other hand, were constantly being tried for proceeding too slowly and failing to appear on time. As a result of his successes, Huo

Qubing's favour with the emperor increased day by day until it matched that of his uncle, the general in chief Wei Qing.

In the autumn the *Shanyu*, angry that the Hunye king, who lived in the western part of the Xiongnu realm, had so often been defeated by Huo Qubing's soldiers and had lost 20,000 or 30,000 of his men, sent a summons to the Hunye king, intending to execute him. The Hunye king, the Xiutu king, and others of their group plotted together and decided to surrender to the Han; they sent one of their men ahead to the border as envoy to make the arrangements.

At this time the grand messenger Li Xi was overseeing the construction of fortifications along the Yellow River, and the envoy from the Hunye king was brought to him. He at once hastened off by relay carriage to the capital to report to the emperor. On hearing the report, the emperor, fearing that the surrender offer was only a ruse to launch an attack on the border, dispatched Huo Qubing with a force of soldiers to go to the frontier to meet the Xiongnu.

Huo Qubing crossed the Yellow River and rode to within sight of the army of the Hunye king. Many of the subordinate generals under the Hunye king, however, were opposed to the surrender and when they saw the Han troops advancing, they turned and fled in great numbers. Huo Qubing immediately galloped into the midst of the enemy, met with the Hunye king, and cut down 8,000 of the king's men who were attempting to flee. He placed the Hunye king in a relay carriage and sent him on ahead alone to the emperor's residence, and then led all of the king's followers across the river into Han territory. The Xiongnu who surrendered numbered 30,000 or 40,000, though they were referred to as a force of 100,000. When they reached Chang'an, the emperor handed out rewards and gifts to them amounting to 10,000,000 cash. The Hunye king was enfeoffed as marquis of Teyin with 10,000 households, the petty king Huduni as marquis of Xiamo, Yingbi as marquis of Huiqu, Qinli as marquis of Heqi, and the grand household administrator Tongli as marquis of Changle.

The emperor issued an edict congratulating Huo Qubing on his achievement in these words:

> When the general of swift cavalry Huo Qubing led his forces to attack the Xiongnu, the Hunye king, who is the ruler of the western region, and his multitude of followers all came running to our army to surrender. With the enemy's provisions to feed his army and over 10,000 of their bowmen added to his force, Huo Qubing punished the fierce and violent, capturing or killing over 8,000 of the enemy and receiving the surrender of thirty-two rulers of the foreign tribes. His

fighting men suffered not a single wound, and yet a host of 100,000 of the enemy flocked about him and submitted. Thus has the fame of his numerous military exploits spread to the frontiers along the Yellow River, and we may hope from now on that they will be free from peril and may enjoy lasting peace. He shall therefore be enfeoffed with 17,000 additional households, and the number of soldiers garrisoning the provinces of Longxi, Beidi, and Shang shall be reduced to half in order to lighten the burden of frontier duty upon the empire.

Shortly afterwards the Xiongnu who had surrendered were divided into groups and sent to inhabit the five provinces of Longxi, Beidi, Shang, Shuofang, and Yunzhong which had been created in the region south of the bend of the Yellow River beyond the old frontier of the empire. There they were allowed to follow the customs of their native land and were treated as a subject nation.

The following year the Xiongnu invaded Youbeiping and Dingxiang, killing or carrying off over 1,000 Chinese. The year after, the emperor plotted with his generals, saying, "Since Zhao Xin, the marquis of Xi, has gone over to the enemy, he is acting as adviser to the *Shanyu* and is planning his strategy for him. He is convinced that the Han forces can never cross the desert, and therefore he and the *Shanyu*, despising our might, remain in the same place. Now if we were to dispatch a really large army, we could be sure of accomplishing our aim by force of numbers!" This was in the fourth year of the *yuanshou* era (119 BC).

In the spring of the same year the emperor dispatched the general in chief Wei Qing and the swift cavalry general Huo Qubing to lead a force of 50,000 cavalry each, with several hundred thousand infantry and baggage carriers to follow in their rear. All of the bravest fighters who were daring enough to risk a plunge deep into enemy territory were placed under the command of Huo Qubing. Originally Huo Qubing was supposed to ride north from Dingxiang and attack the *Shanyu*, but when enemy captives revealed that the *Shanyu* was farther east, the emperor ordered He Qubing to ride out of Dai Province. Wei Qing was then ordered to proceed from Dingxiang, while the chief of palace attendants Li Guang led the vanguard, the master of carriage Gongsun He acted as general of the left, the master of titles Zhao Yiji acted as general of the right, and the marquis of Pingyang, Cao Xiang, commanded the rear. All were under the command of Wei Qing. When the troops of the various generals had crossed the desert, a force of 50,000 men and horses in all, they were to join with the men of He Qubing and all together attack the *Shanyu*.

Zhao Xin advised the *Shanyu*, saying, "By the time the Han troops have crossed the desert their men and horses will be worn out and we can make prisoners of them without the slightest difficulty!" The *Shanyu* therefore ordered his baggage trains to withdraw far to the north, while he waited with his best troops on the northern edge of the desert.

Wei Qing's army, having ridden over 1,000 *li* beyond the border, emerged from the desert just at the point where the *Shanyu* was waiting. Spying the *Shanyu*'s forces, Wei Qing likewise pitched camp and waited. He ordered the armoured wagons to be ranged in a circle about the camp and at the same time sent out 5,000 cavalry to attack the Xiongnu. The Xiongnu dispatched some 10,000 of their own cavalry to meet the attack. Just as the sun was setting, a great wind arose, whirling dust into the faces of the men, until the two armies could no longer see each other. The Chinese then dispatched more men to swoop out to the left and right and surround the *Shanyu*. When the *Shanyu* saw how numerous the Han soldiers were and perceived that the men and horses were still in strong fighting condition, he realized that he could win no advantage in battle. In the gathering dusk he mounted a team of six mules and, accompanied by several hundred of his finest horsemen, broke straight through the Han encirclement and fled to the northwest.

By this time night had fallen, and the Han and Xiongnu soldiers were jumbled together in complete confusion, both sides suffering an equal number of dead and wounded. One of the Han commanders of the left captured a prisoner who informed him that the *Shanyu* had already fled before dark, and the Han army accordingly dispatched a party of light cavalry to pursue him in the night. Wei Qing and the rest of his army followed after, while the Xiongnu fighters scattered in all directions. By the time dawn came, the Han army had travelled over 200 *li*, but they were unable to overtake the *Shanyu*. All in all, Wei Qing killed or captured over 10,000 of the enemy. He then proceeded to Zhao Xin's fort at Mt. Tianyan, where he seized the Xiongnu's supplies of grain and feasted his men. He and his army remained there only a day, however, and then, setting fire to all the remaining grain, began the journey home.

When Wei Qing encountered the forces of the *Shanyu*, his generals of the vanguard and the right, Li Guang and Zhao Yiji, were making their way around by a separate route to the east, but they lost their way and failed to arrive in time to take part in the attack on the *Shanyu*. It was not until Wei Qing had led his army back south across the desert that he met up with Li Guang and Zhao Yiji. He sent his chief clerk to question Li Guang and draw up a list of charges against him, intending to send a full report to the emperor, but Li Guang committed suicide. When Zhao Yiji returned to the capital he was handed over to the prison officials but was allowed to ransom his life and become a commoner. By the time Wei Qing's army recrossed the border into China he and his men had succeeded in killing or capturing 19,000 of the enemy.

The *Shanyu* in his flight was separated from his forces for over ten days, during which time the Luli King of the Right, learning of his disappearance, set himself up as the new *Shanyu*. When the real *Shanyu* regained possession of his army, however, the Luli king renounced his claim to the title.

Meanwhile, Huo Qubing with his 50,000 cavalry rode more than 1,000 *li* north from Dai and Youbeiping and attacked the forces of the Wise King of the Left. He was accompanied by a force of carriages and baggage similar to that which travelled with Wei Qing's army, but he had no subordinate generals under his command. Instead he appointed men like Li Gan, Li Guang's son, and others to act as division commanders in place of subordinate generals. He succeeded in killing and capturing so many of the enemy that his achievements exceeded those of Wei Qing.

When Huo Qubing's army returned to the capital, the emperor issued an edict which read:

> The general of swift cavalry Huo Qubing has led forth the troops and personally commanded a force of barbarians captured in previous campaigns, carrying with him only light provisions and crossing the great desert. Fording the Huozhangqu, he executed the enemy leader Bijuqi and then turned to strike at the enemy general of the left, cutting down his pennants and seizing his war drums. He crossed over Mt. Lihou, forded the Gonglü, and captured the Tuntou king, the Han king, and one other, three in all, as well as eighty-three generals, ministers, household administrators, and chief commandants of the enemy. He performed the Feng sacrifice at Mt. Langjuxu and the Shan sacrifice at Mt. Guyan, ascending the hills and gazing out across the sea of sand. He seized a great multitude of the enemy, taking 70,443 captives, while only three tenths of his own men were lost in the campaign. He snatched the food supplies of the enemy and penetrated deep into their territory, and his provisions never gave out. Therefore his fief shall be increased by 5,800 households.

The governor of Youbeiping, Lu Bode, arrived on time at his rendezvous with the general of swift cavalry at Yucheng and from there accompanied him as far as Mt. Taoyu, killing or capturing 2,700 of the enemy, for which he shall be enfeoffed as marquis of Fuli with 1,600 households. The chief commandant of Beidi, Xing Shan, accompanied the general of swift cavalry in capturing the enemy kings, for which he shall be enfeoffed as marquis of Yiyang with 1,200 households. The Yinchun king Fuluzhi and the Louzhuan king Yijijian, Xiongnu leaders who have come over to the side of the Han, both accompanied the general of swift cavalry and won distinction in the campaign. Therefore Fuluzhi shall be enfeoffed as Zhuang marquis with 1,300 households, and Yijijian shall be enfeoffed as Zhongli marquis with 1,800 households. The Congpiao marquis Zhao Ponu and the marquis of Changwu, An Ji, both won distinction under the command of the general of swift cavalry and their fiefs shall be increased by 300 households each. The subordinate commander Li Gan captured the enemy pennants and drums and shall be made a marquis within the Pass with the revenue from 200 households. The subordinate commander Xu Ziwei shall be awarded the rank of superior chief of the multitude.

In addition, a great many of Huo Qubing's officers and men were appointed as officials and presented with rewards. Wei Qing, on the other hand, received no increase in his fief, and not one of the men in his army was made a marquis.

When the armies of the two generals rode out across the border, they had with them a total of 140,000 horses, both government-owned and private, but when they recrossed the border they had less than 30,000 horses left. The emperor created a new rank of grand marshal and appointed both Wei Qing and Huo Qubing to it. In this way he made it possible for Huo Qubing to enjoy the same rank and salary as Wei Qing. From this time on Wei Qing day by day retired farther into the background, while Huo Qubing enjoyed ever-increasing honour. Many of Wei Qing's old friends and followers deserted him and went to serve Huo Qubing, where they were immediately awarded offices and titles. Only Ren An refused to follow their example.[4]

Huo Qubing was a man of few words and was little given to idle talk, but he possessed great daring and initiative. The emperor once tried to teach him the principles of warfare as expounded by the ancient philosophers Sun Zi and Wu Zi, but he replied, "The only thing that matters is how one's own strategies

---

[4]Ren An was the friend to whom Sima Qian wrote his famous letter explaining why he chose to suffer castration rather than commit suicide.

are going to work. There is no need to study the old-fashioned rules of warfare!"

Another time the emperor had a mansion built for Huo Qubing and summoned him to look at it, but he only commented, "While the Xiongnu have still not been wiped out there is no time to think about houses!" Because of such incidents the emperor regarded him with even greater favour.

Huo Qubing had become an attendant in the palace when he was still young, and after he became honoured he took little thought for the men in his command. Whenever he went on a campaign, the emperor would send his own steward along with twenty or thirty carriages full of provisions for Huo Qubing's private consumption. When the army returned to the capital, the baggage carts would still be full to overflowing with grain and meat, although the soldiers would be starving. Again, when he was campaigning beyond the border there were times when his men were so short of provisions that many of them did not have the strength to stand up, and yet Huo Qubing would make them dig out a playing field for him so he could amuse himself at football. He did many other things of a similar nature.

Wei Qing, on the other hand, was a kindly, retiring man, who attempted to ingratiate himself with the emperor by being mild and compliant. Yet no one in the empire had a good word to say for him.

Huo Qubing died in the sixth year of *yuanshou* (117 BC), three years after taking part in the campaign described above. The emperor was deeply grieved and ordered soldiers from the tribes of Xiongnu who had submitted to Han rule to be called to the capital and ranged along the road from Chang'an to Mouling bearing iron weapons. At Mouling he had a grave mound constructed in the shape of the Qilian Mountains. In recognition of Huo Qubing's military achievements and his services in extending the borders of the empire, the emperor awarded him the double posthumous name of Jinghuan or "Righteous and Martial" marquis.

His son Huo Shan or Huo Zihou succeeded to the marquisate. The emperor was very fond of him and wanted to make him a general when he grew up, but six years later, in the first year of *yuanfeng* (110 BC), the boy died. He was given the title of Ai or "Pitiful" marquis. He left no heir and the fief was abolished.

Sometime after Huo Qubing died, Wei Qing's oldest son, Wei Kang, the marquis of Yichun, was tried for some offense and deprived of his marquisate. Five years later Wei Kang's two younger brothers, Wei Buyi, the marquis of Yin'an, and Wei Deng, the marquis of Fagan, were accused of having presented faulty tribute money and were likewise deprived of their marquisates. (It was two years after this that Huo Qubing's son died and his marquisate was abolished.) Four years later, the general in chief Wei Qing died and was given the posthumous title of Lie or "Ardent" marquis. His son Wei Kang was allowed to succeed his father and become marquis of Changping.

Wei Qing died fourteen years after he led the great expedition against the Xiongnu and surrounded the *Shanyu*. The reason he made no further attacks on the Xiongnu was that the Han at this time was short of horses and its troops were busy putting down the rebellion in the two kingdoms of Yue, attacking Korea in the east and the Qiang and other barbarian tribes in the southwest. Therefore the attacks on the Xiongnu were suspended for a considerable time.

Wei Qing's wife was Princess Pingyang, the younger sister of Emperor Wu, and for this reason their son Wei Kang, although he had been deprived of his own marquisate, was allowed to succeed to his father's title. (Six years later Wei Kang was tried for some offence and deprived of the marquisate a second time.)[5]

The following is a brief résuméof the accomplishments of Wei Qing and Huo Qubing and the generals who served under them:

General in chief Wei Qing, who achieved the highest distinction. Made seven attacks on the Xiongnu, capturing or killing over 50,000 of the enemy. Fought one encounter with the *Shanyu*, brought the region south of the bend of the Yellow River under Han control, and established the province of Shuofang. Fief increased twice, reaching a final total of 11,800 households. Three sons also enfeoffed as marquises with 1,300 households each, making a grand total of 15,700 households for the family. Nine subordinate commanders and generals who served under him became marquises, and fourteen were made full generals in their own right. Among his subordinate generals were the following men:

Li Guang. He has his own biography and will not be treated here.

General Gongsun He. A native of Yiqu whose ancestors were barbarians. His father, Gongsun Hunye, became marquis of Pingqu during the reign of Emperor Jing but was later tried for some offence and deprived of the title. When Emperor Wu was still heir apparent, Gongsun He served in his household. Eight years after Emperor Wu came to the throne, Gongsun He, who held the post of master of carriage, was appointed general of light carriage and sent to garrison Mayi. Four years later went on a campaign out of Yunzhong. Five years

---

[5]The sentence in parentheses is a later addition.

later was made cavalry general and served in an expedition under Wei Qing. Was enfeoffed as marquis of Nanpao because of his achievements. A year later again accompanied Wei Qing as general of the left in an expedition north from Dingxiang but failed to win any merit. Four years later was accused of some fault in tribute money and deprived of marquisate. Was appointed Fuju General eight years later and rode over 2,000 *li* north from Wuyuan but failed to achieve any distinction. Eight years later was promoted from post of master of carriage to that of chancellor and was enfeoffed as marquis of Geyi. Served as a general in seven attacks on the Xiongnu but never won any outstanding merit. Was twice enfeoffed as a marquis and later became chancellor. (His son Gongsun Jingsheng was accused of adultery with Princess Yangshi and of practising black magic. The entire family was wiped out and no heir left to succeed to the marquisate.)[6]

General Li Xi. A native of Yuzhi. Served Emperor Jing and, eight years after Emperor Wu came to the throne, was appointed general of bowmen and sent to garrison Mayi. Six years later was made a general in a campaign out of Dai and three years later accompanied Wei Qing out of Shuofang. Won no merit in any of these actions. Served as a general three times; later acted as grand messenger.

General Gongsun Ao. A native of Yiqu; served as palace attendant to Emperor Wu. In the twelfth year after Emperor Wu's accession to the throne was made general of light cavalry and sent out of Dai. Lost 7,000 men; condemned to death but on payment of fine was made a commoner. Five years later accompanied Wei Qing as subordinate commander and won distinction. Enfeoffed as Heqi marquis. One year later was appointed general of the centre and accompanied Wei Qing on two campaigns out of Dingxiang but won no merit. Two years later was appointed general on a campaign out of Beidi. Failed to reach rendezvous with Huo Qubing at appointed time; condemned to death but on payment of fine was made a commoner. Two years later accompanied Wei Qing as subordinate commander; no merit. Fourteen years later appointed Yinyu General and ordered to build the "City for Receiving Surrender". Several years later again made two attacks on Xiongnu as Yinyu General. Reached Yuwu but lost most of his men. Thrown into prison and condemned to death (but managed to escape by feigning death and lived in hiding among the common people for five or six years. Was later discovered and thrown into

---

[6]This and other passages in parentheses are later additions.

prison again. Tried on charges that his wife was practising black magic; he and his entire family executed). Served as a general four times in attacks on the Xiongnu; enfeoffed as marquis once.

General Li Ju. Native of Yunzhong; served under Emperor Jing. In seventeenth year after Emperor Wu's accession, while holding post of left prefect of the capital, was appointed general of strong bowmen. One year later he again served as general of strong bowmen.

General Li Cai. Native of Chengji; served Emperors Wen, Jing, and Wu. Accompanied Wei Qing as general of light carriage and won distinction. Enfeoffed as marquis of Lean. Later became chancellor but was tried for an offence and committed suicide.

General Zhang Cigong. Native of Hedong. Served as subordinate commander to Wei Qing and won merit. Enfeoffed as marquis of Antou. After death of Empress Dowager Wang was made general and put in charge of the Northern Garrison. One year later accompanied Wei Qing. Served as general twice but was tried for some offence and deprived of marquisate. His father, Zhang Long, a skilful archer, served as armed archer of the light carriage division and enjoyed favour with Emperor Jing.

General Su Jian. Native of Duling. Served as subordinate commander to Wei Qing and won merit. Enfeoffed as marquis of Pingling. Appointed general and sent to garrison Shuofang. Four years later was appointed scouting and attacking general and accompanied Wei Qing out of Shuofang. One year later, as general of the right, accompanied Wei Qing on two attacks out of Dingxiang. Allowed Zhao Xin to escape and lost his own army; condemned to death but permitted to pay fine and become a commoner. Later became governor of Dai Province and died in office. Grave situated in Dayou County.

General Zhao Xin. Formerly a high minister of the Xiongnu but surrendered to the Han and was enfeoffed as marquis of Xi. In seventeenth year after Emperor Wu's accession was appointed general of vanguard and attacked *Shanyu*; surrendered to the Xiongnu.

General Zhang Qian. Sent as envoy to Bactria; on return was appointed subordinate commander in campaign under Wei Qing. Won merit and was enfeoffed as Bowang marquis. Three years later was made general and went on campaign out of Youbeiping. Failed to arrive at rendezvous point on time; condemned to death but allowed to pay fine and become a commoner. Later sent as envoy to Wusun barbarians. Became grand messenger and died in office. Grave situated in Hanzhong.

General Zhao Yiji. Native of Daixu. In twenty-second year after Emperor Wu's accession was made general of right while holding post of master of titles; accompanied Wei Qing out of Dingxiang. Lost his way; condemned to death but allowed to pay fine and become a commoner.

General Cao Xiang. Marquis of Pingyang. Appointed general of rear and accompanied Wei Qing on campaign out of Dingxiang. He was a grandson of Cao Can, the famous statesman.

General Han Yue. Illegitimate grandson of marquis of Gonggao.[7] Won distinction as a subordinate commander under Wei Qing. Enfeoffed as marquis of Longwo but later accused of irregularity in tribute money and deprived of title. In sixth year of *yuanding* (112 BC) was summoned and appointed General Who Traverses the Sea and sent to attack Eastern Yue. Won distinction and was enfeoffed as marquis of Andao. In third year of *taichu* (102 BC) was appointed scouting and attacking general and sent to garrison the string of forts beyond Wuyuan. (Appointed superintendent of the imperial household. Dug up the palace of Crown Prince Wei and discovered the charms by which the prince was attempting to bewitch the emperor. Murdered by the crown prince.)

General Guo Chang. Native of Yunzhong. Served as subordinate commander under Wei Qing. In fourth year of *yuanfeng* (107 BC), while serving as palace counsellor, was made Barbarian Quelling General and sent to garrison Shuofang. Returned and attacked the kingdom of Kunming. Failed to achieve any merit and was relieved of post.

General Xun Zhi. Native of Guangwu in Taiyuan. Won audience with the emperor because of skill as carriage driver and was appointed to serve in the palace. Several times served as subordinate commander under Wei Qing. In third year of *yuanfeng* (108 BC) was appointed general of left and sent to attack Korea. No merit. Was tried and executed on charges of having arrested his fellow commander, Yang Pu.

General of Swift Cavalry Huo Qubing, who achieved highest distinction. Made six attacks on Xiongnu, four as a general. Killed or captured 110,000 of the enemy. When the Hunye king surrendered with 30,000 or 40,000 followers, he opened up the regions of Hexi and Jiuquan and greatly decreased the

---

[7] A Xiongnu leader who came over to the side of the Chinese and was enfeoffed as a marquis. He was said to be a descendant of Hann Xin, the king who rebelled and fled to the Xiongnu in the time of Gaozu.

incursions of the western barbarians. Fief was four times increased, reaching total of 15,100 households. Six of his officers won merit and were enfeoffed as marquises, and two later became generals.

General Lu Bode. Native of Pingzhou. Governor of Youbeiping; served under Huo Qubing and won merit. Enfeoffed as marquis of Fuli. After death of Huo Qubing became colonel of the guard and was appointed General Who Calms the Waves, and attacked and defeated Southern Yue. Fief increased. Later tried and deprived of marquisate. Appointed chief commandant of strong bowmen and sent to garrison Juyan, where he died.

General Zhao Ponu. Originally from Jiuquan but fled to territory of the Xiongnu. Later came over to the side of the Han and served as marshal under Huo Qubing in campaign out of Beidi. Won distinction in this campaign and was enfeoffed as Congpiao marquis. Tried for irregularity in tribute money and deprived of marquisate. One year later appointed Xionghe General and attacked barbarians, advancing as far as Xionghe River. No merit. Two years later attacked and captured king of Loulan. Again enfeoffed, this time as marquis of Zhuoye. Six years later was appointed Junji General and led 20,000 cavalry in attack on Xiongnu Wise King of Left. Fought Wise King and was surrounded by 80,000 enemy cavalry; taken prisoner and lost his army. (Lived ten years among the Xiongnu but fled with Anguo, the Xiongnu crown prince, and returned to the Han. Later tried on charges of witchcraft and executed along with his family.)

When the Wei family rose to power, the general in chief Wei Qing was the first to be enfeoffed. Later five other members of the family were enfeoffed as marquises. In the course of twenty-four years, however, all five were deprived of their titles, so that in the end not a single member of the family was a marquis.

The Grand Historian remarks; Su Jian has told me that he once reprimanded the general in chief Wei Qing for the fact that, although he occupied a position of honour and trust, he enjoyed no praise among the worthy men of the empire. "You should observe how the famous generals of antiquity worked to select and promote men of worth, and strive to imitate their example!" Su Jian told him. But General Wei Qing declined to accept the advice, saying, "Ever since Dou Ying and Tian Fen by their generosity gathered together their own groups of followers and caused such trouble, the Son of Heaven has been enraged at the thought of anyone doing such a thing. It is the prerogative of the ruler of men to attract others to his service and to decide who is worthy of promotion and who is not. An official's job is simply to obey the laws and fulfil the duties of his post and that is all. What has he to do with the promotion of others?"

Huo Qubing was apparently of the same opinion. That is the kind of generals they were.

SHI JI 20: THE CHRONOLOGICAL TABLE OF MARQUISES ENFEOFFED FROM THE JIANYUAN ERA ON: INTRODUCTION

North they struck at the powerful Xiongnu; south they put down the strong forces of Yue. In the campaigns against the barbarians they won the merits which are set forth here. Thus I made "The Chronological Table of Marquises Enfeoffed from the *Jianyuan* Era (140-135 BC) on".

The Grand Historian remarks: The Xiongnu broke off peaceful relations and attacked the northern border where the roads lead across it. The people of Minyue wilfully marched against Eastern Ou, which begged to surrender to us and receive assistance. Thus the northern and southern barbarians in turn committed outrages against the glory of the powerful Han, whose subjects won merit in battle against them and received fiefs, proving themselves the equals of their ancestors. For do we not read in the *Odes* and *Documents* how the men of the Three Dynasties

> Smote the northern barbarians
> And punished the tribes of Jing and Shu;[1]

have we not heard how Duke Huan of Qi crossed through the state of Yan to strike at the mountain barbarians; how King Wuling of Zhao, though ruler of a small and unimportant state, brought the *Shanyu* to his knees; how Duke Mu of Qin, by following the advice of Boli Xi, became dictator of the western barbarians; and how the rulers of Wu and Chu, feudal lords of the Zhou, marched against the hundred tribes of Yue? How much more so now, therefore, when all China is united under the rule of an enlightened emperor, excelling in both civil and military arts, who has rolled up the land within the four seas like a mat and gathered into his realm a multitude of millions? How could he sit quietly by and not march against those who violate our borders? Therefore he sent forth his

---

[1] "Bigong" of the "Temple Odes of Lu", *Book of Odes*.

armies to strike the powerful Xiongnu in the north and to put down the strong forces of Yue in the south, and enfeoffed his victorious generals as I have recorded here.

SHI JI 112: THE BIOGRAPHIES OF THE MARQUIS OF PINGJIN AND ZHUFU YAN

While the high ministers and members of the imperial family were all outdoing each other in luxurious living, Gongsun Hong, the marquis of Pingjin, alone, by his frugality in dress and food, set an example for the other officials. Thus I made "The Biographies of the Marquis of Pingjin and Zhufu Yan".

The Marquis of Pingjin

The chancellor Gongsun Hong, whose polite name was Ji, was a native of the district of Xue in the state of Zichuan, formerly a part of Qi. In his youth he served as a prison official of Xue but was forced to retire because of some offence. His family was very poor and he made a living by raising pigs on the seacoast. When he was over forty he studied the *Spring and Autumn Annals* and the theories of the various philosophical schools. He took care of his stepmother, treating her with great respect and filial piety.

In the first year of the *jianyuan* era (140 BC), when the present emperor came to the throne, a call was sent out for men of high moral character and literary ability to take service in the government. At this time Gongsun Hong was sixty, but because of his worth he was summoned and appointed as an erudite. He was sent on a mission to the Xiongnu, but when he returned and made his report, his views did not accord with those of the emperor, who grew angry and concluded that he was a man of no ability. Gongsun Hong thereupon retired from his post on grounds of illness and returned to his home.

In the fifth year of *yuanguang* (130 BC) a call was again sent out summoning men of literary ability to court. The state of Zichuan once more recommended Gongsun Hong. Gongsun Hong begged the men of his state not to submit the recommendation, saying, "I have already answered the summons once in the past and journeyed west to the capital, but because of my lack of ability I was dismissed and sent home. I beg you to recommend someone else."

But the people of his state insisted upon sending Gongsun Hong.

When Gongsun Hong and the other Confucian scholars who had answered the summons, 100 men or more, arrived at the office of the master of ritual, they were ordered to write answers to some question of government policy. At the examination Gongsun Hong was seated near the bottom of the group, but when the results were presented to the throne, the emperor selected Gongsun Hong's answer and gave it the highest mark. The emperor then summoned Gongsun Hong for an audience and, struck by his handsome and imposing appearance, once more honoured him with the post of erudite.

At this time the Han government was busy building a road out of China to the lands of the southwestern barbarians and setting up new provinces in the region, undertakings which were causing great hardship to the people of Ba and Shu Provinces in the west. The emperor ordered Gongsun Hong to go on a mission to the area to observe what progress had been made. When he returned and made his report, he strongly criticized the project, insisting that there was no benefit to be gained from establishing communication with the southwestern barbarians. The emperor, however, paid no attention to his views.

Gongsun Hong was a man of broad and unusual ideas and wide learning. He always used to say that the greatest fault in a ruler was lack of breadth and magnanimity, while the greatest failing in ministers was a lack of frugality. Gongsun Hong himself wore the plainest hemp robes and never ate more than one meat dish at a meal. When his stepmother died he mourned for three years. Whenever debates were held at court he would simply state the pros and cons of the question and leave the emperor to make his own decision; he never ventured to contradict the emperor to his face or argue with the other ministers in court.

The emperor observed that he was sincere in action, that his speeches were full of depth, that he was experienced in legal and bureaucratic affairs and in addition gave a strict Confucian garb and trimming to everything he did, all of which pleased the emperor greatly. In the course of two years at court Gongsun Hong advanced to the post of left prefect of the capital.

Whenever he made some proposal at court, if the emperor did not approve of it, he would never attempt to argue his case before the other ministers. Instead he and the master of titles chief commandant Ji An would ask to speak to the emperor in private. Ji An would then begin by explaining the proposal and Gongsun Hong would follow after him and second his opinion. The emperor was invariably pleased by this procedure and would agree to whatever they advised. In this way Gongsun Hong came to enjoy greater and greater favour with the emperor.

Once he made an agreement with the other high ministers that he would support certain proposals that they were going to make, but when the group appeared before the emperor, Gongsun Hong broke all of his promises and simply agreed with whatever opinion the emperor expressed. Ji An began to berate him in front of the whole group at court, saying, "The men of Qi are full of deceit and have no respect for truth! Originally you agreed to cooperate with the rest of us in supporting these proposals, but now you have gone back on your word in every case. This is downright disloyalty!"

When the emperor asked Gongsun Hong what he had to say to this, he apologized and replied, "Those who understand me think I am loyal; those who do not understand me think I am disloyal." The emperor approved of his answer and from then on, whenever any of the emperor's favoured ministers criticized Gongsun Hong, the emperor only treated him with greater favour and generosity.

In the third year of *yuanshuo* (126 BC), when Zhang Ou retired, Gongsun Hong was appointed to succeed him as imperial secretary.

At this time communications were being established with the Southwestern barbarians, the province of Canghai was being set up also in the east, and in the north fortifications were being built in the newly created province of Shuofang. Gongsun Hong several times criticized these moves, saying that the wealth and manpower of China were being exhausted in the service of worthless foreign regions, and begging that the projects be abandoned. The emperor then ordered Zhu Maichen and others of the court ministers to refute Gongsun Hong's opinion. They drew up a list of ten reasons why the establishment of the province of Shuofang would be of advantage to the nation. Gongsun Hong then professed himself unable to refute a single one of their arguments and apologized, saying, "I am a simple country man from east of the mountains. I had no idea that such advantages as these were entailed. I beg therefore that the projects among the southwestern barbarians and in Canghai be abandoned and that the government concentrate upon that in Shuofang." The emperor gave his consent.

One day in court Ji An said to the emperor, "Gongsun Hong occupies one of the three highest offices in the government and enjoys a very large salary, and yet he goes around wearing a plain hemp robe. This is sheer hypocrisy!"

The emperor turned and questioned Gongsun Hong about this, whereupon the latter apologized and replied, "It is true. Among all my friends in high office, none is closer to me than Ji An, and yet today he has accused me before the whole court. There is no doubt that he has put his finger upon my shortcoming. For me to occupy one of the three highest posts and yet wear a plain hemp robe is indeed no more than a hypocritical show by which I had hoped to fish for fame. In the old days, they say, when Guan Zhong was serving as prime minister to the state of Qi, he had a great mansion called the 'Three Returnings'[1] and strove to imitate the luxurious living of his lord, Duke Huan. He helped Duke Huan to become one of the feudal hegemons of the time, and yet he tended to usurp to himself the way of living of his lord. On the other hand, when Yan Ying was acting as prime minister to Duke Jing of Qi he ate no more than one meat dish at a meal and his wife never wore silk robes, and yet at that time also the state of Qi was well governed. In his case he strove to live in the same manner as the common people. Now though I occupy the post of imperial secretary I wear a plain hemp robe so that there will be no difference between myself and any other official down to the lowest clerk in the government. Indeed, it is just as Ji An has said. And if it had not been for his outspoken loyalty, how would Your Majesty have ever become aware of the situation?"

The emperor considered that Gongsun Hong had replied with exemplary modesty and treated him with even greater favour; eventually he enfeoffed him as marquis of Pingjin.

By nature Gongsun Hong was suspicious and envious of others. On the surface he seemed to be magnanimous, but at heart he was a stern man. If he ever had a falling out with anyone, although he pretended to be as friendly with the person as before, he would work in secret to bring about his downfall. The execution of Zhufu Yan and the transfer of Dong Zhongshu to Jiaoxi were both due to his efforts. He himself ate only unpolished grain and no more than one meat dish at a meal, but if any of his old friends or people he liked came to his house and asked for food and clothing, he would supply them with whatever they needed out of his salary, so that his family never accumulated any wealth. For this he won praise among worthy men.

Just at the time when it was discovered that the kings of Huainan and Hengshan were plotting revolt and the investigations of the conspirators were

---

[1] There are various interpretations of the word "three returnings". I have followed the one which regards it as the name of Guan Zhong's mansion, though some commentators take it to mean that he had three wives. Guan Zhong and Yan Ying were famous statesmen of the seventh and sixth centuries BC respectively.

being pressed with the greatest intensity, Gongsun Hong became seriously ill. He considered that he had achieved no merit that warranted his being enfeoffed as a marquis. In addition, he held the post of chancellor at this time and by rights ought to have worked to enlighten the ruler, bring order to the nation, and see to it that the inhabitants conducted themselves as loyal subjects and obedient sons. Instead of this, however, there were feudal lords who were actually plotting revolt, all of which proved, he believed, that he had failed in his duties as chief minister of the nation. He was afraid that if his illness grew worse and he should die he would have no way to atone for his failures, and he therefore wrote a letter to the throne which read:

> I have heard that there are five abiding duties to be observed throughout the world, and three means by which they are put into practice. The five duties are the hierarchical relationships to be observed between ruler and subject, father and son, older and younger brother, husband and wife, and senior and junior. The three abiding virtues by which these are brought to realization are wisdom, benevolence, and courage. Therefore it is said that to be diligent in action is near to benevolence, to be fond of inquiry is near to wisdom, and to understand dishonour is near to courage. He who knows these three will know how to govern himself, and he who knows how to govern himself will then understand how to govern others. There has never been anyone in the world who could govern others without first being able to govern himself. This principle has remained unchanged for a hundred generations.[2]
>
> Now Your Majesty has in person practised the greatest filial piety, surveyed the Three Dynasties of antiquity, established the principles of the Zhou rulers, and shown yourself proficient in both civil and military affairs, encouraging the worthy and rewarding them with stipends, weighing the abilities of others and selecting them for government office.
>
> I, on the other hand, have no more worth than a tired old horse, nor have I ever won any distinction on the field of battle. Your Majesty, in an act of excessive generosity, has selected me from among the rank and file, enfeoffed me as a marquis, and promoted me to one of the

---

[2] In wording and thought, this passage closely parallels the famous Confucian work, the *Zhongyong* or *Doctrine of the Mean*, XX, 8-11.

three highest posts in the government. Yet there has been nothing in my actions or ability that is worthy of praise. From the beginning I have been undeserving of these honours, and now that I am ill, if I should drop dead in service like one of the palace dogs or horses, and end tumbled in a ditch, I would never have the opportunity to repay the generosity I have enjoyed or atone for my faults. I therefore beg to return the seals of the marquisate I have received and be allowed to retire as a commoner so that I may clear the way for true men of ability.

The emperor replied to this as follows:

In ancient times merit was rewarded and virtue praised. When the nation was well ordered, civil accomplishments were honoured, and only when disaster threatened was warfare accorded a higher place. This principle has never changed. Day and night I have thought how I might fulfil the obligations of my high office, fearing always that I would be unable to bring peace to the nation. You who have shared with me the governing of the empire must know this. It is the duty of a gentleman to love good and hate evil, and this too you must know. Your careful and judicious actions are always before my eyes. Now, although you have unfortunately been afflicted with this illness, brought on by frost and dew, what reason is there to despair of recovery? And yet you have submitted a letter, returning your marquisate and begging for retirement: this is only to make clear to everyone my lack of virtue! Now that you have some leisure from your duties, you must reconsider your decision. Do your best to rally your spirits and take what aid you can from medicines.

At the same time the emperor granted Gongsun Hong a vacation and presented him with meat, wine, and various silk goods. After a few months Gongsun Hong recovered his health and was able to resume his duties.

In the second year of *yuanshou* (121 BC), however, he fell ill again and died while holding the office of chancellor. His son Gongsun Du succeeded him as marquis of Pingjin and became governor of Shanyang, but some ten years later he was tried for an offence and deprived of the marquisate.

Zhufu Yan

Zhufu Yan was a native of Linzi in Qi. He studied the diplomatic and military theories of the Warring States period, and in his later years the *Book of*

Changes, the *Spring and Autumn Annals*, and the works of the various philosophers. He travelled about among the scholars of Qi but could find none who would treat him with any liberality. On the contrary they refused to have anything to do with him, so that he could get nowhere in his native state of Qi. His family was very poor and he likewise failed in all attempts to borrow money. Later he travelled north to Yan, Zhao, and the region of Zhongshan, but again was unable to find anyone who would employ him. He suffered great hardship on his travels.

He finally decided that it was no use seeking employment among the feudal lords and during the first year of the *yuanguang* era (134 BC) of the present emperor he journeyed west beyond the Pass to the capital, where he obtained an interview with General Wei Qing.

Wei Qing mentioned him several times to the emperor, but the emperor failed to summon him to court. Although he had very little money, he continued to linger about the capital until many of the officials and their retainers had grown to dislike him. At last he decided to submit a letter directly to the throne. His petition was brought before the emperor in the morning, and that same evening he was summoned for an audience. His memorial dealt with nine items, of which eight were concerned with legal matters. The other item was a criticism of the attacks being made on the Xiongnu. This portion of his letter read as follows:

> I have heard that an enlightened sovereign does not take offence at remonstrances, no matter how severe, so long as they broaden his understanding; and that a loyal subject does not hesitate for fear of the gravest punishment if he feels that outspoken criticism is needed. Only in this way can all matters of policy be effectively disposed of, and the achievements of the ruler passed on to his heirs for ten thousand generations. Now I have not dared to hide my feelings of loyalty for fear of death and have ventured to state these unworthy opinions. I beg Your Majesty to forgive my shortcomings and to deign to consider these words.
>
> In the *Rules of the Marshal* describing the ancient art of warfare it is said that, no matter how large a nation may be, if it is too fond of fighting it is doomed to perish. It is also said that, no matter how peaceful the world may be, if men forget warfare altogether, danger will ensue.
>
> Now the empire has been brought to peace and the Son of Heaven

sings the song of victory, carrying out the great spring and autumn hunts, while the feudal lords review their troops in the spring and train their soldiers in the fall. Thus warfare is not forgotten.

And yet it is said that anger is the thief of virtue, weapons are the tools of evil, and strife is the least noble of actions. In ancient times, if the ruler became truly angry, he did not stop until he had strewn the ground with corpses and loosed a river of blood. Therefore a sage king regards the venting of anger as a grave matter indeed.

No one who has devoted himself to arms and spent all his efforts on military endeavours has ever failed to regret it. In earlier times the First Emperor of the Qin, relying upon his might in battle, gobbled up the whole world, seized the other warring states, and united all within the four seas into a single domain, winning as great distinction as the rulers of the Three Dynasties of antiquity. And yet he would not cease his warfare there, but wanted to go on and attack the Xiongnu.

His minister Li Si reprimanded him, saying, "It is impossible. The Xiongnu have no fixed cities or forts and no stores of provisions or grain. They move from place to place like flocks of birds and are just as difficult to catch and control. Now if we send parties of lightly equipped soldiers deep into their territory, our men will soon run out of food, and if we try to send provisions after them, the baggage trains will never reach them in time. Even if we were to seize control of the Xiongnu lands, they would bring us no profit, and even if we were to win over their people, we could never administer and keep control of them. And if, after we had won victory, we were to massacre them, this would hardly be a fitting action for a Son of Heaven, who must act as a father and mother to the people. Therefore we would only be wearing out the strength of China in an attempt to have our way with the Xiongnu. Surely this is not a wise policy!"

But the First Emperor would not listen to his advice and sent his general Meng Tian with troops to attack the barbarians. He extended the borders of the empire 1,000 *li*, establishing the frontier along the Yellow River, but the land he won over was nothing but brackish swamp, unfit for the cultivation of the five grains.

After this the young men were called up from all over the empire and sent to guard the northern frontier along the river. The troops spent over ten years fighting in the wastes and wildernesses, where they died in untold numbers, and yet they were never able to extend the empire north beyond the Yellow River. Surely this was not because there were not enough fighting men, or because their weapons and equipment were insufficient. Rather it was because the circumstances made any other outcome impossible.

At the same time the whole empire was ordered to rush fodder and grain to the soldiers. Shipments were sent from as far away as the provinces of Huangzhui and Langya along the seacoast, but by the time they had been transported to the northern frontier along the Yellow River, no more than one picul out of an original thirty bushels remained. Though the men worked the fields as hard as they could, they were unable to supply enough provisions, and though the women wove and spun, they could not produce enough tents and hangings for the army. Soon the common people were exhausted; there was no surplus left to feed the orphans and widows, the children and the old people; and the roads were filled with dead and dying. This was why the empire turned in revolt against the Qin.

Later, when Emperor Gaozu had won control of the empire and was working to bring the border areas under control, he heard that the Xiongnu were gathered north of the valley of Dai and decided to attack them. His imperial secretary Cheng Jin advised him against this, saying, "It is impossible. It is the nature of the Xiongnu to swarm together like so many beasts, and to disperse again like flocks of birds. Trying to catch them is like grabbing at a shadow. In spite of all Your Majesty's noble virtue, I fear that any attempt to attack the Xiongnu will only lead to danger!"

But Emperor Gaozu did not heed his advice. Instead he rode north to the valley of Dai and, as Cheng Jin had feared, was surrounded by the enemy at Pingcheng. He regretted deeply what he had done and forthwith dispatched Liu Jing to conclude a peace alliance with the Xiongnu, and from that time on the empire was able to forget the sorrows of war.

It is said in the *Art of War*: "He who raises an army of 100,000 must spend 1,000 pieces of gold a day." The Qin was forever calling together armies and sending its soldiers into the field, 200,000 and 300,000 of them. But although they won distinction by overpowering armies, slaying generals, and taking the *Shanyu* prisoner, such victories served only to insure the hatred of the enemy and deepen their resentment; in no way did they compensate for the expense which they cost the empire. Any policy which empties the treasuries and arsenals and exhausts the strength of the common people merely for the purpose of having one's way with foreign nations is hardly a sound one.

It is not only our generation which finds the Xiongnu difficult to conquer and control. They make a business of pillage and plunder, and indeed this would seem to be their inborn nature. Ever since the times of Emperor Shun and the rulers of the Xia, Shang, and Zhou dynasties, no attempt has ever been made to order or control them; rather they have been regarded as beasts to be pastured, not as members of the human race.

Now Your Majesty does not observe how the Xia, Shang, and Zhou dynasties managed to preserve their rules for so long, but imitates only the mistakes of the recent past, which is a source of grave concern to me and of tribulation and trial to the common people.

Moreover, warfare prolonged over a great period often gives rise to rebellion, and the burden of military service is apt to lead to disaffection, for the people along the border are subjected to great strain and hardship until they think only of breaking away, while the generals and officers grow suspicious of each other and begin to bargain with the enemy. It was circumstances such as these which caused Zhao Tuo to turn against the Qin and make himself an independent ruler in Southern Yue, and the Qin general Zhang Han to desert to the army of the rebellious nobles. The rule of the Qin ceased to be effective because its authority was weakened by the loss of these two men. Such are the results of an erroneous policy. Therefore it is said in the *Book of Zhou*: "The safety of the state depends upon what kind of orders are issued; its preservation depends upon what kind of men are employed."

I beg Your Majesty to examine closely what I have written, to give it some consideration, no matter how slight, and to ponder carefully what steps should be taken!

At this time a man of Zhao named Xu Yue and a man of Qi named Yan An both submitted memorials to the throne on some aspect of current policy. Xu Yue's memorial read as follows:

I have heard that in the past and present alike the greatest danger to the empire is a landslide, not a few falling tiles. What do I mean by a landslide? The end of the Qin dynasty is a good example. Chen She commanded no force of 1,000 chariots, nor did he possess so much as a foot of territory. He was not the descendant of any ruler or famous man, nor did he enjoy any outstanding reputation in his village. He did not have the wisdom of a Confucius, a Mo Zi, or a Zeng Zi, nor the wealth of a Tao Zhu or an Yi Dun. And yet he rose up from the lanes and alleys, grasped his spear, bared his arm, and raised a mighty cry, and the whole empire followed after him as though driven by the wind.[3] Why did it happen thus? Because the people were in misery and their rulers had no mercy, because the governed were full of hatred and the governors lost in ignorance, and because the customs of the nation had been thrown into complete confusion and the rule of the dynasty had ceased to be effective. These three conditions were the material out of which Chen She fashioned success. This is what is called a landslide and therefore I say that it is the greatest danger to the safety of the empire.

What do I mean by a few falling tiles? The armies of Wu, Chu, Qi, and Zhao are an example. When the leaders of the Seven Kingdoms plotted together to overthrow the Han government, everyone of them was what is called a "lord of ten thousand chariots". Their soldiers numbered several hundred thousand, their might was sufficient to insure the strictest obedience within their realms, and their resources plentiful enough to spur their subjects to action. And yet they were unable to advance west and seize a single inch of territory, but instead were taken prisoner on the central plains. Why was this? Surely not because their authority was less than that of Chen She, a mere commoner, or because their armies were weaker than his. Rather it was because at that time the virtue and mercy of the early Han emperors still prevailed in the land and the majority of the people lived in peace and contentment with their lot. Therefore the rebellious lords were

---

[3] This description of Chen She is paraphrased from Jia Yi's famous essay, "The Faults of Qin", part of which is translated in Volume I, at the end of "The Hereditary House of Chen She".

unable to receive any assistance from the people outside their domains. This is what I call a few falling tiles, and therefore I say it is not a real danger to the empire.

From this we may see that, if the conditions in the empire are really ripe for a landslide, then even the poorest and lowliest man in a coarse robe can become the leader of a rebellion and endanger the safety of the entire land within the four seas. Chen She is proof of this, and if he could accomplish so much, how much more could the lords of states such as Hann, Zhao, and Wei at that time?

On the other hand, although the empire may not be completely at peace, if the conditions are not yet ripe for a landslide, then even the strongest lords and the most powerful armies, if they venture to rebel, will suffer defeat and capture before they have time to turn around. The states of Wu, Chu, Qi and Zhao are proof of this. Under such circumstances, then, how could ordinary officials or commoners succeed in carrying out a revolt?

These two conditions represent the crux of safety or peril for the nation, and any enlightened ruler must give them careful thought and profound consideration.

Recently the grain crops east of the Pass have not been good and the harvests have not yet returned to normal, so that many of the people are poor and starving. On top of this they are burdened by the military campaigns along the border. In view of this, if I were to attempt to predict the future on the basis of reason, I would say that the people will soon become restless in their present habitations. Being restless, they will begin to shift about, and shifting about is what brings on landslides.

The wise ruler is primarily concerned in perceiving the sources from which all changes arise, in understanding the keys to safety and peril, and in incorporating this knowledge in his governing of the nation, in order to forestall danger before it has taken form. The important thing for Your Majesty, therefore, is simply to strive to prevent conditions in the empire that would bring about a landslide. If this is done, then, although powerful states and strong armies were to oppose you, Your Majesty would be free to spend your time pursuing galloping beasts in the chase and shooting at fleeting birds, broadening your pleasure parks, giving yourself up to the most carefree wandering, and tasting every pleasure of the hunt with complete security and confidence. The sound of bells and chiming stones, strings and flutes, would never cease to soothe your ears, while within the curtains of your private rooms the antics of actors and comic dwarfs would forever delight your eyes, and yet the empire would never know sorrow. Why must your name be King Tang or King Wu? Why must your rule be that of Kings Cheng or Kang? If I may be so bold, I would say that Your Majesty was a natural born sage, endowed with tolerance and benevolence. If you will only give thought to the governing of the empire, then your name may easily rival those of the sage rulers Tang and Wu, and you may revive in your own time the glorious rules of Kings Cheng and Kang. Then, when you have achieved these two goals, you may rest in true honour and security, spread your fame abroad to the world of your time, and win the loyalty of the empire and the submission of the barbarian tribes which surround it, and the effects of your virtue and generosity will insure the prosperity of your heirs for generations to come, so that they may face south before their screens of state, fold their garments about them, and receive the feudal lords and high officials in audience. This is what Your Majesty should strive for!

I have heard that, though one does not succeed in becoming a true king, yet his efforts will be sufficient to bring him security. And with peace and security, what could Your Majesty seek for that would not be gained, what could you do that would not meet with success, whom could you attack without winning submission?

Yan An's memorial read as follows:

I have heard that when the house of Zhou won control of the empire it was able to rule effectively for over 300 years. The dynasty reached its height in the time of Kings Cheng and Kang, when such order reigned that punishments could be set aside and were not needed for over forty years. Later, although the power of the dynasty declined, it was still able to maintain nominal rule for another 300 years and more. During this latter period the five great feudal hegemons arose one after the other, seeking always to assist the Son of Heaven, to encourage profitable measures and prevent danger to the empire, to punish violence and prohibit evil, and to bring order and justice to the land within the four seas so that the Son of Heaven might enjoy greater honour.

But after the five hegemons had passed away, no more wise men appeared to succeed them. The Son of Heaven was left alone and powerless, his commands ignored, while the feudal lords did as they pleased. The strong tyrannized the weak; the many oppressed the few. Tian Chang usurped the throne of Qi; the six ministers of Jin divided the kingdom of Jin among themselves; and the era of the Warring States ensued. This was the beginning of hardship for the people.

The powerful states devoted themselves to offensive warfare, while the weaker ones strove for self-preservation, some joining the Vertical Alliance, others the Horizontal Alliance. The soldiers dashed into battle in their war chariots, the hubs clashing against each other; they wore their armour day and night until their bodies were covered with lice; and there was no one whom the people could turn to for help.

Then the king of Qin rose to power, gobbling up the empire piece by piece until he had united all the warring states under his command. He assumed the title of Supreme Emperor and became lord of the entire land within the four seas. He razed the fortifications of the feudal lords, and seized their weapons and melted them down to make bells, to show the world that they would never again be needed.

The masses of the common people, believing that they would henceforth be spared the hardships of the Warring States period and be ruled by an enlightened sovereign at last, rejoiced as though each man had been born anew. At this time, if the Qin had only relaxed its punishments, lightened the burden of taxation, and decreased its demands upon the labour of the people; if it had honoured benevolence and righteousness and scorned power and profit; if it had placed more value on sincerity and less on cunning, and had worked to reform the ways and manners of the people and to educate the empire to virtue, then it might have ruled in peace and security for generations. Yet it did none of these, but merely continued to follow its old customs, advancing men who thought only of craft and cunning, power and profit, and pushing aside men of sincerity and good faith. Its laws were stern and its government harsh. A multitude of flatterers and sycophants appeared, day after day singing the praises of the emperor, until his will was blown up and his heart lulled into ease.

Then, vainly desiring to extend his might to foreign lands, he dispatched Meng Tian with an army to attack the barbarians to the north. He broadened the empire, pushed back the frontier, and sent an army to garrison the area north of the Yellow River, dispatching a stream of porters bearing fodder and grain in the wake of the fighting men to keep them supplied.

At the same time the emperor sent the military commander Tu Sui with a force of men in towered ships to sail south and attack the hundred tribes of Yue, and ordered the supervisor Lu to dig a canal to transport supplies for the men so that they could penetrate deep into the region of Yue. But the natives of Yue fled before the invaders, and the Qin soldiers were left to sit idly day after day with no opponent, until their provisions were exhausted. Then the men of Yue launched an attack and inflicted a severe defeat on the Qin army. Finally the emperor was obliged to dispatch the military commander Zhao Tuo with another force of soldiers to occupy Yue.

At this time the Qin was plagued in the north by its involvements with the Xiongnu, and in the south by its entanglements in Yue. For over ten years the armies were camped in worthless tracts of land, able to advance but never to withdraw. The young men were obliged to don armour and the girls to transport provisions; hardship made life no longer worth living and the people hanged themselves from the road-side trees in such numbers that one corpse dangled within sight of another.

Finally, when the First Emperor of the Qin passed away, the whole empire rose up in revolt. Chen She and Wu Guang raised an army in Chen, Wu Chen and Zhang Er in Zhao, Xiang Liang in Wu, Tian Dan in Qi, Jing Ju in Ying, Zhou Shi in Wei, and Han Guang in Yan. In the farthest mountains and the remotest valleys heroes sprang to action in numbers too great to recount. None of them were the descendants of feudal lords; none were high officials. Without so much as a foot of land in their possession, they rose up from the lanes and alleys, grasped their spears, and marched into battle, answering the call of the times. No plots had been laid, and yet they sprang up on all sides; no agreements had been reached, and yet their armies joined together; bit by bit they broadened the areas under their control and increased their territories until they had become self-appointed kings. It was the state of the times which brought it all about. The Qin enjoyed the honour of the imperial title and the wealth of the empire, and yet its heirs were wiped out and its sacrifices cut off, all because of excessive warfare. The Zhou dynasty failed because of its weakness, the Qin because of its strength; both suffered by not changing with the times.

Now Your Majesty wishes to induce the southern barbarians to come to court and to make the land of Yelang acknowledge your sovereignty, to conquer the Qiang and Po tribes, gain control of Huizhou, and build fortified cities there, to invade deep into the territory of the Xiongnu and burn the headquarters of the Xiongnu at Longcheng. Your advisers all applaud these aims, but they are thinking only of their own profit; these are not wise policies for the empire as a whole. Now, when China is not troubled by so much as the bark of a dog, to become involved in wearisome projects in distant lands that exhaust the wealth of the nation — this is hardly right for a ruler whose duty is to be a father to the people. To seek to fulfil endless ambitions, determining to win revenge and incurring the hatred of the Xiongnu — this will not bring peace to the frontier. To incite troubles and leave them unsolved, to disband the armies only to call them up again, bringing sorrow and hardship to those near at hand and alarm to distant lands — this is no way to insure the continuance of the dynasty!

At present the whole empire is engaged in forging armour and sharpening swords, straightening arrows and stringing bows, transporting supplies and hauling provisions without a moment's rest. This is the burden shared by everyone in the empire. But warfare continued too long may give rise to rebellion, and duties which are too burdensome may breed treasonable thoughts. Some of the outlying provinces are almost 1,000 *li* in size, with lines of twenty or thirty fortified cities, situated in strategic areas and with tightly controlled populations, posing a threat to the feudal lords whose territories adjoin them. This is not to the advantage of the imperial house.

We have seen that in ancient times the rulers of Qi and Jin were overthrown because the royal houses in those states had sunk too low and the great ministers were too powerful, while in more recent times we have observed that the Qin was destroyed because its laws were harsh and its ambitions grandiose and endless. Now the power of the governors in the provinces is much greater than that of the high officials of Qi and Jin; their territories of 1,000 *li* offer a far better basis for revolt than the lanes and alleys from which Chen She raised his rebellion; and their weapons and military resources are hardly limited to the homemade spears which Chen She fought with. If, by one chance in ten thousand, a revolt should break out, it would end in consequences so fearful I dare not name them.[4]

When these memorials had been presented to the throne, the emperor summoned the three men, Zhufu Yan, Xu Yue, and Yan An, and said to them, "Gentlemen, where have you been keeping yourselves up till now? Why have we not met sooner?" And he honoured them with the rank of palace attendant. Zufu Yan continued to appear before the emperor from time to time and submit memorials on government policy. The emperor promoted him four times within a single year until he had advanced him to the post of master of guests. He also promoted Xu Yue to the rank of palace counsellor.

On one occasion Zufu Yan advised the emperor, saying, "In ancient times the territories of the feudal lords did not exceed 100 *li* in breadth, so that it was easy to control them and insure that they did not become too strong. Now, however, some of the feudal lords possess lands 1,000 *li* square, dotted by twenty or thirty strong cities. If they are treated with leniency, they may give themselves up to wayward and luxurious living, which leads easily into lasciviousness and moral chaos, while if they are pressed to mend their ways, they are apt to band together and use their might to defy the capital. Any attempt to deprive them of territory by legal means will only nourish the seeds of revolt, as we have seen from the case of Chao Cuo and the revolt of the Seven Kingdoms in the time of Emperor Jing.

"Now, although some of the feudal lords have as many as ten or more sons and younger brothers, only one of them, the recognized heir to the title, receives any inheritance; the others, though of the same flesh and blood as the heir, do not receive a single foot of territory. Surely this is not the way to encourage the practice of benevolence and filial piety.

---

[4]Yan An's memorial, which is mainly a criticism of Emperor Wu's foreign wars, seems to wander from the point at the end in warning of the danger of revolt in the outlying provinces. It should be remembered, however, that the reason the outlying provinces were strong enough to pose a threat to the central government was that the armies were stationed there for the purpose of launching attacks abroad. Anyone familiar with the history of imperial Rome knows what such a situation could mean.

"I beg Your Majesty, therefore, to issue an order allowing the feudal lords to extend the blessings of your generosity by dividing their lands among their sons and younger brothers, enfeoffing each as a marquis with a grant of territory. In this way each one will rejoice in the gratification of his desires and Your Majesty, while performing an act of virtue, will in fact be dividing up the feudal states. Thus, without your resorting to forced deprivations of territory, the feudal lords will be gradually weakened."

The emperor approved this plan and put it into effect.

On another occasion Zhufu Yan said, "Now that Your Majesty's mausoleum has been established at Mouling in the suburbs, it would be advisable to gather together the wealthy and powerful families and the troublemakers among the people from all over the empire and resettle them at Mouling. In this way you will increase the population of the capital area and at the same time prevent the spread of evil and vicious ways in the provinces. This is called preventing danger without resorting to punishments." The emperor put this suggestion into effect as well.

Zhufu Yan also won distinction by the part he played in having Wei Zifu made empress and in exposing the evil deeds of Liu Dingguo, the king of Yan. The other high officials were all terrified of the power of Zhufu Yan's words and presented him with bribes of thousands of gold pieces to win his favour. One of them cautioned him about his actions, saying, "You are being too headstrong!" But Zhufu Yan only replied, "After I bound up my hair and entered manhood I spent over forty years wandering from place to place and studying, never able to win success. My father would not treat me as a son, my brothers refused to have anything to do with me, and my friends rejected me. Many were the days when I knew nothing but hardship. Any real man knows that there are only two alternatives in life — to succeed and dine from rich cauldrons, or to fail and end by being boiled alive in them. Now my days are drawing to a close, and I have no time for virtuous ways. So I do anything I please, no matter how unreasonable, and never worry about the consequences!"

Zhufu Yan spoke strongly in favour of occupying the region of Shuofang in the north. It was a very fertile area, bounded by the Yellow River on the north, he argued, and had been fortified by Meng Tian during the Qin and used as a base in driving out the Xiongnu. If it were occupied once more, it would help to reduce the transportation of supplies and soldiers from the interior of the empire, broaden the territory of China, and serve as a foundation for wiping out the barbarians. The emperor considered his proposal and referred it to the high ministers for discussion, but all of them opposed it as impractical. Gongsun Hong pointed out, "Although the Qin constantly kept a force of 300,000 men in the area to fortify the northern border along the Yellow River, it was never able to accomplish anything and finally had to abandon the project."[5]

But Zhufu Yan continued to urge the advantages of the project, and the emperor finally decided to follow his advice and set up the province of Shuofang.

In the second year of *yuanshuo* (127 BC) Zhufu Yan reported that Liu Zijing, the king of Qi, was guilty of lewd and immoral conduct. The emperor appointed him as prime minister of Qi and sent him to that kingdom to investigate. When he arrived in Qi he summoned all his brothers and friends and scattered gifts amounting to 500 gold pieces among them. Then he reviled them, saying, "Formerly, when I was poor, my brothers would not clothe or feed me and my friends would not let me inside their gates. Now that I am prime minister of Qi, you all come rushing to greet me, some from as far away as 1,000 *li*. But I want nothing more to do with any of you! Don't ever enter my gate again!"

Then he sent men to warn the king to mend his ways, telling him that he knew all about the king's incestuous relations with his older sister. The king, concluding that he would never be able to escape punishment, and fearing that he would be condemned to execution in the same way as Liu Dingguo, the king of Yan, committed suicide. The officials reported his death to the emperor.

In his early days, when Zhufu Yan was still a commoner, he had travelled widely in Yan and Zhao, and after he won favour with the emperor he had utilized his experience to bring to light the misdoings of the king of Yan. The king of Zhao was afraid that he himself might suffer the same fate and wanted to send a letter to the emperor accusing Zhufu Yan of secret misdeeds, but as long as Zhufu Yan was serving at the emperor's side he did not dare to make a move. After Zhufu Yan had been appointed prime minister of Qi and had left the capital and gone beyond the Pass, however, the king of Zhao sent an envoy with a letter to the emperor reporting that Zhufu Yan had accepted bribes of

---

[5] It seems odd that Zhufu Yan would urge expansion into the area of Shuofang when his first memorial showed him strongly opposed to Emperor Wu's wars against the Xiongnu. It should also be recalled that Gongsun Hong, though at first opposing the plan to set up fortifications in Shuofang, later changed his mind and supported it. Apparently both men were capable of altering their views to conform to the wishes of the emperor, which is no doubt one reason why Sima Qian chose to treat them both together in this chapter.

money from the feudal lords. "That is why he urged that so many of the sons and brothers of the feudal lords be enfeoffed!"

Sometime afterwards the emperor received word of the death of the king of Qi and was extremely angry, believing that Zhufu Yan had threatened the king and driven him to suicide. He therefore summoned Zhufu Yan back to the capital and turned him over to the law officials for investigation. Zhufu Yan admitted having accepted gold from the feudal lords, but denied that he had threatened the king of Qi and driven him to suicide.

The emperor was in favour of sparing him the death penalty, but Gongsun Hong, who was imperial secretary at this time, said, "Since the king of Qi has committed suicide and left no heir, his kingdom should be abolished and his territory taken over and made into a province of the central government. As for Zhufu Yan, he was the one who originally started all the trouble. If Your Majesty does not execute him, there will be no way to make amends to the empire for what has happened!"

Accordingly, the emperor in the end ordered the execution of Zhufu Yan and all his family. While Zhufu Yan enjoyed honour and favour, his guests and retainers numbered in the thousands, but when he and his family were executed, none of them was willing to dispose of the corpses. Only one man, Kong Che of Xiao, came forward to accept the bodies and bury them. Later on, when the emperor learned of this, he admired Kong Che as a man of true worth.

The Grand Historian remarks: Although Gongsun Hong was careful to act according to righteous principles, he was also fortunate in having lived at the right time. It had been over eighty years since the dynasty was founded, and the emperor looked with favour on literary accomplishments and invited men of talent and worth to take service in the government in order to spread the teachings of Confucius and Mo Zi. Gongsun Hong won the highest place in the examination.

While Zhufu Yan was in a position of power, men all united in praising him. But when his good name was gone and he had been condemned to execution — alas, they outdid each other in speaking ill of him![6]

---

[6] The remainder of the chapter, dealing with events long after the death of Sima Qian, is a later addition and has therefore been omitted.

SHI JI 113: THE ACCOUNT OF SOUTHERN YUE

After the Han had brought peace to China, Zhao Tuo gained control of the region of Yangyue, guarding the south as a vassal of the Han and sending tribute to the court. Thus I made "The Account of Southern Yue".

The king of Southern Yue, formerly known as military commander Tuo, was a native of Zhending. His family name was Zhao. After the Qin dynasty had unified the empire, it sent troops to invade and seize control of the region of Yangyue, setting up the provinces of Guilin or Cassia Forest, Nanhai or Southern Sea, and Xiang or Elephant, and moving bands of condemned Chinese into the area, where they lived among the natives for the following thirteen years.

Under the First Emperor of the Qin, Zhao Tuo served as magistrate of Dragon River in the province of Nanhai. After the Second Emperor came to the throne the military commander of Nanhai, Ren Xiao, fell ill. Just before he died he summoned Zhao Tuo, the magistrate of Dragon River, and said to him, "I have received news that Chen She and others have started a revolt. The rule of the Qin has been cruel and tyrannous and the whole empire is embittered. Xiang Yu, Liu Ji, Chen She, Wu Guang, and others have gathered bands of men and raised armies in every province, fighting like tigers with each other for the possession of the empire. All of China is in turmoil and no one knows when the fighting will cease, for the powerful leaders have all turned against the Qin and set themselves up as independent rulers. Nanhai is a distant and out-of-the-way region, and yet I am afraid that the rebel soldiers may invade even this far. I had hoped to call out the troops and cut off the new road that connects us with China, fortifying ourselves so that we may be prepared for any move of the feudal leaders. Unfortunately, however, I have contracted this grave illness.

"The region of Panyu[1] is rugged and backed by mountains, and Nanhai measures several thousand *li* from east to west. Moreover, there are a number

---

[1] The site of the capital of Southern Yue in the region of present-day Canton.

of Chinese in the region who can be of assistance. Thus anyone who holds command of this area has in effect a whole prefecture under his control and could easily set it up as an independent kingdom. None of the provincial officials here, however, are worth talking to, and therefore I have summoned you to tell you my ideas."

Ren Xiao drew up a letter empowering Zhao Tuo to act as military commander of Nanhai, and shortly afterwards died.

Zhao Tuo then circulated a notice to the customs barriers at Hengpu, Yangshan, and Huangqi saying, "The rebel troops will soon be here! Close the roads as fast as you can and call together your troops to defend yourselves!"

On one legal pretext or another he little by little did away with the officials appointed by the Qin and filled the posts with temporary appointees belonging to his own party. By the time the Qin dynasty fell, Zhao Tuo had attacked and brought under his command the provinces of Guilin and Xiang as well and had set himself up as King Wu of Southern Yue.

After Gaozu won control of the empire he allowed Zhao Tuo to go unpunished, since China had enough to do to take care of internal troubles, and in the eleventh year of his reign (196 BC) he dispatched Lu Jia to recognize Zhao Tuo as king of Southern Yue, presenting him with the split tallies of a feudal lord. He enjoined Zhao Tuo to unite all the people of Yue in peace and not to cause any disturbance along the southern border, which adjoined that of the kingdom of Changsha.

In the time of Empress Lü the officials requested that all trade in iron goods between Southern Yue and China be prohibited. When Zhao Tuo received word of this, he protested. "Emperor Gaozu set me up as a feudal lord and sent his envoy giving me permission to carry on trade. But now Empress Lü, heeding the advice of slanderous officials, is discriminating against me, treating me as one of the barbarians and breaking off our trade in iron vessels and goods. This must be a plot of Wu Rui, the king of Changsha. He thinks he will be able to use the forces of China to attack and destroy Southern Yue, and then increase his prestige by making himself king of this region as well!"

Zhao Tuo thereupon assumed the title of Emperor Wu of Southern Yue and sent out his troops to attack the towns along the border of Changsha. They succeeded in capturing several district towns before returning to their own territory.

Empress Lü dispatched General Zhou Zao, the marquis of Longlü, to attack Southern Yue, but he encountered such heat and dampness, and so many of his officers and men fell ill, that his army could not cross the mountains into the region. After a year or so Empress Lü passed away and Zhou Zao's troops were recalled to China.

Zhao Tuo began once more to threaten the border with his forces. He sent gifts and bribes to the chiefs of Minyue, Western Ou, and Luoluo, persuading them to submit to his authority, until the region under his control extended over 10,000 *li* from east to west. He then began to ride about in a carriage with a yellow top, decorated with plumes on the left side, and to call his orders "edicts" in imitation of the Han emperor, all of which was intended to show that he was an equal of the ruler of China.

In the first year of Emperor Wen's reign (180 BC), because peace had only recently been restored to the empire, the emperor sent an announcement to the feudal lords and the barbarian chiefs, explaining his reasons for leaving his kingdom of Dai and journeying to the capital to take the throne, and informing them of his virtuous intentions. At the same time, learning that Zhao Tuo's parents were buried in Zhending, he set aside one of the towns in that district to take care of their graves and offer sacrifices at certain times each year. He also summoned Zhao Tuo's cousins to court and appointed them to high offices, treating them with great generosity. He then asked the chancellor Chen Ping and the other high officials to recommend someone to act as envoy to Southern Yue. Chen Ping suggested Lu Jia of Haozhi, who had had experience under the former emperor as envoy to Southern Yue. Emperor Wen summoned Lu Jia, made him a palace counsellor, and sent him to Southern Yue with instructions to reprimand Zhao Tuo for setting himself up as an "emperor" and at the same time failing to send a single envoy to report the fact to the Han court.

When Lu Jia arrived in Southern Yue, Zhao Tuo, thoroughly frightened, wrote a letter of apology. Referring to himself as "Your aged subject Tuo, a barbarian chief," Zhao Tuo explained:

> Some time ago, when Empress Lü cut off trade with Southern Yue and began to discriminate against me, I suspected that it was due to the slanders of the king of Changsha. I also heard rumours that all the members of my clan in China had been executed and the graves of my ancestors dug up and desecrated. Therefore in desperation I dared to violate the borders of the kingdom of Changsha. Moreover, this region of the south is low and damp and inhabited only by barbarian tribes. To the east of me is the chief of Minyue who, with no more than 1,000 subjects, calls himself a king, while to the west are the lands of Western

Ou and Luoluo, whose rulers likewise call themselves kings. So your aged subject, to gratify a whim, presumed in his delusion to call himself "emperor". Yet how could he dare to report such a fact to the Heavenly King of China?

Zhao Tuo bowed his head and apologized, begging that he might be allowed to continue to serve the emperor as a feudal lord, rendering his tribute and labour services as before. He then circulated an order throughout his kingdom which read:

> I have heard that two great men do not stand side by side, and two wise men never appear in the same age. The emperor is in truth a wise Son of Heaven. From this time onward, I relinquish the use of the words "emperor" and "edict" and the yellow covered carriage with plumes on the left side.

Lu Jia returned and reported the success of his mission, which greatly pleased Emperor Wen. Thus, for the remainder of his reign, as well as for that of Emperor Jing, Zhao Tuo called himself a subject of the Han and sent envoys with tribute to the court in the spring and fall. As a matter of fact, however, he continued secretly to use the designations "emperor" and "edict" the same as before within his kingdom, and only referred to himself as a "king" and used the other terms appropriate to a feudal lord when he sent envoys to the rulers of China.

Zhao Tuo died in the fourth year of the era *jianyuan* (137 BC). His grandson Zhao Hu succeeded him as king of Southern Yue. At this time Zou Ying, the king of Minyue, had called out his troops and was attacking the border towns of Southern Yue. Zhao Hu dispatched a messenger to the Han court with a letter to the emperor saying,

> Since the two kings of Southern Yue and Minyue are both vassal lords of the Han, it is not right that they should arbitrarily call out their troops and attack each other. Yet now the king of Minyue has raised his troops and is invading my territory. I do not dare call out my own troops unless the Son of Heaven commands me to.

The emperor, much impressed by the fidelity with which the king of Southern Yue had abided by his duties as a vassal lord, called up an army for his sake and dispatched it under the command of two generals to attack Minyue. Before the Han troops had crossed the mountains into the south, however, Zou

Yushan, the younger brother of Zou Ying, the king of Minyue, murdered his brother and surrendered to the Han forces. The emperor then recalled his troops and dispatched Zhuang Zhu to go and explain his intentions to Zhao Hu, the king of Southern Yue. Zhao Hu bowed his head and replied, "For my sake the Son of Heaven has raised an army and attacked Minyue. Death could not repay the debt of gratitude which I owe him." He sent his son, the crown prince Zhao Yingqi, to return with Zhuang Zhu to the capital and serve as an attendant at the imperial court, telling Zhuang Zhu, "Since my country has suffered recently from these attackers, you had better return at once to the capital, while I for my part will make preparations day and night and follow shortly afterwards to pay my respects in person to the Son of Heaven."

After Zhuang Zhu had returned to China, however, Zhao Hu's high ministers reprimanded him for making such a commitment, saying, "We have just recovered from the excitement caused by the Han armies which came to punish Zou Ying. Now, if you should leave the kingdom and journey to the Han court, it would cause great alarm and unrest in Southern Yue. Moreover the former king used to say that in serving the Son of Heaven, all that was necessary was to avoid a breach of etiquette. The important thing is not to be taken in by friendly words to the point where you commit yourself to a journey to the capital. If you ever go to the capital to visit the Son of Heaven, you will never return again! It will mean the downfall of the kingdom!"

Zhao Hu therefore pleaded illness and in the end never went through with his plans to visit the capital. Some ten or so years later he actually did fall gravely ill, and his son, the crown prince Zhao Yingqi, received permission to return home. Zhao Hu died and was given the posthumous title of Wen, the "Civil King". Zhao Yingqi succeeded to the throne and put away the old seal which Zhao Tuo had used when he called himself by the title "Emperor Wu".

While Zhao Yingqi was at the court in Chang'an he married a daughter of the Jiu family of Handan, by whom he had a son named Xing. After he took the throne he sent a letter to the emperor requesting that his wife be formally declared queen and his son Xing designated as heir to the throne. The Han envoys who came from time to time hinted to Zhao Yingqi that it would be well for him to go to the capital to visit the emperor. But Zhao Yingqi was accustomed to doing as he pleased, murdering people and giving free rein to his passions, and he was afraid that if he went to the capital he would be treated the same as the feudal lords of China proper and tried for his offences under Han law. So he kept insisting that he was too ill to make the journey and never went to the capital, instead sending his second son Zhao Cigong to be an attendant at court. Zhao Yingqi died and was given the posthumous title of Ming, the "Enlightened King".

The crown prince Zhao Xing succeeded to the throne and his mother became queen dowager. Before the queen dowager married Zhao Yingqi she had had an affair with a man of Baling named Anguo Shaoji. After Zhao Yingqi's death, in the fourth year of the era *yuanding* (113 BC), this same Anguo Shaoji was sent as envoy from the Han court to persuade the king of Southern Yue and the queen dowager that they should come to the capital to visit the emperor and conduct themselves the same as the other feudal lords. The admonisher Zhong Jun and others skilled at rhetoric were designated to present the arguments in favour of such a move, with Wei Chen and other men noted for their daring standing by to help out. The colonel of the guard Lu Bode was ordered to lead his troops and station them at Guiyang, where he would wait for the return of the envoys.

The king was still very young, and his mother, the queen dowager, was a native of China. Moreover, as mentioned before, she had once had an affair with Anguo Shaoji, and when he arrived as an envoy from the Han, she resumed the illicit relationship, a fact which was known to quite a number of people of the kingdom. The majority of them therefore had little use for her. The queen dowager, fearing the outbreak of revolt and hoping to use the authority of the Han to strengthen her position, repeatedly urged the king and his ministers to seek closer ties with the Han court. The king asked the Han envoys to forward a letter to the throne requesting that he be treated the same as the feudal lords of China proper and promising to journey to court once every three years to pay his respects. He also asked that the customs barriers on the border between his kingdom and China be removed. The emperor granted his requests and presented the prime minister of Southern Yue, Lü Jia, with a silver seal, along with the seals for the internal secretary, the military commander, and the grand tutor. The king was left to appoint the other officials of his court without consulting the emperor. The old punishments of tattooing and cutting off the nose were abolished and the Han laws put into effect, so that the kingdom would be governed the same as those of the other feudal lords. The envoys from the Han court were to remain in the kingdom to see that no trouble occurred. The king and the queen dowager then set about getting their baggage together and selecting a number of rare gifts to be presented to the emperor when they made their trip to the capital.

The prime minister Lü Jia was an old man and had served as prime minister to three kings of southern Yue. Over seventy members of his family held high posts as officials of the state. His sons were all married to princesses and his daughters were all married to men of the royal family. In addition, he was related by marriage to King Qin of Cangwu. He therefore wielded enormous power in the kingdom. The people of Yue trusted him, and many of them were happy to act as ears and eyes for him; he had a firmer hold on the hearts of the multitude than the king himself.

When the king was preparing to send his letter to the emperor, Lü Jia several times advised him against the move, but the king would not listen. Lü Jia by this time was already contemplating revolt and repeatedly refused to see the Han envoys, claiming that he was ill. The envoys for their part kept a close watch on Lü Jia, but the situation had not yet reached a point where they could take action against him.

The king and the queen dowager also were afraid that Lü Jia and the others of his party would seize the initiative by making a decisive move. They therefore decided to give a banquet and, relying on the support of the Han envoys, to do away with Lü Jia and his party. At the banquet the envoys were all seated facing east. The queen dowager faced south, the king faced north, and Lü Jia and the other high ministers all faced west. Lü Jia's younger brother, who was a general, led his soldiers and stationed them outside the palace.

When the drinking had reached its height, the queen dowager turned to Lü Jia and said, "Obviously all of Southern Yue would profit by being treated as a part of China proper. And yet you as prime minister have bitterly opposed the move. What is the reason?"

She thought in this way she could arouse the envoys to a display of anger, but the envoys hesitated and held back, waiting for each other to make a move, and in the end did not dare do anything. Lü Jia, judging from the faces of those about him that something was afoot, jumped up and started out of the room. The queen dowager in her rage tried to strike him down with a spear, but the king prevented her and Lü Jia succeeded in escaping from the room. Once outside, he got a party of his brother's soldiers to escort him back to his lodging, from which he sent word that he was ill, refusing to meet with the king and the envoys. In the meantime he laid plans in secret with the high ministers to start a revolt.

The king had originally had no intention of doing away with Lü Jia. Lü Jia knew this, and so for several months made no move. The queen dowager tried every way she could to get rid of Lü Jia and his group, but because of her immoral conduct and the fact that the people of the kingdom had no use for her, she could not muster enough support to accomplish her aim.

The emperor soon received word that Lü Jia was refusing to obey the king and the queen dowager and that the queen dowager was alone and powerless to remedy the situation, while the Han envoys were too afraid to make a move. He considered, however, that since the king and queen dowager had already declared their loyalty to the Han, and since it was only Lü Jia who was rebellious, there was no need to send an army against Southern Yue. He therefore decided to dispatch Zhuang Can with 2,000 men to act as his envoy. Zhuang Can declined to accept the mission, however, declaring that it was impossible. "If the mission is a friendly one, then two or three men will be sufficient. But if it is to be a display of force, 2,000 men are not enough to accomplish anything!"

After the emperor had dismissed Zhuang Can, Han Qianqiu, a young man of Jia who had formerly been prime minister to the king of Jibei, stepped forward and exclaimed, "A little, insignificant country like Yue, and in addition we have the support of the queen dowager to count on! The only one who is causing any trouble is the prime minister Lü Jia. Give me 200 brave men and I will cut off his head and bring it back without fail!"

The emperor thereupon dispatched Han Qianqiu, together with the queen dowager's younger brother Jiu Yue, to lead a force of 2,000 men. When they crossed the border of Southern Yue, Lü Jia and his men finally started their revolt. Lü Jia circulated an order throughout the kingdom which read:

> The king is very young and the queen dowager is a Chinese. Moreover she has had immoral relations with one of the Han envoys. Her only thought is to make the kingdom a part of China. She intends to take all of the precious goods and vessels of our former rulers and present them to the Son of Heaven in order to curry favour with him, and as soon as she reaches the capital, the numerous attendants in her party will be seized and sold as slaves. In her haste to snatch a momentary advantage for herself she disregards the sacred altars of the Zhao family and gives no thought to the future of the state!

With the assistance of his brother's soldiers Lü Jia then attacked the palace and murdered the queen dowager and the Han envoys. He sent men to report what he had done to King Qin of Cangwu and to the various provinces and districts, and set up Zhao Jiande, the marquis of Shuyang, the eldest son of Zhao Yingqi by a wife of the Yue people, as king.

After Han Qianqiu and his soldiers had attacked and defeated several small towns, the people of Yue opened up the roads and began to supply food to his soldiers. Then, when Han Qianqiu had marched to within forty *li* of Panyu, the Yue soldiers fell upon him and his men and wiped them out. Lü Jia ordered men to take the imperial credentials of the Han envoys and, sealing them up, deposit them with the officials at the border, giving some sort of false excuse and apologizing for the action he had taken. He also dispatched troops to guard the vital points of the kingdom.

When the emperor received word of what had happened he announced that, although Han Qianqiu had failed in his mission, he had distinguished himself by leading the attack, and therefore he enfeoffed his son Han Yannian as marquis of Cheng'an. In addition, because Jiu Yue's sister, the queen dowager, had been the leader in the movement to make the kingdom of Southern Yue a part of China, he enfeoffed Jiu Yue's son Jiu Guangde as marquis of Longkang. Then he granted a general amnesty to the empire, declaring: "In the *Spring and Autumn Annals* Confucius has expressed his condemnation of a situation in which, the Son of Heaven being weak and the feudal lords engaged in fights among themselves, no one troubles to punish rebels. Now Lü Jia, Zhao Jiande, and the others of their party have revolted and brazenly put themselves in power. Let the convicts who are freed by this amnesty, as well as 100,000 sailors of the towered ships who are stationed south of the Huai and Yangtze rivers, be sent to attack them!"

In the autumn of the fifth year of *yuanding* (112 BC) the colonel of the guard Lu Bode was appointed General Who Calms the Waves and ordered to leave Guiyang and sail down the Hui River. The master of titles chief commandant Yang Pu was made General of the Towered Ships and ordered to sail down the Hengpu River from Yuzhang. Two men of Yue who had surrendered to the Han and been made marquises were appointed as General of the Daggered Ships and General Who Descends the Torrents respectively and sent out of Lingling, one to sail down the Li River and the other to move into Cangwu. Another native of Yue, the Marquis Who Hastens to Duty, was ordered to lead a band of criminals from Ba and Shu and, mobilizing the troops of Yelang, to descend the Zangge River. All were to meet at Panyu, the capital of Southern Yue.

In the winter of the sixth year of *yuanding* (111 BC) Yang Pu, leading his best men, advanced ahead of the others, captured Xunxia, and broke through the line at Shimen. There he seized the Yue grain ships and, moving forward again, drove back the vanguard of the Yue forces. Then he halted with his 20,000 or 30,000 men to await the arrival of Lu Bode. Lu Bode had set out with his army of released convicts as scheduled, but because he had such a long distance to travel he did not reach the rendezvous point as soon as planned, and when he finally joined up with Yang Pu, he had no more than 1,000 or so men with him.

The two armies then advanced together, but since Yang Pu was in front, he reached Panyu first. Zhao Jiande, Lü Jia, and the others of their party were all guarding the city. Yang Pu, selecting the most advantageous site, took up a position facing the southeast side of the city, while Lu Bode was forced to draw up on the northwest side. By this time night had fallen. Yang Pu attacked and defeated a number of the Yue defenders and set fire to the city.

The men of Yue had heard before of Lu Bode's reputation, but since it was already night, they could not tell how many men he had with him. After Lu Bode had set up his camp he sent envoys inviting the men of Yue to surrender and presenting those who did so with the seals of a marquis. Then he sent them back into the city to persuade more of their friends to surrender. In the meantime Yang Pu began attacking the city with force and setting fire to it, which had the unexpected effect of driving the enemy over into Lu Bode's camp. By the time dawn came, therefore, all the defenders of the city had surrendered to Lu Bode.

Lü Jia and Zhao Jiande had already escaped in the night with several hundred of their followers and, embarking in ships, had fled west. Lu Bode, however, questioning one of the noblemen who had surrendered to him, discovered Lü Jia's destination and sent men to pursue him. Thus a colonel named Sima Suhung succeeded in capturing Zhao Jiande, for which he was enfeoffed as marquis of Haichang, and Du Ji, a palace attendant of Yue, captured Lü Jia, for which he was enfeoffed as marquis of Lincai.

King Qin of Cangwu, Zhao Guang, bore the same surname as the kings of Southern Yue. When he heard that the Han forces had arrived, he sent word through Shi Ding, the magistrate of Jieyang, that he was prepared to submit to Han rule. The overseer of Guilin, Ju Weng, also persuaded the chiefs of Western Ou and Luoluo to submit to the Han. All of them were made marquises. Before the forces of the General of the Daggered Ships, the General Who Descends the Torrents, or the soldiers of Yelang mobilized by the Marquis Who Hastens to Duty had even arrived in the area, peace was restored to Southern Yue. The region was eventually divided up into nine provinces. Lu Bode's fief was increased and Yang Pu, because his soldiers had captured a strongly fortified city, was enfeoffed as marquis of Jiangliang. Thus five generations, or ninety-three years, after Zhao Tuo first became king of Southern Yue, the state was destroyed.

The Grand Historian remarks: It was through Ren Xiao that Zhao Tuo originally got to be a king, and when the Han came to power, he ranked among the feudal lords. Because Zhou Zao's men were halted by dampness and disease, Zhao Tuo grew more arrogant than ever. Western Ou and Luoluo fell to fighting, and Southern Yue was filled with unrest until the Han troops appeared on the border and Zhao Yingqi was sent to the capital to attend the emperor. The downfall of the state in later days came about through the queen dowager, a daughter of the Jiu family. Lü Jia also, because of his lack of loyalty, caused Zhao Tuo's line to perish. Yang Pu selfishly chose the best camp site for himself, and his laziness and pride lost him the larger measure of success, but Lu Bode, though in a difficult position, proved himself a clever strategist, turning disaster into good fortune. Thus the shifts of success and failure are entwined like the strands of a rope.[2]

---

[2]Unlike the remarks of the Grand Historian at the end of other chapters, these do little more than summarize the principal points of the narrative; they are in four-character rhyming phrases, a form much used in later literary and historical works for rhymed "epitomes" at the ends of chapters.

SHI JI 114: THE ACCOUNT OF EASTERN YUE

When Liu Pi, the king of Wu, revolted against the Han, the men of Eastern
Ou assassinated him. Later, when they were attacked by Minyue, they
guarded Mt. Fengyu as loyal subjects of the Han. Thus I made "The
Account of Eastern Yue".

Wuzhu, the king of Minyue, and Yao, the king of Donghai in the region of
Yue, were both descendants of Goujian, king of the state of Yue in ancient
times.[1] Their family name was Zou. After the Qin dynasty unified the empire
both were deprived of their rank as kings and given the title of chieftain. Their
lands were made into the province of Minzhong. When the feudal lords rose in
revolt against the Qin, Zou Wuzhu and Zou Yao called out the troops of Yue
and went to join Wu Rui, the magistrate of Boyang (known as the Lord of Bo),
taking part with the other feudal lords in the overthrow of the Qin dynasty. At
that time Xiang Yu was issuing orders to the other leaders of the revolt, but he
failed to make kings of Wuzhu and Yao, and for that reason they refused to give
him their support. Instead, when the king of Han attacked Xiang Yu, they once
more called out the troops of Yue and aided the Han cause.

In the fifth year of the Han (202 BC) Emperor Gaozu reestablished Zou
Wuzhu as king of Minyue, ruling over the region that had formerly been the
province of Minzhong, with his capital at Dongye. In the third year of Emperor
Hui's reign (192 BC) the service rendered by the men of Yue to Gaozu was
brought to the emperor's attention. "Zou Yao, the chief of Min, achieved great
merit and his people supported the Han cause," the emperor announced, and set
up Zou Yao as king of Donghai, with his capital at Dongou or Eastern Ou. For
this reason he is popularly known as the king of Eastern Ou.

After the reigns of several Han rulers, in the third year of Emperor Jing's
reign (154 BC), Liu Pi, the king of Wu, revolted. He tried to persuade the king
of Minyue to join him, but the latter refused; only Zou Yao, the king of Eastern

---

[1] Reigned 496-465 BC.

Ou, sided with the rebels. After the armies of Wu had been defeated, the men of Eastern Ou accepted a bribe from the Han government and murdered the king of Wu at Dantu. For this reason the men of Eastern Ou were allowed to return to their homes without punishment.

Liu Ziju, the son of the king of Wu, fled to Minyue, where, deeply angered at Eastern Ou because of his father's murder, he worked constantly to incite Minyue to an attack on Eastern Ou. In the third year of the *jianyuan* era (138 BC) the king of Minyue finally called out his troops and surrounded the city of Eastern Ou. Food supplies in the city were soon exhausted and the defenders in such distress that they were about to surrender, when the king of Eastern Ou dispatched someone to report his plight to the present emperor. The emperor questioned the grand commandant Tian Fen on what course to follow. Tian Fen replied, "It is a common occurrence for the men of Yue to attack each other. Moreover they have several times proved disloyal to us. There is therefore no reason for China to go to the trouble of rescuing them. It has been the policy since the Qin dynasty to let them go their own way and not to attempt to force them into submission!"

The palace counsellor Zhuang Zhu, however, took exception to Tian Fen's words. "The only thing we should worry about is whether we have strength enough to rescue them and virtue enough to command their loyalty," he said. "If we have, then why should we 'let them go' as you say? As for the Qin dynasty, it 'let go' not only Yue but the whole empire, including the capital itself! Now a small country has come to report its distress to the Son of Heaven. If he does not save it, to whom can it turn for aid? And how can the Son of Heaven claim that the rulers of all other states are like sons to him if he ignores their pleas?"

"It is obvious," said the emperor, "that Tian Fen is not worth consulting in these matters! However, since I have just come to the throne, I do not wish to issue the tiger seals and officially call out the troops of all the provinces and kingdoms." He therefore dispatched Zhuang Zhu with the seals of an envoy to call out only the troops of Kuaiji. The governor of Kuaiji tried to prevent him from carrying out his orders on the grounds that he was not bearing the tiger seals, but Zhuang Zhu cut off the head of one of the marshals to show that he meant business, and eventually managed to call out the troops and transport them by sea to rescue Eastern Ou. Before they reached their destination, the king of Minyue withdrew his troops and departed. The king of Eastern Ou then requested that he be allowed to move the inhabitants of his state to China.

Permission was granted, and he and all his people came and settled in the region between the Yangtze and Huai rivers.

In the sixth year of the era *jianyuan* (135 BC) Minyue attacked Southern Yue. The king of Southern Yue, abiding by his agreement with the Son of Heaven, did not venture to call out his troops on his own authority, but sent word of his predicament to the emperor. The emperor dispatched the grand messenger Wang Hui from Yuzhang and the minister of agriculture Han Anguo from Kuaiji, both of them with the rank of general. Before they had crossed the mountains into the region of Yue, however, Zou Ying, the king of Minyue, sent his troops to block the passes. The king's younger brother, Zou Yushan, began to plot with the prime minister and the other members of his family, saying, "Without requesting permission, the king has arbitrarily sent out his troops to attack Southern Yue. Therefore the armies of the Son of Heaven have come to punish us. The Han armies are numerous and powerful, and even if we should somehow succeed in defeating them, more and more would come to follow, until in the end our country would be wiped out. Now if we were to kill the king and apologize to the Son of Heaven, and if he accepted our apology and withdrew his armies, we could preserve the state as it is now. And should he refuse to listen, we could try our luck in battle. If we lose, we can escape to the sea!"

The others all having agreed to this plan, Zou Yushan ran the king through with a spear and dispatched a messenger with his head to Wang Hui.

"My purpose in coming," said Wang Hui, "was simply to punish the king. Now that you have brought his head, the offence has been atoned for. You have surrendered without a fight — I could ask for no greater victory!" He therefore decided to halt his troops, sending word to Han Anguo of what had happened and dispatching a messenger to hasten back to the capital with the king's head and report to the emperor.

The emperor issued an edict disbanding the armies of the two generals and stating, "Zou Ying and the others of his party were the chief troublemakers. Only Zou Wuzhu's grandson Zou Chou, the chieftain of Yao, refrained from taking any part in the plot." He therefore sent one of his palace attendant generals to set up Zou Chou as king of Yao in the region of Yue so that he could carry on the sacrifices to the former rulers of Minyue.

Zou Yushan, having successfully carried out the assassination of his brother Zou Ying, wielded great power in the kingdom, and the majority of the people favoured him. He therefore secretly declared himself king of the region, while the officially recognized king, Zou Chou, found himself powerless to command his subjects and force obedience to himself. When the emperor received news of this state of affairs, he decided that it was not worth calling out another army to deal with Zou Yushan. Instead he announced, "Although Zou Yushan several times plotted revolt with his brother Zou Ying, he later took the lead in punishing Zou Ying, sparing our armies the trouble of attack," and set up Zou Yushan as king of Eastern Yue, ruling side by side with Zou Chou, the king of Yao.

In the fifth year of *yuanding* (112 BC) the kingdom of Southern Yue rebelled against the Han. Zou Yushan, the king of Eastern Yue, sent a letter to the throne asking that he be allowed to lead a force of 8,000 men and join Yang Pu, the General of the Towered Ships, in attacking Lü Jia and the other rebels. When he had taken his troops as far as Jieyang, however, he halted, claiming that the wind and waves were too high to permit him to embark, and sent an envoy in secret to the rebels in Southern Yue, thus maintaining contact with both sides. Even after the Han armies had succeeded in capturing Panyu, the capital of Southern Yue, he still failed to appear on the scene. Yang Pu sent a letter to the throne asking that he be allowed to lead his troops and attack Eastern Yue to punish Zou Yushan for his perfidy, but the emperor replied that the troops were by this time too exhausted for another campaign and refused to grant permission. Instead he disbanded the armies and instructed the officers to garrison Meiling in Yuzhang and await further orders.

In the autumn of the sixth year of *yuanding* (111 BC) Zou Yushan, learning that Yang Pu had requested permission to attack him and seeing that the Han troops were poised on the border ready to invade his territory, finally determined to revolt, calling out his troops to block the roads by which the Han armies might advance. Appointing Zou Li and others with the title of Generals Who Swallow Up the Han, he invaded Baisha, Wulin, and Meiling, and killed three of the Han commanders.

At this time the Han had sent the minister of agriculture Zhang Cheng and the former marquis of Shanzhou, Liu Chi, to command the garrison, but both of them, not daring to attack the rebels, had instead withdrawn to positions of safety. Both were later tried on charges of cowardice and executed. In the meantime Zou Yushan had a seal carved for himself reading "Emperor Wu" and set himself up with this title, deluding his subjects with all kinds of false assertions.

The emperor dispatched Han Yue, the General Who Traverses the Sea, to embark with his troops from Juzhang and sail around to attack the rebels from the east. Yang Pu marched out of Wulin, the military commander Wang Wenshu advanced from Meiling, and the two Yue marquises known as the General of the Daggered Ships and the General Who Descends the Torrents proceeded from Ruoye and Baisha. In the winter of the first year of *yuanfeng* (Nov.-Dec., 111 BC)[2] all of them invaded Eastern Yue.

Eastern Yue had earlier dispatched its troops to block the passes and had appointed a General Who Conquers the North to guard Wulin, defeating several of Yang Pu's military commanders and murdering the Han officials in the region. One of Yang Pu's subordinates, Yuan Zhonggu of Qiantang, however, defeated and killed the General Who Conquers the North, for which he was made marquis of Yuer.

Earlier, before the Han armies had arrived, Wu Yang, the marquis of Yan, a native of Yue who made his home in China, had been sent back to Yue by the emperor to persuade Zou Yushan to remain loyal to the Han. Zou Yushan, however, had refused to listen to his advice, and when Han Yue arrived with his troops in the region of Yue, Wu Yang, along with 700 men of his city, turned against his countrymen and attacked the Yue army at Hanyang. Then, joining with Ao, the marquis of Jiancheng, Wu Yang led his troops and placed them under the command of Zou Jugu, the king of Yao. The three of them plotted together, saying, "Zou Yushan is the chief troublemaker and has forced us into defending him. Now the Han armies have come in great strength and number, but if we were to plot together and assassinate Zou Yushan and surrender to the Han general, we might be able to escape punishment." Eventually they joined in murdering Zou Yushan and led his troops to surrender to Han Yue. As a result of this action, Zou Jugu, the king of Yao, was enfeoffed as marquis of Eastern Yue, with 10,000 households; Ao, the marquis of Jiancheng, was newly enfeoffed as marquis of Kailing; and Wu Yang, the marquis of Yan, was newly enfeoffed as marquis of Beishi. Han Yue was enfeoffed as marquis of Andao, and his military commander Liu Fu as marquis of Liaoying. (Liu Fu was a son of King Gong of Chengyang. Formerly he had been marquis of Haichang, but had been tried for some offence and deprived of his title. He had won no particular distinction in his career with the army but was enfeoffed as a marquis because he was a member of the imperial family.) None of the other Han

---

[2] It should be remembered that the official Han year at this time still began with the tenth month, so that although the first year of *yuanfeng* falls largely in 110 BC, the action described here took place in the last months of 111 BC.

generals had won any distinction in the campaign and therefore they were not enfeoffed. Duo Jun, a general of Eastern Yue, abandoned his army and surrendered when the Han troops arrived, and was therefore enfeoffed as marquis of Wuxi.

With the rebellion at an end, the emperor announced, "The region of Eastern Yue is narrow and full of mountain defiles, and the people of Minyue are fickle and have shifted their loyalties numerous times." He therefore commanded the army officials to lead away all the inhabitants of the region and resettle them in the area between the Yangtze and Huai rivers, leaving Eastern Yue a deserted land.

The Grand Historian remarks: Although Yue is a land of barbarians, its former rulers must have treated the people with great wisdom and virtue. Otherwise how could their line have lasted so long? For generation after generation they held the title of chieftain or king, and Goujian even acted for a time as one of the dictator lords of China. And although Zou Yushan, because of his flagrant rebelliousness, brought about the destruction of his kingdom and the resettlement of its inhabitants, yet other descendants of the same line, such as Zou Jugu, the king of Yao, are still enfeoffed as marquises of 10,000 households. The fact that the leaders of Yue have for so many generations been great lords is due, no doubt, to the merit which has come down to them from their distant ancestor, the sage Emperor Yu.[3]

---

[3] The founder of the Xia dynasty and reputed ancestor of the royal family of Yue. The paragraph is a good illustration of Sima Qian's theory that the virtue and merit of a great man are somehow transmitted to and benefit his descendants, even after the lapse of hundreds or thousands of years.

SHI JI 115: THE ACCOUNT OF CHAOXIAN

Dan, the crown prince of Yan, fled to the region of Liao, but later Wei Man gathered together the refugees of Yan and, establishing them in the land of the eastern sea and adding Zhenpan, guarded the frontier as a foreign vassal of the Han. Thus I made "The Account of Chaoxian".

Wei Man, the king of Chaoxian (Korea), came originally from the state of Yan. When Yan was at the height of its power, it invaded and conquered the regions of Zhenpan and Chaoxian,[1] appointing officials to rule the area and setting up fortifications along the frontier. After the Qin dynasty destroyed the state of Yan, the area fell more or less under Qin control, bordering as it did the province of Liaodong. When the Han arose, however, it regarded the region as too far away and difficult to guard, and rebuilt the fortifications at the old border of Liaodong, leaving the area beyond, as far as the Bei (Yalu) River, to be administered by the king of Yan.

When Lu Wan, the king of Yan, revolted and crossed over into the territory of the Xiongnu, Wei Man fled into hiding. He gathered together a band of 1,000 or more followers and, adopting the mallet-shaped hairdo and dress of the eastern barbarians, escaped over the eastern border and, crossing the Bei River, settled down in the region formerly administered by the Qin, moving back and forth along the old border. Little by little he brought under his control the barbarians and Chinese refugees from Yan and Qi who were living in the regions of Zhenpan and Chaoxian, and made himself their king, establishing his capital at Wangxian (Pyongyang).

During the reigns of Emperor Hui and Empress Lü, because peace had only recently been restored to the empire, the governor of Liaodong Province agreed to regard Wei Man as a "foreign vassal" of the Han if he would guard the frontier against the barbarians and prevent them from raiding the border. In addition, if

---

[1] Zhenpan was the region west of the Yalu River; Chaoxian was that east of the river. Although Chaoxian is often used as a name for Korea, it is obvious that Chinese influence at this time did not extend very far down the Korean Peninsula.

any of the barbarian chieftains wished to enter China and pay their respects to the emperor, Wei Man was not to hinder them from making the journey. When word of this agreement was reported to the emperor, he gave his approval. As a result, Wei Man was able to acquire considerable wealth and military power, with which he attacked and conquered the smaller settlements in the area until all of Zhenpan and Lintun were under his control. His territory by this time measured several thousand *li* square.

In time the rule passed to Wei Man's son and then to his grandson Wei Youqu, who induced an increasing number of Han subjects to flee to his kingdom. Neither he nor his father or grandfather had ever journeyed to the capital to visit the emperor and, when the chiefs of Zhenpan or any of the other various states in the area sent a letter to the throne requesting an audience with the Son the Heaven, they blocked the way and refused to let them pass.

In the second year of *yuanfeng* (109 BC) the Han dispatched She He to rebuke Wei Youqu and warn him to mend his ways, but the latter refused to obey the imperial edict. She He left the capital of Chaoxian and began his journey home but, when he reached the border and was about to cross the Bei River, he stabbed and killed Zhang, the assistant king of Chaoxian, who had been sent to escort him out of the kingdom. Then he made a dash across the river and back into Han territory, where he sent a report to the emperor stating that he had killed a general of Chaoxian. The emperor, pleased by this feat, asked no questions but honoured him with the post of chief commandant of the eastern sector of Liaodong Province. The king of Chaoxian, angered at this treachery, called out his troops and attacked and killed She He, whereupon the emperor gathered together a force of ex-convicts to make an assault on Chaoxian.

In the autumn Yang Pu, the General of the Towered Ships, embarked from Qi and crossed the Gulf of Bohai with a force of 50,000 soldiers, while the general of the left Xun Zhi marched out of Liaodong to aid in punishing Wei Youqu. Wei Youqu called out his troops and blocked the passes.

One of Xun Zhi's battalion commanders named Duo took it upon himself to lead a large number of the troops of Liaodong on ahead of the rest, and as a result suffered a severe defeat. Many of his men were routed and fled back to Liaodong, and Duo was tried under military law and executed. As a result Yang Pu and 7,000 of his men from Qi succeeded in reaching Wangxian, the capital of Chaoxian, first. Wei Youqu had withdrawn into the city, but when he observed that Yang Pu's force was very small, he marched out and attacked, defeating and routing Yang Pu's army. Yang Pu, having lost most of his men, was forced to flee to the mountains, where he spent ten days or more rounding up the remnants of his army, until he had gathered together a sizable force again. Xun Zhi in the meantime was attacking the Chaoxian army west of the Bei River, but was unable to break their line or advance any farther.

The emperor, seeing that neither of his generals was accomplishing much, dispatched Wei Shan to threaten Wei Youqu with further military action if he did not submit. When Wei Youqu received the Han envoy, he bowed his head and apologized for his actions: "I wanted to surrender, but I was afraid that the two generals would go back on their promises of safety and kill me. Now that I see you bear the seals of a genuine envoy, I beg to surrender." To make amends, he also agreed to send his son, the crown prince, to the capital to wait on the emperor, and to present a gift of 5,000 horses, as well as provisions for the Han armies.

The crown prince set off, accompanied by a force of 10,000 men bearing arms, and was about to cross the Bei River, but the Han envoy and Xun Zhi, suspecting his intentions, told him that, since he had already surrendered, he ought to order his men to lay down their arms. The crown prince in turn began to suspect that the envoy and Xun Zhi were plotting to murder him and so he did not cross the river, but instead turned around and went back to Wangxian. The Han envoy Wei Shan then returned to Chang'an and reported to the emperor on his mission. The emperor executed him.

Xun Zhi once more attacked the Chaoxian army west of the Bei River and, defeating it, advanced to Wangxian, camping in a semicircle around the northwest corner of the city. Yang Pu arrived at the same time with his forces and took up a position south of the city. Wei Youqu, however, guarded his city well, and though several months passed, the Han forces had still not succeeded in taking it.

Xun Zhi had formerly served at court and had enjoyed favour with the emperor. Leading an army made up of men from Yan and Dai, he had plunged forward on a wave of victory and many of his soldiers had grown proud and reckless. Yang Pu, on the other hand, had come by sea with his band from Qi and had already suffered a number of times from defeat and desertion. In his earlier encounter with Wei Youqu he had been shamefully trounced and had lost many of his men, so that his soldiers were all afraid of the enemy and he himself was deeply mortified. Thus, although he was now taking part in the siege against Wei Youqu, he did everything he could to bring about a peaceful settlement.

Xun Zhi in the meantime made a sudden attack on the city, whereupon the high minister of Chaoxian sent men in secret to discuss plans for a surrender agreement with Yang Pu. Messengers were sent back and forth several times between the two parties, but no final agreement was reached. Xun Zhi repeatedly set a date with Yang Pu for a joint attack on the city, but Yang Pu, anxious to complete arrangements for the surrender as soon as possible, failed each time to put in an appearance. Xun Zhi then began sending envoys of his own to spread discord among the men of Chaoxian and effect a surrender. The men of Chaoxian, however, refused to listen to his offers and continued to favour negotiating with Yang Pu. As a result, relations between the two generals became strained. Xun Zhi, considering the fact that Yang Pu had earlier committed the military sin of losing his army and observing that he was now secretly on good terms with the men of Chaoxian and was making no effort to capture their city, began to suspect that Yang Pu was planning to revolt, but he did not dare at this point to announce his suspicions publicly.

Meanwhile the emperor declared, "Formerly these two generals were unable to make any progress in their campaign, and so I sent Wei Shan as my envoy to persuade Wei Youqu to surrender and send the crown prince of Chaoxian to court. But because Wei Shan was not able to conclude the negotiations on his own, he consulted with Xun Zhi and the two of them acted wrongly and in the end upset the whole agreement. Now Xun Zhi and Yang Pu are besieging the city of Wangxian and again there seems to be a clash of opinions. That is the reason the affair has dragged on so long without reaching a settlement!" He then dispatched Gongsun Sui, the governor of Ji'nan, to go and straighten things out, giving him authority to take what measures might be necessary to clear up the matter.

When Gongsun Sui arrived on the scene, Xun Zhi said to him, "The men of Chaoxian should have given in a long time ago. There appears to be some reason why they refuse to capitulate." He then told him how Yang Pu had failed to appear at the times agreed upon for an attack and related in detail all the doubts that he harboured concerning Yang Pu. "If some action is not taken at once, I am afraid a major disaster will result. The emperor will lose not only Yang Pu and his men, but they will take sides with Chaoxian and wipe out my army as well!"

Gongun Sui agreed with him and, using the imperial credentials which he carried, summoned Yang Pu to come to Xun Zhi's camp to plan the next move. Once there, he ordered Xun Zhi's subordinates to arrest Yang Pu and combine the armies of the two generals. When Gongsun Sui reported his actions to the emperor, the emperor sent back orders to have Gongsun Sui executed.

With both armies now under his own command, Xun Zhi began to press his attacks on Chaoxian. At this point the prime ministers of Chaoxian, Luren, and Han Yin; Can, the prime minister of Niqi; and a general named Wang Jia, began to plot together, saying, "Originally we had planned to surrender to Yang Pu, but now he has been arrested and Xun Zhi, who is in command of both armies, is pressing his attacks with increasing intensity. It is unlikely that we can win out against him, and at the same time the king refuses to surrender!" Han Yin, Wang Jia, and Luren then fled from the city; Luren was killed on the way, but the others succeeded in surrendering to the Han forces.

In the summer of the third year of *yuanfeng* (108 BC) Can, the prime minister of Niqi, sent men to assassinate Wei Youqu, the king of Chaoxian, and to announce the surrender of the state. The city of Wangxian, however, had not yet capitulated, and the former high minister of Wei Youqu named Chengsi declared the country once more in revolt and sent men to attack the Han officers. Xun Zhi then dispatched Zhang, the son of Wei Youqu, and Zui, the son of the prime minister Luren, to persuade the people to submit and to execute Cheng Si. Thus Chaoxian was at last conquered and the territory divided into four provinces.

Can, the prime minister of Niqi, was enfeoffed as marquis of Huaqing; Han Yin as marquis of Diju; Wang Jia as marquis of Pingzhou; and Wei Zhang as marquis of Ji. Because his father had been killed and because he had rendered signal service, Zui was made marquis of Nieyang. Xun Zhi was recalled to the capital and, on his arrival, tried on charges of inordinate striving for distinction, jealousy of his associates, and betrayal of strategy. He was executed and his corpse exposed in the market place. Yang Pu was also tried on charges of having arbitrarily advanced against the enemy when he reached Liekou instead of waiting for the arrival of Xun Zhi, and thereby losing many of his men. He was sentenced to execution but on payment of a fine was allowed to become a commoner.

The Grand Historian remarks: Wei Youqu trusted in the natural barriers protecting his land, but brought an end to the sacrifices of the state. She He achieved distinction through treachery and became the cause of the bloodshed. Yang Pu, leading a meagre army, met with hardship and blame; regretting his failure to win distinction in the siege of Panyu some years before, he sought for it this time, but instead aroused suspicion. Xun Zhi contended for glory, but he and Gongsun Sui suffered execution. Both armies disgraced themselves and none of their leaders were enfeoffed as marquises.[2]

---

[2] Like the remarks at the end of "The Account of Southern Yue", these are in four-character phrases with occasional end rhymes.

SHI JI 123: THE ACCOUNT OF DAYUAN

After the Han had sent its envoy to open up communications with the state of Daxia (Bactria), all the barbarians of the distant west craned their necks to the east and longed to catch a glimpse of China. Thus I made "The Account of Dayuan".

Zhang Qian was the first person to bring back a clear account of Dayuan (Ferghana).[1] He was a native of Hanzhong and served as a palace attendant during the *jianyuan* era (140-135 BC). At this time the emperor questioned various Xiongnu who had surrendered to the Han and they all reported that the Xiongnu had defeated the king of the Yuezhi people (Indo-scythians) and made his skull into a drinking vessel. As a result the Yuezhi had fled and bore a constant grudge against the Xiongnu, though as yet they had been unable to find anyone to join them in an attack on their enemy.

The Han at this time was engaged in a concerted effort to destroy the Xiongnu, and therefore, when the emperor heard this, he decided to try to send an envoy to establish relations with the Yuezhi. To reach them, however, an envoy would inevitably have to pass through Xiongnu territory. The emperor accordingly sent out a summons for men capable of undertaking such a mission. Zhang Qian, who was a palace attendant at the time, answered the summons and was appointed as envoy to the Yuezhi.

He set out from Longxi, accompanied by Ganfu, a Xiongnu slave who belonged to a family in Tangyi. They travelled west through the territory of the Xiongnu and were captured by the Xiongnu and taken before the *Shanyu*. The *Shanyu* detained them and refused to let them proceed. "The Yuezhi people live north of me," he said. "What does the Han mean by trying to send an envoy to them! Do you suppose that if I tried to send an embassy to the kingdom of Yue in the southeast the Han would let my men pass through China?"

---

[1] As in previous chapters, the better-known western equivalents of Chinese geographical names have been added in brackets where possible. Some of these identifications, however, are still a matter of dispute among scholars.

The Xiongnu detained Zhang Qian for over ten years and gave him a wife from their own people, by whom he had a son. Zhang Qian never once relinquished the imperial credentials that marked him as an envoy of the Han, however, and after he had lived in Xiongnu territory for some time and was less closely watched than at first, he and his party finally managed to escape and resume their journey toward the Yuezhi.

After hastening west for twenty or thirty days, they reached the kingdom of Dayuan. The king of Dayuan had heard of the wealth of the Han empire and wished to establish communication with it, though as yet he had been unable to do so. When he met Zhang Qian he was overjoyed and asked where Zhang Qian wished to go.

"I was dispatched as envoy of the Han to the Yuezhi, but the Xiongnu blocked my way and I have only just now managed to escape," he replied. "I beg Your Highness to give me some guides to show me the way. If I can reach my destination and return to the Han to make my report, the Han will reward you with countless gifts!"

The king of Dayuan trusted his words and sent him on his way, giving him guides and interpreters to take him to the state of Kangju (Trans-Oxiana). From there he was able to make his way to the land of the Great Yuezhi.

Since the king of the Great Yuezhi had been killed by the Xiongnu, his son had succeeded him as ruler and had forced the kingdom of Daxia (Bactria) to recognize his sovereignty. The region he ruled was rich and fertile and seldom troubled by invaders, and the king thought only of his own enjoyment. He considered the Han too far away to bother with and had no particular intention of avenging his father's death by attacking the Xiongnu. From the court of the Yuezhi, Zhang Qian travelled on to the state of Daxia, but in the end he was never able to interest the Yuezhi in his proposals.

After spending a year or so in the area, he began to journey back along the Nanshan or Southern Mountains, intending to re-enter China through the territory of the Qiang barbarians, but he was once more captured by the Xiongnu and detained for over a year.

Just at this time the *Shanyu* died and the Luli King of the Left attacked the *Shanyu*'s heir and set himself up as the new *Shanyu* (126 BC). As a result of this the whole Xiongnu nation was in turmoil and Zhang Qian, along with his Xiongnu wife and the former slave Ganfu, was able to escape and return to China. The emperor honoured Zhang Qian with the post of palace counsellor and awarded Ganfu the title of "Lord Who Carries Out His Mission".

Zhang Qian was a man of great strength, determination, and generosity. He trusted others and in turn was liked by the barbarians. Ganfu, who was a Xiongnu by birth, was good at archery, and whenever he and Zhang Qian were short of food he would shoot birds and beasts to keep them supplied. When Zhang Qian first set out on his mission, he was accompanied by over 100 men, but after thirteen years abroad, only he and Ganfu managed to make their way back to China.

Zhang Qian in person visited the lands of Dayuan, the Great Yuezhi, Daxia, and Kangju, and in addition he gathered reports on five or six other large states in the neighbourhood. All of his information he related to the emperor on his return. The substance of his report was as follows:

> Dayuan lies southwest of the territory of the Xiongnu, some 10,000 *li* directly west of China. The people are settled on the land, plowing the fields and growing rice and wheat. They also make wine out of grapes. The region has many fine horses which sweat blood;[2] their forebears are supposed to have been foaled from heavenly horses. The people live in houses in fortified cities, there being some seventy or more cities of various sizes in the region. The population numbers several hundred thousand. The people fight with bows and spears and can shoot from horseback.
>
> Dayuan is bordered on the north by Kangju, on the west by the kingdom of the Great Yuezhi, on the southwest by Daxia, on the northeast by the land of the Wusun, and on the east by Yumi and Yutian (Khotan).
>
> West of Yutian, all the rivers flow west and empty into the Western Sea, but east of there they flow eastward into the Salt Swamp (Lob Nor). The waters of the Salt Swamp flow underground and on the south form the source from which the Yellow River rises. There are many precious stones in the region and the rivers flow into China. The Loulan and Gushi peoples live in fortified cities along the Salt Swamp. The Salt Swamp is some 5,000 *li* from Chang'an. The western branch of the Xiongnu occupies the region from the Salt Swamp east to a point south of the Great Wall at Longxi, where its territory adjoins that of

---

[2] The "bloody sweat" was apparently the result of parasites which caused small running sores in the hides of the horses.

the Qiang barbarians, thus cutting off the road from China to the West.

The Wusun live some 2,000 *li* northeast of Dayuan, moving from place to place in the region with their herds of animals. Their customs are much like those of the Xiongnu. They have 20,000 or 30,000 skilled archers and are very daring in battle. They were originally subjects of the Xiongnu, but later, becoming more powerful, they refused any longer to attend the gatherings of the Xiongnu court, though still acknowledging themselves part of the Xiongnu nation.

Kangju is situated some 2,000 *li* northwest of Dayuan. Its people likewise are nomads and resemble the Yuezhi in their customs. They have 80,000 or 90,000 skilled archer fighters. The country is small, and borders Dayuan. It acknowledges nominal sovereignty to the Yuezhi people in the south and the Xiongnu in the east.

Yancai lies some 2,000 *li* northwest of Kangju. The people are nomads and their customs are generally similar to those of the people of Kangju. The country has over 100,000 archer warriors, and borders a great shoreless lake, perhaps what is known as the Northern Sea (Caspian Sea?).

The Great Yuezhi live some 2,000 or 3,000 *li* west of Dayuan, north of the Gui (Oxus) River. They are bordered on the south by Daxia, on the west by Anxi (Parthia), and on the north by Kangju. They are a nation of nomads, moving from place to place with their herds, and their customs are like those of the Xiongnu. They have some 100,000 or 200,000 archer warriors. Formerly they were very powerful and despised the Xiongnu, but later, when Maodun became leader of the Xiongnu nation, he attacked and defeated the Yuezhi. Some time afterwards his son, the Old *Shanyu*, killed the king of the Yuezhi and made his skull into a drinking cup.

The Yuezhi originally lived in the area between the Qilian or Heavenly Mountains and Dunhuang, but after they were defeated by the Xiongnu they moved far away to the west, beyond Dayuan, where they attacked and conquered the people of Daxia and set up the court of their king on the northern bank of the Gui River. A small number of their people who were unable to make the journey west sought refuge among the Qiang barbarians in the Southern Mountains, where they are known as the Lesser Yuezhi.

Anxi is situated several thousand *li* west of the region of the Great

Yuezhi. The people are settled on the land, cultivating the fields and growing rice and wheat. They also make wine out of grapes. They have walled cities like the people of Dayuan, the region containing several hundred cities of various sizes. The kingdom, which borders the Gui River, is very large, measuring several thousand *li* square. Some of the inhabitants are merchants who travel by carts or boats to neighbouring countries, sometimes journeying several thousand *li*. The coins of the country are made of silver and bear the face of the king. When the king dies, the currency is immediately changed and new coins issued with the face of his successor. The people keep records by writing horizontally on strips of leather. To the west lies Tiaozhi (Mesopotamia) and to the north Yancai and Lixuan (Hyrcania).

Tiaozhi is situated several thousand *li* west of Anxi and borders the Western Sea (Persian Gulf?). It is hot and damp, and the people live by cultivating the fields and planting rice. In this region live great birds which lay eggs as large as pots. The people are very numerous and are ruled by many petty chiefs. The ruler of Anxi gives orders to these chiefs and regards them as his vassals. The people are very skilful at performing tricks that amaze the eye. The old men of Anxi say they have heard that in Tiaozhi are to be found the River of Weak Water and the Queen Mother of the West, though they admit that they have never seen either of them.[3]

Daxia is situated over 2,000 *li* southwest of Dayuan, south of the Gui River. Its people cultivate the land and have cities and houses. Their customs are like those of Dayuan. It has no great ruler but only a number of petty chiefs ruling the various cities. The people are poor in the use of arms and afraid of battle, but they are clever at commerce. After the Great Yuezhi moved west and attacked and conquered Daxia, the entire country came under their sway. The population of the country is large, numbering some 1,000,000 or more persons. The capital is called the city of Lanshi (Bactra) and has a market where all sorts of goods are bought and sold.

Southeast of Daxia is the kingdom of Shendu (India). "When I was in Daxia," Zhang Qian reported, "I saw bamboo canes from Qiong

---

[3] The Queen Mother of the West was an immortal spirit who was said to live in some fabulous region of the west. According to later writers the River of Weak Water was so called because it would not float even a goose feather.

and cloth made in the province of Shu. When I asked the people how they had gotten such articles, they replied, 'Our merchants go to buy them in the markets of Shendu.' Shendu, they told me, lies several thousand *li* southeast of Daxia. The people cultivate the land and live much like the people of Daxia. The region is said to be hot and damp. The inhabitants ride elephants when they go into battle. The kingdom is situated on a great river.

"We know that Daxia is located 12,000 *li* southwest of China. Now if the kingdom of Shendu is situated several thousand *li* southeast of Daxia and obtains goods which are produced in Shu, it seems to me that it must not be very far away from Shu. At present, if we try to send envoys to Daxia by way of the mountain trails that lead through the territory of the Qiang people, they will be molested by the Qiang, while if we send them a little farther north, they will be captured by the Xiongnu. It would seem that the most direct route, as well as the safest, would be that out of Shu."

Thus the emperor learned of Dayuan, Daxia, Anxi, and the others, all great states rich in unusual products whose people cultivated the land and made their living in much the same way as the Chinese. All these states, he was told, were militarily weak and prized Han goods and wealth. He also learned that to the north of them lived the Yuezhi and Kangju people who were strong in arms but who could be persuaded by gifts and the prospect of gain to acknowledge allegiance to the Han court. If it were only possible to win over these states by peaceful means, the emperor thought, he could then extend his domain 10,000 *li*, attract to his court men of strange customs who would come translating and retranslating their languages,[4] and his might would become known to all the lands within the four seas.

The emperor was therefore delighted, and approved Zhang Qian's suggestion. He ordered Zhang Qian to start out from Jianwei in Shu on a secret mission to search for Daxia. The party broke up into four groups proceeding out of the regions of Mang, Ran, Xi, and Qiong and Po. All the groups managed to advance 1,000 or 2,000 *li*, but they were blocked on the north by the Di and Zuo tribes and on the south by the Sui and Kunming tribes. The Kunming tribes have no

---

[4] A stock phrase in Han rhetoric meaning that such people come from so far away that they have no knowledge of the Chinese language and their words must therefore be "translated and retranslated" through a number of intermediary languages before being put into Chinese.

rulers but devote themselves to plunder and robbery, and as soon as they seized any of the Han envoys they immediately murdered them. Thus none of the parties were ever able to get through to their destination. They did learn, however, that some 1,000 or more *li* to the west there was a state called Dianyue whose people rode elephants and that the merchants from Shu sometimes went there with their goods on unofficial trading missions. In this way the Han, while searching for a route to Daxia, first came into contact with the kingdom of Dian.

Earlier the Han had tried to establish relations with the barbarians of the southwest, but the expense proved too great and no road could be found through the region and so the project was abandoned. After Zhang Qian reported that it was possible to reach Daxia by travelling through the region of the southwestern barbarians, the Han once more began efforts to establish relations with the tribes in the area.

Zhang Qian was made a subordinate commander and sent to accompany the general in chief Wei Qing on expeditions against the Xiongnu. Because he knew where water and pasture were to be found in the Xiongnu territory, he was able to save the army from hardship. He was enfeoffed as Bowang or "Broad Vision" marquis. This occurred in the sixth year of the *yuanshuo* era (123 BC).

The following year he was appointed colonel of the guard and sent with General Li Guang on an expedition out of Youbeiping to attack the Xiongnu. The Xiongnu surrounded Li Guang's army and wiped out most of the men. Zhang Qian was accused of having arrived late at his rendezvous with Li Guang and was sentenced to execution, but on payment of a fine he was allowed to become a commoner. This same year the Han sent the swift cavalry general Huo Qubing against the Xiongnu. He defeated and killed 30,000 or 40,000 of the Xiongnu in the western region[5] and rode as far as the Qilian Mountains. The following year the Hunye king led his barbarian hordes and surrendered to the Han, and the Xiongnu completely disappeared from the region from Jincheng and Hexi west along the Southern Mountains to the Salt Swamp. Occasionally Xiongnu scouts would appear, but even they were rare. Two years later the Han armies attacked the *Shanyu* and chased him north of the desert.

During this time the emperor occasionally questioned Zhang Qian about Daxia and the other states of the west. Zhang Qian, who had been deprived of his marquisate, replied, "When I was living among the Xiongnu I heard about the king of the Wusun people, who is named Kunmo. Kunmo's father was the

---

[5] Following the reading in *Han shu* 61.

ruler of a small state on the western border of the Xiongnu territory. The Xiongnu attacked and killed his father, and Kunmo, then only a baby, was cast out in the wilderness to die. But the birds came and flew over the place where he was, bearing meat in their beaks, and the wolves suckled him, so that he was able to survive. When the *Shanyu* heard of this, he was filled with wonder and, believing that Kunmo was a god, he took him in and reared him. When Kunmo had grown to manhood, the *Shanyu* put him in command of a band of troops and he several times won merit in battle. The *Shanyu* then made him the leader of the people whom his father had ruled in former times and ordered him to guard the western forts. Kunmo gathered together his people, looked after them and led them in attacks on the small settlements in the neighbourhood. Soon he had 20,000 or 30,000 skilled archers who were trained in aggressive warfare. When the *Shanyu* died, Kunmo led his people far away, declared himself an independent ruler, and refused any longer to journey to the meetings of the Xiongnu court. The Xiongnu sent surprise parties of troops to attack him, but they were unable to win a victory. In the end the Xiongnu decided that he must be a god and left him alone, still claiming that he was a subject of theirs but no longer making any large-scale attacks on him.

"Now the *Shanyu* is suffering from the recent blow delivered by our armies, and the region formerly occupied by the Hunye king and his people is deserted. The barbarians are well known to be greedy for Han wealth and goods. If we could make use of this opportunity to send rich gifts and bribes to the Wusun people and persuade them to move farther east and occupy the region which formerly belonged to the Hunye king, then the Han could conclude an alliance of brotherhood with them and, under the circumstances, they would surely do as we say. If we could get them to obey us, it would be like cutting off the right arm of the Xiongnu! Then, once we had established an alliance with the Wusun, Daxia and the other countries to the west could all be persuaded to come to court and acknowledge themselves our foreign vassals."

The emperor approved of this suggestion and, appointing Zhang Qian as a general of palace attendants, put him in charge of a party of 300 men, each of whom was provided with two horses. In addition the party took along tens of thousands of cattle and sheep and carried gold and silk goods worth 100,000,000 cash. Many of the men in the party were given the imperial credentials making them assistant envoys so that they could be sent to neighbouring states along the way.

When Zhang Qian reached the kingdom of the Wusun, the king of the

Wusun, Kunmo, tried to treat the Han envoys in the same way that the *Shanyu* treated them. Zhang Qian was greatly outraged and, knowing that the barbarians were greedy, said, "The Son of Heaven has sent me with these gifts, but if you do not prostrate yourself to receive them, I shall have to take them back!"

With this Kunmo jumped up from his seat and prostrated himself to receive the gifts. The other details of the envoys' reception Zhang Qian allowed to remain as before. Zhang Qian then delivered his message, saying, "If the Wusun will consent to move east and occupy the region of the Hunye king, then the Han will send you a princess of the imperial family to be your wife."

But the Wusun people were split into several groups and the king was old. Living far away from China, he had no idea how large the Han empire was. Moreover, his people had for a long time in the past been subjects of the Xiongnu and still lived nearer to them than to China. The high ministers of the king were therefore all afraid of the Xiongnu and did not wish to move back east. The king alone could not force his will upon his subjects, and Zhang Qian was therefore unable to persuade him to listen to his proposal.

Kunmo had over ten sons, among them one named Dalu who was very strong and skilful in leading the people. He lived in a separate part of the realm and had over 10,000 horsemen under his command.

Dalu's older brother, who had been designated as heir to Kunmo, had a son name Cenqu. The heir apparent died early and on his deathbed he begged his father, Kunmo, to make Cenqu the new heir. "Do not allow anyone to take his position away from him!" he pleaded. Kunmo, moved by grief, gave his permission and designated his grandson Cenqu as the new heir apparent.

Dalu was furious that he himself had not been appointed heir and, persuading his other brothers to join him, led his forces in a revolt, planning to attack Cenqu and Kunmo. Kunmo, who was old and lived in constant fear that Dalu would attack and kill his grandson, gave Cenqu a force of over 10,000 horsemen and sent him to live in another part of the realm, while he himself kept over 10,000 horsemen for his own protection. Thus it happened that when Zhang Qian arrived the Wusun people were split into three factions, though the large part of them acknowledged the leadership of Kunmo. Kunmo for this reason did not dare make any promises to Zhang Qian on his own authority.

Zhang Qian dispatched his assistant envoys to Dayuan, Kangju, the Great Yuezhi, Daxia, Anxi, Shendu, Yutian, Yumo, and the other neighbouring states, the Wusun providing them with guides and interpreters. Then he returned to China, accompanied by twenty or thirty envoys from the Wusun and a similar number of horses which the Wusun sent in exchange for the Han gifts. The Wusun envoys thus had an opportunity to see with their own eyes the breadth and greatness of the Han empire.

On his return Zhang Qian was honoured with the post of grand messenger, ranking him among the nine highest ministers of the government. A year or so later he died.

The Wusun envoys, having seen how rich and populous the Han was, returned and reported what they had learned to their own people, and after this the Wusun regarded the Han with greater respect. A year or so later the envoys whom Zhang Qian had sent to Daxia and the other states of the west all returned, accompanied by envoys from those states, and for the first time relations were established between the lands of the northwest and the Han. It was Zhang Qian, however, who opened the way for this move, and all the envoys who journeyed to the lands in later times relied upon his reputation to gain them a hearing. As a result of his efforts, the foreign states trusted the Han envoys.

After Zhang Qian's death the Xiongnu learned that the Han had established relations with the Wusun and, infuriated by the news, decided to make an attack on the Wusun. By this time the Han had already sent envoys to the Wusun, as well as the Dayuan, the Great Yuezhi, and the other states to the south, and the Wusun, frightened by the threat of a Xiongnu attack, sent an envoy with a gift of horses to the Han court to ask that a Han princess be granted to the Wusun leader and an alliance of brotherhood concluded. The emperor referred the matter to his ministers for debate, and they all replied, "The princess should not be sent until the betrothal gifts have been duly received."

Sometime earlier the emperor had divined by the *Book of Changes* and been told that "divine horses are due to appear from the northwest". When the Wusun came with their horses, which were of an excellent breed, he named them "heavenly horses". Later, however, he obtained the blood-sweating horses from Dayuan, which were even hardier. He therefore changed the name of the Wusun horses, calling them "horses from the western extremity", and used the name "heavenly horses" for the horses of Dayuan.

At this time the Han first built fortifications west of the district of Lingju and established the province of Jiuquan in order to provide a safe route to the lands of the northwest, and as a result more and more envoys were sent to Anxi, Yancai, Lixuan, Tiaozhi, and Shendu. The emperor was very fond of the Dayuan horses and sent a constant stream of envoys to that region to acquire them.

The largest of these embassies to foreign states numbered several hundred persons, while even the smaller parties included over 100 members, though later, as the envoys became more accustomed to the route, the number was gradually reduced. The credentials and gifts which the envoys bore with them were much like those supplied to the envoys in Zhang Qian's time. In the course of one year anywhere from five or six to over ten parties would be sent out. Those travelling to distant lands required eight or nine years to complete their journey, while those visiting nearer regions would return after a few years.

At this time the Han had already overthrown the kingdom of Yue in the southeast, and the barbarian tribes living southwest of Shu were all filled with awe and begged to be ruled by Han officials and to be allowed to pay their respects at court. The Han therefore set up the provinces of Yizhou, Yuesui, Zangge, Chenli, and Wenshan, hoping to extend the area under Han control so that a route could be opened to Daxia. The Han sent Bo Shichang, Lü Yueren, and others, over ten parties in the space of one year, out of these new provinces to try to get through to Daxia. The parties were all blocked by the Kunming barbarians, however, who stole their goods and murdered the envoys, so that none of them were ever able to reach Daxia.

The Han then freed the criminals of the three districts of the capital area and, adding to them 20,000 or 30,000 soldiers from Ba and Shu, dispatched them under the command of two generals, Guo Chang and Wei Guang, to go and attack the Kunming tribes that were blocking the Han envoys. The army succeeded in killing or capturing 20,000 or 30,000 of the enemy before departing from the area, but later, when another attempt was made to send envoys to Daxia, the Kunming once more fell upon them and none were able to reach their destination. By this time, however, so many envoys had journeyed to Daxia by the northern route out of Jiuquan that the foreign states in the area had become surfeited with Han goods and no longer regarded them with any esteem.

After Zhang Qian achieved honour and position by opening up communications with the lands of the west, all the officials and soldiers who had accompanied him vied with one another in submitting reports to the emperor telling of the wonders and profits to be gained in foreign lands and requesting to become envoys. The emperor considered that, since the lands of the west were so far away, no man would choose to make the journey simply for his own pleasure, and so when he had listened to their stories he immediately presented them with the credentials of an envoy. In addition he called for volunteers from among the people and fitted out with attendants and dispatched anyone who came forward, without inquiring into his background, in an effort to broaden the area that had been opened to communication.

When the envoys returned from a mission, it invariably happened that they had plundered or stolen goods on their way or their reports failed to meet with the approval of the emperor. The emperor, who was very practised at handling such matters, would then have them summarily investigated and accused of some major offence so that they would be spurred to anger and would volunteer to undertake another mission in order to redeem themselves. Thus there was never any lack of men to act as envoys, and they came to regard it as a trifling matter to break the law. The officials and soldiers who had accompanied them on a mission would in turn start at once enthusiastically describing the wealth to be found in the foreign nations; those who told the most impressive tales were granted the seals of an envoy, while those who spoke more modesty were made assistants. As a result all sorts of worthless men hurried forward with wild tales to imitate their example.

The envoys were all sons of poor families who handled the government gifts and goods that were entrusted to them as though they were private property and looked for opportunities to buy goods at a cheap price in the foreign countries and make a profit on their return to China. The men of the foreign lands soon became disgusted when they found that each of the Han envoys told some different story and, considering that the Han armies were too far away to worry about, refused to supply the envoys with food and provisions, making things very difficult for them. The Han envoys were soon reduced to a state of destitution and distress and, their tempers mounting, fell to quarrelling and even attacking each other.

The states of Loulan and Gushi, though very small, lay right across the path that the envoys travelled, and they attacked and plundered the parties of Wang Hui and other envoys with extreme ferocity. In addition, raiding parties of Xiongnu from time to time appeared in the region to swoop down on the envoys to the western states and block their advance. The envoys hastened to the emperor with complaints of all the hardships which they suffered and suggested that, although the inhabitants of the western regions lived in fortified cities, they were poor in combat and could easily be attacked.

As a result of their complaints, the emperor dispatched Zhao Ponu, the former Congpiao marquis, with a force of 20,000 or 30,000 troops recruited from the dependent states and the provinces. He advanced as far as the Xionghe River, hoping to attack the Xiongnu, but they withdrew.

The following year an attack was made on Gushi. Zhao Ponu, with a force of 700 or more light horsemen, led the attack, captured the king of Loulan, and succeeded in conquering Gushi. At the same time he used his armies to intimidate the Wusun, Dayuan, and the other states in the region. On his return Zhao Ponu was enfeoffed as marquis of Zhuoye.

Wang Hui, who had several times acted as an envoy and been mistreated by the people of Loulan, took his complaint to the emperor. The emperor called out a force of troops and appointed Wang Hui as aide to Zhao Ponu, in which capacity he attacked and defeated Loulan. He was enfeoffed as marquis of Hao. After this a series of defence stations was established from Jiuquan west to the Jade Gate Pass.

The Wusun sent 1,000 horses to the Han as a betrothal gift for the Han princess whom they had been promised. The Han then sent a princess of the imperial family, the daughter of the king of Jiangdu, to be the wife of the Wusun leader. Kunmo, the king of the Wusun, made her his Bride of the Right. The Xiongnu also sent one of their women to marry Kunmo, and he made her his Bride of the Left. Later, saying that he was too old, he gave the Han princess to his grandson Cenqu to be his bride. The Wusun have a great many horses, the wealthy men among them owning as many as 4,000 or 5,000.[6]

When the Han envoys first visited the kingdom of Anxi, the king of Anxi dispatched a party of 20,000 horsemen to meet them on the eastern border of his kingdom. The capital of the kingdom is several thousand *li* from the eastern border, and as the envoys proceeded there they passed through twenty or thirty cities inhabited by great numbers of people. When the Han envoys set out again to return to China, the king of Anxi dispatched envoys of his own to accompany them, and after the latter had visited China and reported on its great breadth and might, the king sent some of the eggs of the great birds which live in the region, and skilled tricksters of Lixuan, to the Han court as gifts. In addition, the smaller states west of Dayuan, such Huanqian and Dayi, as well as those east of Dayuan, such as Gushi, Yumi, and Suxie, all sent parties to accompany the Han envoys back to China and present gifts at court. The emperor was delighted at this.

The emperor also sent envoys to trace the Yellow River to its source. They found that it rises in the land of Yutian among mountains rich in precious stones,

---

[6]The purpose of this last statement is no doubt to indicate that 1,000 horses was not by any means a very lavish betrothal gift to send in exchange for the Han princess. The parallel passage in *Han shu* 96B gives a much more elaborate account of the princess's attendants and her reception at the Wusun court and includes a famous poem supposedly written by her lamenting her exile to a strange and distant land.

many of which they brought back with them. The emperor studied the old maps and books and decided to name these mountains, where the Yellow River has its source, the Kunlun Mountains.

At this time the emperor made frequent tours east to the seacoast, and at such times he would take all the visitors from foreign lands along in his party, passing through large and populous cities on the way, scattering gifts of money and silk among the visitors, and supplying them with generous accommodation in order to impress upon them the wealth of the Han empire. He would hold great wrestling matches and displays of unusual skills and all sorts of rare creatures, gathering together large numbers of people to watch. He entertained the foreign visitors with veritable lakes of wine and forests of meat and had them shown around to the various granaries and storehouses to see how much wealth was laid away there, astounding and overwhelming them with the breadth and greatness of the Han empire. After the skills of the foreign magicians and tricksters had been imported into China, the wrestling matches and displays of unusual feats developed and improved with each year, and from this time on entertainments of this type became increasingly popular.

In this way party after party of envoys from the foreign lands of the northwest would arrive in China and, after a while, take their leave. Those from the states west of Dayuan, however, believing that their homelands were too far away from China to be in any danger, continued to conduct themselves with great arrogance and self-assurance; it was impossible to make them conform to proper ritual or to compel them to obey the wishes of the Han court.

The lands from that of the Wusun on west to Anxi were situated nearer to the Xiongnu than to China, and it was well known that the Xiongnu had earlier caused the Yuezhi people great suffering. Therefore, whenever a Xiongnu envoy appeared in the region carrying credentials from the *Shanyu*, he was escorted from state to state and provided with food, and no one dared to detain him or cause him any difficulty. In the case of the Han envoys, however, if they did not hand out silks or other goods they were given no food, and unless they purchased animals in the markets they could get no mounts for their riders. This was because the people considered the Han too far away to bother about. They also believed that the Han had plenty of goods and money and it was therefore proper to make the envoys pay for whatever they wanted. As may be seen, they were much more afraid of the Xiongnu envoys than of those from the Han.

The regions around Dayuan make wine out of grapes, the wealthier inhabitants keeping as much as 10,000 or more piculs stored away. It can be kept for as long as twenty or thirty years without spoiling. The people love their wine and the horses love their alfalfa. The Han envoys brought back grape and alfalfa seeds to China and the emperor for the first time tried growing these plants in areas of rich soil. Later, when the Han acquired large numbers of the "heavenly horses" and the envoys from foreign states began to arrive with their retinues, the lands on all sides of the emperor's summer palaces and pleasure towers were planted with grapes and alfalfa for as far as the eye could see.

Although the states from Dayuan west to Anxi speak rather different languages, their customs are generally similar and their languages mutually intelligible. The men all have deep-set eyes and profuse beards and whiskers. They are skilful at commerce and will haggle over a fraction of a cent. Women are held in great respect, and the men make decisions on the advice of their women. No silk or lacquer is produced anywhere in the region, and the casting of coins and vessels was formerly unknown. Later, however, when some of the Chinese soldiers attached to the Han embassies ran away and surrendered to the people of the area, they taught them how to cast metal and manufacture weapons. Now, whenever the people of the region lay their hands on any Han gold or silver they immediately make it into vessels and do not use it for currency.

By this time a number of embassies had been sent to the west and even the lesser attendants who went along on the expeditions had become accustomed to appearing before the emperor and relating their experiences. "Dayuan has some fine horses in the city of Ershi (Sutrishna)," they reported, "but the people keep them hidden and refuse to give any to the Han envoys!"

The emperor had already taken a great liking to the horses of Dayuan, and when he heard this he was filled with excitement and expectation. He dispatched a party of able young men and carriage masters with 1,000 pieces of gold and a golden horse to go to the king of Dayuan and ask him for some of the fine horses of Ershi.

But Dayuan by this time was overflowing with Han goods, and the men of the state therefore plotted together, saying, "The Han is far away from us and on several occasions has lost men in the salt-water wastes between our country and China. Yet if the Han parties go farther north, they will be harassed by the Xiongnu, while if they try to go to the south they will suffer from lack of water and fodder. Moreover, there are many places along the route where there are no cities whatsoever and they are apt to run out of provisions. The Han embassies that have come to us are made up of only a few hundred men, and yet they are always short of food and over half the men die on the journey. Under such circumstances how could the Han possibly send a large army against us? What have we to worry about? Furthermore, the horses of Ershi are one of the most valuable treasures of our state!"

In the end, therefore, they refused to give the Han envoys any horses. Enraged, the Han envoys cursed the men of Dayuan, smashed the golden horse with a mallet, and departed.

The nobles of Dayuan were furious, complaining that the Han envoys had treated them with the utmost contempt. After the Han party had left, therefore, they sent orders to the people of Yucheng on the eastern border of the kingdom to attack and kill the envoys and seize their goods.

When the emperor received word of the fate of the envoys, he was in a rage. Yao Dinghan and others, who had acted as envoys to Dayuan in the past, assured the emperor that the kingdom was militarily weak and that it would not require a force of more than 3,000 Han soldiers equipped with powerful crossbows to conquer it and take the entire population captive. Earlier, when the emperor had dispatched Zhao Ponu to attack Loulan, Zhao had led an advance party of only 700 horsemen and had taken the king of Loulan prisoner. The emperor therefore believed the assurances of Yao Dinghan and the others and, wishing to have some excuse to enfeoff the relatives of his favourite, Lady Li, he honoured her brother Li Guangli with the title of Ershi General and dispatched him with a force of 6,000 horsemen recruited from the dependent states, as well as 20,000 or 30,000 young men of bad reputation rounded up from the provinces and kingdoms, to launch an attack on Dayuan. The title of Ershi General was given to Li Guangli because it was expected that he would reach the city Ershi and capture the fine horses there. Zhao Shicheng was appointed director of martial law for the expedition, and Wang Hui, the former marquis of Hao, was ordered to act as guide. Li Che was made a subordinate commander and put in charge of various military affairs. This was in the first year of the *taiyuan* era (104 BC). At this time great swarms of locusts rose up in the area east of the Pass and flew west as far as Dunhuang.

General Li and his army passed the Salt Swamp and were advancing west when they found that the inhabitants of the small states along the way, terrified by their approach, had all shut themselves up tightly in their walled cities and refused to supply any food to the army. Even attacks on the cities did not always prove successful. The army was able to obtain provisions from some of the cities that submitted, but in the case of others, if a few days of attack did not bring capitulation, the army would move on its way. Thus by the time Li Guangli reached Yucheng he had no more than a few thousand soldiers left, and all of these were suffering from hunger and exhaustion.

He attacked Yucheng, but was severely beaten and a great many of his men were killed or wounded. General Li then consulted Li Che, Zhao Shicheng, and his other officers and decided that, if they could not even conquer the city of Yucheng, there was absolutely no hope that they could make a successful attack on Ershi, the king's capital, farther to the west. They therefore decided to lead their troops back to China. The journey to Dayuan and back had taken them two years, and by the time they reached Dunhuang they had no more than one or two tenths of their original force left.

Li Guangli sent a messenger to the emperor explaining that the distance had been so great and he had been so short of provisions that his men, though brave enough in battle, had been defeated by hunger and not enough of them had survived the journey to make an attack on Dayuan possible. He asked that the army be disbanded for a while and a larger force recruited for another expedition later on.

When the emperor received word of this, he was enraged and sent an envoy with orders to close the pass at Jade Gate, saying that anyone from General Li's army who attempted to enter the country would be cut down on the spot.

General Li, afraid to move, remained for the time being at Dunhuang. This same summer over 20,000 Han soldiers under the command of Zhao Ponu were surrounded by the Xiongnu and forced to surrender.

The high ministers and court advisers all wanted the emperor to disband the army that had been sent to attack Dayuan and concentrate the strength of the empire on attacking the Xiongnu. But the emperor had already undertaken to punish Dayuan for its outrage and he was afraid that if his armies could not conquer even a small state like Dayuan, then Daxia and the other lands would come to despise the Han. No more fine horses could ever be obtained from Dayuan, the Wusun and Luntou people would scorn and mistreat the Han envoys, and China would become a laughing-stock among the foreign nations. He therefore had Deng Guang and the others who were most outspoken in their opposition to the Dayuan campaign handed over to the law officials for investigation, freed all the skilled bowmen who were in prison, and called out more young men of bad reputation and horsemen from the border states. By the end of a year or so he had sent 60,000 new men to Dunhuang to reinforce the army there, not counting porters and personal attendants. The army was provided with 100,000 oxen, over 30,000 horses, and tens of thousands of donkeys, mules, and camels, as well as plentiful provisions and a great number of crossbows and other weapons. The whole empire was thrown into a turmoil, relaying orders and providing men and supplies for the attack on Dayuan. Over fifty subordinate commanders were appointed to direct the army.

It was known that there were no wells in the capital city of Dayuan, the city drawing its water supply from rivers that flowed outside the walls. The emperor therefore sent water engineers to join the army so that when the time came they could divert the streams which flowed by the city and deprive the inhabitants of their water. A force of 180,000 soldiers was also dispatched to garrison the district of Juyan and Xiutu, which had been established north of Jiuquan and Zhangye in order to provide greater protection for Jiuquan. All men in the empire who came in the seven classes for reprobated persons[7] were called out and sent to transport supplies of dried boiled rice to Li Guangli's forces. The lines of transport wagons and marching men stretched without a break all the way west to Dunhuang. In addition, two men who were skilled in judging horses were appointed as commanders in charge of steeds so that, when the conquest of Dayuan had been accomplished, they would be on hand to select the finest horses to take back to China.

When all of this had been done, Li Guangli set off once again. This time he had far more men, and in every little state he came to the inhabitants came out to greet him with gifts of food for his army. When he reached Luntou, however, the people there refused to submit. He besieged the city for several days and, after taking it, massacred the inhabitants, and from there on west to Ershi, the capital of Dayuan, his advance was unhindered.

He reached Ershi with a force of 30,000 soldiers. The men of Dayuan came forward to attack, but the Han soldiers overwhelmed them with their arrows and forced them to flee into the city, where they mounted the battlements and prepared to defend the city.

General Li's men had wanted to attack Yucheng on the way, but he was afraid that if he halted his advance it would only give the men of Ershi more time to think up plots to save their lives. He therefore pressed on to Ershi, where he broke down the banks of the rivers and springs and diverted them from their

---

[7] Petty officials who had committed crimes, fugitives, adopted sons-in-law, resident merchants, those formerly registered as merchants, those whose fathers or mothers had been registered as merchants, and those whose grandfathers or grandmothers had been registered as merchants.

courses so that they no longer supplied water to the city. This move caused the inhabitants of the city extreme distress and hardship.

After surrounding and besieging the city for over forty days, he managed to break down the outer wall and capture one of the enemy leaders, a noble of Dayuan named Jianmi who was noted for his bravery. The inhabitants were thoroughly terrified and fled within the inner wall, where the nobles of Dayuan gathered to plot the next move. "The reason the Han has sent troops to attack us is simply that our king Wugua hid his best horses and killed the Han envoys," they said. "Now if we kill the king and hand over the horses, the Han troops will most likely withdraw. Should they refuse, that will be the time to fight to the death for our city!"

All having agreed that this was the best plan, they killed the king and sent one of the nobles to carry his head to General Li and ask for an agreement. "If the Han soldiers do not attack us," the nobleman said, "we will bring out all the finest horses so that you may take your pick, and will supply food to your army. But if you refuse to accept these terms we will slaughter all the best horses. Moreover, rescue troops will soon be coming to aid us from Kangju, and when they arrive the Han will have to fight both our men within the city and their forces on the outside. You had better consider the matter well and decide which course to take!"

At this time scouts from Kangju were keeping a watch on the Han troops, but since the latter were still in good condition, the Kangju forces did not dare to advance against them.

Li Guangli consulted with Zhao Shicheng, Li Che, and his other officers on what to do. "I have received word," he said, "that the people within the city have just obtained the services of a Chinese who knows how to dig wells. Moreover, they still seem to have plenty of food. Our purpose in coming here was to punish the chief offender, Wugua, and now that we have obtained his head, our task has been accomplished. If under these circumstances we refuse to withdraw our troops, the inhabitants will defend the city to the last man. Meanwhile the scouts from Kangju, seeing our soldiers wearied by the siege, will come with troops to rescue Dayuan and the defeat of our army will be inevitable."

His officers all agreed with this opinion, and General Li sent word that he was willing to accept Dayuan's proposal. The men of Dayuan then brought out their finest horses and allowed the Han officers to choose the ones they wanted. They also produced large stores of provisions to feed the Han army. The Han officers selected twenty or thirty of the choicest horses, as well as over 3,000 stallions and mares of less high quality, and set up one of the nobles named Micai, who had treated the earlier Han envoys with kindness, as the new king of Dayuan, promising that they would withdraw their troops. In the end the Han soldiers never entered the inner wall of the city, but withdrew according to their promise and began the journey home.

When Li Guangli first started west from Dunhuang, he considered that his army was too numerous to be provided with food by the lands along the way and he therefore divided it up into several parties, some of them taking the northern route and some the southern. One of these separate groups, comprising 1,000 or more men and led by the subordinate commander Wang Shensheng, the former grand herald Hu Chongguo, and others, arrived at Yucheng. The men of Yucheng withdrew into the city and refused to provide any food to Wang Shensheng's soldiers. Though he was 200 *li* away from the main army of General Li, Wang Shensheng examined the city and, deciding that he had nothing to fear, began to berate the inhabitants for failing to give him any food. The inhabitants could see that Wang Shensheng's army was growing smaller day by day, and finally one day at dawn they sent out a force of 3,000 men who attacked and killed Wang Shensheng and the other commanders and defeated his army. Only a few of the Han soldiers managed to escape and flee to the army of General Li.

General Li thereupon dispatched Shangguan Jie, his chief commandant in charge of requisitioning grain, who attacked and conquered the city of Yucheng. The king of Yucheng fled to Kangju, where Shangguan Jie pursued him. When the men of Kangju heard that the Han armies had already conquered Dayuan, they handed the king of Yucheng over to Shangguan Jie. The latter ordered four of his horsemen to bind the king and take him under guard to the headquarters of the commander in chief, General Li.

The four horsemen consulted together, saying, "The king of Yucheng is the archenemy of the Han. Now we have been given the task of escorting him alive to the general's headquarters, but if he should suddenly escape it would go very badly with us!" They therefore decided to kill the king, but none of them dared to strike the first blow. Finally one of the horsemen from Shanggui named Zhao Di, the youngest of the group, drew his sword and cut down the king. Then, bearing the king's head, he and Shangguan Jie and the rest of the group set out after and overtook General Li.

Earlier, when General Li started out on the second expedition against

Dayuan, the emperor sent envoys to announce the fact to the Wusun and ask them to send a large force to cooperate in the attack. The Wusun did in fact send 2,000 horsemen but, not willing to alienate either party, they held back and refused to join in the attack.

When General Li and his army returned east, the rulers of all the small states they passed through, having heard of the defeat of Dayuan, sent their sons or brothers to accompany the army to China, where they presented gifts, were received by the emperor, and remained at the Han court as hostages.

In General Li's campaign against Dayuan, the director of martial law Zhao Shicheng achieved the greatest merit. In addition, Shangguan Jie won distinction by daring to venture far into enemy territory and Li Che by his skill in planning. When the army re-entered the Jade Gate Pass, it numbered something over 10,000 men, with over 1,000 military horses. During General Li's second expedition the army had not suffered from any lack of provisions, nor had many of the soldiers been killed in battle. The generals and other officers, however, were a greedy lot, most of them taking little care of their men but abusing and preying upon them instead. This was the reason for the large number of lives lost.

Nevertheless the emperor, considering that it had been such a long expedition, made no attempt to punish those who were at fault, but enfeoffed Li Guangli as marquis of Haixi, and Zhao Di, the horseman who had cut off the head of the king of Yucheng, as marquis of Xinzhi. He appointed Zhao Shicheng as superintendant of the imperial household, Shangguan Jie as as privy treasurer, and Li Che as governor of Shangdang. Three of the officers who had gone on the campaign were appointed to posts ranking among the nine highest ministers; over 100 were enfeoffed as marquises or appointed as chancellors, governors, or 2,000 picul officials; and more than 1,000 were appointed to posts paying 1,000 piculs or less. Those who had volunteered to join the army were given posts which far exceeded their expectations, while the convicts who had been pressed into service were all pardoned and released from penal servitude. The common soldiers were rewarded with gifts valued at 40,000 catties of gold.

The expedition against Dayuan in its two phases required four years to carry out, after which the army was disbanded. A year or so after the Han conquered Dayuan and set up Micai as the new king, the nobles of Dayuan, considering Micai a servile flatterer who had brought about the destruction of his own country, joined forces and murdered him. In his place they set up Chanfeng, the brother of Wugua, the former king. Chanfeng sent his son as a hostage to the

Han court, whereupon the Han dispatched an envoy to Dayuan to present gifts to the new ruler and make sure that he restored peace and order to the kingdom. The Han also sent over ten parties of envoys to the various countries west of Dayuan to seek for rare objects and at the same time to call attention in a tactful way to the might which the Han had displayed in its conquest of Dayuan.

The government set up a chief commandant of Jiuquan in Dunhuang and established defence stations at various points from Dunhuang west to the Salt Swamp. A force of several hundred agricultural soldiers was sent to set up a garrison at Luntou, headed by an ambassador who saw to it that the fields were protected and stores of grain laid away to be used to supply the Han envoys who passed through on their way to foreign countries.

The Grand Historian remarks: the *Basic Annals* of Emperor Yu[8] records that the source of the Yellow River is in the Kunlun Mountains, mountains over 2,500 *li* high where the sun and moon in turn go to hide when they are not shining. It is said that on their heights are to be found the Fountain of Sweet Water and the Pool of Jade. Yet, since Zhang Qian and the other envoys have been sent to Daxia, they have traced the Yellow River to its source and found no such Kunlun Mountains as the *Basic Annals* records. Therefore, what the *Book of Documents* states about the mountains and rivers of the nine ancient provinces of China seems to be nearer the truth, while when it comes to the wonders recorded in the *Basic Annals of Emperor Yu* or the *Classic of Hills and Seas*,[9] I cannot accept them.

---

[8] An ancient text now lost.

[9] A geography of ancient China filled with legends and descriptions of fabulous beasts and other wonders. This is the earliest mention of the work. It is from works such as these that Emperor Wu selected the name Kunlun to apply to the range of mountains discovered by his envoys.

SHI JI 116: THE ACCOUNT OF
THE SOUTHWESTERN BARBARIANS

Tang Meng was sent as imperial envoy to invade the southwest and open up communication with Yelang, and as a result the chiefs of the Qiong and Zuo peoples begged to become subjects of the Han and to be ruled by Chinese officials. Thus I made "The Account of the Southwestern Barbarians".[1]

There are dozens of chiefs ruling among the southwestern barbarians, but the most important is the ruler of Yelang. To the west of Yelang live the chiefs of the Mimo, of which the most important is the ruler of Dian. North of Dian live numerous other chiefs, the most important being the ruler of Qiongdu. All of the tribes ruled by these chiefs wear their hair in the mallet-shaped fashion, work the fields, and live in settlements. Beyond them to the west, in the region from Tongshi east to Yeyu, are the tribes called Sui and Kunming, whose people all braid their hair and move from place to place with their herds of domestic animals, having no fixed homes and no chieftains. Their lands measure several thousand *li* square. Northeast of the Sui live twenty or thirty chiefs, the most important being those of Xi and Zuodu. Among the numerous chiefs northeast of Zuo, those of Ran and Mang are most important. Some of their people live a settled life on the land, while others move about from place to place. Their territory is west of the province of Shu. Northeast of Ran and Mang are numerous other chiefs, the most important being the ruler of Baima. All of them belong to the Di tribe. These are all the barbarian groups living in the area southwest of Ba and Shu.

In earlier times, when King Wei ruled the state of Chu (339-328 BC), he sent his general Zhuang Qiao to lead an army along the upper reaches of the Yangtze River and invade Ba, Shu, Qianzhong, and the regions to the

---

[1] The tribes described in this chapter lived in western China in the area of present day Sichuan, Guizhou, and Yunnan Provinces.

west. (Zhuang Qiao was a descendant of King Zhuang, a former ruler of Chu.)[2] Zhuang Qiao advanced as far as Lake Dian, a body of water 300 *li* in circumference, surrounded by several thousand *li* of rich flatland. Having used his military might to subdue the region and bring it under the rule of Chu, he started back to Chu to report his success when the armies of Qin attacked Chu and seized the provinces of Ba and Qianzhong, cutting off his way. Unable to get through to Chu, he returned to Lake Dian and with the men under his command made himself ruler of Dian, adopting native dress, following the customs of the people, and acting as their chief.

In the time of the Qin dynasty, Chang An invaded the region and opened up the so-called five-foot-wide road. Qin officials were set up to administer most of the numerous native states in the area. Some ten years later, however, the Qin dynasty was overthrown.

When the Han came to power, it abandoned all relations with these states and re-established the old frontier defences along the border of Shu. The people of Ba and Shu often crossed the frontier on unofficial trading expeditions, however, bringing back horses from Zuo and slaves and long-haired oxen from Po. These expeditions brought great wealth to the provinces of Ba and Shu.

In the sixth year of the era *jianyuan* (135 BC) the grand messenger Wang Hui was sent to attack Zou Ying, the king of Eastern Yue, who was in revolt. Shortly afterwards the men of Eastern Yue murdered Zou Ying and reported their willingness to submit to Han rule. Wang Hui, relying upon his military might to bring the region under control, dispatched Tang Meng, the magistrate of Poyang, to visit the king of Southern Yue and persuade him to remain loyal to the Han. While Tang Meng was at the court of Southern Yue, he was given some *ju* berry sauce to eat. When he inquired where it came from, he was told, "It is brought down the Zangge River from the northwest. The Zangge is several *li* wide and flows past Panyu, the capital of Southern Yue." When Tang Meng returned to Chang'an he questioned a merchant of Shu on the matter and the merchant replied, "Shu is the only place that makes *ju* berry sauce. Large quantities of it are exported in secret to the markets of Yelang, which is situated on the Zangge. The Zangge at that point is over 100 paces across, wide enough to allow boats to move up and down it. The king of Southern Yue sends money and goods in an effort to gain control of Yelang, extending his efforts as far west

---

[2] *Ca.* 600 BC.

as Tongshi, but so far he has not succeeded in getting Yelang to acknowledge his sovereignty."

Tang Meng then sent a letter to the throne, saying, "The king of Southern Yue rides about in a yellow canopied carriage with plumes on the left side, like the Son of Heaven, ruling a region that measures over 10,000 *li* from east to west. He is referred to as a 'foreign vassal' of the Han, but in fact he is the lord of a whole vast territory. If troops were sent from Changsha and Yuzhang to attack him, they would find most of the rivers impassable and would have great difficulty in advancing. I have received information, however, that over 100,000 first-rate soldiers could be recruited from the region of Yelang. If these were transported down the Zangge River in ships and deployed against the king of Southern Yue while he was still unprepared, it would be an excellent way to bring his territory under control. With the strength of the Han forces and the wealth of Ba and Shu to support the undertaking, it would be an easy task to open up communications with Yelang and establish officials in the region."

The emperor approved of this plan and, appointing Tang Meng as a general of palace attendants, put him in command of a force of 1,000 soldiers and over 10,000 porters. With these he marched out through the Zuo Pass in Ba and visited Duotong, the marquis of Yelang.

Tang Meng presented Duotong with generous gifts and, describing the might and virtue of the Han dynasty, urged him to permit Han officials to be sent to the area, promising that Duotong's son would be appointed as governor. The small towns in the neighbourhood of Yelang were all anxious to obtain silk from the Han, and Duotong, considering that the road between his territory and China was too steep and perilous to be kept open for long, agreed for the time being to listen to Tang Meng's demands. Tang Meng then returned to the capital to report on his mission. As a result, the province of Jianwei was established in the area and troops from Ba and Shu were sent out to work on the road, extending it through Po in the direction of the Zangge River.

Sima Xiangru, a native of Shu, also urged the emperor to set up provinces in the western barbarian regions of Qiong and Zuo. The emperor therefore appointed Sima Xiangru a general of palace attendants and sent him to these regions to negotiate with their rulers. Over ten districts were set up under a chief commandant and attached to the province of Shu, the natives being treated in the same way as the barbarians of the region farther south.

In connection with the building of the road to the lands of the southwestern barbarians, the four provinces in the region of Ba and Shu were obliged at this time to send out men to guard the supply lines and transport provisions to the workmen. But though the work went on for several years, the road was still not completed, while the men engaged in the project, exhausted by starvation and plagued by dampness, died off in great numbers. In addition, the barbarians frequently rebelled against Han rule and forces had to be called out to combat them, using even more money and material and accomplishing little in the way of military success.

The emperor, worried by the way things were going, sent Gongsun Hong to the region to observe the situation. On his return he advised the emperor that the project was impractical. Shortly afterwards, he was made imperial secretary. By this time the emperor was busy building fortifications in Shuofang in an attempt to drive the Xiongnu out of the region south of the Yellow River. Gongsun Hong repeatedly emphasized the dangers involved in attempting to open up communication with the southwestern barbarians and urged the emperor to abandon the project and concentrate his strength on combating the Xiongnu. The emperor accordingly gave up the idea, keeping only the two districts of Nanyi and Yelang, with one chief commandant, and leaving the province of Jianwei more or less to take care of itself.

In the first year of *yuanshou* (122 BC) Zhang Qian, the Bowang marquis, returned from his mission to the land of Daxia (Bactria) and reported that while he was there he had seen cloth produced in Shu and bamboo canes from Qiong. On inquiring how they had arrived in Daxia, he was told, "They come from the land of Shendu (India), which lies some several thousand *li* west of here. We buy them in the shops of the Shu merchants there." He was also told that Shendu was situated some 2,000 *li* west of Qiong. "Daxia, which is situated southwest of our country," Zhang Qian reported to the emperor with enthusiasm, "is eager to open relations with China and is much distressed that the Xiongnu are blocking the road in between. If we could find a new route from Shu via the land of Shendu, however, we would have a short and convenient way to reach Daxia which would avoid the danger of the northern route!"

The emperor therefore ordered Wang Ranyu, Bo Shichang, Lü Yueren, and others to go on a secret expedition through the region of the southwestern barbarians and on to the west to search for the land of Shendu. When they got as far as Dian, Changqiang, the king of Dian, detained them and sent a party of ten or twelve men to the west to find out the way to Shendu for them. The Chinese party waited over a year, but all the roads to the west had been closed off by the inhabitants of Kunming, so that none of the men who had been sent ahead were able to reach Shendu.

In the course of his talks with the Han envoys, the king of Dian asked, "Which is larger, my domain or that of the Han ruler?" and the marquis of Yelang asked the same question. Because there were no roads open between their lands and China, each considered himself the supreme ruler of a vast territory and had no idea of the breadth and greatness of the Han empire.

When the Han envoys returned to the capital, they stressed that Dian was a large state and ought to be bound by closer ties to China. The emperor gave the matter serious consideration.

Some years later, when the kingdom of Southern Yue rebelled, the emperor ordered the Marquis Who Hastens to Duty to raise an army among the southwestern barbarians in the province of Jianwei and aid in the attack on southern Yue. The chief of one of the barbarian states in the region, Julan, was afraid, however, that if he and his men went on such a distant expedition the inhabitants of neighbouring states would invade his territory and seize the old men and boys who had been left behind. He and his people therefore revolted and killed the Han envoys and the governor of Jianwei. The emperor had ordered a force of released criminals from Ba and Shu to join in the attack on Southern Yue, and he now detached eight commanders from this force and sent them to put down the revolt in Julan. In the meantime the resistance in Southern Yue was brought to an end, and the eight commanders, instead of proceeding downriver to the coast, turned back north and on their way executed the chief of Toulan. Toulan was another small state in the region which had constantly been hindering communications with Dian. Thus Toulan and the other tribes of the southwestern barbarians were brought under control and the region made into the province of Zangge.

The marquis of Yelang had originally sided with the king of Southern Yue, but when Southern Yue was wiped out, he proceeded to execute all those who had advised him to revolt against the Han. Eventually he journeyed to Chang'an to pay his respects to the emperor, who bestowed on him the title of king of Yelang.

After the Han forces had defeated Southern Yue, executed the chiefs of Julan and Qiong, and killed the marquis of Zuo, all the native rulers in the regions of Ran and Mang were struck with terror and begged to become vassals of the Han, with Chinese officials to govern their lands. The emperor therefore converted Qiongzuo into the province of Yuesui, Zuodu into the province of Chenli, Ran and Mang into the province of Wenshan, and Baima, west of

Guanghan, into the province of Wudu.

The emperor also sent Wang Ranyu to persuade the king of Dian to pay a visit to the capital, pointing out to him the fate that Southern Yue and the chiefs of the southwestern barbarians had suffered at the hands of the Han forces. The king of Dian possessed a force of some 20,000 or 30,000 men, while to the northeast of him lived the tribes of Laojin and Mimo which were ruled by members of the same clan as himself and were in a position to aid him. He was therefore not inclined to listen to the threats of the Han envoy. Moreover, the men of Laojin and Mimo frequently made attacks on the Han envoys and soldiers. In the second year of *yuanfeng* (109 BC) the emperor dispatched troops from Ba and Shu to attack and wipe out the Laojin and Mimo states and take up a position on the border of Dian. Because the king of Dian had originally been friendly toward the Han, they were not ordered to execute him. The king of Dian, Linan,[3] then surrendered to the Han forces with all his people, asking that officials be sent to govern his territory and that he be allowed to visit the emperor. His lands were made into the province of Yizhou and he was presented with the seals of the king of Dian and restored to the position of leader of the people. Thus, of the hundreds of native rulers among the southwestern barbarians, only those of Yelang and Dian were granted the seals of kings. Dian, although a relatively small fief, still enjoys the highest favour with the emperor.

The Grand Historian remarks: The ancestors of the state of Chu must certainly have received the blessing of Heaven! At the founding of the Zhou dynasty, one of them served as a general under King Wen and his descendants were enfeoffed in Chu. Even when the glory of the Zhou had waned, the state of Chu still boasted an area of 5,000 *li*. The Qin dynasty wiped out all of the other feudal families; only the descendants of Chu continued to rule as kings of Dian. And although the Han punished many of the barbarians of the southwest and destroyed their states, the ruler of Dian alone was favoured and allowed to continue as a king.

The whole affair of Han relations with the southwestern barbarians came about because someone saw some *ju* berry sauce in Panyu, and because the people of Daxia carried canes made of Qiong bamboo! Later the western barbarians were split up into two groups and their lands made into seven provinces.

------

[3] The text of the first part of the sentence appears to be corrupt and the translation is highly tentative.

SHI JI 117: THE BIOGRAPHY OF SIMA XIANGRU

Sima Xiangru's prose poem on The Mighty One and his discussions of Sir Fantasy, although couched in extravagantly rich and exaggerated language, are actually satirical in intent and have their basis in the philosophy of non-action. Thus I made "The Biography of Sima Xiangru".

Sima Xiangru was a native of Chengdu in the province of Shu. His polite name was Sima Changqing. When he was young he loved to read books. He also studied swordsmanship, and for this reason his parents gave him the name of "Dog Boy".[1] In the course of his studies, however, he developed a great admiration for the famous statesman of antiquity, Lin Xiangru,[2] and he accordingly changed his name to Xiangru. Because of the wealth of his family, he was made a palace attendant and served Emperor Jing as a mounted guard. He did not care for this position, but as it happened that Emperor Jing had no liking for literature, he had no alternative.

During this time King Xiao of Liang came to court to pay his respects to the emperor, bringing with him in his retinue a number of wandering rhetoricians such as Zou Yang of Qi, Mei Sheng of Huaiyin, and Master Zhuang Ji of Wu. Xiangru had an opportunity to meet these men and was so delighted with their company that he retired from his post on grounds of illness and journeyed to Liang to become a guest retainer at the king's court. King Xiao gave orders that Xiangru was to be quartered in the same lodge with the other scholars, so that for several years he was able to live with the scholars and guest rhetoricians of Liang. It was at this time that he wrote his prose poem entitled *Zixu* or *Sir Fantasy*. With the death of King Xiao, he left Liang and returned to his home in Chengdu, but by this time his family had grown very poor and he had no

---

[1] Commentators suggest that the Han pronunciation of the words "dog" and "sword" was sufficiently close to make the name sound like "Sword Boy".

[2] High minister of the state of Zhao in pre-Qin times who was noted for his bravery. His biography is recorded in *Shi ji* 81.

means of making a living.

Xiangru had formerly been on close terms with Wang Ji, the magistrate of the district of Linqiong, and Wang Ji sent word saying, "Since your long journey in search of official position has proved unsuccessful, why don't you come to see me?"

Xiangru accordingly went to Linqiong and stayed at the officials' lodge in that city. The magistrate made a great show of treating him with respect and honour, going every morning to call upon Xiangru. For the first few times Xiangru received him, but after that he pleaded illness and sent one of the attendants to convey his apologies to Wang Ji. Wang Ji, however, only treated him with greater deference.

There were a number of wealthy men living in Linqiong, among them Zhuo Wangsun, whose household included 800 servants and slaves, and Cheng Zheng, who also had several hundred servants. These two rich men conferred together and decided, "Since the magistrate seems to have a highly honoured guest visiting him, it would be well if we were to give a party for him and invite the magistrate to come along." When the magistrate arrived at the Zhuo residence on the day of the party, he found it filled with hundreds of guests. As noon approached the host dispatched a messenger inviting Xiangru to join the party, but he sent back word that he was ill and could not come. At this news the magistrate declined to join the feast, but instead went in person to fetch Xiangru. Xiangru, unable to find any further excuse, was forced to appear at the party, and soon all eyes were fixed on him.

When the drinking was at its height the magistrate came forward with a lute and, presenting it to Xiangru, said, "I have heard that you are fond of this instrument. I wonder if you could be persuaded to amuse yourself with a selection?"

Xiangru politely declined, but finally consented to strum a few selections for the company. It happened that Zhuo Wangsun had a daughter named Wenjun who was very fond of music and had only recently been widowed, and although Xiangru pretended to be playing only out of deference to the magistrate, in reality he used the lute to pour out his heart in an effort to win the young girl's attentions. When Xiangru arrived in Linqiong with his carriage riders, Wenjun had heard, he had displayed a figure of most elegant poise and refinement, and now that he was in her own home drinking and playing the lute, the young girl secretly peered in through the door at him and her heart was filled with delight; she felt an instant love for him, and her only fear was that she could not have him for her husband.

After the party was over Xiangru sent someone with lavish presents to Wenjun's ladies in waiting and requested them to inform their mistress of his deep respect. That night Wenjun ran away from home and joined Xiangru, and the two of them galloped off to Chengdu. There they took up residence in Xiangru's house, four bare walls with nothing inside.

Her father Zhuo Wangsun was in a rage. "What a piece of trash — this daughter of mine!" he exclaimed. "I have not the heart to kill her outright, but I will see to it that she never gets a penny of my money!" A number of people tried to talk him into reason, but he absolutely refused to listen to them.

After a while Wenjun grew unhappy with her new life and said to her husband, "The only thing for us to do is to go to Linqiong together. There we can borrow some money from my relatives and find a way to make a living. Why should we force ourselves to live in misery like this?"

She and Xiangru accordingly went to Linqiong, where they sold their carriage and all their riding equipment and bought a wine-shop. Xiangru left Wenjun to mind the counter while he himself, dressed in a workman's loincloth, went off on errands with the other hired men or washed the wine vessels at the well in the market place.

When Zhuo Wangsun heard the way his daughter was living, he was filled with shame and, shutting his gates, refused to leave the house. His relatives and the other gentlemen of the town once more attempted to reason with him. "You have only one son and two daughters," they said, "so you cannot say that you lack the funds to help your daughter. It is true that she has ruined her reputation by running off with Sima Xiangru, but he spent a good deal of time in the past travelling about the country, and though he is poor, he surely has the talent and ability to win success eventually. Moreover, he was a guest of the magistrate. Why do you insist upon bringing shame to both him and yourself like this?"

Persuaded that there was no other way out, Zhuo Wangsun finally gave his daughter Wenjun 100 servants, 1,000,000 cash, and the clothing, quilts, and other articles that she had received as a dowry at the time of her first marriage. Wenjun and Xiangru then returned to Chengdu, where they purchased a house and some fields and lived a life of ease.

Some time after this a man from Shu named Yang Deyi was appointed to serve Emperor Wu as keeper of the imperial hunting dogs. The emperor happened to come into possession of Sima Xiangru's prose poem, *Sir Fantasy*, which he read with great pleasure, and remarked to Yang Deyi, "What a pity that I could not have lived at the same time as the author of this!"[3]

"There is a man named Sima Xiangru who comes from the same city as myself," replied Yang Deyi, "and he claims that he himself wrote this prose poem!" The emperor was astonished and, summoning Xiangru to the capital, questioned him about it.

"The poem is mine," said Xiangru, "but it concerns the affairs of the feudal lords and is not worthy of Your Majesty's attention. If I may be permitted, however, I would like to compose a prose poem about the imperial hunt and present it to Your Majesty when it is completed."

The emperor gave his consent and ordered the master of documents to provide Xiangru with the necessary writing tablets. In the poem, Sir Fantasy, so called because his words are all fantasy, is made to praise the state of Chu; Master No-such (that is, no such thing ever happened) criticizes the claims of Sir Fantasy and speaks on behalf of the state of Qi, while Lord Not-real (not a real person) states the case for the Son of Heaven.[4] Thus the poet utilizes the words of these three imaginary characters to describe the hunting parks of the feudal lords of Chu and Qi and of the Son of Heaven, and at the close makes a

---

[3] Although the text does not say so, the implication is that Sima Xiangru had asked Yang Deyi to bring his poem to the emperor's attention.

[4] It would appear that what Sima Xiangru did was to use the poem, or at least part of it, which he had composed earlier for King Xiao of Liang, and add a final section on the hunting park of the emperor. The poems in this chapter are all in the *fu* or rhyme-prose style, already familiar to the reader from the examples in "The Biographies of Qu Yuan and Jia Yi" in Volume I. They are composed of rhymed lines of varying lengths and strong rhythmical beat, at times introduced by or interspersed with short passages in prose. Arthur Waley, in his introduction to *The Temple and Other Poems*, a book which has been of great assistance in making these translations, characterizes this type of poetry as a kind of "incantation" or "word-magic" which achieves its effect "not by argument nor even by rhetoric, but by a purely sensuous intoxication of rhythm and language". The reader should keep this apt description in mind in judging what follows. Waley also remarks, in speaking of this first poem of Sima Xiangru's, that its "eloquence cannot be described, much less translated". In spite of this warning, I have nevertheless undertaken the task of translation because Sima Xiangru is such an important figure in the cultural history of the period and because his poetry so well conveys the boundless energy and delight in richness and variety that characterize this era of the Han. I should warn the reader that many of the precious stones, flowers, trees, birds, etc. mentioned in the poems cannot be identified with any certainty and my translations are intended to be no more than rough equivalents. I must beg the indulgence of specialists if in places the translations constitute scientific impossibilities. The poet is obviously less concerned in conveying information than in creating a feeling of lush and exotic language, and for this reason I hope a certain freedom in the translation may be excused.

plea for greater frugality. The poem as a whole is intended therefore as a satirical reprimand. When it was completed, Sima Xiangru presented it to the emperor, who was exceedingly pleased. The text reads:

> When Chu dispatched Sir Fantasy as its envoy to the state of Qi, the king of Qi called out all the knights within his domain and, providing the party with carriages and horsemen, went out with the envoy on a hunt. After the hunt was over, Sir Fantasy was describing the wonders of the event to Master No-such, while Lord Not-real stood by. When the three of them had taken their seats, Master No-such asked, "Did you enjoy the hunt today?" "Very much!" replied Sir Fantasy. "Did you have a large catch?" Master No-such asked, to which Sir Fantasy answered, "No, the catch was rather meagre." "If the catch was small, then what did you find so enjoyable?" he pressed. "What I enjoyed was the way the king of Qi was endeavouring to impress me with the great number of carriages and horsemen, while for my part I described to him the hunts which we have at Yunmeng in Chu." "Would you perhaps tell us about these hunts of Qi and Chu?" asked Master No-such, to which Sir Fantasy replied:
>
> "Surely!
> The king of Qi rode forth with a thousand carriages,
> Selecting to accompany him ten thousand horsemen,
> To hunt on the borders of the sea.
> The ranks of men filled the lowlands;
> Their nets and snares covered the hills.
> They seized the hares and ran down the deer,
> Shot the tailed deer with arrows and snared the feet of the unicorns.
> They raced along the briny coves,
> The new-felled game staining their carriage wheels.
> Their arrows found their mark and the catch was plentiful;
> The king grew proud and began to boast of his achievements.
> He turned in his carriage and said to me,
> " 'Does the state of Chu also have its hunting lands, its wide plains and stretching lowlands, as rich and joyous as these? Can the hunts of the king of Chu rival these of mine?'
> "I dismounted from my carriage and replied, 'I am only a humble inhabitant of the land of Chu. I have served the king ten years or more,

and at times have accompanied him on his travels; I have attended him in the hunting parks of the capital of Chu and seen in person what they are like; yet I have not seen all by any means, and I can hardly speak of his hunts in the distant lowlands.'

" 'Be that as it may,' said the king of Qi, 'tell me in general what you have seen and heard!' and I replied, 'Of course, of course.

" 'In Chu, they say, there are seven lowlands. Of these I have visited only one; the other six I have never seen. The one I have visited is the smallest of them all, called Yunmeng. It is nine hundred *li* square, and in the centre there is a mountain.

" 'A mountain which winds and twists upward,
Rearing its lofty crags on high,
Covered with ragged jutting peaks
That blot out the sun and moon
And entangle them in their folds;
Its crest pierces the blue clouds,
Its slopes roll and billow downward,
Reaching to the Yangtze and the rivers around.
Its soil is coloured cinnabar and blue, copper and clayey white,
With yellow ochre and white quartz,
Tin and jade, gold and silver,
A mass of hues, glowing and shining,
Sparkling like the scales of a dragon.
Here too are precious stones: carnelians and garnets,
Amethysts, turquoises, and matrices of ore,
Chalcedony, beryl, and basalt for whetstones,
Onyx and figured agate.
To the east stretch fields of gentians and fragrant orchids,
Iris, turmeric, and crow-fans,
Spikenard and sweet flag,
Selinea and angelica,
Sugar cane and ginger.
On the south lie broad plains and wide lowlands,
Rising and falling in gentle slopes,
Secluded hollows and rolling leas,
Hemmed in by the great Yangtze
And bounded by Witch's Mountain.

On the high, dry crests grow
Indigo, broom, and sage,
Basil, sweet fern, and blue artemisia;
Marsh roses and bog rhubarb,
Water lilies, cress and mare's-tail,
Wormwood and swamp cabbage.
All manner of plants are here,
Too numerous to be counted.
To the west, bubbling springs and clear pools
Spread their restless waters,
Lotus and water chestnut blooming on their borders,
Huge rocks and white sand hidden in their depths,
Where live sacred turtles, dragons, and water lizards,
Terrapins and tortoises.
Northward rise dense forests and giant trees —
Medlar, cedar, and camphor,
Cinnamon, prickly ash, and anise tree,
Chinese cork, wild pear, red willow,
Hawthorn, chinaberry, jujube, and chestnut,
Mandarins and citrons, breathing forth their fragrance.
In their branches live apes, gibbons, and langurs,
Phoenixes, peacocks, and pheasants,
Flying lizards and lemurs.
Beneath their shade prowl white tigers and black panthers,
Leopards, lynxes, and jackals.[5]
The king of Chu orders his brave warriors
To seize these beasts with their bare hands,
While he mounts behind four piebald horses,
Riding in a carriage of carved jade.
From pliant staffs of whalebone
Stream banners studded with moon-bright pearls.
He grasps his stout lance forged by Gan Jiang.
At his left side hangs the painted bow of the Yellow Emperor;

---

[5]Two lines, mentioning rhinoceroses and elephants and repeating the name of one of the beasts above, have been omitted, as they appear to be a later addition.

On his right are strong arrows in a quiver of the Xia kings.
A companion as wise as Yangzi of old stands by his side;
A driver as skilled as Xian'a holds the reins.
Though the steeds are reined in to an easy pace,
They gain on the wily beasts;
The carriage wheels run down asses,
The steeds kick at onagers,
Spears pierce wild horses, axle points cut down wild mares,
As the hunters behind their powerful steeds shoot at fleeing jackasses.
Swiftly, relentlessly,
Like thunder they move, like the whirlwind they advance,
Streaming like comets, striking like lightning.
No shot leaves their bows in vain
But each must pierce the eye of the game,
Burrow in the breast, strike through the side,
And sever the cords of the heart,
Till the catch becomes a rain of beasts,
Covering the grass and filling the ground.
With this the king of Chu slackens his pace and gazes about,
Raising his head with lofty composure;
He looks toward the dark forest,
Observes the fierceness of his brave huntsmen
And the terror of the wild beasts,
Then spurs after the exhausted game, striking those that are spent,
Watching the aspect of every creature.
Next come the lovely maidens and fair princesses,
Robed in fine silk cloth
And trailing rich silks and crêpes,
Girdled in sheer netting
And draped with scarves like mist,
Beneath which their skirts, gathered in close pleats,
Gently swirl and sway,
Falling in deep and pliant folds,
So long and full
That they must gather up the hems demurely.
With flying beads and dangling pendants,

They bend and sway in their carriages,
Their robes and scarves rustling softly,
Brushing the heads of the orchids below
Or fluttering against the feathered carriage tops,
Tangling in their kingfisher hairpins
Or twining about the jewelled carriage cords.
Lightly and nimbly they come
Like a vision of goddesses.
Together the groups set out to hunt in the fields of marsh orchids;
Scrambling through the thick grasses
And ascending the stout embankments of the river,
They surprise kingfishers
And shoot crow pheasants,
Fix fine cords
To their short arrows
To shoot the white geese
And the wild swans,
Bring down a pair of egrets
Or a black crane.
Tiring of these sports, they embark
To sail upon the clear lake,
And drift over the surface in their pelican-prowed boats.
They lift their cassia oars,
Spread kingfisher curtains,
And raise feathered canopies;
With nets they snare terrapins
And angle for purple molluscs;
They strike golden drums
And sound the wailing flutes,
As the songs of the boatmen
Echo across the water.
The lake insects are startled
By the waves of their wake,
As the bubbling springs gush forth,
A turmoil of water,
And the boulders in the depths grate together
With a dull, reverberating roar

Like the voice of thunder
Resounding a hundred miles.
To signal the huntsmen to rest from their labours,
The sacred drums are sounded
And beacon fires raised;
The carriages draw up in ranks,
The horsemen form in battalions,
And all take their places in proper order,
Range themselves once more in position.
Then the king of Chu ascends the Terrace of the Bright Clouds,
Where he rests in perfect repose,
Takes his leisure in perfect ease
And, flavouring his dishes with herbs and spices,
Sits down to feast.
The king of Chu is not like Your Highness,
Who counts it a pleasure to race all day,
Never descending from your carriage to rest,
Slashing at game and staining your carriage wheels with blood.
If I may speak from what I have seen,
The hunts of Qi cannot match those of Chu!' "

"With this the king of Qi fell silent and did not answer me."

"How can you speak in such error?" exclaimed Master No-such. "You have not considered a thousand miles too long a journey, but have been gracious enough to visit our state of Qi. On this occasion the king of Qi, calling out all the knights within his domain and providing them with a multitude of carriages and horsemen, has set forth to the hunt, hoping that by these efforts he might secure a plentiful catch and bring enjoyment to the guests at his court. How can you call it a mere boastful show? When he inquired whether you have such hunting lands in Chu, it was his wish to hear of the stalwart customs of your great kingdom and to listen to your discourses. Now, instead of praising the virtues of the king of Chu, you lavish your words on the glories of Yunmeng and describe to us in rich phrases the wanton pleasures and reckless extravagances which take place there. For your sake, I cannot help wishing you had not done this. Even if these entertainments are as you describe them, they hardly reflect to the credit of Chu. If they exist, for

you to speak of them is only to spread abroad the fame of your ruler's
faults; and if your reports are false, then you do but injure the trust we
bear you. To expose the evils of one's ruler or to place trustworthiness
in jeopardy — neither action can be approved. By speaking as you
have, you must certainly invite contempt from the king of Qi and cause
embarrassment to the state of Chu.

"As for Qi, it is bounded on the east by the vast ocean,
And on the south by the mountains of Langya.
We may take our pleasure upon Mt. Cheng
And shoot game on the slopes of Zhifu,
Sail upon the Gulf of Bohai
And roam the marsh of Mengzhu.
Northeast of us lies the land of the Sushen,
And east of this we border the Valley of Boiling Water.
In autumn we hunt in the region of the Green Hills,
Sailing far away over the seas;
Our state could swallow eight or nine of your Yunmengs
And they would never even tickle its throat.
As for the wonders and marvels you speak of,
The strange creatures of other regions,
The rare beasts and odd birds —
All manner of beings are gathered here in Qi
In such abundance within our borders
That I could not finish describing them,
Nor could the ancient sage Emperor Yu give them names
Or his minister Xie write them all down.
Yet, since the king of Qi is but a vassal of the emperor,
He does not consider it right to speak of the joys of travel
Or describe the magnificence of his parks and gardens.
Moreover, you are here as his guest,
And this is why he declined to reply to your words.
How could you think it was because he had no answer?"

Thereupon Lord Not-real broke into a smile and said, "The
spokesman for Chu has spoken in error, while the case for Qi leaves
much to be desired. When the emperor demands that the feudal lords
bear their tribute to his court, it is not that he desires the goods and
articles they bring, but that his vassal may thereby 'report on the

administration of their offices';[6] and when he causes mounds to be raised on the borders of states and their boundaries to be marked off, these are not for the purpose of defence, but so that the feudal lords may not trespass upon each other's lands. Now, although the king of Qi has been enfeoffed in the east to serve as a bastion to the imperial house, he is carrying on secret contacts with the Sushen and jeopardizing his own state by crossing his borders and sailing over the sea to hunt in the Green Hills, actions which are a violation of his duties. Both of you gentlemen, instead of attempting in your discussions to make clear the duties of lord and subject and striving to rectify the behaviour of the feudal lords, vainly dispute with each other over the joys of hunting and the size of parks, each attempting to outdo the other in descriptions of lavish expenditures, each striving for supremacy in wanton delights. This is no way to win fame and gain praise, but will only blacken the names of your rulers and bring ruin to yourselves. Moreover, what do the states of Qi and Chu possess, that they are worth speaking about? You gentlemen perhaps have never laid eyes upon true splendour. Have you not heard of the Shanglin Park of the Son of Heaven?

"To the east of it lies Cangwu,
To the west the land of Xiji;
On its south runs the Cinnabar River,
On its north, the Purple Deeps.
Within the park spring the Ba and Chan rivers,
And through it flow the Jing and Wei,
The Feng, the Hao, the Lao, and the Jue,
Twisting and turning their way
Through the reaches of the park;
Eight rivers, coursing onward,
Spreading in different directions, each with its own form.
North, south, east, and west
They race and tumble,
Pouring through the chasms of Pepper Hill,

---

[6] A reference to *Mencius* IB, IV, 5.

Skirting the banks of the river islets,
Winding through the cinnamon forests
And across the broad meadows.
In wild confusion they swirl
Along the bases of the tall hills
And through the mouths of the narrow gorges;
Dashed upon boulders, maddened by winding escarpments,
They writhe in anger,
Leaping and curling upward,
Jostling and eddying in great swells
That surge and batter against each other;
Darting and twisting,
Foaming and tossing,
In a thundering chaos;
Arching into hills, billowing like clouds,
They dash to left and right,
Plunging and breaking in waves
That chatter over the shallows;
Crashing against the cliffs, pounding the embankments.
The waters pile up and reel back again,
Skipping across the rises, swooping into the hollows,
Rumbling and murmuring onward;
Deep and powerful,
Fierce and clamorous,
They froth and churn
Like the boiling waters of a cauldron,
Casting spray from their crests, until,
After their wild race through the gorges,
Their distant journey from afar,
They subside into silence,
Rolling on in peace to their long destination,
Boundless and without end,
Gliding in soundless and solemn procession,
Shimmering and shining in the sun,
To flow through giant lakes of the east
Or spill into the ponds along their banks.
Here horned dragons and red hornless dragons,

Sturgeon and salamanders,
Carp, bream, gudgeon, and dace,
Cowfish, flounder, and sheatfish
Arch their backs and twitch their tails,
Spread their scales and flap their fins,
Diving among the deep crevices;
The waters are loud with fish and turtles,
A multitude of living things.
Here moon-bright pearls
Gleam on the river slopes,
While quartz, chrysoberyl,
And clear crystal in jumbled heaps
Glitter and sparkle,
Catching and throwing back a hundred colours
Where they lie tumbled on the river bottom.
Wild geese and swans, graylags, bustards,
Cranes and mallards,
Loons and spoonbills,
Teals and gadwalls,
Grebes, night herons, and cormorants
Flock and settle upon the waters,
Drifting lightly over the surface,
Buffeted by the wind,
Bobbing and dipping with the waves,
Sporting among the weedy banks,
Gobbling the reeds and duckweed,
Pecking at water chestnuts and lotuses.
Behind them rise the tall mountains,
Lofty crests lifted to the sky;
Clothed in dense forests of giant trees,
Jagged with peaks and crags;
The steep summits of the Nine Pikes,
The towering heights of the Southern Mountains,
Soar dizzily like a stack of cooking pots,
Precipitous and sheer.
Their sides are furrowed with ravines and valleys,
Narrow-mouthed clefts and open glens,

Through which rivulets dart and wind.
About their base, hills and islands
Raise their tall heads;
Ragged knolls and hillocks
Rise and fall,
Twisting and twining
Like the coiled bodies of reptiles;
While from their folds the mountain streams leap and tumble,
Spilling out upon the level plains.
There they flow a thousand miles along smooth beds,
Their banks lined with dikes
Blanketed with green orchids
And hidden beneath selinea,
Mingled with snakemouth
And magnolias;
Planted with yucca,
Sedge of purple dye,
Bittersweet, gentians, and orchis,
Blue flag and crow-fans,
Ginger and turmeric,
Monkshood, wolfsbane,
Nightshade, basil,
Mint, ramie, and blue artemisia,
Spreading across the wide swamps,
Rambling over the broad plains,
A vast and unbroken mass of flowers,
Nodding before the wind;
Breathing forth their fragrance,
Pungent and sweet,
A hundred perfumes
Wafted abroad
Upon the scented air.
Gazing about the expanse of the park
At the abundance and variety of its creatures,
One's eyes are dizzied and enraptured
By the boundless horizons,
The borderless vistas.

The sun rises from the eastern ponds
And sets among the slopes of the west;
In the southern part of the park,
Where grasses grow in the dead of winter
And the waters leap, unbound by ice,
Live zebras, yaks, tapirs, and black oxen,
Water buffalo, elk, and antelope,
'Red-crowns' and 'round-heads',
Aurochs, elephants, and rhinoceroses.
In the north, where in the midst of summer
The ground is cracked and blotched with ice
And one may walk the frozen streams or wade the rivulets,
Roam unicorns and boars,
Wild asses and camels,
Onagers and mares,
Swift stallions, donkeys, and mules.
Here the country palaces and imperial retreats
Cover the hills and span the valleys,
Verandahs surrounding their four sides;
With storied chambers and winding porticos,
Painted rafters and jade-studded corbels,
Interlacing paths for the royal palanquin,
And arcaded walks stretching such distances
That their length cannot be traversed in a single day.
Here the peaks have been levelled for mountain halls,
Terraces raised, storey upon storey,
And chambers built in the deep grottoes.
Peering down into the caves, one cannot spy their end;
Gazing up at the rafters, one seems to see them brush the heavens;
So lofty are the palaces that comets stream through their portals
And rainbows twine about their balustrades.
Green dragons slither from the eastern pavilion;
Elephant-carved carriages prance from the pure hall of the west,
Bringing immortals to dine in the peaceful towers

And bands of fairies to sun themselves beneath the southern
eaves.[7]

Here sweet fountains bubble from clear chambers,
Racing in rivulets through the gardens,
Great stones lining their courses;
Plunging through caves and grottoes,
Past steep and ragged pinnacles,
Horned and pitted as though carved by hand,
Where garnets, green jade,
And pearls abound;
Agate and marble,
Dappled and lined;
Rose quartz of variegated hue,
Spotted among the cliffs;
Rock crystal, opals,
And finest jade.
Here grow citrons with their ripe fruit in summer,
Loquats, persimmons,
Wild pears, tamarinds,
Jujubes, arbutus,
Peaches and grapes,
Almonds, damsons,
Mountain plums and litchis,
Shading the quarters of the palace ladies,
Ranged in the northern gardens,
Stretching over the slopes and hillocks
And down into the flat plains;
Lifting leaves of kingfisher hue,
Their purple stems swaying;
Opening their crimson flowers,
Clusters of vermilion blossoms,
A wilderness of trembling flames
Lighting up the broad meadow.

---

[7]In much the same way as the European aristocrats delighted in picturing themselves as rustic shepherds and shepherdesses, their Chinese counterparts loved to imagine that they were carefree immortals riding about on dragons and sipping dew in airy mountain retreats.

Here crab apple, chestnut and willow,
Birch, maple, sycamore and boxwood,
Pomegranate, date palm,
Betel nut and palmetto,
Sandalwood, magnolia,
Cedar and cypress
Rise a thousand feet,
Their trunks several arm-lengths around,
Stretching forth flowers and branches,
Rich fruit and luxuriant leaves,
Clustered in dense copses,
Their limbs entwined,
Their foliage a thick curtain
Over stiff and bending trunks,
Their branches sweeping to the ground
Amidst a shower of falling petals.
They tremble and sigh
As they sway with the wind,
Creaking and moaning in the breeze
Like the tinkle of chimes
Or the wail of flageolets.
High and low they grow,
Screening the quarters of the palace ladies;
A mass of sylvan darkness,
Blanketing the mountains and edging the valleys,
Ascending the slopes and dipping into the hollows,
Overspreading the horizon,
Outdistancing the eye.
Here black apes and white she-apes,
Drills, baboons, and flying squirrels,
Lemurs and langurs,
Macaques and gibbons,
Dwell among the trees,
Uttering long wails and doleful cries
As they leap nimbly to and fro,
Sporting among the limbs
And clambering haughtily to the treetops.

Off they chase across bridgeless streams
And spring into the depths of a new grove,
Clutching the low-swinging branches,
Hurtling across the open spaces,
Racing and tumbling pell-mell,
Until they scatter from sight in the distance.
Such are the scenes of the imperial park,
A hundred, a thousand settings
To visit in the pursuit of pleasure;
Palaces, inns, villas, and lodges,
Each with its kitchens and pantries,
Its chambers of beautiful women
And staffs of officials.
Here, in late fall and early winter,
The Son of Heaven stakes his palisades and holds his hunts,
Mounted in a carriage of carved ivory
Drawn by six jade-spangled horses, sleek as dragons.
Rainbow pennants stream before him;
Cloud banners trail in the wind.
In the vanguard ride the hide-covered carriages;
Behind, the carriages of his attendants.
A coachman as clever as Sun Shu grasps the reins;
A driver as skilful as the Duke of Wei stands beside him.
His attendants fan out on all sides
As they move into the palisade.
They sound the sombre drums
And send the hunters to their posts;
They corner the quarry among the rivers
And spy them from the high hills.
Then the carriages and horsemen thunder forth,
Startling the heavens, shaking the earth;
Vanguard and rear dash in different directions,
Scattering after the prey.
On they race in droves,
Rounding the hills, streaming across the lowlands,
Like enveloping clouds or drenching rain.
Leopards and panthers they take alive;

They strike down jackals and wolves.
With their hands they seize the black and tawny bears,
And with their feet they down the wild sheep.
Wearing pheasant-tailed caps
And breeches of white tiger skin
Under patterned tunics,
They sit astride their wild horses;
They clamber up the steep slopes of the Three Pikes
And descend again to the river shoals,
Galloping over the hillsides and the narrow passes,
Through the valleys and across the rivers.
They fell the 'dragon sparrows'
And sport with the *xiezhi*,
Strike the *xiage*[8]
And with short spears stab the little bears,
Snare the fabulous *yaoniao* horses
And shoot down the great boars.
No arrow strikes the prey
Without piercing a neck or shattering a skull;
No bow is discharged in vain,
But to the sound of each twang some beast must fall.
Then the imperial carriage signals to slacken pace
While the emperor wheels this way and that,
Gazing afar at the progress of the hunting bands,
Noting the disposition of their leaders.
At a sign, the Son of Heaven and his men resume their pace,
Swooping off again across the distant plains.
They bear down upon the soaring birds;
Their carriage wheels crush the wily beast.
Their axles strike the white deer;
Deftly they snatch the fleeting hares;
Swifter than a flash
Of scarlet lightning,
They pursue strange creatures

---

[8] These appear to be mythical beasts. From this point on Sima Xiangru's description of the hunt becomes more and more fanciful.

Beyond the borders of heaven.
To bows like the famous Fanruo
They fit their white-feathered arrows,
To shoot the fleeing goblin-birds
And strike down the griffins.
For their mark they choose the fattest game
And name their prey before they shoot.
No sooner has an arrow left the string
Then the quarry topples to the ground.
Again the signal is raised and they soar aloft,
Sweeping upward upon the gale,
Rising with the whirlwind,
Borne upon the void,
The companions of gods,
To trample upon the black crane
And scatter the flocks of giant pheasants,
Swoop down upon the peacocks
And the golden roc,
Drive aside the five-coloured *yi* bird
And down the phoenixes,
Snatch the storks of heaven
And the birds of darkness,
Until, exhausting the paths of the sky,
They wheel their carriages and return.
Roaming as the spirit moves them,
Descending to earth in a far corner of the north,
Swift and straight is their course
As they hasten home again.
Then the emperor ascends the Stone Gate
And visits the Great Peak Tower,
Stops at the Magpie Turret
And gazes afar from the Dew Cold Observatory,
Descends to the Wild Plum Palace
And takes his ease in the Palace of Righteous Spring;
To the west he hastens to the Xuanqu Palace
And poles in a pelican boat over Ox Head Lake.
He climbs the Dragon Terrace

And rests in the Tower of Lithe Willows,
Weighing the effort and skill of his attendants
And calculating the catch made by his huntsmen.
He examines the beasts struck down by the carriages,
Those trampled beneath the feet of the horsemen
And trod upon by the beaters;
Those which, from sheer exhaustion
Or the pangs of overwhelming terror,
Fell dead without a single wound,
Where they lie, heaped in confusion,
Tumbled in the gullies and filling the hollows,
Covering the plains and strewn about the swamps.
Then, wearied of the chase,
He orders wine brought forth on the Terrace of Azure Heaven
And music for the still and spacious halls.
His courtiers, sounding the massive bells
That swing from the giant bell rack,
Raising the pennants of kingfisher feathers,
And setting up the drum of sacred lizard skin,
Present for his pleasure the dances of Yao
And the songs of the ancient Emperor Ge;
A thousand voices intone,
Ten thousand join in harmony,
As the mountains and hills rock with echoes
And the valley waters quiver to the sound.
The dances of Bayu, of Song and Cai,
The Yuzhe song of Huainan,
The airs of Dian and Wencheng,
One after another in groups they perform,
Sounding in succession the gongs and drums
Whose shrill clash and dull booming
Pierce the heart and startle the ear.
The tunes Jing, Wu, Zheng, and Wei,
The Shao, Huo, Wu, and Xiang music,
And amorous and carefree ditties
Mingle with the songs of Yan and Ying,
'Onward Chu!' and 'The Gripping Wind'.

Then come actors, musicians and trained dwarfs,
And singing girls from the land of Didi,
To delight the ear and eye
And bring mirth to the mind;
On all sides a torrent of gorgeous sounds,
A pageant of enchanting colour.
Here are maidens to match
The goddesses Blue Lute and Princess Fu:
Creatures of matchless beauty,
Seductive and fair,
With painted faces and carved hairpins,
Fragile and full of grace,
Lithe and supple,
Of delicate feature and form,
Trailing cloaks of sheerest silk
And long robes that seem as though carved and painted,
Swirling and fluttering about them
Like magic garments;
With them wafts a cloud of scent,
A delicious perfume;
White teeth sparkle
In engaging smiles,
Eyebrows arch delicately,
Eyes cast darting glances,
Until their beauty has seized the soul of the beholder
And his heart in joy hastens to their side.

"But then, when the wine has flowed freely and the merriment is at its height, the Son of Heaven becomes lost in contemplation, like one whose spirit has wandered, and he cries, 'Alas! What is this but a wasteful extravagance? Now that I have found a moment of leisure from the affairs of state, I thought it a shame to cast away the days in idleness and so, in this autumn season, when Heaven itself slays life, I have joined in its slaughter and come to this hunting park to take my ease. And yet I fear that those who follow me in ages to come may grow infatuated with these sports, until they lose themselves in the pursuit of pleasure and forget to return again to their duties. Surely this is no way for one who has inherited the throne to carry on the great task of his forbears and insure the rule of our imperial house!'

"Then he dismisses the revellers, sends away the huntsmen, and instructs his ministers, saying, 'If there are lands here in these suburbs that can be opened for cultivation, let them all be turned into farms in order that my people may receive aid and benefit thereby. Tear down the walls and fill up the moats, that the common folk may come and profit from these hills and lowlands! Stock the lakes with fish and do not prohibit men from taking them! Empty the palaces and towers, and let them no longer be staffed! Open the storehouses and granaries to succour the poor and starving and help those who are in want; pity the widower and widow, protect the orphans and those without families! I would broadcast the name of virtue and lessen punishments and fines; alter the measurements and statutes, change the colour of the vestments, reform the calendar and, with all men under heaven, make a new beginning!'

"Then, selecting an auspicious day and fasting in preparation,
He dons his court robes
And mounts the carriage of state,
With its flowery pennants flying
And its jade bells ringing.
He sports now in the Park of the Six Arts,
Races upon the Road of Benevolence and Righteousness,
And scans the Forest of the *Spring and Autumn Annals*.
His archery now is to the stately measures of 'The Fox Head'
And 'The Beast of Virtue';[9]
His prey is the Dance of the Black Cranes,
Performed with ceremonial shield and battle axe.
Casting the heavenly Cloud Net,[10]
He snares the songs of the *Book of Odes*,
Sighs over 'The Felling of the Sandalwood'[11]
And delights in the ruler who 'shares his joy with all'.[12]

---

[9] Musical compositions supposed to have been played at the archery contests of the king and the feudal lords respectively in ancient times.

[10] The name of a constellation.

[11] A song from "Airs from the State of Wei", in the *Book of Odes*, said to express censure of a greedy ruler who fails to make use of wise men.

[12] From the song "Sanghu", "Lesser Odes", *Futian* section, in the *Book of Odes*.

He mends his deportment in the garden of *Rites*
And wanders in the orchard of the *Book of Documents*.
He spreads the teachings of the *Book of Changes*,
Sets free the strange beasts penned in his park,
Ascends the Bright Hall,
And seats himself in the Temple of the Ancestors.

"Then may his ministers freely present before him their proposals for the betterment of the empire, and within the four seas there is no one who does not share in the 'spoils' of this new hunt.[13] Then is the empire filled with great joy; all men turn their faces toward the wind of imperial virtue and harken to its sound. As though borne upon a stream, they are transformed to goodness; with shouts of gladness they set forth upon the Way and journey to righteousness, so that harsh punishments are set aside and no longer used. Finer is this ruler's virtue than that of the Three Sages of antiquity, more plenteous his merits than those of the Five Emperors. When a ruler has achieved such virtue, then may he enjoy himself at the hunt without incurring blame. But to gallop from morn to night in sunshine or rain, exhausting the spirit and tiring the body, wearing out the carriages and horses, draining the energies of the huntsmen and squandering the resources of the treasury; to think only of one's own pleasure before sufficient benefits have been bestowed upon others; to ignore the common people and neglect the government of the nation, merely because one is greedy for a catch of pheasants and hares — this no truly benevolent ruler would do! Thus, from what I can see, the kings of Qi and Chu merit only pity. Though their domains are no more than a thousand *li* square, their hunting parks occupy nine tenths of the area, so that the land cannot be cleared and the people have no space to grow food. When one who is no more than a feudal prince attempts to indulge in extravagances fit only for the supreme ruler, then I fear it is the common people who will suffer in the end!"

---

[13] In the passage above the poet uses the hunting metaphor to describe the ideal ruler: a student of the Classics and the arts, amusing himself with the stately dances and songs of antiquity and thinking always of the welfare of his people instead of indulging in extravagant pleasures. Thus, after having dazzled the emperor with his rhetoric, the poet delivers his "message".

At these words Sir Fantasy and Master No-such abruptly changed countenance and looked uneasily about, quite at a loss for words. Then, backing off and rising from their places, they replied, "We are uncouth and ignorant men who do not know when to hold our tongues. Fortunately today we have received your instruction, and we shall do our best to abide by it."

When the poem was presented to the emperor, he appointed Sima Xiangru to the post of palace attendant. To the passages in which Lord Not-real tells of the vastness of the emperor's hunting park at Shanglin with its hills and valleys and its rivers and countless creatures, as well as Sir Fantasy's description of the great size and richness of Yunmeng in Chu, however, it was objected that the extravagant language of the poet had overstepped the bounds of reality and displayed too little respect for the dictates of reason and good sense. As a result only the essential parts of the poem were accepted, and it was discussed in the light of the final passage which shows the ruler returning to just ways of government.[14]

After Sima Xiangru had been a palace attendant for several years, it happened that Tang Meng was dispatched to invade the regions of Yelang and Western Po to the west of China and open up relations with them. To accomplish this, he recruited 1,000 officers and men from the provinces of Ba and Shu. In addition, these provinces took it upon themselves to send along a force of 10,000 or more men to transport provisions.[15] When he encountered any difficulties in carrying out his plans, Tang Meng took advantage of the military supply law to execute the ringleaders of the opposition, a step which threw the people of Ba and Shu into extreme panic. When the emperor got wind of the affair, he dispatched Sima Xiangru to reprimand Tang Meng and to explain to the inhabitants of Ba and Shu that it had not been his intention to inflict any such penalties upon them. Xiangru issued a proclamation to them which read:

---

[14] Fortunately, Sima Qian seems to have quoted the entire poem, without omitting the passages that the emperor and his court found objectionable. It should be noted that, although Chinese literature contains many fine works of fantasy, Chinese literary criticism, at least in those periods when it was dominated by Confucian thought, has been suspicious of anything that was too obviously opposed to "reason and good sense", such as the passage in the poem just quoted in which the emperor and his huntsmen mount into the sky and pursue the birds on the wing. The critics tend to regard such flights of fancy as useless and irresponsible, if not actually morally unsound.

[15] With a view, it would seem from what follows, to making a profit from the expedition.

Let this be known to the governors of Ba and Shu. For a long time now the barbarians have been left to conduct themselves as they please and no steps have been taken to punish them; time and again they have invaded and plundered our borders and made trouble for our soldiers and officials. Since His Majesty came to the throne, he has done his best to preserve his people and to bring peace to China. For this purpose he has in recent years raised his armies and called out the troops. To the north he has dispatched them to attack the Xiongnu until the *Shanyu*, filled with terror, has come with clasped hands to receive our orders, with bent knee to beg for peace. Kangju (Trans-Oxiana) and the other regions of the west, translating and retranslating their strange tongues, have come to pay their respects, bowing their heads to the ground and bringing gifts of tribute to our court. Our ruler has dispatched his armies to the east to rescue Eastern Yue from the attacks of Minyue, consenting for the sake of the king of Eastern Yue to send them as far as the city of Panyu, so that the king in gratitude sent his heir to our court. Thus the princes of the eastern barbarians, as well as the chieftains of the Western Po, have not dared to be lax in the presentation of their customary tribute and services; standing on tiptoe with necks outstretched, they gasp like little fishes, each striving to outdo the other in the execution of his duties, all begging to become our subjects.

Yet the way to their lands is very far and blocked by precipitous mountains and deep rivers, so that they cannot be trusted to make the journey of themselves. Now His Majesty has already punished those who failed to acknowledge his sovereignty, but he has not yet rewarded those who have acted in good will, and for this reason he has dispatched his general of palace attendants Tang Meng to journey to these lands and welcome their rulers as guests of China. He has recruited 500 soldiers from each of the provinces of Ba and Shu and provided them with gifts so that they may act as a bodyguard for his envoy in case of any unforeseen event. There is no reason to believe that this is a matter of open warfare or to fear that the men will become involved in a conflict.

Now it has come to His Majesty's attention that in the calling out of troops and the application of the supply laws the envoy has acted in such a way as to bring panic to the young men and fear and foreboding to the elders. In addition, it appears that the provinces have, on their own initiative, undertaken to transport grain and supplies to the party. None of these actions, I assure you, are in accordance with His Majesty's will. Again, some of those who have been chosen to make the expedition have run away or taken it upon themselves to rob and kill. This, needless to say, is not in accord with the duties of a subject.

The brave men of the other border provinces of our empire, as soon as they see the beacon fires burning or the smoke signals rising, all seize their bows and gallop off, shoulder their weapons and hasten on foot, dashing off in sweaty haste, each fearful only that he will be last. Plunging upon the bare blades of the foe, braving the rain of arrows, they forget all else in the pursuit of duty, nor do they think for a moment to turn aside their steps; each in his breast is burning with anger, as though he were avenging a private wrong. Yet can you say that these men hate life and delight in death? Are they not ordinary citizens like yourselves? Do they serve some other ruler than you men of Ba and Shu? No! It is only that, considering the future and taking deep thought for the dangers which threaten the state, they delight in fulfilling their duty as subjects. Therefore they are rewarded with the split tallies of enfeoffment, the jade emblems of nobility; they take their place among the ranking marquises and reside in the mansions east of the imperial palace; and when their days are ended, they have a name for later ages to remember, and their lands are handed down to their sons and grandsons. In the execution of their duties they display the utmost fidelity; they dwell in peace and comfort; their fame is sung for endless ages; and the glory of their achievements never fades. This is the reason that wise men and gentlemen do not hesitate at the call to arms, though they may spill their bowels upon the broad plains and drench the wild grasses with their blood.

In contrast to these, however, the men who have now been entrusted with the mission of bearing gifts to the southern barbarians and who rob and kill of their own will, or incur punishment because they run away, will find themselves deprived of both life and fame. Their posthumous name will be "Supreme Stupidity", their shame will reflect upon their fathers and mothers, and they will become the laughing stock of the world. How far apart in wisdom and judgement are these two groups of men!

And yet the fault does not lie wholly with the members of the expedition themselves. You, the elders of Ba and Shu, have failed in your duty to instruct them, and the young men have not been diligent in carrying out your teachings. You are poor in modesty and lacking in shame, and the ways of your people are neither just nor generous. Is it not inevitable, then, that your men should suffer punishment?

His Majesty the emperor is distressed that his envoy Tang Meng and the other officials have behaved as they have, and he is full of pity for men such as these who have shown themselves to be ignorant and unworthy. He has therefore sent me as his personal messenger to explain to the common people his reasons for calling out the troops, and at the same time to reprimand those have proved themselves disloyal in the face of death and to censure the elders and mentors of the people for failing to give them proper instruction.

It is now the season when you are most busy in the fields, and I would not add to the burdens of the common people by calling them together to address them. I have been in person to visit the men of the nearby districts, but I am afraid that there are many people living in remote valleys and mountain regions who may not receive word of this. I have therefore issued this proclamation to be delivered with all speed to the districts and marches, so that everyone may be informed of His Majesty's will. Pay heed to what it says!

By the time Sima Xiangru completed his mission and returned to report to the emperor, Tang Meng had invaded and opened up communication with the region of Yelang. It was decided to use this opportunity to make contact with the roads in the territory of the barbarians of the southwest. More soldiers were called out from Ba, Shu, and Guanghan, and a labour force of 20,000 or 30,000 men put to work building a road. At the end of two years, however, the road had still not been completed. A number of men died in the course of the construction and the expense reached staggering proportions, so that many of the people of Shu, as well as the Han officials connected with the project, began to complain that it was impractical. At the same time the local chieftains of the regions of Qiong and Zuo, hearing that the other southern barbarians had entered into relations with the Han empire and were receiving many fine gifts, asked to become subjects of the emperor and requested the officials to grant them the same treatment as the southern barbarians.

The emperor asked Sima Xiangru's opinion on the question, to which he replied, "The lands of Qiong, Zuo, Ran, and Mang are situated near Shu and it is an easy task to open up roads to them. In earlier times the Qin dynasty was in contact with these regions and divided them up into provinces and districts, but they were abandoned after the rise of the Han. Now if it were actually possible to re-establish these provinces and districts, it would prove of even greater advantage than communications with the southern barbarians.

The emperor approved his opinion and, appointing him a general of palace attendants, sent him with the imperial credentials to act as envoy to these regions. Accompanied by Wang Ranyu, Hu Chongguo, and Lü Yueren as assistant envoys, he set off in haste by four-horse relay carriage with orders to collect gifts from the officials of Ba and Shu and present them to the western barbarians.

When Xiangru reached Shu, the governor of the province and his subordinates all came out to the suburbs to greet him, and the magistrates of the districts, bearing crossbows and arrows on their backs, rode before his carriage, for the men of Shu considered him a person of great honour. Xiangru's father-in-law Zhuo Wangsun, as well as the various distinguished men of Linqiong, flocked to his gate with presents of meat and wine to express their warm-hearted friendship. Zhuo Wangsun was filled with remorse that he had been so late in recognizing his daugther's marriage to Xiangru, and to make up for it he presented her with a generous portion of his estate, so that her inheritance equalled that of her brother.

Sima Xiangru proceeded to carry out his mission of invading and pacifying the lands of the western barbarians, and the chiefs of Qiong, Zuo, Ran, Mang, and Siyu all begged to become subjects of the Han. He abolished the gates along the old border and moved them farther out, establishing the new frontier at the Mo and Ruo rivers in the west and Zangge in the south. In addition he opened up a road through the Ling Pass, built a bridge across the Sun River, and established communication with the capital of Qiong. When he returned and reported on his mission, the emperor was overcome with delight.

While Sima Xiangru was carrying out this mission, he received complaints from many of the elders of Shu that the whole idea of opening up communications with the barbarians of the southwest was a waste of time, and he learned in addition that even one of the high court ministers, Gongsun Hong, was opposed to the plan. He would have liked to urge the emperor to abandon the idea, but since he was the one who had first suggested it, he did not dare. Instead he composed a letter in which he used the words of the elders of Shu to express his own disapproval of the plan in order to criticize the actions of the emperor, and at the same time explained the purpose of his mission and made known the emperor's wishes in the matter. The letter read as follows:

For seventy-eight years the Han had flourished, its virtue resplendent in the reigns of six sovereigns, glorious in their might and majesty, their deep mercy and blessing spreading far and wide, nourishing all creatures and overflowing beyond the borders of the empire. At that time an envoy[16] was sent by imperial order to carry out an expedition to the west, following the rivers and driving back the enemy, and wherever he went there were none who failed to bow, like grass before the wind, to the word of our sovereign. Thus Ran journeyed to court and Mang followed after; Zuo was conquered and Qiong pacified; Siyu was invaded and Baoman forced to its knees. Then the envoy halted his attack, wheeled his carriage about, and headed toward the east to return and make his report to the throne. But when he reached the capital of the province of Shu, a number of elderly statesmen, gentlemen, and teachers, twenty-seven in all, stern and correct in their behaviour, came to call upon him. When they had exchanged a word of greeting, the men of Shu came forward and said:

"We have heard it said that the Son of Heaven in his relations with the barbarian tribes should be like one who holds an animal by the halter, merely leading it on without stop. For three years now the men of the provinces of Ba, Shu, and Guanghan have wearied themselves with the task of building a road to Yelang, and still it is not completed. The soldiers are worn out and the common people are in want, and yet on top of this we are told we must open up communications with the western barbarians. The strength of the people is exhausted, and we fear that the undertaking can never be carried out. The blame for this lies partly with His Majesty's envoy, and we are secretly afraid for the safety of the advisers who urged this plan upon the ruler.

"Moreover, the lands of Qiong, Zuo, and Western Po have existed side by side with China for more years than it is possible to reckon, and yet during that period no benevolent ruler has ever succeeded in winning them over by virtue, nor any powerful ruler in annexing them

---

[16]Namely, Sima Xiangru himself.

by force. In our opinion the task is next to impossible. The present plan does no more than deprive the common people of China in order to benefit the barbarians, exhausting those who are the support of the nation in the service of worthless foreigners. Ignorant and rustic men that we are, we are unable to comprehend the reasons for such a policy!"

The envoy replied, "How can you make such an assertion? If what you say were true, then the men of Shu as well would be following barbarian customs![17] Even a man of my own poor capabilities must reject such arguments as these!

"This is a large-scale undertaking, and for that reason it is hardly the kind of thing that mere bystanders like yourselves can comprehend. I am in a hurry to be on my way and I have no leisure to go into details, but I should like at least to give you gentlemen a general outline of the plan.

"In this world there must first be extraordinary men before there can be extraordinary deeds, and there must be extraordinary deeds before extraordinary results can be achieved. Whatever is extraordinary is always regarded with suspicion by ordinary men. Therefore it is said, 'The common folk are terrified by the start of anything extraordinary, but when it has reached completion, the whole world enjoys the benefits thereof.'

"Thus in ancient times a great flood arose, spilling its waters across the whole land; the people were forced to flee over hill and dale in terror, and nowhere could they find refuge. Then Emperor Yu of the house of Xia, taking pity upon their plight, set about to stem the flood, opening up the rivers and channelling off the streams, dividing and deepening their beds to rescue the people from disaster; he led the waters east to the sea and all the world found peace and safety. Do you suppose that the people accomplished such a task by themselves? The mind of the emperor was fraught with care, and he himself took part in their labours, until his skin was calloused and brown and the hair no longer grew on his body. Thus the glory of his achievements has shone

---

[17] I.e., the region of Shu itself would never have been wrested from the barbarians and made a part of the Chinese empire.

through countless ages and his praises are sung to this very day.

"When a truly wise ruler has ascended the throne, how can you expect him to give his attention only to petty deeds and trifles, to be bound by the letter of custom and led by common ways, to abide only by the stories and traditions of the past, seeking nothing more than the approval and delight of his own generation? Rather will he honour lofty ideals and farsighted proposals, embark upon new undertakings to insure the continuance of the dynasty, and provide a model for ten thousand ages to admire. Thus will he strive with all his might to bring new lands and people beneath his sway and expend every thought to match the virtue of the life-giving earth, and with earth and heaven to form a triad! Is it not said in the *Odes*,

Beneath all heaven
There is no land that is not the king's;
Throughout the borders of the earth,
None who are not his subjects![18]

"Therefore, within the six directions and beyond the eight corners of the earth, wherever his virtue flows, if there is any creature that is not touched and transformed by his mercy, the wise ruler considers it a source of shame.

"Now, within the borders of the nation, the men of China with their hats and girdles all enjoy the highest blessing, and none are excluded or left out. But in the lands of the strange-mannered barbarians, in the distant regions of the foreigners, where our boats and carriages cannot penetrate and our people seldom set foot, the teachings of our government are as yet unknown and the wind of virtue which issues from our sovereign blows but faintly. Therefore, when they enter our borders they turn their backs upon duty and insult propriety, while within their own lands they commit all manner of wanton evil, banishing or assassinating their leaders. Among them, ruler and subject change places, and honourable and lowly are confounded; fathers and elders suffer for crimes they have not committed, and children and orphans are taken as slaves, bound and weeping. Then do they look toward our land and cry out in anger, saying, 'We have heard that in China there is a ruler of supreme benevolence, whose

---

[18]"Shanbei", *Gufeng* Section, "Lesser Odes", in the *Book of Odes*.

virtue is manifold and whose mercy is all-embracing, so that under him all beings find their just place. Why are we alone deprived of his blessing?' On tiptoe they stand, gazing longingly like men in drought at a distant rainstorm. Even the cruellest of men would shed tears for them; how much more, then, must a great sage like our ruler be moved to pity by their plight!

"For this reason he sent his armies north to attack the powerful Xiongnu, dispatched his envoys to hasten south and reprimand the headstrong rulers of Yue, extending his virtue to the lands on every side. Then the chieftains of the west and southwest came to him by the millions, swarming together like fish that battle their way upstream, begging to receive titles from the ruler of China. It was for this reason that he extended the boundaries to the Mo and Ruo rivers, moved the frontier to Zangge, opened up a way through Ling Mountain, and bridged the source of the Sun, building a new road for justice and virtue and establishing for the sake of posterity a new regime of benevolence and righteousness. Then may his mercy extend far and wide, bringing succour to every foreign land, and the remote regions will no longer be shut up; the dark and inaccessible places will be illumined with a great light of understanding, so that we in China may at last lay down our weapons and the barbarians may find rest from invasion and punishment; near and far will become one body, and China and the lands beyond it will together enjoy good fortune. Will that not be a joyous day indeed?

"To rescue the people from the sea of troubles in which they flounder and to serve the cause of the highest and most beautiful virtue; to turn back a dying age from the course of decay and ruin and to carry on the dynastic labours of the Zhou kings which were cut off: these are the urgent tasks which confront the Son of Heaven. Though the execution of them may mean toil for the common people, how can he cease on that account?

"Every task undertaken by a ruler must begin in sorrow and toil, but as surely will it end in ease and joy. The proof that our ruler has received the mandate of Heaven lies in this very undertaking to the west. When it has been completed, he will increase his glory by performing the Feng sacrifice upon Mt. Tai and the Shan sacrifice at Liangfu; the phoenix bells on his carriage will ring with joy; odes of praise will peal forth in his honour; and he will be acclaimed the equal of the Five Emperors of ancient times and mount to greater heights than the rulers of the Three Dynasties.

"And yet you, the watchers, have not understood his intentions; the listeners do not comprehend his voice. Like a bright swan, he soars to the dome of heaven, but the spreaders of nets still search for him, alas, in the marshy wastes!"

At this the elders of Shu looked about in confusion, forgetting what it was they had come to say and no longer able to make their proposal. With a sigh they replied as in one voice, "Wonderful indeed is the virtue of the Han! This is what we came to hear! Though the common people should be idle in their labours, we beg to lead the way ourselves!"

Then, abashed and at a loss for words, they took their leave and hastily withdrew.

Sometime after this, someone sent a report to the throne accusing Sima Xiangru of having accepted bribes when he was acting as imperial envoy. As a result, he was dismissed from office, but a year or so later was recalled to the post of palace attendant.

Xiangru stuttered when he spoke, but was very fond of composing works of literature. He also suffered constantly from diabetes. Because of his marriage to the daughter of the Zhuo family, he enjoyed considerable wealth. Though he was promoted to various offices at court, he never ventured to discuss affairs of state with the high ministers but, pleading ill health, lived a life of retirement. He had no desire for high offices or noble titles.

It was his custom to accompany the emperor on hunting parties to the Palace of Old Poplars. At such times the emperor delighted in shooting down bears and wild boars in person and galloping after the various wild beasts. Xiangru, distressed at this, submitted a memorial reprimanding the emperor for such conduct. It read as follows:

I have heard that even creatures of the same species differ in their abilities. Thus, when we talk of great strength, we mention the famous strong man Wu Hu of Qin; for outstanding swiftness we cite Qing Ji of Wu, and for bravery the ancient heroes Meng Ben and Xia Yu. If this is true of men, may I venture to suggest, then, that it must be true of beasts as well?

Now Your Majesty delights in racing through the dangerous mountain defiles and shooting ferocious beasts. But should you suddenly encounter some creature of extraordinary size and strength, should some startled beast spring out from an unexpected quarter and charge down upon the vehicles of your attendants, your carriages would have no room to wheel about, nor would your men have time to employ their skill and, though they might have the strength of Wu Hu and the skill of the archer Feng Meng, they would be powerless to aid you. Like so many dead limbs or rotten stumps, they would all suffer injury. Were the Xiongnu or Yue barbarians to spring up from beneath your hubs, or the Qiang and Yi barbarians fling themselves at your crossboard, the situation could not be more perilous. And even if it were absolutely certain that there was no danger involved, it is not the sort of situation in which the Son of Heaven should place himself to begin with!

Even when the roads have been cleared for your passing and your carriage gallops down the middle of the way, there are times when a horse slips the bit or wrenches free of its bridle and runs wild. How much more so, then, when you are racing through the tall grasses or galloping over the hills, with your eyes set only upon the pleasure of the catch before you and your mind forgetful of sudden mishaps that might occur? How easy would it be to meet with misfortune! To make light of the importance of your high position and find no peace in it, but to count it a joy to set out on paths that threaten even a particle of danger is, if I may venture to say so, hardly the way for Your Majesty to act.

An enlightened man sees the end of things while they are still in bud, and a wise man knows how to avoid danger before it has taken shape. Misfortune often lurks in the shadowy darkness and springs forth when men are off their guard. Thus the homely proverb says: "The heir to an estate of a thousand pieces of gold should not sit on the edge of the porch!" This is a trifling remark, and yet it can apply to great affairs. I beg Your Majesty to give it thought and to be kind enough to consider my words!

The emperor was pleased with this memorial. On the way back from the hunt, the emperor stopped for a visit at the Palace of Righteous Spring, nearby which stood the grave mound of the Second Emperor of the Qin. Sima Xiangru thereupon composed a poem in the rhyme-prose style in which he lamented the erroneous ways of the Second Emperor. It read:

> I climb the winding face of the long slope
> And enter the lofty halls of the many-storeyed palace;
> Looking down upon the banks of the crooked streams
> Or gazing far off at the ragged crests of the Southern Mountains,
> I see the deep stillness of cliff-bound glens
> And the spreading mouths of spacious valleys,
> Where the racing torrents endlessly leap and tumble,
> Spilling their waters abroad upon the wide plain.
> I scan the dark and massive forests,
> The dense groves of bamboo;
> To the east I gallop up the earthen mound,
> To the north, wade across the stony shallows,
> And with slackened pace and solemn mien
> I pay my respects to the memory of the Second Emperor.
> He failed to conduct himself with discretion
> And lost his empire and his throne;
> He heeded slander and would not wake to truth
> And brought destruction to the temples of his ancestors.
> Alas, how pitiful
> That he went so far astray!
> Now his grave mound is untended, a tangle of weeds,
> And his spirit wanders homeless and unfed.[19]
> With the fleeting years, his tomb falls further into ruin;
> With the passing seasons, it sinks deeper into darkness;
> While his soul like a shadow wings upward,
> Ascending to the ninth heaven, to depart from the world forever.
> Alas, how pitiful!

After this Sima Xiangru was honoured with the post of keeper of the funerary park of Emperor Wen.

Emperor Wu had earlier expressed admiration for the poet's work on Sir Fantasy. Sima Xiangru, observing that the emperor was fond of anything dealing with immortal spirits, took occasion to remark, "My description of the Shanglin

---

[19] Because his descendants are no longer living to offer sacrifices to him.

Park is hardly deserving of praise. I have something that is still finer. In the past I began a poem in rhyme-prose style on 'The Mighty One'. It is not completed yet, but when I have finished it, I beg to present it to Your Majesty."

The older legends of famous immortals always pictured them as emaciated creatures who dwell among the hills and swamps, but Sima Xiangru judged that this was not the type of immortal that would take the emperor's fancy. He therefore completed his "*Fu* on The Mighty One", which read as follows:

> In this world there lives a Mighty One
> Who dwells in the Middle Continent.[20]
> Though his mansion stretches ten thousand miles,
> He is not content to remain in it a moment
> But, saddened by the sordid press of the vulgar world,
> Nimbly takes his way aloft and soars far away.
> With crimson carriage flags interwoven with crystal rainbows,
> He mounts upon the clouds and wanders on high;
> He raises his long standard of yellow flame
> Tipped with multicoloured plumes of shimmering radiance,
> Streaming with starry pennants
> And banderoles of comets' tails.
> Drifting with the wind, he threads his way;
> With banners fluttering, he wanders aloft.
> He snatches a shooting star for a flag
> And sheathes his flagstaff in a broken rainbow.
> A blaze of vermilion, dazzling the eyes,
> He whirls before the gale and drifts upon the clouds.
> His elephant-carved chariot is drawn by winged dragons,
> With red serpents and green lizards writhing at their sides.
> High and low they gallop,
> Lifting their heads in lordly pride;
> Lithely bending and rearing their backs,
> They slither and curl their winding way.
> Now they stretch their necks and peer about,
> Raising their heads and pausing in passage;
> Now with fearless and lofty assurance
> They bolt forward in tumultuous flight.

---

[20] I.e., China. The Mighty One is of course intended to be Emperor Wu himself.

Onward they bound, twisting and turning,
Left side and right leaping in harmony,
Tumbling forward in dauntless array,
Prancing in unison.
Straining at the bridle and uttering strange cries,
They swoop down to tread the earth;
Springing upward in breathless flight,
They careen wildly across the sky.
Pressing forward, chasing after,
They swirl like sparks, they stream like lightning,
Plunging boldly into the mists
And fading out of sight among the clouds.[21]
Thus the Mighty One crosses to the eastern limit and ascends to
the end of the north,
Searching out other immortal spirits.
Together they wheel about and drive far to the right;
Slanting across the Valley of Leaping Springs, they turn again
east.
He summons all the fairies of the Magic Garden
And a host of gods to ride behind him on the Star of Pure Light.
He orders the Emperors of the Five Directions to be his guides,
Beckons to his side the Great Single Star and the immortal Ling
Yang.
On his left rides the deity Black Night, on his right, the Thunder
Bearer,
While before and behind the gods Luli and Yuhuang attend him.
He has the War Earl Qiao as his footman, the genie Xianmen as
his page,
And the physician Qibo to prepare his medicine cup.
The god of fire Zhurong goes in front to clear the road
And disperse the foul vapours before his coming.
His cortège boasts ten thousand carriages,
Their canopies woven of cloud, their flowered pennants flying.
He calls the god of the east Jumang to wait upon him,

---

[21] In this passage, a mass of obscure onomatopoeic compounds, commentators are able
to give only tentative suggestions as to the exact meaning of the words.

Saying, "I would journey south to take my pleasure!"
He visits the sage Emperor Yao on Mt. Chong
And Emperor Shun on the Mountain of Nine Peaks.
In endless massive ranks his retinue advances;
Pressing upon each other, they gallop on their way,
Veering and jostling
Amidst a tangle of chariots,
Swooping onward in eternal procession
Like a mighty river rolling by;
Spurring forward in serried ranks,
A host of countless numbers advancing,
Fanning out across the heavens,
Their columns scattered and broken.
Straight they ride into the din and clangour of the Thunder
Hall
And swoop through the craggy confines of Devil Valley.
They survey the eight directions and the four outer wastes,
Ford the Nine Rivers and pass over the Five Streams,
Traverse the Flaming Mountain and the River of Weak
Waters,
Embark among the floating islets and cross the drifting sands;
They rest upon the Congling Ranges and idle by their waters,
While the goddess Nügua strikes the lute and the Lord of the River
dances.
At times, when the sky grows dark and threatening,
They summon Pingyi, the messenger of the gods,
And send him to chastise the Wind Earl and punish the Rain
Master.
They gaze west to the hazy contours of the Kunlun Mountains,
Then gallop off to the Mountain of the Three Pinnacles.
They batter at the gates of Heaven, enter the palace of the Celestial
Emperor,
And invite the goddess Jade Maiden to return in their chariots.
They roam the slopes of Langfeng and sit down to rest,
Like ravens that circle on high and come to roost again.
They wander among the Dark Hills,
Winging their way in crooked flight.

"Behold!" cries the Mighty One, "the Queen Mother of the West,[22]
With her hair of silvery white
And her burden of hairpins, living in a cave!
Fortunately she has her three-legged crow to bring her food.
Yet if she must live in this state forever,
Though it be for ten thousand ages, what joy can she find?"
Then he wheels his carriage about and departs from her abode,
Making his way across Mt. Buzhou.
He stops to dine at the Hill of the Sombre City;
He sucks up the midnight vapours of the northland
And feasts on golden morning mists;
He nibbles the blossoms of the herb of immortality
And savours the flowers of the Ruby Tree.
Then he rises and resumes his journey,
His chariot dancing wildly towards the heavens.
He threads through the streams of lightning that pour from Heaven's portals
And traverses the drenching torrents of the Cloud Master.
With his attendant carriages, he gallops the long road downward,
Racing through the mists and off into the distance.
He presses beyond the borders of the narrow universe
And, with slackened pace, emerges beyond the bounds of the north.
He leaves his attendants behind at the Dark Pass
And rides ahead of them out of the Cold Gate of the North.
Beneath him in the vastness, the earth has disappeared;
Above his head the heavens vanish in endless space.
Gazing about, his eyes swim and grow sightless;
His ears are deafened and discern no sound.
Riding upon the Void, he mounts on high,
Above the world of men, companionless, to dwell alone.

When Sima Xiangru presented his ode in praise of the Mighty One, the emperor was overcome with delight, declaring that it made him feel as though

---

[22] An immortal spirit whose cult was very popular in Han times, said to dwell in a cave west of the Kunlun Mountains. The poet makes fun of her constrained way of life, contrasting it with the freedom and luxury of The Mighty One.

he were already whirling away over the clouds and filled him with a longing to wander about the earth and the heavens.

Xiangru had retired from his post at court sometime earlier because of ill health and was living at his home in Mouling. "Xiangru's illness seems to be very serious," the emperor announced to his attendants. "It would be well if someone went to his house and gathered up all of his writings. If it is not done now, they are very likely after his death to become scattered and lost." He dispatched Suo Zhong to carry out the task, but when Suo Zhong reached Mouling he discovered that Xiangru was already dead. Finding no manuscripts in the poet's house, he questioned Xiangru's wife, who replied, "My husband never kept any books or writings around the house. From time to time he used to compose pieces, but someone always came and took them away, so that there is nothing left here now. Before he died, however, he did write one piece and told me that if a messenger came from His Majesty looking for books, I was to present it to him. But outside of that there is nothing else!"

She then gave Suo Zhong the manuscript her husband had left behind, written on slips of wood, which dealt with the Feng and Shan sacrifices. Suo Zhong in turn presented it to the emperor, who regarded it very highly. It read:[23]

> From the beginnings of highest antiquity, when august Heaven first created the people, until the time of the Qin, how many have been the lords who ruled generation after generation! When we survey the records of recent ages and hark back to the legends of far-off times, we find but a vast and shadowy confusion of figures whose names are no longer spoken, their numbers too great to be reckoned. Yet from the reigns of Shun and Yu, among those who were honoured with titles and posthumous names, we may still count a total of seventy-two rulers. And of all these, there were none who practised good and yet failed to prosper; none who wrought evil and yet escaped destruction!
>
> Of those who went before the Yellow Emperor, aeons removed from us today, we can learn nothing in detail; but the history of the Five Emperors and the Three Dynasties has been handed down to us in the Classics and other writings for all to peruse. Thus the *Book of Documents* says:

---

[23] The purpose of this piece is to persuade Emperor Wu to perform the Feng and Shan sacrifices. In places the poet uses a pseudo-historical style, as though the emperor had already agreed to perform them.

Enlightened is the Lord of the Multitude!
Good the great ministers, his arms and legs![24]

From this we may see that among rulers there was none more glorious than Emperor Yao of Tang, and among ministers, none wiser than his minister Hou Ji, the ancestor of the Zhou kings. Hou Ji laid the foundations of their glory in the age of Emperor Yao; Gong Liu increased the power of the family among the western barbarians; and King Wen instituted the changes appropriate to a new dynasty, opening the way for the flourishing might of the Zhou. Thus was their great undertaking brought to completion and, though in later ages the power of the Zhou lords waned and their virtue declined, yet for a thousand years they ruled without ill repute. Did they not make, as the saying puts it, "a good beginning and a good end"?

There was but one reason for their glory: they were careful to preserve the ways of those who went before them and diligent in handing down their teachings to posterity. Thus their ways were just and easy to follow; their bounty was far-reaching and easily flourished; their laws were manifest and easy to obey; and their method of choosing successors to the throne was logical and easy to maintain. So the dynasty reached its height under King Cheng, who came to the throne when he was still in swaddling clothes, and its glory surpassed that of the Xia and Shang, the two dynasties that had preceded it.

If we examine the origins and survey the later history of the Zhou, we find no wonders or extraordinary deeds worthy to compare with those of our present age today. Nevertheless, the Zhou kings journeyed to Liangfu and ascended Mt. Tai, performing the Feng and Shan sacrifices, to publish abroad their glory and proclaim to the world their honour and fame.

The virtue of our great Han, however, is like a mighty fountain of waters, bubbling forth and spreading abroad; to the four borders it extends like a sheltering cloud, an enveloping mist, reaching upwards to the nine levels of the sky, stretching here below to the eight corners of the earth. All living creatures are bathed in its waters. Its harmony flows out in all directions; its might swirls onward to distant lands. Those nearby sport in its springs; those far off swim in its margins.

---

[24] *Yiji*, "Documents of Yu".

Thus have all evil-doers vanished beneath its surface and the dark places have been flooded with light; the very insects and reptiles stir with joy and turn their heads toward the source of this blessing.

In response to our ruler's virtue, auspicious creatures such as the fabulous *zouyu*[25] come to play in his gardens, and strange beasts like the musk deer appear on his borders. A wonderful variety of grain with six heads growing miraculously out of one stalk is brought to his kitchens and used for offerings, and a beast with a two-pronged horn growing from one base is used for his sacrifices. Marvellous tortoises, still living from the days of the Zhou dynasty, have been captured among the rivers of Qi, and dragons of blue and gold have been called forth from the lakes. Spirits and gods come to his Garden of Immortals: he receives them as his guests in the Lodge of Leisure. Strange creatures in astonishing profusion, extraordinary occurrences of every description — how manifold are the auspicious signs that come in answer to his virtue! And yet the Son of Heaven protests that he is unworthy and dares not speak of undertaking the Feng and Shan sacrifices. In the days of King Wu of Zhou, when a white fish leaped into his boat as he was crossing the Yellow River, he marvelled at the wonder and offered it as a burnt offering to Heaven. With only this trifling portent as a sign of his worth, he dared to ascend the great mountain and perform the Feng and Shan sacrifices. Was this not presumptuous of him? How far removed was his presumption from the modesty of our own ruler!

Then the grand marshal came forward and said, "Your Majesty's benevolence has brought succour to all living creatures and your righteousness has punished the evil-doers. The clans of China in joy bear tribute to court and the hundred barbarians come with gifts. Your virtue equals that of the rulers of highest antiquity and your achievements are unparalleled. Your goodness and glory have spread far and wide, calling forth a host of auspicious omens; not on one occasion alone have they appeared, but time and again. So it is the opinion of the officials that Your Majesty should order altars erected on Mt. Tai and Liangfu to await your coming, and there increase the glory of your

---

[25] Described by commentators as "a white tiger with black markings" which appears when there is a virtuous ruler in the land.

fame. Then will the Lord on High send down his blessing, and good fortune in abundance to crown your labours!

"So long as Your Majesty modestly declines to take this step, the three deities of Heaven, Earth, and the Mount are robbed of their fulfilment, and the ceremonies proper to a true king are left incomplete, bringing shame to all your ministers.

"Some say that the ways of Heaven are dark and silent, and therefore the auspicious omens, which are the expressions of its will, cannot be ignored. If the rulers of antiquity had similarly declined to heed the meaning of the omens, then there would be no records of the Feng Sacrifice on the summit of Mt. Tai and none of the Shan Sacrifice at Liangfu. If each had been content only to enjoy glory in his own time and had thought of nothing but the fulfilment of his days in this world, then what fame would they have enjoyed in generations after, and how could the orators speak of the seventy-two rulers of antiquity? Your Majesty has diligently practised virtue and been rewarded with these omens from Heaven; if you now respectfully heed them and carry out the measures which they indicate, you will in no sense be overstepping propriety. Thus it was that the sage kings of ancient times did not neglect these steps but carried out their rituals before the Lord of the Earth, manifested their truthfulness to the God of Heaven, and engraved their achievements upon the Central Peak, in order to make known their supreme worth, extend their abundant virtue, spread abroad their fame and honour, and receive generous blessings from above whereby to enrich their people. Ah, how marvellous is this act! The spectacle of the world, the supreme undertaking of a king — it must not be neglected!

"We beg Your Majesty to complete this ritual and make use of the plans drawn up by the officials and court scholars, so that they may be enlightened by the rays of your virtue, which is like the sun and moon, and be warmed by the distant fires of your worth, thereby fulfilling their duties. We beg you at the same time to set forth a true record of the deed, couched in rich and sonorous language, so that it may stand beside the *Spring and Autumn Annals*. Then will a seventh Classic be added to the former six, to be handed down for ages everlasting, that all posterity may be washed by the clear currents of your virtue and lifted upon its spreading waves; that the fame of such virtue may be noised abroad and its precious worth be known to all. The reason the sages of old have for so long maintained their glorious reputations and have constantly been praised as chief among the virtuous was solely that they carried out this ritual. Your Majesty should order the master of ancient affairs to draw up a complete set of rules for the ceremony for you to peruse!"

The Son of Heaven, moved by his words, changed countenance and cried, "You have spoken well. I will try it!" Then he began to consider the matter and to lay his plans, gathering together all the proposals of his high ministers, weighing how best to carry out the Feng and Shan sacrifices, spreading abroad in song his great blessing, and making known to all the wealth of auspicious omens which had appeared. He composed a song of praise which read:

"From the sheltering heavens of my virtue
The clouds come rolling forth,
The sweet dews and seasonable rains fall
To make glad the earth;
What creature lives not succoured
By their rich showers and soaking mists?
My harvest is replete
With the auspicious six-headed grain.
I not only send the rain,
But soak the earth with life-giving moisture;
I not only dampen the earth,
But cause the waters to flow abroad!"[26]
All beings in harmony
Turn their thoughts in longing to him;
The great Mt. Tai illumines its heights
And watches expectantly for the coming of its lord.
Oh prince, oh prince!
Why do you tarry?
The dappled *zouyu* beast
Sports in our lord's park;
Black markings on its white hide,
Emblems of its auspicious nature;

---

[26] In the first section of this poem the emperor is imagined as speaking in his own words.

Gentle and austere,
With the manners of a prince.
It has heard of our lord's virtue
And has come now to observe it;
Over trackless roads it journeyed,
A fair omen sent by Heaven,
As it came before in the time of Emperor Shun,
Heralding his rise to glory.
Likewise the merry unicorn
Was found rambling among the sacred altars
When, in the tenth month, the beginning of winter,
Our lord went to conduct the suburban sacrifices.
It galloped before our lord's carriage
And when he sacrificed to it, the deities of Heaven sent rich
blessings.
Even the days before the Three Dynasties
Knew no such wonders as these!
The writhing yellow dragon,
Drawn by his virtue, has ascended from the depths,
Shimmering with a dozen hues,
Sparkling like fire,
Showing to all its form and face,
That the people might be awakened to the worth of their lord.
Thus it is written in the ancient records:
"Dragon-drawn is the carriage of the Heaven-ordained ruler"
The will of Heaven is thus made clear;
There is no need for reiterated pronouncements.
By these signs is the commandment conveyed
To carry out the Feng Sacrifice at Mt. Tai!

If we open the Classical texts and study their meaning, we find
that, even when the will of Heaven and the deeds of mankind have
reached accord and those here below have acted in such a way as to
call forth a true response from on high, still the virtue of the sage king
is to act with caution and utmost reverence. So the saying has it that
"in times of prosperity, one must consider decline; in safety, one must
think of danger!" Thus it is said that Kings Tang and Wu, the founders
of the Shang and Zhou dynasties, though they held the most honoured

positions, did not fail to exercise cautious reverence; and Emperor Shun, while carrying out the great rituals, constantly reflected whether he were committing some oversight.

In the fifth year after Sima Xiangru's death, the Son of Heaven for the first time sacrificed to the Earth Lord, and in the eighth year he proceeded first to the Middle Peak, Mt. Song, to perform rituals there, then to Mt. Tai to carry out the Feng Sacrifice, and finally to Liangfu to carry out the Shan Sacrifice on the hill called Suran. Sima Xiangru wrote other works besides those which I have quoted here, such as the "Letter to Su Jian," the marquis of Pingling, and the "Letter to the Five Lords" on the relative merits of grasses and trees, but I have not included them here. The only works of his I have quoted are those which are best known among the high officials.

The Grand Historian remarks: The *Spring and Autumn Annals*, by relating matters that are familiar and mundane, manages to convey the most subtle principles. The *Book of Changes*, while dealing with essentially abstruse affairs, is yet perfectly clear in its application. The "Greater Odes" of the *Book of Odes* praise the virtue of kings and powerful men, but nevertheless extend their attention to the virtues of the common people. The "Lesser Odes" criticize the deeds of petty officials, but their criticisms implicate the men in highest office. Thus all these works choose different modes of expression, and yet they are alike in dealing primarily with virtue. Similarly the works of Sima Xiangru, although often couched in fantastic and extravagant language, are in the end essentially concerned with moderation and frugality. Can we say, then, that they are any different from the satires and reprimands of the *Book of Odes*?[27] Accordingly, I have selected from among his works those that I consider worthy of discussion and recorded them in this chapter.

---

[27]The text at this point contains some remarks by Yang Xiong, a poet who lived some hundred years after Sima Qian, which have been inserted by later editors. They have been omitted in the translation.

SHI JI 120: THE BIOGRAPHIES OF JI AN AND ZHENG DANGSHI

When he donned his formal robes and cap and appeared at court, none of the other officials dared to propound any foolish theories: such was the effect of Ji An's dignity. Fond of recommending others and praised as a worthy man: such was the character of Zheng Dangshi. Thus I made "The Biographies of Ji An and Zheng Dangshi".

JI AN

Ji An, whose polite name was Ji Changru, was a native of Puyang. His ancestors won favour with the rulers of the state of Wey and for seven generations, down to the time of Ji An, served without break as high officials.

During the reign of Emperor Jing, Ji An, on the recommendation of his father, was appointed as a mounted guard to the heir apparent. Because of his stern bearing he was treated with deference. Later, when Emperor Jing passed away and the heir apparent ascended the throne, Ji An was appointed master of guests.

When the tribes of Eastern and Southern Yue began to attack each other, the emperor dispatched Ji An to go to the area and observe the situation. He did not journey all the way, however, but went only as far as Wu and then turned around and came back to the capital to make his report. "The Yue people have always been in the habit of attacking each other," he said. "There is no reason for the Son of Heaven's envoy to trouble himself about such matters!"

When a great fire broke out in Henei and destroyed over 1,000 houses, the emperor once more sent Ji An to observe the situation. On his return he reported, "The roofs of the houses were so close together that the fire spread from one to another; that is why so many homes were burned. It is nothing to worry about. As I passed through Henan on my way, however, I noted that the inhabitants were very poor, and over 10,000 families had suffered so greatly from floods and droughts that fathers and sons were reduced to eating each other. I therefore took it upon myself to use the imperial seals to open the granaries of Henan and relieve the distress of the people. I herewith return the seals and await punishment for overstepping my authority in this fashion."

The emperor, impressed with the wisdom he had shown, overlooked the irregularity of his action and transferred him to the post of governor of Xingyang. Ji An, however, felt that he was unworthy of a governorship and, pleading illness, retired to his home in the country. When the emperor heard of this, he summoned him to court again and appointed him a palace counsellor. But because he sharply criticized the emperor on several occasions, it proved impossible to keep him around the palace for long. The emperor therefore transferred him to the post of governor of Donghai.

Ji An studied the doctrines of the Yellow Emperor and Lao Zi. In executing his duties and governing the people he valued honesty and serenity, selecting worthy assistants and secretaries and leaving them to do as they saw fit. In his administration he demanded only that the general spirit of his directives be carried out and never made a fuss over minor details. He was sick a great deal of the time, confined to his bed and unable to go out, and yet after only a year or so as governor of Donghai he had succeeded in setting the affairs of the province in perfect order and winning the acclaim of the people.

The emperor, hearing of his success, summoned him to court and appointed him master of titles chief commandant, promoting him to one of the nine highest offices in the government. In this post, as well, Ji An emphasized a policy of *laissez-faire*, interpreting his duties very broadly and not bothering with the letter of the law.

Ji An was by nature very haughty and ill-mannered. He could not tolerate the faults of others and would denounce people to their faces. Those who took his fancy he treated very well, but those who didn't he could not even bear to see. For this reason most men gave him a wide berth. On the other hand he was fond of learning and liked to travel about doing daring and generous things for others, and his conduct was always above reproach. He was also fond of outspoken criticism and his words frequently brought scowls to the emperor's face. His constant ambition was to be as direct and outspoken as the Liang general Fu Bo and Emperor Jing's minister Yuan Ang. He was on very friendly terms with Guan Fu, Zheng Dangshi, and the director of the imperial clan Liu Qi. Because of his frank criticisms, however, it was impossible for him to stay in one position for long.

At this time Empress Dowager Wang's younger brother Tian Fen, the marquis of Wuan, was serving as chancellor. When officials of 2,000 picul rank would appear before Tian Fen, they would prostrate themselves in obeisance, but Tian Fen would never deign to return their greeting. When Ji An went to see Tian Fen, however, he never prostrated himself, but always just gave a low bow.

The emperor at the time was busy summoning scholars and Confucians to court and telling them, "I want to do thus-and-so, I want to do thus-and-so." Commenting on this, Ji An said to the emperor, "On the surface Your Majesty is practising benevolence and righteousness, but in your heart you have too many desires. How do you ever expect to imitate the rule of the sage emperors Yao and Shun in this way?"

The emperor sat in silence, his face flushed with anger, and then dismissed the court. The other high officials were all terrified of what would happen to Ji An. After the emperor had left the room, he turned to his attendants and said, "Incredible — the stupidity of that Ji An!"

Later, some of the officials reproached Ji An for his behaviour, but he replied, "Since the Son of Heaven has gone to the trouble of appointing us as his officials and aides, what business have we in simply flattering his whims and agreeing with whatever he says, deliberately leading him on to unrighteous deeds? Now that we occupy these posts, no matter how much we may value our own safety, we cannot allow the court to suffer disgrace, can we?"

Ji An was frequently ill, and if it appeared that he would be laid up for as long as three months, the emperor would always grant him a vacation from his duties. This happened several times, but Ji An could never seem to get completely well. When his illness persisted, Zhuang Zhu, one of the other officials, appeared in his place before the emperor and requested a leave of absence for him.

"What sort of man is Ji An anyway?" the emperor asked, to which Zhuang Zhu replied, "As long as he is employed in some ordinary post as an official, he will do no better than the average person. But if he were called upon to assist a young ruler or to guard a city against attack, then no temptation could sway him from his duty, no amount of entreaty could make him abandon his post. Even the bravest men of antiquity, Meng Ben and Xia Yu, could not shake his determination!"

"Yes," said the emperor. "In ancient times there were ministers who were deemed worthy to be called the guardians of the altars of the nation. And men like Ji An come near to deserving the same appellation."

When the general in chief Wei Qing was at court, the emperor would sometimes receive him while lounging informally on the couch, and when the chancellor Gongsun Hong came to see the emperor on some private affair, the emperor would often not bother to don his hat for the interview. But if Ji An came for an audience, the emperor would never receive him without his hat on.

The emperor was once seated in his curtained armour hall when Ji An appeared to present a memorial on some affair. The emperor caught sight of him from a distance and, because he did not have his hat on at the time, quickly withdrew behind the curtains and sent someone else to accept and approve the memorial. Such was the respect and courtesy that he showed Ji An.

At this time Zhang Tang had just been promoted to the post of commandant of justice because of his services in revising and systematizing the penal code. Ji An several times launched sharp attacks on Zhang Tang in the presence of the emperor. "Here you are, one of the highest officials in the government, and yet you have not succeeded in doing anything to carry on and broaden the accomplishments of the former emperors or to repress the evil desires of the people of the empire. You have not enriched the nation and its inhabitants, nor cleared the jails of malefactors. None of these things have you done, but instead you excel in evil and cruelty and win merit by wantonly destroying the old ways. What right have you to tamper with the old code of laws given to the nation by Emperor Gaozu? For such actions you and your family deserve to be wiped out!"

Ji An frequently engaged in arguments with Zhang Tang. Zhang Tang would always base his case on the letter of the law, paying strict attention to the most petty details, while Ji An would fight sternly and stubbornly for general principles, but, unable to persuade his opponent, in the end would become so enraged that he would begin cursing Zhang Tang. "People say that petty clerks with their brushes and scrapers have no business becoming high government officials. How right they are! It is men like this Zhang Tang who have gotten the empire into such a state that men are afraid to look each other in the eye or to put one foot down beside the other for fear of breaking the law!"

At this time the dynasty was busy attacking the Xiongnu and trying to force the other barbarian tribes surrounding China to acknowledge allegiance to the Han. Ji An did his best to get the government to reduce its activities in this direction, catching the emperor whenever he could in moments of leisure and urging him to make peace with the Xiongnu and stop sending out the troops. But the emperor at this time favoured Confucian principles and esteemed the advice of Gongsun Hong. As the number of government undertakings increased, the petty officials and the people grew skilful at evading the law and twisting it around to satisfy their own ends. The emperor himself took a great interest in legal matters, and Zhang Tang and other officials won his favour by frequently submitting memorials to the throne on law cases. Ji An for his part constantly disparaged Confucian teachings and denounced Gongsun Hong and the others to their faces. "With hearts full of deceit and a facade of learning, all you do is flatter the whims of the ruler! A bunch of brush-and-scraper clerks, intent only on making the laws more severe and thinking up clever ways to ruin people — trapping them into committing some offence, making it impossible for them to tell the truth, and then gloating over your victory!"

The emperor, however, continued to heap greater and greater honour on Gongsun Hong and Zhang Tang. These two, for their part, had a profound hatred for Ji An, and even the emperor himself was displeased with Ji An and would have liked to find some excuse to execute him.

Gongsun Hong, who was chancellor at this time, one day said to the emperor, "The area under the jurisdiction of the right prefect of the capital includes the homes of many prominent men and members of the imperial family and is therefore difficult to govern. Only an official of longstanding importance is capable of handling the task. May I suggest that Ji An be transferred to the post of right prefect?"

Ji An was accordingly appointed to the position and filled it for several years without a break. By this time the general in chief Wei Qing enjoyed great honour and his sister had been designated empress, and yet Ji An treated Wei Qing in a very casual manner as though he were an equal. Someone cautioned him about this, saying, "It is obviously the emperor's wish that the other officials should all humble themselves before General Wei Qing. Therefore he keeps heaping greater honours on him. It is hardly right for you alone to refuse to prostrate yourself before him."

To this Ji An replied, "But the very fact that the general has a visitor whom he permits to greet him with only a bow — does this not in itself increase his prestige?"

When Wei Qing heard about this, he was more than ever convinced of Ji An's worth. On various occasions he consulted Ji An on questions concerning the nation and the court and treated him with even greater favour than before.

The king of Huainan was plotting revolt but was afraid of Ji An. "A man who is fond of outspoken criticism and willing to die for his principles is very hard to tempt into doing evil," he commented. "As for persuading men like Gongsun Hong to come over to my side, that is as easy as lifting the lid off a jar or shaking down dry leaves from a tree!"

By this time the emperor had sent several expeditions against the Xiongnu and won considerable success, so that he paid less attention than ever to Ji An's recommendations. Formerly, when Ji An held one of the nine highest posts in the government, Gongsun Hong and Zhang Tang were only petty clerks. Later, Gongsun Hong and Zhang Tang rose step by step until they were equal in rank with Ji An, but Ji An continued to criticize them as before. Finally Gongsun Hong became chancellor and was enfeoffed as a marquis, and Zhang Tang reached the post of imperial secretary. By this time all of Ji An's former assistants and secretaries had advanced as high as Ji An himself, and some even outranked him. Ji An, rather petty-minded as he was, could not keep from feeling a certain resentment at this, and when he appeared before the emperor one day, he remarked, "Your Majesty appoints officials just the way one stacks firewood — whatever comes to hand last is piled on the top!"

The emperor was silent, and after a little while Ji An retired. When he had gone, the emperor said, "After all, it doesn't do for a man to be without learning! Listening to Ji An's words, I find that they are getting more outrageous every day!"

Shortly afterwards the Hunye king, one of the Xiongnu chiefs, led his troops to the border and surrendered to the Han. The Han decided to send 20,000 carriages to the border to transport them to the capital, but since the government officials had no cash on hand, they were obliged to requisition horses from the common people on promise of future payment. As a result, many people hid their horses and it was impossible to get hold of the necessary number. The emperor was enraged and wanted to execute the governor of Chang'an, but Ji An, who was right prefect of the capital at this time, said, "The governor of Chang'an has done nothing wrong. Since he is under my jurisdiction, it will be enough if I alone am executed. Then I think the people will be willing to bring out their horses. Moreover, we must not forget that these Xiongnu have turned against their own ruler in order to surrender to the Han. It should be sufficient if the Han arranges for them to be transported from province to province by easy stages. What need is there to turn the whole empire upside down and exhaust the resources of China merely to accommodate a bunch of barbarians?"

The emperor received his words in silence.

After the Hunye king had arrived in Chang'an some 500 or more merchants and market traders were condemned to death for having sold contraband goods to the Xiongnu. Ji An thereupon asked to speak to the emperor in a moment of leisure and was granted an audience with him in the High Gate Hall of the Eternal Palace. "The Xiongnu have attacked the main roads along the border and broken off peaceful relations with us," said Ji An. "Therefore China has called up troops to punish them, suffering innumerable dead and wounded in the process and spending cash by the billions. In my unworthy opinion any Xiongnu that Your Majesty captures should be treated as slaves and presented to the families of the men who died in the fighting, along with whatever spoils were taken, in order to repay the empire for the hardships it has borne and gratify the hearts of the common people. Even if that is impossible at the moment, what is the reason, when the Hunye king comes with his 30,000 or 40,000 followers and surrenders to the Han, for emptying the treasuries and showering gifts on him, and ordering out faithful Chinese subjects to wait on him as though he were a favourite child? Moreover, how are the common people in their ignorance to know that goods which are sold in the markets of Chang'an will be regarded as contraband by the law officials when they are transported to the border and traded to the barbarians? Now, although Your Majesty may not be in a position to distribute the wealth of the Xiongnu to the empire in payment for its troubles, do you intend to execute 500 or more ignorant men simply because of some petty law? This is what is known as protecting the leaves but injuring the branches. If I may say so, I trust Your Majesty will not adopt such a course as this!"

The emperor listened to his words in silence and expressed no approval. Later he said, "It has been a long time since I have heard anything from Ji An, and now he comes to me again with these absurd suggestions!"

Several months later Ji An was tried for some minor infraction of the law; his offence was pardoned, but he was obliged to resign his post. He retired to his home in the country.

After a few years the government put into circulation the new five-*shu* cash currency. Many of the people began minting the coins illegally, the region of Chu being particularly notorious for counterfeiting. The emperor, considering that the province of Huaiyang was a key point in Chu, summoned Ji An to come to court and receive appointment as governor of Huaiyang. Ji An declined the appointment with great humility and refused to accept the seals of office, but the emperor continued to send edicts urging him to accept until finally he agreed to obey. He was then summoned for an audience, and when he appeared before the emperor, he wept and said, "I expected to die and be tossed into a ditch without ever seeing Your Majesty again. But now, contrary to all my expectations, you have deigned to call me into service once more. However, I am constantly troubled by this miserable illness of mine and have not the strength to undertake the administration of a province. I beg instead to be appointed as a palace attendant so that I may come and go at Your Majesty's side and work to repair defects in government policy. This is my desire!"

"Do you think the governorship of Huaiyang is too insignificant a post?" said the emperor. "Never mind, I will call you back to court in a little while. It is just that the officials and the people of Huaiyang are not getting along well with each other and I thought that, with your weight and prestige, you would be able to straighten things out without having to make any particular effort."

When Ji An had accepted the appointment and was about to leave the capital, he went to visit the grand messenger Li Xi and remarked, "I am now being cast off and sent to live in the provinces so that I will not be able to take part in the deliberations at court. I should warn you, however, that the imperial secretary Zhang Tang has wisdom enough to block any worthwhile criticism and deceit enough to put a plausible facade on his misdeeds. His only concern is to talk cleverly and ingratiatingly and to argue effectively. He will never consent to speak for the good of the empire, but cares only to flatter the will of the ruler. Whatever the emperor does not desire, he condemns; whatever the emperor wishes to do, he praises. He delights in proposing new undertakings and manipulating the laws to satisfy his ends. With deceit in his heart he bends the emperor to his will, and with his harsh officials supporting him in the provinces he increases his power and authority. Now you occupy one of the nine highest offices. If you do not quickly speak out against him, you yourself will end up by sharing the punishment that is bound to come to him!"

But Li Xi was too afraid of Zhang Tang and never had the courage to speak out against him. Ji An took up his duties as governor and carried them out as he had in the past in Donghai, administering the province of Huaiyang and setting its government to rights again. Later, as Ji An had predicted, Zhang Tang fell from power. When the emperor learned that Ji An had urged Li Xi to oppose Zhang Tang, he condemned Li Xi to punishment for having failed to follow the advice. He promoted Ji An to a rank equivalent to that of prime minister to one of the feudal lords and kept him on in Huaiyang. Seven years later, Ji An died.

After his death, and in recognition of his services, the emperor made his younger brother Ji Ren an official and gradually promoted him until he held one of the nine highest offices. Ji An's son Ji Yan also advanced as high as prime minister to one of the feudal lords.

Sima An, the son of Ji An's father's elder sister, had served in his youth as a mounted guard to the heir apparent along with Ji An. Sima An was a man of cultured bearing but of cruel disposition and was very clever at getting along in the official world. Four times he advanced to the rank of the nine highest ministers, and he died while holding the office of governor of Henan. Because of Sima An's influence, ten of his brothers at one time held posts paying 2,000 piculs.

Duan Hong who, like Ji An, also came from Puyang, served originally under Wang Xin, the marquis of Gai and older brother of Empress Dowager Wang. Wang Xin recommended him to the emperor, and as a result Duan Hong was twice ranked among the nine highest ministers. All of those other men from the region of Wey who served in the government, however, were terrified of Ji An and never managed to rival his fame.

ZHENG DANGSHI

Zheng Dangshi, whose polite name was Zheng Zhuang, was a native of Chen. His grandfather Zheng Jun once served as a general under Xiang Yu, but after Xiang Yu was killed he went over to the side of the Han. Emperor Gaozu ordered all of Xiang Yu's former officials to refer to Xiang Yu by his familiar name,[1] Ji, but Zheng Jun alone refused to obey the order. Later, Gaozu summoned all men who had used the familiar name Ji and appointed them as court officials, but Zheng Jun was sent into exile, where he died.

During the reign of Emperor Wen, Zheng Dangshi amused himself by wandering about and performing daring exploits. After he succeeded in rescuing the Liang general Zhang Yu from difficulty, he achieved considerable fame in the area of Liang and Chu.

In the time of Emperor Jing, Zheng Dangshi was made a retainer in the household of the heir apparent. Every five days, when his bath and hair washing day came around,[2] he would order post horses to be held in readiness for him in the suburbs of Chang'an so that he could ride about and visit his friends, or else he would invite guests to his home and entertain them right through the night until dawn, his constant fear being that he would not get around to chatting with

---

[1] To refer to a man by his familiar name, particularly when one had formerly been in his service, was a mark of great disrespect.

[2] The periodic holiday of court officials when they were allowed to leave the palace dormitory and return to their homes to "bathe and wash their hair".

them all. He was fond of the teachings of the Yellow Emperor and Lao Zi, and sought the company of worthy men as though he feared he would never meet enough of them. Although he was still young and held a rather insignificant post, the people he associated with were all of his grandfather's generation and included some of the most famous men of the empire.

After Emperor Wu came to the throne Zheng Dangshi gradually advanced, holding such posts as palace military commander of Lu, governor of Ji'nan, and prime minister of Jiangdu, until he ranked with the nine highest officials, being appointed as right prefect of the capital. At the time of the quarrel between Tian Fen and Dou Ying, he was demoted to the post of steward of the household of the empress and heir apparent, but was later promoted to that of minister of agriculture.

While Zheng Dangshi was acting as a high official, he instructed his gatekeeper that, whenever visitors came to the house, regardless of whether they were of high or low rank, he was not to keep them waiting at the gate but to show them in with all due courtesy. This was the way that Zheng Dangshi, in spite of his high position, humbled himself before others. In addition, he was a man of strict integrity and did nothing to increase the wealth of his family, depending upon his salary and gifts from the emperor to supply the funds needed to entertain his guests. When he sent a present of food to someone, it was never more than a simple dish in a bamboo container.

Every time he appeared at court he would wait until he could catch the emperor in a moment of leisure and then speak to him, always recommending some person of worth in the empire. The ways he used to boost his subordinate officials and assistants into higher positions were truly admirable. When he was recommending someone, he would always take care to show that the person was more worthy than himself. He never addressed his officials by their familiar names, and when he had to speak to one of his subordinates, he took great care not to hurt the man's feelings. If he heard of some worthwhile suggestion that someone else had made, his only thought was to report it to the emperor as quickly as possible. For this reason, gentlemen and men of prominence from east of the mountains all flocked about him and praised him highly.

Once, when the emperor appointed him as envoy to go and observe the break in the dikes of the Yellow River, Zheng Dangshi requested that he be given five days to prepare for the journey. The emperor replied, "I had always heard that you did not bother to take along provisions even for a journey of 1,000 *li*. What do you mean by asking for five days to make preparations?"

Ordinarily, however, when Zheng Dangshi appeared in court he was always careful to take cognizance of the emperor's wishes and go along with them, and never ventured to argue very forcibly for or against any particular measure.

When he was already well along in years, the Han began to launch attacks on the Xiongnu and work to force the submission of the various barbarian tribes, putting the empire to great expense and exhausting the fiscal resources of the government. On Zheng Dangshi's recommendation one of his friends was appointed as a transportation official in the ministry of agriculture, but the man appropriated large sums of money without making any reparation to the government. When Sima An became governor of Huainan, he brought the affair to light, and Zheng Dangshi was implicated in the offence. On payment of a fine he was pardoned and reduced to the status of commoner. A short while later he was appointed to act as chief secretary to the chancellor, but the emperor decided that he was too old for this job and appointed him instead as governor of Runan. After a few years he died in office.

Zheng Dangshi and Ji An at one time ranked among the nine highest officials of the state. They were men of great integrity who always acted with scrupulous honesty. Both men, however, lost their positions in middle age and, their families being poor, their former guests and friends little by little deserted them. Later they went to live in the provinces and died there, leaving no wealth or estate for their sons to inherit. As a result of Zheng Dangshi's merit, six or seven of his brothers and descendants rose to the position of 2,000 picul officials.

The Grand Historian remarks: As long as Ji An and Zheng Dangshi wielded power, they had friends by the score, but when their power vanished, their friends vanished with it. If even worthy men such as they suffered this fate, how must it be with ordinary people!

Lord Di of Xiagui tells this story. Formerly, he says, when he was commandant of justice, he had so many guests that they completely filled his gate. Later, however, when he lost his position, he might have spread a sparrow net in front of his gate without fear of anyone stumbling into it. Sometime afterwards, Lord Di was once more appointed as commandant of justice and all his old visitors wanted to come to see him again, but Lord Di wrote in large letters over the top of his gate the following inscription:

> When you're alive one moment, all but dead the next, then you
> know who your real friends are.

When you're rich one moment, poor the next, then you know the quality of friendship.

When you're lordly one moment, lowly the next, then friendship shows its true face.

Alas! Ji An and Zheng Dangshi might well have said the same thing!

Part III

THE PLOTTERS OF REVOLT

SHI JI 118: THE BIOGRAPHIES OF THE KINGS OF HUAINAN AND HENGSHAN

Because Qing Bu rebelled against the throne, Emperor Gaozu's son Liu Chang was made ruler of his territory, bringing peace to the region south of the Huai and Yangtze rivers. But his son Liu An robbed the common people of Chu. Thus I made "The Biographies of the Kings of Huainan and Hengshan".

The King of Huainan

Liu Chang, posthumously known as King Li of Huainan, was one of the youngest of Emperor Gaozu's sons. His mother was originally a concubine of Zhang Ao, the king of Zhao. In the eighth year of Gaozu's reign, when Gaozu visited the state of Zhao on his way back from Dongyuan, the king of Zhao gave this concubine to him. She won the favour of the emperor and soon became pregnant. After the emperor had gone on his way, the king did not dare to take her back into his own palace, but had a separate palace built to accommodate her.

Shortly afterwards it was discovered that Guan Gao and the other ministers of Zhao were plotting revolt and had intended to assassinate the emperor at Boren. They were arrested, along with the king of Zhao, and brought to the capital for trial; at the same time the king's mother, his brothers, and his concubines were all seized and taken in chains to Henei. Liu Chang's mother was among those seized. She told the officials, "I have won favour with the emperor and I am pregnant!" but although they reported this to the emperor, he was at the time enraged with the king of Zhao and did nothing to rescue her from prison.

Her younger brother Zhao Jian managed to get Shen Yiji, the marquis of Biyang, to speak to Empress Lü on her behalf, but Empress Lü was jealous and refused to mention the matter to the emperor, while Shen Yiji for his part did nothing to press it.

In due time the lady gave birth to her child, the future King Li, but immediately afterwards committed suicide in rage over the treatment she had received. The officials then took the boy and brought him to the emperor, who regretted his behaviour and ordered Empress Lü to raise him as though he were her own child. He also gave instructions for the boy's mother to be buried at her old home in Zhending, where her ancestors had lived for generations.

In the tenth month of the eleventh year of Gaozu's reign (196 BC), after Qing Bu, the king of Huainan, had revolted, the emperor appointed his son Liu Chang as king of Huainan to rule the territory that had formerly belonged to Qing Bu, four provinces in all. The emperor in person led the troops in attacking and defeating Qing Bu. Thus King Li became ruler of Huainan.

Because he had lost his mother at a very early age and had thereafter been constantly cared for by Empress Lü, he enjoyed great favour during the reigns of Emperor Hui and Empress Lü and was able to escape any harm. In his heart he nursed an undying hatred for Shen Yiji, though he did not dare to reveal his feelings.

When Emperor Wen came to the throne Liu Chang, being the only surviving brother of Emperor Wen, considered himself very close to the emperor and began to behave in an arrogant and wilful manner, several times failing to obey the law. Because they were brothers, however, the emperor always pardoned him.

In the third year of Emperor Wen's reign (177 BC), when Liu Chang journeyed to court to pay his respects, he behaved most presumptuously, joining the emperor on hunts and trips to the pleasure parks, riding in the same carriage with him, and constantly addressing him as "Elder Brother".

Liu Chang was a very powerful man, so strong that he could lift a cauldron. He went to call on Shen Yiji, the marquis of Biyang, and requested an interview, and when Shen Yiji appeared, he smashed him over the head with an iron mallet which he had concealed in his sleeve. Then he ordered his attendant Wei Jing to cut off Shen Yiji's head. This done, he mounted his carriage and hurried to the palace gate, where he bared his arms and apologized for his action. "My mother should never have been held guilty along with the others in the Zhao affair," he said. "At that time the marquis of Biyang exercised great influence with Empress Lü and could have saved her, but he failed to press the matter. This was his first crime. Neither Liu Ruyi, the young king of Zhao, nor his mother Lady Qi, were guilty of any offence, and yet the marquis of Biyang stood by and let Empress Lü murder them without saying a word. This was his second crime. Empress Lü made kings of the members of her own clan, endangering the safety of the Liu family, and yet again the marquis of Biyang did not protest. This was his third crime. For the sake of the empire I have respectfully taken upon myself the task of punishing this evil minister and avenging the wrong which my mother suffered. Now with all due respect I bow before the palace gate and beg to receive punishment."

Emperor Wen, moved by the resolution Liu Chang had shown in avenging his mother's death, did not punish him but pardoned his offence. At this time Empress Dowager Bo, the heir apparent, and the various high officials were all terrified of Liu Chang. Liu Chang returned to his kingdom and behaved more wilfully than ever. He paid no attention to the Han laws but had attendants to cry "Clear the way! Attention!" whenever he went in or out of his palace, called his orders "edicts", and issued whatever decrees he pleased, all in imitation of the Son of Heaven.

In the sixth year of Emperor Wen's reign (174 BC), Liu Chang ordered Dan and others, seventy men in all, to join with Chai Qi, the heir of Chai Wu, the marquis of Jipu, in plotting a revolt. They set off in forty large carriages and gathered in a place called Valley Mouth to plan their rebellion. Liu Chang also dispatched envoys to negotiate with the Minyue barbarians of the south and the Xiongnu. When these actions came to light and steps were taken to punish the offenders, the emperor sent an envoy to summon Liu Chang to the capital.

When Liu Chang arrived in Chang'an, the high ministers presented the following memorial to the throne:

> Your servants, the chancellor Zhang Cang, the director of guests Feng Jing, the imperial secretary and director of the imperial clan Yi, the commandant of justice He, and Fu, the palace military commander in charge of suppressing rebels, dare to risk death in speaking these words. Liu Chang, the king of Huainan, has cast aside the laws of the former emperors and refused to obey the edicts of the Son of Heaven. He shows no restraint in his manner of living, riding about in a carriage with a yellow canopy and in his comings and goings imitating the prerogatives of the Son of Heaven. He arbitrarily issues his own commands and pays no attention to the laws of the Han. In appointing his officials he has taken it upon himself to elevate his palace counsellor Chun to the post of chancellor. At his court he has gathered together men from the other fiefs of the Han and fugitives from justice whom he hides from the law, building houses for them and showering them with gifts of wealth, titles, salaries, and lands, even enfeoffing some

of them with the title of marquis within the Pass and paying them stipends of 2,000 piculs. Though he knows that such actions are not proper for a feudal lord, he persists in them, and would like to do even worse!

In addition, the counsellor Dan, the gentleman of the ranks Kaizhang, and others, seventy men in all, plotted a revolt with Chai Qi, the heir of the marquis of Jipu, intending to endanger the ancestral temples and sacred altars of the dynasty. Chai Qi sent Kaizhang in secret to report his plans to the king of Huainan, inviting him to join the revolt and to send envoys to the Minyue tribes and the Xiongnu to persuade them to send out their troops. When Kaizhang journeyed to Huainan for this purpose and appeared before the king, the king sat feasting and talking with him on numerous occasions and even gave him a house, a bride, and a salary of 2,000 piculs. Kaizhang then sent a man to report to Dan that he had discussed their plans for revolt with the king, and the chancellor Chun likewise sent a man to confirm this report to Dan and the other conspirators.

When the officials learned of the affair, they dispatched Qi and several other law officers from Chang'an to go to Huainan and arrest Kaizhang. The king, however, refused to hand Kaizhang over to the authorities, but kept him in hiding and eventually conspired with his former military commander Jian Ji to murder him in order to prevent him from talking. The king put off the officials as long as he could, declaring that he did not know where Kaizhang was and then finally buried a coffin and some grave clothes at the city of Feiling and attempted to deceive them by constructing a grave mound and setting up a notice saying, "Kaizhang is buried here."

In addition, Liu Chang himself killed an innocent man in cold blood and got his officials to condemn six other innocent men to death; he sheltered a criminal who had been condemned to die in the market place and arrested an innocent man instead, handing him over to the authorities as the fugitive and letting the real fugitive go without punishment. In the case of fourteen persons he passed arbitrary and unreasonable sentences, carried out punishments without reporting them to the central government, and had them bound and cross-examined and condemned to serve in the men's or women's labour gangs or to worse punishments. He also pardoned criminals without proper authority, including eighteen persons who had been sentenced to death and fifty-eight persons who had been sentenced to the labour gangs or lesser punishments. Finally he handed out titles, honouring ninety-four men with various ranks ranging from marquis within the Pass on down.

Some time earlier, when Liu Chang was ill, Your Majesty, troubled about the state of his health, sent an envoy to him with a letter and gifts of jujubes and dried meat. But Liu Chang was unwilling to accept the presents and refused to receive the envoy and bow before him.

Again, when the tribes living on the border of Lujiang Province in Nanhai revolted and the soldiers of Huainan were called out to attack them, Your Majesty, considering that the people of Huainan had been put to great hardship and expense by the campaign, dispatched an envoy to present Liu Chang with 5,000 rolls of silk which he in turn was to present to the soldiers in recompense for their labours. But Liu Chang again did not wish to accept the gift and put off the envoy, saying, "No one here has suffered any hardship!"

When Zhi, the ruler of the people of Nanhai, sent a letter to the throne accompanied by an offering of jade, Liu Chang's former official Jian Ji arbitrarily intercepted it, burned the letter, and failed to forward any report. The officials asked that Jian Ji be handed over to them for investigation, but Liu Chang refused to send him to them, attempting to deceive them by saying that Jian Ji was ill.

Finally, when Chun, the chancellor of Huainan, asked the king for permission to journey to the capital for an audience with Your Majesty, Liu Chang flew into a rage and replied, "Do you want to leave me and go over to the side of the Han?"

It is clear from these charges that Liu Chang deserves to be executed and his corpse exposed in the market place. We beg that sentence be passed upon him in accordance with the law.

The emperor replied to their memorial with an edict which read:

I cannot bear to inflict upon the king of Huainan the penalty prescribed by law. You must debate the matter further with the feudal lords and the 2,000 picul officials.

The ministers responded as follows:

Your servants Cang, Jing, Yi, Fu, and He dare to risk death in speaking these words. We have respectfully discussed the matter with

Xiahou Ying and the other feudal lords and 2,000 picul officials, consulting forty-three persons in all. Their unanimous opinion is that Liu Chang has failed to uphold the laws and obey the edicts of the Son of Heaven. He has secretly gathered together a band of conspirators and revolutionaries, treating fugitives from justice with great generosity in hopes that he may fulfil his ambitions. We and the others therefore recommend that sentence be passed in accordance with the law.

The emperor's edict in reply read:

I cannot bear to inflict the legal penalty upon the king. Let him be pardoned from the death sentence but deprived of his title of king.

The ministers responded once more:

Your servants Cang and the rest risk death in speaking these words. Liu Chang has committed crimes which are eminently deserving of death. Your Majesty, however, cannot bear to enforce the law but would graciously pardon him and deprive him of the position of king. We therefore request that he be exiled to Qiongyou in Yandao in the province of Shu. The mothers of his children shall be allowed to accompany him. The district officials shall provide him with the necessary housing and see to his food supplies, providing him with firewood, vegetables, salt, bean preserves, cooking and eating utensils, and mats. We dare risk death to ask that the details of the matter be published throughout the empire.

The emperor replied with an edict which read:

Concerning the food rations of Liu Chang, let him be provided with five catties of meat a day and two measures of wine. Ten of his former palace ladies who have won favour with him shall be allowed to accompany him. The other conditions of his exile shall be as originally proposed. All those who took part with him in the conspiracy shall be executed.

Thus the king of Huainan was sent into exile. He was placed in a covered baggage cart and orders were given to the districts along the way to pass him on from one to the other.

At this time Yuan Ang reprimanded Emperor Wen, saying, "The king of

Huainan has always been wilful by nature and yet Your Majesty failed to appoint strict tutors and chancellors for him. That is the reason things have come to this pass. Moreover, the king is a man of stubborn spirit. Now you have suddenly struck him down, and I fear that, exposed to the dew and damp of the road, he may eventually become ill and die. What would happen if Your Majesty should incur the name of a fratricide?"

But the emperor replied, "I only want to teach him a lesson. Later on I will call him back again."

As the king was passed along from district to district, the attendants were all too terrified of him to break the seals on his prison cart and open it up. "Is it because you fools take me for a man of daring that you are so afraid?" the king said to the attendants. "What have I to do with deeds of bravery? I have come to this because I was too wilful to learn my own faults. Who can bear, in the little space of time which is man's life, to suffer such sorrow as this?"

He refused thenceforth to eat any food and died. When his cart reached Yong, the magistrate of Yong broke open the seals and reported his death to the emperor.

The emperor wept with profound grief and said to Yuan Ang, "I would not listen to your advice and now I have lost my brother!"

"There is nothing that can be done about it," replied Yuan Ang. "I beg Your Majesty to take heart and not to be too hard on yourself."

"But what should I do now?" asked the emperor.

"The only thing to do is to execute the chancellor and the imperial secretary in order to make amends to the empire for what they did to the king!"

The emperor did not follow this advice, but instead ordered the chancellor and the imperial secretary to arrest and examine the attendants in the various districts along the king's route who had failed to open up his cart and urge him to eat. All were condemned to be executed and their corpses exposed in the market place. The emperor then had the king buried at Yong with the funeral rites of a feudal lord and established thirty households to act as guardians of his grave mound.

In the eighth year of his reign (172 BC) Emperor Wen, out of pity for the king of Huainan, enfeoffed his four sons, all of whom were around seven or eight years old at the time. Liu An was enfeoffed as marquis of Fuling, Liu Bo as marquis of Anyang, Liu Ci as marquis of Zhouyang, and Liu Liang as marquis of Dongcheng.

The common people made up a song about the emperor and the king of

Huainan which went:

> Though it's only a foot of cloth,
> We can sew it into something;
> Though it's only a peck of grain,
> We'll grind it together.
> But what of those two brothers,
> Older and younger,
> Who could not spare
> A little land for each other?[1]

When Emperor Wen heard of this, he sighed and said, "The ancient rulers Yao and Shun exiled their own kin, and the duke of Zhou killed his brothers Guan and Cai, and yet the whole world calls them sages. This is because, in whatever they did, they did not allow their personal feelings to interfere with the public good. Do the people of the empire now suppose that I acted as I did because I was greedy for my brother's territory?"

Accordingly, in the twelfth year of his reign (168 BC), Emperor Wen removed Liu Xi from his position as king of Chengyang and made him ruler of the territory that had formerly belonged to the king of Huainan. He also awarded the king of Huainan the posthumous title of Li, the "Cruel King", and set up a funerary park for him like those of the other deceased feudal lords.

In the sixteenth year (164 BC) Emperor Wen, still grieved over the fact that King Li of Huainan, by his lawless and wanton behaviour, had lost his kingdom and died an early death, moved Liu Xi back to his former position as king of Chengyang and, dividing the old territory of Huainan into three parts, set up Liu Chang's three sons as rulers there. Liu An, the marquis of Fuling, was named king of Huainan; Liu Bo, the marquis of Anyang, was made king of Hengshan; and Liu Ci, the marquis of Zhouyang, was made king of Lujiang. (Liu Chang's youngest son, Liu Liang, the marquis of Dongcheng, had died earlier and left no heir.)

In the third year of Emperor Jing's reign (154 BC) when Wu, Chu, and the other members of the conspiracy began the so-called revolt of the Seven Kingdoms, an envoy from Wu came to visit Liu An, the king of Huainan. The king decided to call out his troops and join the rebellion, whereupon his prime

---

[1] Though the wording is deliberately ambiguous, the meaning is that the older brother, Emperor Wen, could not spare a little land for his younger brother to live on in peace, but sent him into exile.

minister said, "If Your Highness is determined to call out the troops and aid Wu, I beg to be appointed to command them." The king thereupon turned the soldiers over to the prime minister. After the prime minister had gotten command of the troops, however, he guarded the city from the rebels and refused to listen to anything the king said, remaining loyal to the Han government. Meanwhile, the Han dispatched Chong Jie, the marquis of Qucheng, with a force of troops to rescue Huainan from the rebels. Thus the kingdom of Huainan suffered no ill consequences from the revolt.

Envoys from Wu also visited the king of Lujiang, but he refused to take part in the conspiracy and instead sent his own envoys back and forth to communicate with the kingdom of Yue. The king of Hengshan likewise remained unshakably loyal to the dynasty and spurned the overtures of the Wu envoys.

In the fourth year of Emperor Jing's reign (153 BC), after the rebel states of Wu and Chu had been conquered, Liu Bo, the king of Hengshan, journeyed to the capital to pay his respects to the emperor. The emperor wished to do something to repay him for the loyalty he had shown at the time of the revolt. "The region in the south where you rule at present is too damp and unhealthy!" he declared, and transferred Liu Bo to the position of king of Jibei as a reward. Later, when Liu Bo died, the emperor awarded him the posthumous title of Zhen, the "Loyal King".

The region of the king of Lujiang adjoined the barbarian kingdom of Yue, and the king frequently exchanged envoys with Yue. The emperor, fearing that such a situation might lead to trouble, transferred him to the position of king of Hengshan, ruling the territory north of the Yangtze River. The king of Huainan remained as before.

Liu An, the king of Huainan, was by nature fond of reading books and playing the lute; he took no interest in shooting, hunting, or dashing about with dogs and horses.[2] He hoped to win the support of his people by doing secret favours for them and to achieve a reputation throughout the empire. He would often recall with bitterness the death of his father, King Li, and at times even contemplated revolt, but as yet he had had no opportunity to fulfil his desires.

In the second year of *jianyuan* (139 BC), shortly after Emperor Wu came to the throne, Liu An journeyed to the capital to pay his respects. The king had

---

[2] It was at his court that the *Huainan zi*, a predominantly Taoist work on philosophy and statecraft, was compiled by scholars whom he had summoned.

long been friendly with Tian Fen, the marquis of Wuan, who at this time was acting as grand commandant. Tian Fen came out as far as Bashang to meet the king and, in the course of his conversation, remarked, "As you know, the present emperor has no son whom he could designate as heir apparent. Your Highness is a grandson of Emperor Gaozu and there is no one who has not heard of your reputation for benevolence and righteous conduct. If some day the empire should be faced with the sorrow of an imperial demise, who but Your Highness would be fit to succeed to the throne?"

The king of Huainan was delighted at these words and showered Tian Fen with lavish gifts of money and goods. He also began to gather a band of followers in secret and to work to win the support of the people in preparation for a revolt.

In the sixth year of *jianyuan* (135 BC) a comet appeared in the sky. The king of Huainan was secretly wondering what it portended when someone said to him, "Some years ago, when the armies of Wu rose in revolt, a comet appeared. Its tail was no more than a few feet long, and yet the battles which raged at that time drenched the earth with blood for 1,000 miles. Now a comet has appeared which is so long it fills the sky. It must portend a great uprising of the armies of the empire!"

The present emperor has no heir, thought the king to himself, and if there should be a revolt, the feudal lords would be pitted against one another. He therefore began to manufacture the weapons and tools needed for aggressive warfare in ever increasing quantities, set aside stores of gold and cash, and sent bribes and gifts to wandering knights and men of unusual ability in the provinces and other feudal kingdoms. The rhetoricians and strategists came forward with the most reckless and absurd pronouncements in order to flatter the king who, delighted with their words, awarded them large sums of money and plunged even deeper into plans for revolt.

The king had a daughter named Liu Ling, an intelligent girl and a clever talker. The king loved her and kept her constantly supplied with money, sending her to Chang'an to spy on the emperor and win supporters for his cause among the emperor's attendants.

In the third year of *yuanshuo* (126 BC) the emperor granted a stool and cane to the king of Huainan, indicating that he was excused because of old age from his obligation to journey to court to pay his respects.

The king's consort was named Queen Tu. She enjoyed great favour with the king and had borne him a son named Liu Qian who was designated crown prince. Liu Qian was married to the granddaughter of Empress Dowager Wang, the mother of the emperor. (His wife was a daughter of Lady Xiucheng, the empress dowager's daughter by her first marriage.)

When the king began to lay plans and make preparations for his revolt, he was afraid that the crown prince's wife would find out about them and give away the secret. The king therefore plotted with the crown prince and instructed him to feign indifference toward his wife. For three months the crown prince refused to share the same mat with her, whereupon the king in turn pretended to be angry with the crown prince and shut him up in the same room with his wife for a similar length of time. During the whole time the crown prince would not go near her until finally the girl asked to be allowed to leave the kingdom. The king thereupon wrote a letter of apology to the emperor and sent her back to her own home.

Meanwhile Queen Tu, the crown prince Qian, and the king's daughter Ling, presuming upon the king's favour, began to misuse the power of the state for their own ends, seizing lands and houses from the common people and ordering innocent men to be thrown into prison.

The fifth year of *yuanshuo* (124 BC): The crown prince Liu Qian had studied swordsmanship and considered that no one could rival him. When he heard that one of the palace attendants named Lei Bei was skilful with a sword, he summoned him to a fencing match. Lei Bei yielded twice before the thrusts of the crown prince, but in the third encounter he accidentally struck the prince. The prince flew into a rage, and Lei Bei was terrified of what the consequences would be.

At this time there was a ruling that anyone who volunteered for service in the army should be sent immediately to the capital. Lei Bei therefore expressed his wish to take part in the campaigns against the Xiongnu. The crown prince meanwhile spoke ill of Lei Bei to the king, until the king ordered the chief of palace attendants to remove Lei Bei from his post and see to it that no one in the future should attempt to imitate his example.

Lei Bei, however, eventually managed to escape from the kingdom and make his way to Chang'an, where he submitted a letter to the throne explaining exactly what had happened. The emperor issued an edict referring the matter to the commandant of justice and the officials of Henan. The officials of Henan conducted an investigation and sent an order for the arrest of the crown prince.

The king and queen plotted what to do next and finally decided not to hand the crown prince over to the authorities, but instead to call out the troops in revolt. They hesitated over their plans, however, and ten days or more passed while they were still trying to reach a decision. Meanwhile, an edict arrived from the emperor ordering the officials to cross-examine the crown prince.

At this time the prime minister of Huainan, angry with the law officer of the city of Shouchun for holding up the crown prince's arrest warrant and failing to seize him and turn him over to the authorities, filed charges against the law officer on grounds of failure to respect orders. The king asked the prime minister to drop the charges, but he refused to listen, whereupon the king sent an envoy with a letter to the throne bringing charges against the prime minister. The emperor referred the matter to the commandant of justice for investigation, and it was soon found that the king was deeply involved in the affair. The king then sent another envoy to the capital to determine how the Han ministers stood on the matter. The Han ministers for their part requested the emperor to arrest the king and conduct an investigation.

The king by this time was afraid that the whole plot would come to light, but the crown prince said to him, "If the Han envoys come to arrest you, you should order your men to dress up as bodyguards and station them around the courtyard with spears. Then, if any of the envoys attempts to make a move toward you, they can strike him dead. I myself will at the same time send someone to stab the palace military commander of Huainan and it will still not be too late to call out the troops and start a revolt."

At this time the emperor had not followed the recommendation of the high ministers to arrest the king, but instead had sent the Han palace military commander Yin Hong to go to Huainan and question the king. Hearing that an envoy had arrived from the capital, the king proceeded to station armed bodyguards in the courtyard as the crown prince had suggested. But when Yin Hong appeared, he addressed the king in a mild and friendly manner and only questioned him about Lei Bei's removal from office. The king therefore assumed that there was nothing to worry about and did not give the order to begin the revolt.

The palace military commander Yin Hong returned to the capital and made his report, whereupon the ministers who were in charge of the investigation announced, "Liu An, the king of Huainan, is guilty of having detained Lei Bei and others who volunteered to join in the attacks on the Xiongnu, and of defying the imperial command. He deserves to be executed and his corpse exposed in the market place."

When the emperor refused to approve this recommendation, the ministers requested that the king be removed from his position. The emperor refused this request as well, and the ministers then suggested that the king be deprived of five districts of his territory. The emperor reduced the number to two districts and sent the palace military commander Yin Hong to announce to the king that his offence had been pardoned and that he would be punished by being deprived of a part of his lands.

As soon as Yin Hong crossed the border into Huainan he began to publish word abroad that the king had been pardoned. The king, however, had heard earlier that the ministers had proposed the death penalty for him, and he did not know that the sentence had been reduced to deprivation of territory. When word reached him that an envoy from the Han was on the way, he was afraid that he was going to be arrested and once more plotted with the crown prince to station assassins in the courtyard as they had done before. When Yin Hong finally arrived, however, he merely congratulated the king on his pardon and the king once more refrained from giving the order to revolt.

After the envoy had gone the king complained bitterly of his fate: "I have practised benevolence and righteousness and yet I am deprived of territory! What greater shame could I suffer?"

After the two districts had been taken away from him the king plunged deeper and deeper into his plans for revolt. Whenever his envoys returned from the capital, if they spoke only outrageous nonsense, assuring the king that the emperor had no son to be his heir and that the government was in a state of chaos, he was pleased. But if anyone dared to say that the Han government was functioning smoothly and a son had been born to the emperor, the king would fly into a rage and accuse the person of telling wanton lies.

Day and night the king sat over his maps and charts with Zuo Wu and his other ministers,[3] deciding how he should dispose his troops for the invasion of Han territory. "Since the emperor has no heir," he said, "if anything happens to him the court ministers will undoubtedly summon one of his half-brothers — either the king of Jiaodong or the king of Changshan — to take the throne. At that time the feudal lords will begin struggling with each other for power, and of course I cannot afford to be unprepared. Moreover, I am a direct grandson of Emperor Gaozu and have always practised benevolence and righteousness. His Majesty has treated me generously, and so I am willing to bear my present situation. But if his years should come to an end, how could I ever bring myself

---

[3] Following the reading in *Han shu* 44.

to face north and acknowledge sovereignty to some contemptible child?"

The king one day seated himself in the eastern palace and summoned his minister Wu Bei to join him in laying plans for the revolt. "Come in, general," he said when Wu Bei appeared.

With an air of grave regret Wu Bei said, "The emperor has graciously pardoned Your Highness's offences. How is it that you once again employ titles such as 'general' which are reserved for the officers of the central government alone? Such words as these presage the doom of the kingdom!

"I have heard that my namesake in ancient times, Wu Zixu, admonished the king of Wu, but when the king refused to listen to his advice, Wu Zixu said, 'I foresee the day when the wild deer will sport over the ruins of the Gusu Terrace!'[4] Now I too fear that the day will come when weeds and thorns will grow over this palace and the dew will fall through its shattered roof to wet men's robes!"

The king was furious and ordered Wu Bei's father and mother to be bound and thrown into prison for three months. Then he once more summoned Wu Bei. "Now, general, are you ready to go along with me?" he asked.

"No!" replied Wu Bei. "I have come only to try to suggest a plan for Your Highness. I have heard it said that the truly keen-eared man can hear what has not yet made a sound, and the truly keen-eyed can see what has not yet taken form. Therefore, though the sage may launch ten thousand undertakings, he is sure of ten thousand successes. King Wen in ancient times made only one decisive move, the first step towards the founding of the Zhou dynasty, and yet his merit brought glory to a thousand generations, and he ranks with the founders of the Xia and Shang dynasties as one of the three greatest kings of antiquity. This is called moving in accordance with the heart of Heaven. If a move is of this kind, then, though there has been no previous agreement, everyone within the four seas will rise up to follow. This is the example of success we find in the history of 1,000 years ago. Now if we look back 100 years to the defeat of the Qin, or a generation ago to the fate of Wu and Chu in the revolt of the Seven Kingdoms, we will see where the difference lies between the preservation and

---

[4]Wu Zixu was a famous warrior and statesman of the late sixth and early fifth centuries BC whose biography is the subject of *Shi ji* 66. He aided the king of Wu in conquering the neighbouring state of Yue. When the king of Yue begged for peace, Wu Zixu urged the king of Wu not to accept the offer, warning him that Yue would one day rise again and destroy Wu. The king refused to listen to his warning, which later proved correct, but instead ordered Wu Zixu to commit suicide. The Gusu Terrace was a famous pleasure palace of Wu.

the downfall of a state. I am not afraid to suffer the same punishment as Wu Zixu; I only hope that Your Highness will be better at listening to advice than the king of Wu was!

"In the years before the Han dynasty the First Emperor of the Qin abandoned the way of the sages, killed the practitioners of the way, burned the *Odes* and *Documents*, and cast aside the principles of correct behaviour, honouring deceit and physical force instead and trusting to harsh punishments. He had grain transported from the seacoast all the way to the upper reaches of the Yellow River, but at that time, although the men worked the fields as hard as they could, they could not scrape together enough to make a meal of chaff and dregs, and though the women wove and spun, they had not enough cloth left to cover their bodies. Then he sent Meng Tian to build the Great Wall, stretching several thousand *li* from east to west. He exposed his armies to the hardships of the frontier, never keeping less than 20,000 or 30,000 in the field, until the dead reached incalculable numbers, the corpses lay strewn for a thousand *li*, and streams of blood soaked the plains. The strength of the common people was exhausted, and five families out of every ten longed to revolt.

"Then the First Emperor of the Qin sent Xu Fu to sail over the sea in search of the spirits, and he returned and lied to the emperor, saying, 'In the midst of the sea I met a great spirit who asked me if I were the envoy from the Emperor of the West. When I answered that I was, he asked me what I was seeking for. "I am looking for the medicine which increases one's years and brings long life," I said.

" 'Your King of Qin," replied the spirit, "is too stingy with his courtesy! You may see the medicine, but you cannot take it back with you!"

" 'Then he led me to the southeast, to the mountain of Penglai, where I saw palaces and towers surrounded by lawns of grass. There was a messenger there, copper-coloured and shaped like a dragon, with streams of light pouring from his body and lighting up the sky. When I saw him I bowed before him twice and asked, "What sort of offerings should I bring?" and the Sea God (for that was what he was) replied, "If you will bring me the sons of good families, and beautiful maidens, along with the products of your various craftsmen, then you may have the medicine!" ' '

"When the First Emperor heard this, he was overjoyed and immediately sent Xu Fu back east again, accompanied by 3,000 boys and girls of good families and bearing presents of seeds of the five types of grains and articles produced by the various craftsmen. But when Xu Fu reached Pingyuan and

Guangze, he halted his journey, made himself king of the region, and never returned to the Qin. With this, the people were filled with sorrow and bitterness and six families out of every ten favoured revolt.

"Then the First Emperor sent the military commander Zhao Tuo south across the Five Ranges to attack the hundred tribes of Yue. Zhao Tuo knew that the people of China had reached the limit of their endurance, and so he stayed where he was and made himself king of the region instead of returning. He dispatched an envoy with a letter asking the emperor to send 30,000 unmarried women to sew uniforms for his soldiers. The emperor of the Qin approved his request and sent half the number, 15,000 women of China. With this, the last bit of loyalty in the hearts of the people crumbled away and seven families out of every ten longed for revolt.

"Someone said to the future Emperor Gaozu of the Han, 'The hour has come!' but he replied, 'Let us wait. In time a sage shall arise in the southeast!' Before a year had passed, Chen She and Wu Guang began their rebellion.

"Soon afterwards, Gaozu raised the cry of revolt in Feng and Pei and, though there had been no previous arrangement, the whole empire answered his call, flocking about him in countless numbers. This is what is called waiting for an opening and using the mistakes of others as a stepping-stone. He waited until the Qin was doomed before making a move, and the people longed for his coming as men long for rain in time of drought. Thus he was able to rise from the ranks of the common people and ascend the throne of the Son of Heaven; his achievements excelled those of the founders of the Three Dynasties and his inexhaustible virtue has been handed down to his descendants.

"Now Your Highness sees that it was easy for Emperor Gaozu to win the empire. But have you not also seen what happened to the kings of Wu and Chu in more recent years?

"Liu Pi, the king of Wu, was granted the title of master of sacrificial wine for the Liu clan[5] and was not required to journey to the capital to pay his respects at court. He ruled the multitudes of four provinces, and his territory measured several thousand *li* square. He mined copper within his kingdom and melted it down to mint cash, and in the east he boiled the sea water and extracted salt. In the north he cut down the trees of Jiangling and made boats, and each one of them could carry as large a load as twenty or thirty of the carts of China. His

---

[5] A mark of the highest honour. At feasts and gatherings the person with this title began the proceedings by pouring out a libation of sacrificial wine to the earth god.

kingdom was rich and his people numerous and he was able to scatter bribes of pearls and precious stones, gold and silk among the feudal lords, the members of the imperial family, and the high ministers. Only the members of the Dou family refused to accept his gifts.

"When he had completed his plans and made his preparations for revolt, he called out his troops and marched west, but his armies were smashed at Daliang; he suffered defeat at Hufu and was forced to turn and flee east again. When he reached Dantu, he was taken prisoner by the men of Yue. He was killed, the sacrifices of his state were cut off, and he ended as the laughing-stock of the world. Why is it that, with all the men of Wu and Yue under his command, he could not achieve success? Simply because he violated the way of Heaven and did not understand the times!

"Now Your Highness's troops do not number a tenth of those of Wu and Chu, while the empire is ten thousand times more peaceful and contented then it was under the Qin. I beg you therefore to listen to my advice. If you do not listen but persist in your plans, I assure you that your undertaking will fail, and indeed the news of your plans will leak out before you even have a chance to put them into action!

"I have heard that when Weizi visited the site of the old Shang capital, he was filled with grief and composed the song called 'The Thick-growing Grain'.[6] He was embittered that Emperor Zhou did not listen to the good advice of Prince Bi Gan. Therefore Mencius has said, 'While he lived, Emperor Zhou was honoured as the Son of Heaven, but once dead, he was less respected than a common farmer!'[7] Emperor Zhou did not lose the empire the day he died; he had long before cut himself off from it by his evil deeds!

"Now I too grieve to think that Your Highness may in similar fashion cast away your position as ruler of a state of a thousand chariots. I beg you to bestow upon me the suicide order, as the king of Wu did to Wu Zixu, so that I may lead the way for the other ministers and die here in the Eastern Palace!"

As he listened the king was overwhelmed with a great sadness that he could not shake off; tears filled his eyes and ran down his cheeks. Wu Bei, when he had finished speaking, rose, descended the stairway with faltering steps, and left the hall.

---

[6] Weizi was a half-brother of Emperor Zhou, the last ruler of the Shang who, by his evil and headstrong ways, brought about the destruction of the dynasty.

[7] No such passage is found in the present text of the *Mencius*, though the sense is much the same as *Mencius* IB, VIII.

The king of Huainan had a son named Buhai whose mother was a concubine. Buhai was actually older than the crown prince, but the king had no love for him and neither he, the queen, nor the crown prince treated Buhai as a member of the family. Buhai had a son named Liu Jian, an able and spirited boy who bore a constant grudge against the crown prince for treating his father with such coldness. He also resented the fact that, although the king of Huainan had only two sons, the crown prince and his father, his father had never been made a marquis, although at this time it was customary for all the sons of the feudal lords to be made marquises. Liu Jian plotted in secret with his friends and followers, hoping to bring charges against the crown prince and contrive his downfall so that his father could replace him as heir. The crown prince was aware of this and several times had Liu Jian thrown into prison and flogged.

Jian knew all about the crown prince's plans to revolt and the fact that he had suggested assassinating the Han palace military commander. In the sixth year of *yuanshuo* (123 BC) Jian got a friend from Shouchun named Zhuang Zhi to present a letter to the throne which read:

> Bitter medicine burns the mouth but cures the disease; loyal words sting the ears but profit the conduct. Now Liu Jian, the grandson of the king of Huainan, is a man of great ability, and yet the king's consort Queen Tu and her son the crown prince Qian constantly treat him with the greatest ill will. Though his father Buhai has committed no crime, they have several times arbitrarily arrested Jian and thrown him into prison, hoping to do away with him. Now while Jian is still alive it would be well to summon him for questioning so that all of the secret doings of the kingdom of Huainan may be brought to light.

When the emperor received the letter, he referred it to the commandant of justice, who in turn ordered the officials of Henan to take appropriate action.

At this time Shen Qing, the grandson of Shen Yiji, the marquis of Biyang, was on close terms with the chancellor Gongsun Hong. Shen Qing bore a deep grudge against the king of Huainan because his father Liu Chang had murdered Shen Qing's grandfather Shen Yiji. He therefore did everything he could to convince Gongsun Hong that there was something wrong with the affairs of Huainan. Gongsun Hong began to suspect the king of Huainan of plotting a revolt and urged the officials to make a thorough investigation.

When the officials of Henan called Liu Jian for questioning, they found that the information he gave implicated the crown prince and his fellow conspirators.

The king of Huainan, filled with apprehension, decided to call out his troops. He asked Wu Bei, "Would you say that the Han court is well ordered or in a state of confusion?"

"The entire empire is well ordered," replied Wu Bei.

This was not what the king had wanted to hear. "Why do you say that the empire is well ordered?" he demanded.

"From what I have observed of the government of the Han court," replied Wu Bei, "the duties of ruler and subject, the love between father and son, the distinction between husband and wife, and the hierarchical order between senior and junior are all observed in accordance with what is right. In promoting men to office the emperor honours the principles of antiquity, and there is no fault to be found in the customs or administration of the empire. No region is without its roads over which the rich merchants with their heavy loads of goods travel to every part of the empire. Thus the way has been opened up for foreign trade. The people of Southern Yue acknowledge their allegiance to the Han, the Qiang and Po tribes come bearing tribute, and the men of Eastern Ou have surrendered. The frontier has been extended to Changyu, the province of Shuofang opened up, and the Xiongnu, their feathers plucked and their wings broken, have lost their allies and cannot rise again. Although ours may not be compared to the era of great peace in ancient times, yet it is worthy to be called a well-ordered age!"

The king was furious and Wu Bei was obliged to apologize, admitting that he deserved death for his words. The king then questioned Wu Bei once more. "If there is an uprising east of the mountains, the Han will surely send the general in chief Wei Qing to attempt to put it down. What sort of man would you say Wei Qing is?"

"One of my friends named Huang Yi served under Wei Qing in the campaign against the Xiongnu," replied Wu Bei, "and when he returned he told me, 'The general in chief treats his officers with great courtesy and is good to his men, so that all of them are happy to serve under him. He dashes up and down the hills on horseback as though he had wings, and his ability far outshines that of other men!' In my opinion, therefore, a man with such capacity, plus the experience gained from numerous campaigns, would be very hard to stand up against!

"Again, when the master of guests Cao Liang returned from a mission to Chang'an, he told me that Wei Qing showed great intelligence in his orders and bravery in the face of the enemy, always leading his men in an attack. When he pitches camp, if the wells that are dug fail to bring up much water, he will wait until all his men have had their fill before he ventures to drink, and when the army is in retreat he will not cross a river until every one of his men has reached the other bank. All the gifts of gold and silk which the empress dowager has given him he has distributed among his officers. Even the most famous generals of antiquity could not surpass such acts as these!"

The king received these words in silence.

He knew that Liu Jian had already been summoned and questioned by the officials, and he was afraid that all the secrets of the state would soon come to light. He was therefore anxious to begin the revolt, but Wu Bei continued to oppose the move. The king once more summoned Wu Bei and said, "Do you think the king of Wu was right or wrong in starting his uprising some years ago?"

"Wrong!" replied Wu Bei. "The king of Wu enjoyed the greatest possible wealth and honour, and yet he began his uprising and, failing to win success, was killed at Dantu; his head ended up in one place and his feet in another, and every one of his descendants was wiped out. I have heard that the king of Wu regretted very deeply what he had done. I beg Your Highness to consider well so that you too will not have cause to regret like the king of Wu!"

"Once a man has given his word that he will do something," said the king, "there is nothing left for him but to die in the attempt! Moreover, what did the king of Wu know about revolt? He failed to block the pass at Chenggao, and as a result over forty Han generals attacked him in one day. Now I have ordered Lou Huan first of all to close the pass at Chenggao. At the same time Zhou Bei will lead down the troops from Yingchuan and block the roads at the Huanyuan and Yi passes, and Chen Ding will call out the troops from Nanyang and guard the Wu Pass. This will leave the governor of Henan in possession of nothing but the city of Luoyang, so there will be nothing to worry about from him. Of course we will still have the Linjin Pass, Hedong, Shangdang, Henei, and the kingdom of Zhao in the north to consider. But people say that if you shut off the pass at Chenggao, the rest of the empire can never get at you. Thus if we hold the strong points of Sanchuan in this way and then invite all the soldiers east of the mountains to join the uprising, what would you say to the scheme?"

"I can see how it could lead to disaster," replied Wu Bei, "but I cannot see how it could bring good fortune!"

"Zuo Wu, Zhao Xian, Zhu Qiao, and the others all believe the outcome will be fortunate and consider that we have nine chances out of ten for success!" said the king. "How is it that you alone foresee disaster instead of fortune?"

Wu Bei replied, "Among Your Highness's ministers and advisers, all those who had any ability in leading the people have already been summoned before the emperor's law officials and thrown into prison. Those who are left will be of no use to you."

"In earlier times," said the king, "when Chen She and Wu Guang revolted against the Qin, they did not possess enough territory to stick the point of an awl into. With a band of only 1,000 men they began their uprising in Daze, but when they raised their arms and sounded the cry of revolt, the whole empire responded, and by the time they had advanced west to Xi they had a force of 1,200,000 men. Now, although my kingdom is small, it can provide over 100,000 fighting men, and they are no band of convict labourers armed only with sickles, chisels, and spear handles such as Chen She and Wu Guang commanded. Why then do you say that I will meet with disaster instead of fortune?"

Wu Bei replied, "In former times the Qin emperor ruled with utter disregard for principles, plundering and enslaving the empire. He made lavish journeys accompanied by 10,000 carriages, built the huge Epang Palace, demanded over half the people's produce in taxes, and called out the poor in every village to perform forced labour. Fathers could not look after their children nor brothers help each other; the government was harsh, its punishments stern, and the whole empire writhed as though consumed in flame. The people all stretched their necks in search of aid, bent their ears to listen for help, cried out piteously to Heaven and beat their breasts in hatred for their rulers. Therefore Chen She was able to sound his cry of revolt and the whole empire rose to answer him.

"Now, however, His Majesty the emperor orders the world and has joined all within the four seas under a single rule; his love embraces the common people, and his virtue and bounty spread abroad. Without uttering a word, his voice goes forth with the swiftness of lightning to all the world; without issuing a command, his virtue transforms the people as though by supernatural power. The thoughts of his innermost mind are translated into a might and majesty which extend ten thousand miles, for the governed respond to their governors like shadows or echoes. Moreover, the abilities of the general in chief Wei Qing are far superior to those of Zhang Han and Yang Xiong, the generals who attempted to defend the Qin dynasty against the rebels. Therefore I believe you are mistaken in comparing your own situation to that of Chen She and Wu Guang."

"If it is as you say," said the king, "then do you think there is no chance at all?"

"I have a plan I could suggest," said Wu Bei.

"What is that?"

"At present the feudal lords show no signs of disaffection and the common people have no cause for anger. However, the province of Shuofang, which has recently been opened in the north, embraces a large extent of land with fine pastures and good water, and the people who have so far moved there are not sufficient in number to populate it fully. According to my plan, therefore, you could forge a letter from the chancellor and the imperial secretary to the emperor requesting that the powerful and troublesome families from the various kingdoms and provinces, along with men accused of minor offences, men whose offences have been pardoned by a general amnesty, and those whose fortunes amount to 500,000 cash or over, be resettled in the province of Shuofang along with their kin, with a large force of soldiers to be called out to see that those designated for resettlement start on their way as soon as possible. You could also forge letters from the prison officials of the legal offices in the capital and the Shanglin Park ordering the arrest of the heirs and favourite ministers of the various feudal lords. In this way the people would be enraged, the feudal lords terrified, and you could then send skilled rhetoricians to persuade them to join your cause. In such a case I think you might have one chance in ten of succeeding."[8]

"That would be good, too," said the king, "though I doubt that I will have to go to such lengths."

The king then ordered some of the government slaves to take up residence in his palace and set them to work forging the imperial seal, the seals of the chancellor, the imperial secretary, the general in chief, the army officials, the 2,000 picul officials, and the secretaries of the law offices, as well as the seals of the governors and chief commandants of the neighbouring provinces, and making imitations of the credentials and hats of the imperial envoys, so that he would be able to put Wu Bei's plan into effect. He also pretended to accuse several men of crimes and then had them escape west to Chang'an; there they were to take service under the general in chief Wei Qing and the chancellor Gongsun Hong. Whenever the king should call out his troops in revolt, these

---

[8] This plan seems so absurd that one must suppose Wu Bei only suggested it to delay the king's preparations for revolt.

men were to assassinate Wei Qing and talk Gongsun Hong into joining the revolt, a task which the king supposed would be as easy as lifting the lid off a jar.

The king wanted to call out his troops, but he was afraid that the prime minister and 2,000 picul officials of the state would not consent to such a move. He therefore plotted with Wu Bei and decided to murder them. He and Wu Bei were to pretend that a fire had broken out in the palace, and when the prime minister and 2,000 picul officials arrived on the scene to try to put it out, they would kill them. They had not yet worked out the exact details of the plan, however.

The king also decided to dress some of his men up as thief-seekers[9] and have them come rushing into his capital from the east bearing requests from the local authorities for immediate aid and shouting that the troops of Southern Yue were invading the border. In this way he would have an excuse for calling out his army. He therefore sent men to Lujiang and Kuaiji to take office as thief-seekers, but had not yet ordered the plan put into execution.

The king said to Wu Bei, "If I raise my troops and march west, there are sure to be others of the feudal lords who will join my cause. But what shall I do if some if them refuse to join?"

Wu Bei replied, "You must gain control of Hengshan in the south, attack Lujiang and seize the boats at Xunyang, guard the city of Xiazhi, keep the rivers of Jiujiang open, block the pass at Yuzhang, and station your strong bowmen along the Yangtze to guard it and prevent the enemy from marching down from Nan Province. Then, if you seize control of Jiangdu and Kuaiji in the east, open up communication with the powerful tribes of Yue in the south, and keep a firm grip on the region between the Yangtze and Huai rivers, you should be able to hold on for quite a long time."

"Good!" said the king. "I see no reason to depart from this plan. And if the worst comes I can always flee to Yue."

Meanwhile, the commandant of justice had reported to the emperor the information which he had received from Liu Jian, the king's grandson, incriminating the crown prince. The emperor then appointed the commandant of justice as military commander of Huainan and sent him to Huainan to investigate the affair and arrest the crown prince.

When the commandant of justice arrived in Huainan, the king, having heard

---

[9] Police officials charged with keeping order in the outlying districts.

of his mission, consulted with the crown prince on what to do next and decided to summon the prime minister and 2,000 picul officials, kill them, and call out the troops. The prime minister answered the summons and appeared at the palace, but the internal secretary pretended to be out when the summons arrived and the military commander replied that, since he was acting as an envoy from the emperor, he was not allowed to have an audience with the king. The king realized that, so long as the internal secretary and the military commander refused to appear, he would gain nothing by killing the prime minister, and so he sent the prime minister home again. The king hesitated and could not make up his mind what to do.

The crown prince considered that if he were tried it would be on charges of having plotted to kill the Han military commander. Since he had been the one who suggested the plot to the king, he assumed that if he himself were dead there would be no one left to inform against the king. He therefore said to the king, "All of the ministers who might have been of some use to us have already been thrown into prison by the law officials. Now there is no one left who is capable of helping us in our uprising. Moreover, I am afraid that if you attempt to call out the troops when the time is not right you will not be able to succeed. I beg you, therefore, to let me answer the summons for my arrest."

The king was by this time anxious to find some excuse to abandon the whole undertaking, and he therefore gave the crown prince permission to go. Instead, however, the crown prince tried to commit suicide by cutting his throat, but failed in the attempt.

Meanwhile, Wu Bei went to the authorities on his own accord and informed them that he had been plotting revolt with the king, describing to them all the details of the plot. The officials proceeded to arrest the crown prince and the queen and to surround the king's palace. They also arrested all the king's followers throughout the kingdom who had been party to the plot and searched until they had brought to light the weapons which were to be used in the revolt. When the report of their findings was brought to the emperor, he referred the matter to the high officials for action. Several thousand men, including feudal lords, 2,000 picul officials, and members of powerful families, were found to be involved in the plot and all were punished according to the gravity of their offences.

The king of Huainan's younger brother Liu Ci, the king of Hengshan, as a member of the immediate family, would ordinarily have been held responsible for the crime along with the king of Huainan, but when the authorities asked for permission to arrest Liu Ci, the emperor replied, "The feudal lords should all be considered as existing separately in their own territories. They should not be held responsible for each other's offences. Let the matter be discussed with those among the kings and marquises who have in the past studied legal affairs and precedents with the chancellor!"

Forty-three men, including Liu Pengzu, the king of Zhao, Marquis Rang, and others, discussed the matter and unanimously replied, "Liu An, the king of Huainan, is guilty of the most treasonable and unprincipled conduct. It is clear that he was plotting revolt and he should therefore be subjected to punishment."

Liu Duan, the king of Jiaoxi, after taking part in the discussion, gave his opinion as follows: "Liu An, the king of Huainan, has ignored the laws and committed evil, harbouring deceit in his heart and attempting to bring chaos to the empire, misleading the common people, turning his back upon the ancestral temples of the dynasty, and uttering all manner of falsehoods. The *Spring and Autumn Annals* says: 'A subject must not even harbour the intention of evil. If he has the intention he should be punished.'[10] Yet Liu An's crime is far more serious than that of mere intention, for he had already completed preparations for revolt. I have seen the letters, credentials, seals, and maps which he prepared, as well as clear evidence of his other treasonable and unprincipled acts, and because of the enormity of his crime it is obvious that he should be punished according to the law. As for the officials of his kingdom who receive a salary of 200 piculs or more or those of equivalent rank, as well as his favourites and ministers of the imperial family, although legally they may not be guilty of any direct connection with the plot, they have failed in their duty to instruct him and should all be removed from their posts, deprived of their titles, and reduced to the rank of commoners, and should be forbidden to hold office again. All those close to the king who were not officials should be required to pay two catties and eight taels of gold to ransom their lives. In this way Liu An's guilt will be made clear, the empire will understand how a proper subject and son should behave, and no one will again dare to harbour thoughts of evil and rebellion!"

The chancellor Gongsun Hong, the commandant of justice Zhang Tang,

---

[10] This passage is not found in the *Spring and Autumn Annals* itself, but in the *Gongyang Commentary* on the *Annals* (Duke Zhuang, thirty-second year and Duke Zhao, first year), where the wording is slightly different.

and the other high officials reported these opinions to the emperor, who presented the director of the imperial clan with the seals of an imperial envoy and sent him to deal with the king. Before he had reached Huainan, however, the king cut his throat and died. Queen Tu, the crown prince Liu Qian, and all the others who had been involved in the plot were executed, along with the members of their families.

The emperor considered that Wu Bei in his frequent addresses to the king had done a great deal to point out to him the excellence of the Han dynasty, and therefore he did not wish to punish Wu Bei. But the commandant of justice Zhang Tang said, "Wu Bei was one of the leaders in plotting the revolt for the king. His crime cannot be pardoned!" Eventually, therefore, Wu Bei also was executed. The kingdom of Huainan was abolished and the territory made into the province of Jiujiang.

The King of Hengshan

Liu Ci, the king of Hengshan, had three children by his consort, Queen Chengshu; the eldest was a boy named Shuang who was designated crown prince, the second a boy named Xiao, and the third a girl named Wucai. The king also had four children by a concubine named Xulai and two by a lady in waiting named Jueji.

The king of Huainan and the king of Hengshan, though brothers, were not on good terms, each angrily accusing the other of failing to behave with the proper respect and courtesy. When the king of Hengshan heard that his brother was making preparations to start a revolt, he too began to gather a band of followers about him, secretly intending to join in, though he was afraid that his territory might be taken over by his brother.

In the sixth year of *yuanguang* (129 BC) the king of Hengshan journeyed to the capital to pay his respects to the emperor. His master of guests Wei Ching, who had some knowledge of medicine, divination, and similar arts, wanted to send a letter offering his services to the emperor, but the king, angry at his intention, accused him of some crime deserving death and beat him into acknowledging his guilt. The internal secretary of Hengshan, however, considering the charges unjust, dismissed the case. The king then sent a letter to the throne bringing charges against the internal secretary. When an investigation was made, the internal secretary reported the unjust action of the king. It was also found that the king had on various occasions seized lands from his subjects and destroyed grave mounds to make fields for farming. The authorities requested that they be allowed to arrest the king of Hengshan, but the emperor refused permission, decreeing instead that all officials of the 200 picul rank or over in the kingdom of Hengshan should be appointed directly by the central government.[11]

The king of Hengshan resented this deeply and began to plot with Xi Ci and Zhang Guangchang, searching about for men who were skilled in planning military campaigns and predicting the future by observing the stars and clouds. Day and night these men urged the king on, laying secret plans for a revolt.

In time Queen Chengshu died and the king's concubine Xulai was designated as the new queen. She and Jueji shared the affections of the king, but they were jealous of each other. Jueji began to speak ill of Queen Xulai to the crown prince Liu Shuang, saying, "Xulai ordered her maids to put a curse on your mother and kill her and that is why she died!" Because of this the crown prince came to hate Xulai, and when Xulai's older brother visited Hengshan and was drinking with the crown prince one time, the prince wounded him with his sword. Queen Xulai was furious at this and repeatedly spoke ill of the crown prince to the king.

Liu Wucai, the crown prince's younger sister, had formerly been married, but her husband rejected her and sent her back home, where she carried on illicit relations with a slave and with one of the retainers of the house. The crown prince several times reprimanded her, but she only grew angry and refused to have anything more to do with him.

When Queen Xulai heard of this, she immediately began to treat Wucai very kindly, and since Wucai and her older brother Xiao had lost their mother at an early age, they soon became quite attached to Queen Xulai. The queen for her part deliberately treated them affectionately so that they would assist her in slandering the crown prince. As a result of their slanders the king on several occasions beat the crown prince.

In the fourth year of *yuanshuo* (125 BC) someone attacked and injured Queen Xulai's stepmother. The king suspected that the assailant had been employed by the crown prince and proceeded to beat him. Later, when the king fell ill, the crown prince refused to care for him, claiming that he himself was

---

[11]Ordinarily the feudal lords themselves were allowed to appoint all but the highest officials in their states, such as the prime minister, internal secretary, etc.

ill. Queen Xulai and the crown prince's younger brother and sister, Xiao and Wucai, again took the opportunity to speak ill of him to the king, saying, "The crown prince is not really ill. He only says he is, but he looks perfectly well and happy!" The king was furious at this and decided to remove the crown prince from his position and set up his younger brother Xiao as heir instead.

Queen Xulai knew that the king had made up his mind to deprive Liu Shuang of the position of crown prince and give it to his brother Xiao; her next thought was how she could get him to pass over Xiao as well. One of the queen's ladies in waiting was a skilful dancer and enjoyed the attentions of the king. She therefore decided to get this girl to commit an indiscretion with Xiao so as to ruin Xiao's reputation. In this way she hoped that the king would reject both Shuang and Xiao and set up her own son Guang as crown prince instead.

Crown Prince Shuang knew what she was planning and considered that there would be no end to her slanders if he did not do something. He therefore decided to commit adultery with her in order to silence her. One day when the queen was drinking and feasting, the crown prince came forward and proposed a toast to her. Then, pressing up against her thigh, he asked her to go to bed with him. The queen, however, was furious and reported his action to the king.

The king summoned the prince and was preparing to tie him up and beat him when the prince, who knew that the king had long ago decided to deprive him of the position of heir and give it to Xiao, said, "My brother Xiao is having an affair with your favourite dancing girl and my sister Wucai has been sleeping with a slave! You had better eat hearty and take care of yourself while you can, father — with your leave I intend to report what is going on here to the emperor!" With this he turned his back on the king and walked out.

The king sent someone to stop him, but the prince was not to be detained. The king himself then got into his carriage, dashed after him, and seized him. While the prince cursed and abused his father, the king had him bound and fettered and imprisoned in the royal palace.

From this time on Xiao enjoyed increasing favour with the king. The king, impressed by his unusual ability, allowed him to wear the seals of a king, addressed him as "general", and gave him a separate house to live in, allotting him large sums of money so that he could attract his own band of followers. The followers who gathered about him had heard rumours that the kings of Huainan and Hengshan were plotting a revolt, and day and night they urged Xiao to action.

The king ordered Jiu He and Chen Xi, two of Xiao's followers from Jiangdu, to make armoured carriages and barbed arrowheads and to carve forgeries of the imperial seal and the seals of the various generals and officials. Day and night the king sought out men whose daring was like that of Zhou Qiu,[12] discussed with them the various strategies that had been used at the time of the revolt of Wu and Chu, and made them promise to assist him in his rebellion.

The king of Hengshan did not dare, like his brother the king of Huainan, to aspire to the throne of the Son of Heaven. As a matter of fact, he was afraid that if the king of Huainan started a revolt, the latter might seize possession of his own kingdom of Hengshan. He had decided therefore that, if the king of Huainan should march west, he would call out his own troops and attempt to seize and maintain possession of the region between the Yangtze and Huai rivers. This was the extent of his ambitions.

In the autumn of the fifth year of *yuanshuo* (124 BC) the king of Hengshan was due to visit the capital to pay his respects at court. When the new year came, however, he visited Huainan instead, where he talked with his brother, the king of Huainan, and the two of them, forgetting their previous differences, agreed to make preparation for a revolt. He then sent a letter to the throne pleading illness and received in reply a letter from the emperor releasing him from his obligation to come to court.

During the sixth year of *yuanshuo* (123 BC) the king of Hengshan sent an envoy with a letter to the emperor asking that he be allowed to remove Liu Shuang from the position of crown prince and set up Liu Xiao instead. When Liu Shuang heard of this, he asked a friend of his named Bai Ying to go to Chang'an and present a letter to the throne accusing Xiao of manufacturing armoured chariots and barbed arrowheads and of having illicit relations with one of the king's dancing girls, hoping in this way to bring about Xiao's downfall.

Bai Ying arrived in Chang'an but had not yet presented the letter when the officials arrested him in connection with the planned revolt of the king of Huainan. Meanwhile, the king of Hengshan, having learned that Liu Shuang had sent Bai Ying with a letter to the emperor, was afraid that it contained a report of all the secret doings of the kingdom. He hastily sent a letter of his own,

---

[12] A military adventurer who served the king of Wu at the time of the revolt of the Seven Kingdoms. See "The Biography of Liu Pi", *Han Dynasty* Volume I, p. 411.

therefore, accusing Liu Shuang of committing crimes of sufficient gravity to deserve execution in the market place. The matter was referred to the officials of Pei Province for investigation.

In the winter of the seventh year of *yuanshuo* (122 BC) the authorities and high ministers instructed the officials of Pei Province to round up and arrest all those who had been plotting revolt with the king of Huainan. In the course of their search they arrested Chen Xi in the house of Xiao, the son of the king of Hengshan, and accused Xiao of having taken the lead in concealing Chen Xi from the authorities. Xiao knew that Chen Xi had repeatedly discussed plans for revolt with the king of Hengshan, and he was afraid that the whole affair would come to light. He had heard that, according to the law, those who voluntarily confessed and gave information on their crimes would be let off without punishment and, since he suspected that the letter which Liu Shuang had entrusted to Bai Ying to give to the emperor would bring everything to light anyway, he took the lead by confessing to the officials that he had plotted revolt with Jiu He, Chen Xi, and the others. When the commandant of justice investigated the matter, he found full evidence to support his confession.

The high ministers requested that the king of Hengshan be arrested and brought to trial, but the emperor forbade his arrest and instead dispatched the palace military commander Sima An and the grand messenger Li Xi to go to Hengshan and question the king. The king gave a full and truthful account of the affair, whereupon the officials of the state were ordered to surround his palace and keep him under guard while Sima An and Li Xi returned to the capital to report to the emperor. The high ministers then requested that the director of the imperial clan and the grand messenger be dispatched to pass sentence on the king and, in cooperation with the officials of Pei Province, on Liu Xiao as well. When the king heard of this, he cut his throat and died. Liu Xiao, because he had confessed on his own initiative, was pardoned from the accusation of revolt; instead he was tried on charges of having had illicit relations with one of his father's maids and was executed in the market place. Queen Xulai was also accused of having killed the former queen, Chengshu, by black magic, while Crown Prince Liu Shuang was accused of having acted contrary to filial piety by reporting on his own father. Both were executed in the market place. All those who had taken part in the planned revolt with the king were executed along with their families. The kingdom of Hengshan was abolished and the territory taken over by the central government and made into the province of Hengshan.

The Grand Historian remarks: How apt are the words of the *Book of Odes*:

> He smote the northern barbarians
> And punished the men of Jing and Shu.[13]

The kings of Huainan and Hengshan were of the same flesh and blood as the emperor and ruled domains 1,000 *li* square, ranking among the highest feudal lords of the nation. And yet they did nothing to honour their position as protector vassals or to aid the Son of Heaven, but gave themselves up wholly to schemes of evil, plotting revolt and treason until father and sons alike had all in turn lost their kingdoms. Each was forced to cut off his life before his allotted days were spent, and ended as the laughing-stock of the world!

Yet this was not the fault of the kings alone, for the customs of the region where they lived were corrupt, and their ministers step by step led them into evil. From ancient times the historical records have shown us that the men of Jing and Chu are rash and foolhardy, fickle and fond of revolt!

---

[13] From "Bigong", the temple Odes of Lu. Jing and Shu, as well as Chu at the end of the passage, are all names for the region in the south occupied in Han times by the kingdoms of Huainan and Hengshan.

PART IV

THE COLLECTIVE BIOGRAPHIES

SHI JI 121: THE BIOGRAPHIES OF THE CONFUCIAN SCHOLARS

From the time of Confucius' death there was no one even in the capital who honoured the teachings of the ancient schools. Only in the early years of the present emperor's reign did literature once more begin to flourish. Thus I made "The Biographies of the Confucian Scholars".

The Grand Historian remarks: Whenever I read over the rules for the educational institutions and see what has been done to encourage and open up the way for official scholars, I never fail to lay aside the book with a sigh. Alas, when the house of Zhou declined in ancient time, the song of the "Crying Ospreys" was composed.[1] With Kings You and Li, the power of the Zhou dynasty began to wane, and rites and music fell into disuse; the feudal lords conducted themselves as they pleased, and the actual rule of the empire passed into the hands of the powerful feudal states. Confucius was saddened that the path of the ancient kings had been abandoned and that evil ways flourished, and therefore he discussed and edited the *Book of Odes* and the *Book of Documents* and worked to revive rites and music. "When he went to Qi and heard the ancient Shao music, he did not recognize the taste of meat for three months," and "after he returned to Lu from Wei, the music was reformed and the various sections of the *Book of Odes* were all put in their proper places."[2] But it was an age of confusion and turmoil, and no one was willing to make use of Confucius. Thus, although he sought employment with over seventy different rulers, he could not find a welcome anywhere. "If someone would employ me," he remarked, "I could accomplish something worthwhile in no more than a year!"[3] But when a unicorn was captured at the western hunt, he said, "My way is ended!"[4]

---

[1] The first song in the *Book of Odes*. Sima Qian apparently took it to be a satirical attack on the weak Zhou kings, though it is usually regarded as a hymn of praise.

[2] Quoted from *Analects* VII, 13, and IX, 14.

[3] *Analects* XIII, 10.

[4] *Gongyang Commentary* on the *Spring and Autumn Annals*, Duke Ai, fourteenth year.

Therefore he used the records of the historians to make the *Spring and Autumn Annals*, in order to set forth the laws of a true king. Its words are subtle and its ideas profound; many are the scholars in later times who have written commentaries on it.

After the death of Confucius, his band of seventy disciples broke up and scattered among the feudal lords, the more important ones becoming tutors and high ministers to the rulers, the lesser ones acting as friends and teachers to the lower officials, while some went into retirement and were never seen again. Thus Zilu went to live in Wei, Zizhang in Chen, Ziyu of Tantai in Chu, and Zixia in Xihe, while Zigong died in Qi. Tian Zifang, Duangan Mu, Wu Qi, Qin Huali, and others of their group all received instruction from Zixia's companions and became the tutors of kings. Among the feudal lords, however, only Marquis Wen of Wei had any fondness for literature. Conditions continued to deteriorate until the time of the First Emperor of the Qin; the empire was divided among a number of states, all warring with each other, and no one had any use for the arts of the Confucians. Only in Qi and Lu did scholars appear to carry on the teachings and save them from oblivion. During the reigns of Kings Wei and Xuan of Qi (378-323 BC), Mencius and Xun Qing and their respective groups both honoured the doctrines of the Master and worked to expand and enrich them, winning prominence among the men of the time by their learning.

Then followed the twilight days of the Qin emperor,[5] who burned the *Odes* and *Documents* and buried the scholars alive, and from this time on the texts of the Six Classics of the Confucians were damaged and incomplete.

Later, when Chen She became a king, the Confucian scholars of Lu gathered up the ritual vessels that had belonged to Confucius and went to serve under "King Chen". Thus Kong Jia[6] became an erudite under Chen She and died with him. Chen She rose from among the common people, rounded up a motley band of border guards, and in the space of a month managed to become a king in the region of Chu, though before half a year had passed, he and the uprising he led had been completely wiped out. He and his men were of the most humble origin, and yet gentlemen and scholars did not hesitate to take up the vessels of Confucius and journey to his side, where they presented gifts and

---

[5] So called because in the opinion of Han writers the evil reign of the Qin represented the close of the great cycle of growth and decay that had begun with the founding of the Zhou dynasty.

[6] The eighth-generation descendant of Confucius.

begged to become his ministers. Why was this? Because they were incensed at the Qin dynasty for having burned their books and interrupted their labours, and they hoped that King Chen would help them to vent their rage and accomplish their revenge.

Later, when Gaozu had defeated Xiang Yu, he marched north and surrounded the state of Lu with his troops, but the Confucian scholars of Lu went on as always, reciting and discussing their books, practising rites and music, and never allowing the sound of strings and voices to die out. Is it not because of the teachings and influence which the Sage left behind him that the state of Lu loves rites and music so? Thus, when Confucius was in Chen he said, "Let me return! Let me return to Lu! The little children of my school are ambitious and too hasty. They are accomplished and complete so far, but they do not know how to restrict and shape themselves."[7]

Since ancient times the people of the region of Qi and Lu have had a natural talent for literature. And when the Han came to power, these scholars were at last allowed to study and teach their Classics freely and to demonstrate the proper rituals for the archery matches and community banquets.

Shusun Tong drew up the ceremonial for the Han court and was rewarded with the post of master of ritual, while all the other scholars who assisted him were likewise given preferential treatment in the government. The emperor sighed over the neglected state of learning and would have done more to encourage its revival, but at the time there was still considerable turmoil within the empire and the region within the four seas had not yet been set at peace. Likewise, during the reigns of Emperor Hui and Empress Lü there was still no leisure to attend to the matter of government schools. Moreover, the high officials at this time were all military men who had won their distinction in battle.

With the accession of Emperor Wen, Confucian scholars began little by little to be summoned and employed in the government, although Emperor Wen himself rather favoured the Legalist teachings on personnel organization and control. Emperor Jing made no effort to employ Confucian scholars, and his mother, Empress Dowager Dou, was an advocate of the teachings of the Yellow Emperor and Lao Zi. Thus various scholars were appointed to fill the posts

---

[7] *Analects* V, 21. The usual interpretation is that Confucius, while recognizing the faults of his "little children" or disciples in Lu, is anxious to return from his travels so that he may devote his full time to their instruction. This seems to be the way Sima Qian understood the passage.

of court erudite and to answer questions, but they had no prospects of advancement.

When the present emperor came to the throne there were a number of enlightened Confucian scholars such as Zhao Wan and Wang Zang at court. The emperor was much attracted by their ideas and accordingly sent out a summons for scholars of moral worth and literary ability to take service in the government. From this time on we find that all scholars who taught the *Book of Odes* belonged either to the Lu school of Master Shen Pei, the Qi school of Master Yuan Gu, or the Yan school of the grand tutor Han Ying. The teaching of the *Book of Documents* derived from Master Fu of Ji'nan, that of ritual derived from master Gao Tang of Lu, and that of the *Book of Changes* from Master Tian of Zichuan. For the *Spring and Autumn Annals* there were the Lu and Qi schools deriving from Master Huwu, and the Zhao school of Dong Zhongshu.

After Empress Dowager Dou passed away, the marquis of Wuan, Tian Fen, became chancellor. He rejected the doctrines of the Taoists, the Legalists, and the other philosophical schools, and invited several hundred Confucian scholars and literary men to take service in the government. Among them was Gongsun Hong who, because of his knowledge of the *Spring and Autumn Annals*, advanced from the rank of commoner to that of one of the three highest ministers in the government and was enfeoffed as marquis of Pingjin. Scholars throughout the empire saw which way the wind was blowing and did all they could to follow his example.

As a scholar official, Gongsun Hong, who held the post of imperial secretary, was disturbed that the teachings of Confucius were being neglected and not put into greater practice and he therefore submitted the following memorial:

> The chancellor and the imperial secretary wish to make this statement. Your Majesty has issued an edict which reads:
>
> "I have heard that the people are to be guided by rites and led to the practice of virtue through music, and that the institution of marriage is the basis of the family. Yet at the present time rites have fallen into disuse and music has declined, a fact which grieves me deeply. Therefore I have invited men of outstanding moral worth and wide learning from all over the empire to come and take service at court. Let the officials in charge of ritual encourage learning, hold discussions, and gather all the information they can to encourage the revival of rites in order to act as leaders of the empire. Let the master of ritual consult

Competing schools of thought

with the erudites and their students on how to promote the spread of virtue in the countryside and open the way for men of outstanding talent."

In accordance with this edict we have respectfully discussed the matter with the master of ritual Kong Zang, the erudite Ping, and others, and they have told us that, according to their information, it was the custom under the Three Dynasties of antiquity to set up schools for instruction in the villages. In the Xia dynasty these were called *xiao*, in the Shang dynasty *xu*, and in the Zhou dynasty *xiang*. These schools encouraged goodness by making it known to the court and censured evil by applying punishments. Thus it was the officials of the capital who took the initiative in instructing and educating the people, and virtue spread from the court outwards to the provinces.

Now Your Majesty, manifesting supreme virtue and displaying a profound intelligence worthy to rank with that of heaven and earth, has sought to rectify human relations, encourage learning, revive the former rites, promote instruction in goodness, and open the way for men of worth so that the people of the four directions may be swayed to virtue. This is indeed the way to lay the foundations for an era of great peace.

In earlier times, however, the instruction provided by the government was incomplete and the rites were not fully carried out. We therefore beg that the previous official system be utilized to increase the spread of instruction. In order to fill the offices of erudite we suggest that fifty additional students be selected and declared exempt from the usual labour services. The master of ritual shall be charged with the selection of these students from among men of the people who are eighteen years of age or older and who are of good character and upright behaviour. In order to supply candidates for the selection, the governors, prime ministers, heads, and magistrates of the various provinces, kingdoms, districts, marches, and feudal cities shall recommend to the 2,000 picul officials in their respective regions any men who are fond of learning, show respect for their superiors, adhere to the teachings of the government, and honour the customs of their village, and whose actions in no way reflect discredit upon their reputations. The 2,000 picul officials shall in turn make a careful examination of the men recommended; those found worthy shall then be sent in company with the local accounting officials when the latter come to the capital to make their reports, and shall there be presented to the master of ritual. They shall then receive instruction in the same manner as the regular students of the erudites.

At the end of a year, all of them shall be examined. Those who have mastered one or more of the Classics shall be assigned to fill vacancies among the scholar officials in the provinces or among the officers in charge of precedents who serve under the master of ritual. If there are any outstanding students who qualify for the post of palace attendant, the master of ritual shall present their names to the throne. In this way men of exceptional talent and ability will be brought at once to the attention of the ruler. If, on the contrary, there are any who have not applied themselves to their studies, whose ability is inferior, or who have failed to master even one Classic, they shall be summarily dismissed. In addition, if there are any among the recommending officials who have failed to carry out their duties properly, we suggest that they be punished.

We have respectfully examined the edicts and laws which have been handed down to us by Your Majesty and we find that they distinguish clearly the provinces of heaven and man and combine the best principles of ancient and modern times. Their wording is stately and orthodox, their instructions profound, and the bounty displayed in them most beautiful. Nevertheless we, being petty officials of shallow understanding, have been unable to spread them abroad and therefore they have not been fully publicized and understood by those through-out the empire.[8] Now the officials who handle ritual affairs are ranked below those in charge of precedents, and although men may be selected for office because of their knowledge of literature and ritual, they must remain in the same posts and have no opportunity for advancement. We therefore request that men be selected from among those who have a rank of 200 piculs or over, or those who have a rank of 100 piculs

---

[8] The meaning of this curious burst of humility, it would seem, is that the emperor's edicts and laws are couched in such elegant language that the present officials on the lower levels are unable to understand them. Therefore Gongsun Hong recommends that men with special literary training be assigned as secretaries to the prefects and governors. This is also the reason for the emphasis, later on in the paragraph, on familiarity with the Classics, since imperial edicts were often made up largely of difficult and abstruse quotations from the Classics.

and who have mastered one Classic or more, to act as secretaries to the left and right prefects of the capital and the grand messenger; and that men be selected from among those who rank below 100 piculs to act as secretaries to the governors of provinces, two for regular provinces and one for provinces on the border. In the selection, preference shall be given to those who can recite from memory the longest passages from the Classics. If the number of men available should prove insufficient to fill all the posts, selections should be made from among the officials in charge of precedents to fill the secretaries of the prefects and grand messenger, and from these and the scholar officials to fill the offices in the provinces. We request that these provisions be added to the rules for educational institutions, and that in all other matters the present rules remain in effect.

The emperor signified his approval of this proposal, and from this time on the number of literary men who held positions as ministers and high officials in the government increased remarkably.

Master Shen Pei was a native of Lu. When Gaozu visited Lu, Shen Pei went with his teacher to visit Gaozu at the Southern Palace of Lu. During the reign of Empress Lü he journeyed to Chang'an, where both he and Liu Ying, Gaozu's nephew, studied under the same teacher. Later, when Liu Ying became king of Chu, he summoned Master Shen to act as tutor to his son Liu Wu, the crown prince of Chu. But Liu Wu had no taste for learning and hated Master Shen, and when his father died and he succeeded to the throne of Chu, he had Master Shen bound and condemned to convict labour. Master Shen, deeply shamed by such treatment, returned to Lu where he lived in retirement at home and spent his time teaching. For the rest of his life he never left his house, nor would he receive guests who came to see him; only a summons from the king of Lu himself could induce him to go out. Men travelled great distances from all directions to become his disciples, and over 100 students received instructed from him. The only instruction he gave was oral exegesis of the *Book of Odes*; he used no written commentary on the Classic. Any points that he was doubtful about he left unexplained and did not attempt to comment on.

Wang Zang of Lanling received instruction in the *Odes* from Master Shen and was employed by Emperor Jing. He was appointed lesser tutor to the heir apparent for a time, but later retired from the post. When the heir apparent, the present emperor, ascended the throne, Wang Zang submitted a letter to him and was awarded the post of palace guard. The emperor continued to advance Wang

Zang from one post to another until in the space of a single year he had become chief of palace attendants.

Later, when Zhao Wan of Dai, who had also studied the *Odes* under Master Shen, was appointed imperial secretary, he and Wang Zang joined in urging the emperor to set up a Bright Hall in which to hold audiences with the feudal lords. When their proposal failed to gain acceptance, they recommended their teacher, Master Shen, to the emperor. The emperor thereupon dispatched an envoy with gifts of bolts of silk and jewels and sent a comfortable carriage drawn by four horses to fetch Master Shen. His two disciples Wang Zang and Zhao Wan went along in smaller carriages to accompany their teacher on his journey.

When Master Shen arrived in the capital and appeared before the emperor, the latter questioned him on how to achieve good government. Master Shen was by this time an old man of over eighty, and he replied, "Good government does not require a lot of talk. The only thing to worry about is whether one has the power to carry out one's policies!"

The emperor at this time was very fond of florid speeches and he therefore received Master Shen's answer in silence. But since he had already gone to the trouble of inviting Master Shen to the capital, he appointed him to a post as palace counsellor and quartered him at the official residence of the royal family of Lu, where he was to discuss plans for the construction of a Bright Hall.

Empress Dowager Dou, the emperor's grandmother, favoured the teachings of Lao Zi and had no use for Confucian theories. She managed to discover some fault which Zhao Wan and Wang Zang had committed and made an accusation about them to the emperor, who accordingly abandoned the Bright Hall project and turned Zhao Wan and Wang Zang over to the law officials for trial. Both of them committed suicide shortly afterwards, and Master Shen, pleading illness, retired from his post and returned to Lu, where he died a few years later.

His disciples included over ten men who became erudites, among them Kong Anguo, who became governor of Linhuai; Zhou Ba, who became internal secretary of Jiaoxi; Xia Kuan, who became internal secretary of Chengyang; Lu Ci of Dang, who became governor of Donghai; Master Miao of Lanling, who became internal secretary of Changsha; Xu Yan, who became military commander of Jiaoxi; and Quemen Qingji, a native of Zou, who became internal secretary of Jiaodong. All of these men displayed great honesty and integrity in fulfilling the duties of office and governing the people and were renowned for their love of learning.

Among Master Shen's disciples who became scholar officials there were

some whose conduct was not always perfect; yet 100 or more of them advanced
to posts of counsellor, palace attendant, or officer in charge of precedents.
Although they frequently disagreed in their interpretations of the *Odes*, their
doctrines were based largely upon the teachings of Master Shen.

*Mandate of
Heaven.
discussions*

Master Yuan Gu, grand tutor to the king of Qinghe, was a native of Qi.
Because of his knowledge of the *Book of Odes*, he was appointed an erudite at
the court of Emperor Jing. Once he was having an argument with a certain
Master Huang[9] in the presence of Emperor Jing. "King Tang, the founder of the
Shang dynasty, and King Wu, the founder of the Zhou, did not receive any
'mandate of Heaven' to do what they did," declared Master Huang. "They
simply assassinated their sovereigns and set up their own dynasties!"

"That is not so!" protested Master Yuan Gu. "Jie, the last ruler of the Xia,
and Zhou, the last ruler of the Shang, were both cruel tyrants, and the people of
the empire turned away from them in their hearts and gave their allegiance to
Tang and Wu. Tang and Wu were acting in accordance with the hearts of the
empire when they overthrew and punished Jie and Zhou. The subjects of Jie and
Zhou refused to serve them any longer, but gave their allegiance to Tang and
Wu, who had no other choice than to set up their own dynasties. Is this not what
it means to receive the mandate of Heaven?"

But Master Huang replied, "A hat, no matter how old, belongs on the head,
and shoes, no matter how new, belong on the feet! Why? Because there is a
difference between top and bottom ! Now, although Jie and Zhou were unprincipled men, they were still sovereigns, and although Tang and Wu were sages,
they were still subjects. When a ruler commits some fault, if his subjects fail to
correct his words and reform his actions in order to restore the position of the
Son of Heaven to its full dignity, but instead use his errors as an excuse to
'punish' him and set themselves up in his place, facing south and calling
themselves the new rulers, what is this but a case of assassination of one's liege
lord?"

"If what you say is true," said Master Yuan Gu, "then was Emperor Gaozu
likewise at fault when he replaced the ruler of the Qin dynasty and became Son
of Heaven?"

At this point Emperor Jing intervened. "No one accuses a man of lacking
good taste in food because he eats other meats but refrains from eating horse

---

[9] A scholar of Taoism. Sima Qian mentions in his autobiography that his father Sima Tan
"studied the theories of Taoism with Master Huang".

liver," he said, "and no one considers a scholar stupid because he discusses other questions but does not discuss the matter of whether or not Tang and Wu received the mandate of Heaven!'[10]

He thereupon dismissed the two men, and after this scholars no longer dared to engage openly in debates on who had received the mandate and who was guilty of assassinating his sovereign.

Empress Dowager Dou was fond of the writings of Lao Zi, and she once summoned Master Yuan Gu and asked him what he thought of Lao Zi's book. "The sayings of a menial, nothing more!" he replied.

Empress Dowager Dou was furious. "And pray tell me, where can I get one of your Confucian books on the Director of Public Works and the convict labour system?"[11] she asked. Then she ordered Yuan Gu to be thrown into the pigpen to fight the pigs.

Emperor Jing knew that she was angry and that Yuan Gu had merely given a frank answer and was guilty of no offence, and he therefore lent Yuan Gu a sharp knife to take with him into the pigpen. Yuan Gu stabbed the pig and pierced it through the heart, bringing it to the ground with one blow. The empress dowager watched in silence, but could think of no excuse to punish him further and was obliged to let him go.

Shortly afterwards Emperor Jing, impressed by Yuan Gu's honesty and directness, appointed him grand tutor to his son Liu Sheng, the king of Qinghe. After holding this post for a considerable time Yuan Gu retired because of illness.

When the present emperor first came to the throne he summoned Yuan Gu

---

[10] Horse liver was believed to be deadly poison. Emperor Jing is hinting that the discussions on the question of who has the right to overthrow his sovereign are equally perilous. Mencius had maintained that King Wu was completely justified in overthrowing Zhou, the last ruler of the Shang, and setting up his own dynasty, since Zhou had by his wicked deeds forfeited the right to be called a true sovereign and King Wu had received the "mandate of Heaven" to punish him. This principle of the "right of revolution" was naturally very useful to men who were attempting to found new dynasties, but could hardly be applauded by rulers such as Emperor Jing who were working to maintain a dynasty that had already been established.

[11] Some of the Confucian works such as the "Institutes of Zhou" dealt with the bureaucratic system of the Zhou dynasty and its officials, such as the Director of Public Works, etc. The empress dowager is here deriding this attention to bureaucratic and legal details which seems to have absorbed much of the time of Han Confucian scholars. From the Taoist point of view the Confucians were hopelessly concerned with such "artificial" means of government.

to service in the government again because of his wisdom. Many of the Confucian flatterers at court hated him, however, and did all they could to slander him, complaining that "Yuan Gu is much too old!" until the emperor finally dismissed him and sent him home. By this time Yuan Gu was over ninety.

Summoned at the same time as Yuan Gu was a man from Xue named Gongsun Hong, who was very shy in Yuan Gu's presence and only ventured now and then to cast a glance at him out of the corner of his eye. Yuan Gu said to him, "Master Gongsun! Always strive to base your words on correct learning. Never twist your learning around in order to flatter the age!"

From this time on the scholars of Qi who expounded the *Book of Odes* all derived their interpretations from the teachings of Master Yuan Gu, and all the men of Qi who achieved distinction and honour because of their knowledge of the *Odes* were disciples of his.

Master Han Ying was a native of Yan who became an erudite at the court of Emperor Wen. During the reign of Emperor Jing he was made grand tutor to Liu Shun, the king of Changshan. Master Han studied the meaning of the *Odes* and complied an "inner" and an "outer" commentary, running to 20,000 or 30,000 words.[12] Although his interpretations very often differed from those of the scholars of Lu and Qi, his general approach to the Classic was the same as theirs. Master Bi of Huainan carried on his teachings, and from that time on all scholars in the region of Yan and Zhao who expounded the *Odes* derived their interpretations from Master Han. Master Han's grandson Han Shang is an erudite at the court of the present emperor.

Master Fu Sheng was a native of Ji'nan and once served as an erudite at the court of the Qin emperor. During the reign of Emperor Wen a search was made for someone who had a knowledge of the *Book of Documents*, but no one could be found throughout the whole empire. The emperor then learned that Master Fu had studied the Classic and decided to summon him to court. However, Master Fu was by this time over ninety and was too old to make the journey. The emperor therefore ordered the master of ritual to send Chao Cuo, one of his officers in charge of precedents, to go to Master Fu's home and receive instruction from him.

During the Qin dynasty, when the First Emperor had ordered the burning

---

[12]Only the "outer commentary" is extant today, the *Hanshi waizhuan*, a collection of anecdotes from earlier works in which a line or two from the *Odes* is used to point the moral of the story.

of the books, Master Fu had hidden his copy of the *Documents* in the wall of his house; later, because of the great military uprisings, he had been forced to flee from his home. After the Han restored peace to the empire, Master Fu looked for his book, but he found that several tens of chapters were missing. All he could recover were twenty-nine chapters, which he taught to the men in the region of Lu and Qi. As a result of his efforts, scholars were able to expound the *Book of Documents* in considerable detail, and all the important teachers east of the mountains studied the Classics and included it among their teachings.

Master Fu taught Master Zhang and Master Ouyang of Ji'nan, and Master Ouyang in turn taught Ni Kuan of Qiancheng. Ni Kuan, after having mastered the *Book of Documents*, was recommended by his province for his ability in literature and was sent to receive instruction under the erudites at court. There he studied under Kong Anguo. Ni Kuan was poor and had no money for living expenses. To make up for this he always used to take charge of the preparation of the meals for the other students and occasionally, when he had some free time, would hire himself out as a day labourer in order to earn money for food and clothing. Wherever he went he always carried a volume of the Classics about with him, and if he had a spare moment he would practise reading it over to himself. Because of his good marks in the examination he was appointed as a secretary to Zhang Tang, the commandant of justice.

At this time Zhang Tang favoured men of literary ability and treated Ni Kuan with great kindness, appointing him clerk in charge of presenting petitions to the throne so that he could cite the ancient laws in presenting judgements on difficult and important cases.[13]

Ni Kuan was a warmhearted and kind man, honest, wise, and capable of looking out for himself. He was very good at composing memorials and petitions to the throne, being clever at writing, though in speech he could never make his meaning clear. Zhang Tang considered him a man of exceptional worth and often praised him.

When Zhang Tang became imperial secretary he appointed Ni Kuan as his clerk and recommended him to the emperor. The emperor called him in and, after questioning him on various affairs, found him much to his liking. Six years

---

[13] The *Book of Documents*, it should be noted, includes a section on the ancient penal code of the Zhou dynasty, the "Code of Marquis Lü", from which Ni Kuan no doubt quoted in such cases.

after Zhang Tang died, Ni Kuan was advanced to the position of imperial secretary; he held the post for nine years and died in office.

Although Ni Kuan held one of the three highest posts in the government, he managed to get along with the emperor because of his gentle and compliant disposition and had no difficulty maintaining his position. But as long as he was in office he did nothing to reform abuses in the government or reprimand the emperor, and the officials who served under him accordingly regarded him with contempt and were unwilling to exert themselves for him.

Master Zhang, Master Fu's other disciple, became an erudite, and a grandson of Master Fu was also summoned to court because of his knowledge of the *Book of Documents*, but on examination proved to be unable to explain the work.

From this time on Zhou Ba and Kong Anguo of Lu and Jia Jia of Luoyang were noted for their thorough expositions of the *Book of Documents*. The Kong family possessed a copy of the *Documents* written in archaic characters which Kong Anguo would explain in modern characters, and in this way he started his own school of interpretation. The Kong family text consisted of ten or more chapters from an otherwise lost copy of the work. Thus the number of versions of the *Book of Documents* in circulation was increased. [14]

Many scholars have taught the rites, but among them Master Gao Tang of Lu was the most eminent. If we look into the history of rites, we find that even in the time of Confucius the texts on ritual were not complete. Later, when the Qin dynasty instituted its burning of the books, more of the works on ritual were lost, so that today we have only the rites pertaining to the lower nobility. It was these that Master Gao Tang expounded.

Master Xu of Lu was very good at ceremonies, and during the reign of Emperor Wen, because of this knowledge, was appointed a palace official in charge of rites. His learning was passed on to his son, and eventually to his grandsons Xu Yan and Xu Xiang. Xu Xiang was born with a natural talent for performing the ceremonies well, but he had no understanding of the Classic on

---

[14] "Archaic characters" refers to the type of characters in use before the Qin dynasty's standardization of writing. Kong Anguo's school, as well as schools devoted to other Classics which used texts written in archaic characters, came to be known as the "Old Text" schools, as opposed to the "New Text" schools which used texts written in the regular Han style characters. Ban Gu (*Han shu* 88) states that Sima Qian questioned Kong Anguo about his text of the *Book of Documents* and incorporated some of the "old text" versions into the early parts of the *Shi ji*.

ritual, while Xu Yan had mastered the Classic but was not good at the ceremonies. Because of his ability Xu Xiang was appointed a palace official in charge of ritual at the Han court and eventually reached the position of internal secretary of Guangling. Xu Yan, and Gonghu Manyi, Master Huan, and Shan Ci, who were disciples of the Xu family, were all appointed ritual officials, while Xiao Fen of Xiaqiu, because of his familiarity with the ritual texts, was made governor of Huaiyang. From this time on, all those who taught the rites or performed ceremonies derived their knowledge from the Xu family.

Expositions of the *Book of Changes* began with Shang Qu of Lu, who studied the Classic under Confucius. After Confucius died, Shang Qu's learning was handed down for six generations, until it reached a man of Qi named Tian He or Tian Zizhuang.[15] At the beginning of the Han dynasty, Tian He transmitted his learning to a man of Dongwu named Wang Tong or Wang Zizhong, and Wang Zizhong in turn handed it on to Yang He of Zichuan. In the first year of the era *yuanguang* (134 BC) Yang He was summoned to take service in the government because of his knowledge of the *Book of Changes*, and advanced to the post of palace counsellor.

Jimo Cheng, a scholar of Qi, advanced to the post of prime minister of Chengyang because of his knowledge of the *Changes*, while Meng Dan of Guangchuan was made a lord of the gate to the heir apparent for the same reason. Zhou Ba of Lu, Heng Hu, a native of Ju, and Zhufu Yan of Linzi all obtained service because of their knowledge of this Classic and advanced to posts with a salary of 2,000 piculs. On the whole, however, all the men who expounded the *Changes* derived their learning from the school of Yang He.

Dong Zhongshu was a native of Guangchuan. He studied the *Spring and Autumn Annals*, and in the reign of Emperor Jing was made an erudite. He used to lower the curtains of his room and lecture from within them, and his older disciples would pass on what they had learned to the newer ones, so that some of his students had never seen his face. Three years he taught in this way and never once took the time even to look out into his garden; such was his devotion to his task. In all his activities he never did anything that was not in accord with ritually prescribed behaviour, and all the other scholars looked up to him as their teacher.

When the present emperor came to the throne he appointed Dong Zhongshu

---

[15] Because it was concerned with divination, the *Book of Changes* was exempted from the Qin's burning of the books and its line of transmission was therefore not interrupted.

to the post of prime minister of Jiangdu. Dong Zhongshu studied the various natural disasters and portentous happenings recorded in the *Spring and Autumn Annals* and on the basis of this study attempted to discover the principles behind the operations and interactions of the *yin* and *yang*. Thus he concluded that if one wished rain to fall, one should shut off the *yang* forces and free those of the *yin*, while if one wished the rain to cease, one should do the reverse. He put his theories into practice in the kingdom of Jiangdu and never failed to achieve the results he sought.[16]

In the midst of his career he was removed from the post of prime minister of Jiangdu and made a palace counsellor. He lived in the dormitory for officials and devoted himself to compiling a record of natural disasters and portentous happenings. Shortly before this, the mortuary temple of Emperor Gaozu in Liaodong had burned down. Zhufu Yan, who hated Dong Zhongshu, managed to get hold of his work on disasters and portents and presented it to the emperor, who summoned the court scholars and showed them the work. Many of them criticized it, among them Lü Bushu, a disciple of Dong Zhongshu who, unaware that the book was his teacher's, pronounced it utterly stupid and worthless. Dong Zhongshu was accordingly turned over to the law officials for punishment and was condemned to death, but was pardoned by imperial edict. After this Dong Zhongshu no longer dared to express his opinions on disasters and portents.[17]

Dong Zhongshu was an honest and forthright man. At this time the Han was busy driving back the barbarian tribes which surrounded its borders. Gongsun Hong, although no match for Dong Zhongshu in his knowledge of the *Spring and Autumn Annals*, had succeeded, by following the trend of the times

---

[16] Dong Zhongshu's philosophical views are preserved in a work called the *Chunqiu fanlu*, a series of essays by Dong or his disciples on history, ethics, and the metaphysical operations of the *yin* and *yang* and the five elements, including a chapter on how to make rain fall. His opinions were extremely influential in moulding Han Confucian thought.

[17] To understand this incident it should be remembered that, in the Han theory of portents, it was customary to assign some human fault as the cause of all natural disasters or unusual happenings such as fires, earthquakes, droughts, etc. Since the emperor bore the heaviest responsibility in the government, the faults assigned were usually actions of the emperor himself, or at least of his immediate family or high ministers. Most likely Dong Zhongshu had designated some such "error" as the cause of the fire in Liaodong, and Zhufu Yan was therefore able to arouse the emperor's enmity by showing him the book. The other court scholars, anxious to save their own skins, would naturally pronounce the book worthless and stupid. "Stupid", *yu* in Chinese often means simply "imprudent", i.e., behaviour which is likely to get one into trouble.

and supporting the undertakings of the emperor, in reaching the position of a high minister in the government. Dong Zhongshu for his part considered Gongsun Hong no more than a servile flatterer. Gongsun Hong hated Dong Zhongshu for this reason and told the emperor, "Only Dong Zhongshu is worthy to be appointed as prime minister to the king of Jiaoxi!"[18] The king of Jiaoxi had long heard of Dong Zhongshu's worthy actions, however, and when Dong Zhongshu was appointed as his prime minister, he treated him very well. Dong Zhongshu was afraid that if he remained in Jiaoxi for long he would be accused of some crime and so he resigned his post on grounds of illness and lived the rest of his life at home. He never gave any thought to accumulating wealth for his family but devoted himself entirely to studying and writing books. Thus, from the rise of the Han down to the reign of the fifth ruler, only Dong Zhongshu achieved real distinction for his understanding of the *Spring and Autumn Annals*. In interpreting the Classic he followed the *Gongyang Commentary*.

Master Hu Wu was a native of Qi who became an erudite under Emperor Jing. In his old age he returned to his home and devoted himself to teaching. Many of the scholars of Qi who expound the *Spring and Autumn Annals* received their instruction from him. Gongsun Hong also owed a great deal to his teachings. Master Jiang of Xiaqiu studied the *Guliang Commentary* on the *Spring and Autumn Annals*.[19] Gongsun Hong, after taking office in the government, collected the explanations of Master Jiang, along with those of Dong Zhongshu, and compared them, but decided in the end to follow those of Dong Zhongshu.

Among Dong Zhongshu's disciples who achieved fame were Chu Da of Lanling, Yin Zhong of Guangchuan, and Lü Bushu of Wen. Chu Da became prime minister of Liang, while Lü Bushu became a chief secretary. He was given the imperial seals and sent as envoy to settle legal affairs in Huainan, where he

---

[18] Liu Duan, the king of Jiaoxi, was noted for his violent and unruly temperament, and brought about the death of innumerable officials of the central court who were sent to restrain him. (See his biography in *Han Dynasty* Volume I, "Hereditary Houses of the Five Families", p. 400). Gongsun Hong no doubt thought that this would be a sure way to get rid of Dong Zhongshu.

[19] At this time there were two main commentaries on the *Spring and Autumn Annals*, the *Gongyang* and the *Guliang*, though it is obvious that the former enjoyed wider favour. Sima Qian himself studied the *Gongyang* interpretation of the *Annals* under Dong Zhongshu. The third famous commentary, the *Zuo zhuan*, undoubtedly existed as a separate work at this time but does not seem to have been used as a commentary on the *Annals*.

reprimanded the feudal lords for arbitrarily acting on their own authority and failing to report their actions to the central government, pointing out that such actions were not in accordance with the principles laid down in the *Spring and Autumn Annals*. The emperor highly approved of both Chu Da and Lü Bushu. In addition to these some hundred or more disciples of Dong Zhongshu achieved fame as palace counsellors and attendants, masters of guests, and officials in charge of precedents. Dong Zhongshu's sons and grandsons all won high office because of their learning.

SHI JI 119: THE BIOGRAPHIES OF THE REASONABLE OFFICIALS[1]

The officials who upheld the law and carried out their duties in a reasonable fashion did not boast of their accomplishments nor brag of their ability. Though they won no particular praise from the common people, neither did they commit any glaring errors. Thus I made "The Biographies of the Reasonable Officials".

The Grand Historian remarks: Laws are made to guide the people and punishments carried out to prevent evil. Both must be adequately attended to if people of good character are not to live in fear. Yet men of truly sound moral conduct will never go wrong no matter what public position they are appointed to. Those who fulfil the duties of their office and behave in a reasonable way are also carrying out the work of government. What need is there for officials to be so stern?

Sunshu Ao was a gentleman who lived in retirement in the state of Chu. Yu Qiu, the prime minister, recommended him to King Zhuang of Chu (ca.600 BC) and suggested that he be appointed prime minister in his own place. Three

---

[1] In this brief chapter Sima Qian for a moment seems to forget the harsh realities of life under Emperor Wu as he relates a series of anecdotes about some officials who lived many centuries earlier, during the middle of the Zhou dynasty, and were noted for their just and reasonable conduct. But this mask of the garrulous teller of old tales only faintly conceals Sima Qian's real purpose. As history these anecdotes are practically worthless. Their function here can only be understood when the chapter is read in conjunction with the following one on "Harsh Officials" and the description of Emperor Wu's economic policies in "The Treatise on the Balanced Standard". Not only does Sima Qian make an over-all satirical point by making all his "reasonable officials" men of the Zhou and his "harsh officials" men of his own day; each anecdote in the chapter — the official who objected to the change in currency, the official who would not accept gifts and was so careful not to compete with the occupations of the common people, the law officials whose sense of responsibility drove them to suicide — is calculated to contrast with and satirize some policy or characteristic of official life under Emperor Wu.

months later Sunshu Ao was made prime minister of Chu. He instructed and guided the people so that all ranks of society lived in peace and harmony, and the customs of the people were raised to an admirable level. Though the government was lenient, it was able to prevent evil; the officials did not indulge in corrupt activities, and bandits and robbers disappeared from the kingdom. In autumn and winter Sunshu Ao encouraged the people to gather wood in the mountains, and in spring and summer to make use of the resources of the rivers and lakes. Thus everyone obtained the benefits of his surroundings and the people delighted in life.

One time King Zhuang, deciding that the coins then in use were too light, had them replaced by larger ones, but the people found the new currency inconvenient and all of them abandoned their occupations. The master of the market place came to Sunshu Ao and said, "The market is in complete confusion! The people are milling around restlessly and no one knows where to set up shop."

"How long has it been this way?" asked Sunshu Ao.

"For the past three months," replied the master of the market.

"You may go now," said Sunshu Ao. "I will see that things are put back the way they were."

Five days later Sunshu Ao appeared at court before the king and said, "Some time ago the currency was changed because it was thought that the old coins were too light, but now the master of the market place comes and tells me that the market is in complete confusion and that the people are milling around restlessly and cannot decide where to set up their shops. I beg that things be put back the way they were before."

The king gave his consent, and three days after the order was issued the market had returned to normal.

The people of Chu liked to use very low-slung carriages, but the king did not think that such low carriages were good for the horses and wanted to issue an order forcing the people to use higher ones. Sunshu Ao said, "If orders are issued too frequently to the people they will not know which ones to obey. It will not do to issue an order. If Your Majesty wishes the people to use high carriages, then I suggest that I instruct the officials to have the thresholds of the community gates made higher. Anyone who rides in a carriage must be a man of some social position, and a gentleman cannot be getting down from his carriage every time he has to go through the community gate."

The king gave his approval, and after half a year had passed all the people had of their own accord made their carriages higher so that they could drive over the threshold without difficulty. In this way, without instructing the people, Sunshu Ao led them to change their ways. Those near at hand observed his ways and imitated them; those far off in surrounding states heard of them and took them for their model.

Three times Sunshu Ao was appointed prime minister, but he did not rejoice because he knew that it was no more than the natural result of his ability. Three times he was dismissed from the post, but he had no regrets, for he knew that his dismissal was not due to any fault of his own.

Zichan was one of the high ministers of the state of Zheng. When Lord Zhao of Zheng (seventh century BC) was ruler, he appointed his favourite, Xu Zhi, as prime minister of Zheng, but before long the state was in confusion, superiors and inferiors were at odds with each other, and fathers and sons quarrelled. Dagong Ziqi spoke to the ruler about this and had Zichan appointed as prime minister. After he had been prime minister one year, the children in the state had ceased their naughty behaviour, grey-haired elders were no longer seen carrying heavy burdens, and young boys did not have to work in the fields. After two years, no one overcharged in the markets. After three years, people stopped locking their gates at night and no one ventured to pick up articles that had been left by the roadside. After four years, people did not bother to take home their farm tools when the day's work was finished, and after five years, no more conscription orders were sent out to the knights. As for periods of mourning, people observed them without having to be told to do so. Zichan governed Zheng for twenty-six years, and when he died the young men wept and the old men cried like babies, saying, "Has Zichan gone away and left us? Who is there for the people to turn to now?"

Gongyi Xiu was an erudite of Lu. Because of his outstanding ability he was made prime minister. He upheld the law and went about his duties in a reasonable manner, not indulging in needless changes of procedure, so that all the officials under him naturally came to be upright. He stopped men who were receiving government salaries from scrambling for profit in competition with the common people and prevented those on generous stipends from accepting petty gifts and bribes.

Once one of his retainers sent him a fish, but he refused to accept the gift. "I always heard that you were fond of fish," said another of his retainers. "Now that someone has sent you a fish, why don't you accept it?"

"It is precisely because I am so fond of fish that I do not accept it," replied

Gongyi Xiu. "Now that I am prime minister I can afford to buy all the fish I want. But if I should accept this gift and lose my position as a result, who would ever provide me with fish again? Therefore I have not accepted it."

When he ate some home-grown vegetables and found them very tasty, he immediately pulled up all the vegetables in his garden and threw them away. At the same time, discovering that the cloth being woven by the maids in his house was very fine, he hastily turned them out of the house and burned their looms. "Growing vegetables at home and weaving cloth like this!" he exclaimed. "Do you want to make it so that the farmers and the weaving girls have no place to sell their goods?"

Shi She was prime minister under King Zhao of Chu (ca. 500 BC). He was a man of absolute honesty and integrity and never stooped to favouritism. Once when he was touring the outlying districts, he witnessed a murder on the road, but when he started to pursue the murderer, he discovered that it was his own father. He let his father go and, returning to the capital, had himself put in prison and sent a messenger to report to the king, "I have apprehended a murderer, who turned out to be my father. Now if I administer the legal punishment to my own father, I will be acting contrary to filial piety, while if I disregard the law and pardon him, I will be disloyal. For either offence I deserve the death penalty."

The king replied, "You pursued the murderer but you did not catch him, therefore you need not be punished. Just go about your duties as before!"

But Shi She sent word again, saying, "I would not be a filial son if I did not make an exception in the case of my own father. On the other hand, I would not be a loyal minister if I did not uphold the laws of my sovereign. Your Majesty may bestow mercy upon me by pardoning my offence, but it is still my duty as a subject to submit to punishment and die." In the end he refused to accept the pardon but cut his throat and died.

Li Li was director of prisons under Duke Wen of Jin (late seventh century BC). Once, discovering that an innocent man had been executed because of an error in the investigation conducted at his office, he had himself bound and announced that he deserved the death penalty. Duke Wen said to him, "There are high officials and low officials, and there are light punishments and severe ones. Just because one of the petty clerks in your office made a mistake there is no reason why you should take the blame."

But Li Li replied, "I occupy a position as head of this office and I have made no move to hand the post over to any of my subordinates. I receive a large salary and I have not shared the profits with those under me. Now because of an error in investigation an innocent man has been executed. I have never heard of a man in my position trying to shift the responsibility for such a crime to his subordinate officials!" Thus he declined to accept Duke Wen's suggestion.

"If you insist that, as a superior officer, you yourself are to blame," said Duke Wen, "then do you mean to imply that I too am to blame?"

"The director of prisons," said Li Li, "must abide by the laws which govern his post. If he mistakenly condemns a man to punishment, he himself must suffer punishment; if he mistakenly sentences a man to death, he himself must suffer death. Your Grace appointed me to this post precisely because you believed that I would be able to listen to difficult cases and decide doubtful points of law. But now since I have made a mistake in hearing a case and have executed an innocent man, I naturally deserve to die for my offence." So in the end he refused to listen to the duke's arguments but fell on his sword and died.

The Grand Historian remarks: Sunshu Ao spoke one word and the markets in the capital of Chu were restored to normal. At the death of Zichan the people of Zheng mourned and wept. When Master Gongyi saw the fine cloth the women were weaving, he drove them out of the house. Shi She chose death because he had let his father go, and thus King Zhao's fame spread abroad. Li Li fell on his sword because he had mistakenly executed a man, and so Duke Wen was able to maintain the laws of the state without partiality.

SHI JI 122: THE BIOGRAPHIES OF THE HARSH OFFICIALS

The people scorned agricultural pursuits and turned more and more to deceit, flouting the regulations and thinking up clever ways to evade the law. Good men could not lead them to a life of virtue; only the sternest and most severe treatment had any effect in controlling them. Thus I made "The Biographies of the Harsh Officials".

Confucius says, "If you lead the people with laws and control them with punishments, they will try to avoid the punishments but will have no sense of shame. But if you lead them with virtue and control them with rites, they will have a sense of shame and moreover will become good."[1] Lao Zi states, "The man of superior virtue does not appear to have any virtue; therefore he keeps his virtue. The man of inferior virtue cannot forget his virtue; therefore he has no virtue." He also says, "The more laws are promulgated, the more thieves and bandits there will be."[2]

The Grand Historian remarks: How true these words are! Laws and regulations are only the tools of government; they are not the spring from which flows the purity of good government or the pollution of bad.

Formerly, in the time of the Qin, the net of the law was drawn tightly about the empire and yet evil and deceit sprang up on all sides; in the end men thought of nothing but evading their superiors and no one could do anything to save the situation. At that time the law officials worked to bring about order, battling helplessly as though against fire or boiling water. Only the hardiest and cruellest of them were able to bear the strain of office and derive any satisfaction from the task; those who cared for justice and virtue were left to rot in insignificant posts. Therefore Confucius said, "In hearing litigations, I am no better than

---

[1] *Analects* II, 3.

[2] Lao Zi, *Daode jing* 38 and 57.

anyone else. What is necessary is to make it so that there are no more litigations!"[3] And Lao Zi said, "When the inferior man hears about the Way, he laughs out loud at it."[4]

These are no empty words!

When the Han arose, it lopped off the harsh corners of the Qin code and returned to an easy roundness, whittled away the embellishments and achieved simplicity; the meshes of the law were spread so far apart that a whale could have passed through. The law officials were honest and simple-hearted and did not indulge in evil, and the common people were orderly and content. So we see that good government depends upon virtue, not harshness.

In the time of Empress Lü we find one instance of a harsh official, a man named Hou Feng who oppressed the members of the imperial family and committed outrages against the high officials, but when the Lü clan was overthrown, he and all his family were arrested and done away with. Again, in the reign of Emperor Jing, we have the case of Chao Cuo who, combining learning with natural ability, was noted for his sternness. When the leaders of the Seven Kingdoms rose in revolt, however, they used their resentment against Chao Cuo as an excuse, and in the end Chao Cuo was executed. After him came such men as Zhi Du and Ning Cheng.

ZHI DU

Zhi Du was a native of Yang. He served as a palace attendant under Emperor Wen, and in the time of Emperor Jing was made a general of palace attendants. He had no qualms about voicing his criticisms openly and contradicting the high ministers to their faces at court.

Once he was attending the emperor on an outing to the Shanglin Park. Madam Jia, one of the emperor's concubines, had retired to the toilet when suddenly a wild boar rushed into the privy. The emperor signalled to Zhi Du to do something, but he refused to move, whereupon the emperor himself seized a weapon and was about to go to her rescue in person. Zhi Du flung himself on the ground before the emperor and said, "If you lose one lady in waiting, we will bring you another! The empire is full of women like Madam Jia. But what about Your Majesty? Though you think lightly of your own safety, what will

---

[3] *Analects* XII, 13.
[4] *Daode jing* 41.

become of the temples of your ancestors and of the empress dowager?"

With this, the emperor turned back, and the boar also withdrew. When the empress dowager heard of the incident, she rewarded Zhi Du with a gift of 100 catties of gold. From this time on the emperor treated Zhi Du with great respect.

At this time the Jian clan of Ji'nan, consisting of over 300 households, was notorious for its power and lawlessness, and none of the 2,000 picul officials could do anything to control it. Emperor Jing thereupon appointed Zhi Du as governor of Ji'nan. As soon as he reached the province, he executed the worst offenders among the Jian clan, along with the members of their families, and the rest were all overwhelmed with fear. After a year or so under Zhi Du's rule no one in the province dared even to pick up belongings that had been dropped in the road, and the governors of the ten or twelve provinces in the neighbourhood looked up to Zhi Du with awe as though he were one of the highest ministers of the court.

Zhi Du was a man of great daring and vigour. He was scrupulously honest and public-minded, and would never deign even to break the seal on letters addressed to him by private individuals. He refused to accept gifts from others or to listen to special requests, but always used to say, "I turned my back on parents and kin when I took office. All that remains for me to do is to fulfil my duties and die, if necessary, to maintain my integrity as an official." To the end of his life he never gave a thought to his wife or family.

Later, Zhi Du was moved to the post of military commander of the capital. The chancellor Zhou Yafu, the marquis of Tiao, was at the height of his power and behaved with great arrogance, but whenever Zhi Du appeared before Zhou Yafu, he would only greet Zhou Yafu with a low bow instead of the customary prostration.

At this time the common people were still simple-hearted and ingenuous; they had a genuine fear of breaking the law and took care to stay out of trouble. Zhi Du alone among the officials put sternness and severity above all other qualities and when it came to applying the letter of the law he made no exception even for the emperor's in-laws. The feudal lords and members of the imperial family all eyed him askance and nicknamed him "The Green Hawk".

Liu Rong, the king of Linjiang, was ordered to come to Chang'an and report to the office of the military commander of the capital to answer a list of charges which Zhi Du had drawn up against him. When he arrived, he asked if he might have a brush and scraper to write a letter of apology to the emperor, but Zhi Du forbade the clerks to give him any writing implements. Dou Ying, the marquis of Weiqi, however, sent someone to slip the writing implements to the king in secret, and so he was able to write his letter of apology, after which he committed suicide.[5] When Empress Dowager Dou heard of this she was furious and managed to have charges brought against Zhi Du. He was obliged to resign his post and retire to his home. Emperor Jing then dispatched an envoy bearing the imperial credentials to honour Zhi Du with the post of governor of Yanmen Province on the northern border. Because of the empress dowager's anger, the emperor did not require Zhi Du to come to the capital to receive the appointment but allowed him to proceed directly from his home to Yanmen and to carry out his new duties as he saw fit.

The Xiongnu had long heard of Zhi Du's strict loyalty and integrity, and when he arrived in Yanmen they withdrew their troops from the border; as long as Zhi Du was alive they would not come near the province. The Xiongnu leaders even went so far as to fashion a wooden image of Zhi Du which they ordered their mounted archers to use as a target for practice; but none of them were able to hit it, such was the fear that he inspired in them. He was a constant source of worry to the Xiongnu.

Empress Dowager Dou, however, finally managed to find some legal pretext for bringing charges against Zhi Du once more. "Zhi Du is a loyal subject," the emperor said to her, " and I would like to pardon him." But the empress dowager replied, "And the king of Linjiang — was he not a loyal subject too?" So in the end Zhi Du was executed.

NING CHENG

Ning Cheng was a native of Rang. He served under Emperor Jing as a palace attendant and master of guests. He was a man of great spirit. As long as he was a petty official, he thought of nothing but how he could outdo his superiors, and when he himself became a master of others, he treated the men under him like so much soggy firewood to be bound and bundled into shape. By cunning,

---

[5] Liu Rong was the oldest son of Emperor Jing. Originally the emperor appointed him as heir apparent, but later removed him from that position because of his annoyance at the prince's mother, Lady Li, and made him king of Linjiang instead. From his biography in *Han Dynasty* Volume 1, "Hereditary Houses of the Five Families", p. 398, it is obvious that Zhi Du drove the prince to suicide by his threats and accusations. Empress Dowager Dou never forgave Zhi Du for this harsh treatment of her grandson.

knavery, and displays of might, he gradually advanced until he had reached the post of chief commandant of Ji'nan.

At this time Zhi Du was the governor of Ji'nan. The men who had previously held the post of chief commandant of Ji'nan had always dismounted from their carriages and entered the governor's office on foot, requesting the clerks to grant them an interview with the governor as though they were no more than magistrates of districts; such was the awe with which they approached Zhi Du. When Ning Cheng took over as chief commandant, however, he soon made it clear that he was not only equal to Zhi Du but could outdo him. Zhi Du had long heard of Ning Cheng's reputation and was careful to treat him very well, so that the two became fast friends.

Some years later Zhi Du died, and the emperor, worried about the large number of outrages and crimes being committed by the members of the imperial family living in the capital, summoned Ning Cheng to Chang'an and appointed him as military commander of the capital. In restoring order, he imitated the ways of Zhi Du, though he was no match for Zhi Du in integrity. It was not long, however, before every member of the imperial family and of the other powerful clans was trembling in awe of him.

When Emperor Wu came to the throne he transferred Ning Cheng to the post of prefect of the capital. The emperor's in-laws, however, were assiduous in pointing out Ning Cheng's faults and finally managed to have him convicted of some crime. His head was shaved and he was forced to wear a convict's collar about his neck. At this time it was customary for any of the high officials who had been accused of a capital offence to commit suicide; very few of them would ever submit to actual punishment. Ning Cheng, however, allowed himself to be subjected to the severest punishment. Considering that he would never again be able to hold public office, he contrived to free himself from his convict's collar, forged the credentials needed to get him through the Pass, and escaped to his home in the east.

"An official who can't advance to a salary of 2,000 piculs or a merchant who can't make at least 10,000,000 cash is not fit to be called a man!" he declared. With this he bought 1,000 or so *qing* of hillside farm land on credit and hired several thousand poor families to work it for him. After a few years a general amnesty was issued, absolving him from his former offences. By this time he had accumulated a fortune of several thousand pieces of gold. He did any sort of daring feat that took his fancy, since he knew all the faults of the officials in the area. Whenever he went out he was accompanied by twenty or thirty mounted attendants, and he ordered the people of the area about with greater authority than the governor of the province.

ZHOUYANG YOU

Zhouyang You's father was originally named Zhao Jian. Because he was a maternal uncle of Liu Chang, the king of Huainan, he was enfeoffed as marquis of Zhouyang and consequently changed his family name from Zhao to Zhouyang. Zhouyang You, being related to the imperial family, was employed as a palace attendant and served under Emperors Wen and Jing. During the reign of Emperor Jing he became the governor of a province.

When Emperor Wu first came to the throne, most of the officials still governed with great circumspection and attention to justice, but Zhouyang You alone among the 2,000 picul officials established a new record for violence, cruelty, and wilfulness. In the case of people he liked he would twist the law around to have them set free; in the case of those he hated he would bend the law to any lengths to wipe them out. Whatever province he was appointed to he would not rest until he had brought about the destruction of its powerful families. If he was acting as governor, he would treat the chief commandant of the province as though he were no more than a district magistrate; and if he was acting as chief commandant, it would not be long before he had gone over the head of the governor and seized the power of government right out of his hands. He was fully as stubborn as Ji An, and as good at utilizing the letter of the law for evil ends as Sima An; though all three of these men ranked equally as 2,000 picul officials, if the other two happened to be riding in the same carriage with Zhouyang You, they would never venture to lounge side by side with him on the armrest.

Sometime later, when Zhouyang You was acting as chief commandant of Hedong, he became involved in a struggle for power with the governor of Hedong, Shengtu Gong, each bringing accusations against the other. Shengtu Gong was condemned to suffer punishment, but he cared too much for his honour to undergo the penalty and committed suicide instead. Zhouyang You was executed and his corpse exposed in the market place.

From the time of Ning Cheng and Zhouyang You on, prosecutions became more and more numerous and the people grew very clever at evading the law. The officials for the most part were men of the same type as Ning Cheng and Zhouyang You.

ZHAO YU AND ZHANG TANG

Zhao Yu was a native of Tai. He served originally as a clerk in his district and was later moved to a post in the capital. Because of his honesty he was appointed a clerk under the master of documents and served the grand commandant Zhou Yafu. When Zhou Yafu became chancellor, Zhao Yu was made a secretary to the chancellor. Everyone in the chancellor's office praised Zhao Yu for his honesty and fairness, but Zhou Yafu put little trust in him. "I know perfectly well that Zhao Yu would never do anything unfair," he remarked. "But he is too severe in applying the letter of the law. It would never do to appoint him to an important post such as chancellor!"

Under the present emperor, Zhao Yu continued to work away as a brush-and-scraper clerk, piling up merit and gradually advancing until he became imperial secretary. The emperor considered him a man of ability and even appointed him as a palace counsellor, setting him to work with Zhang Tang discussing and drawing up a number of new laws and statutes. They invented the laws that anyone who knowingly allows a criminal act to go unreported is as guilty as the criminal, and that officials may be prosecuted for the offences of their inferiors or their superiors in the same bureau. From this time on the laws were applied with increasing strictness.

Zhang Tang was a native of Du. His father worked as an aide in the city government of Chang'an. Once his father went out and left Zhang Tang, who was still a young boy at the time, to mind the house. When he returned he discovered that a rat had stolen a piece of meat. He was furious and beat Zhang Tang for his negligence. Zhang Tang set about digging up the rat's hole, caught the rat, and recovered what was left of the piece of meat. He then proceeded to indict the rat, beat it until it told its story, write out a record of its words, compare them with the evidence, and draw up a proposal for punishment. After this he took the rat and the meat out into the yard, where he held a trial, presented the charges, and crucified the rat. When his father saw what he was doing and examined the documents he had drawn up, he found to his astonishment that the boy had carried out the whole procedure like a seasoned prison official. After this he set his son to writing legal documents.

After his father died, Zhang Tang became a clerk in the Chang'an city government. Some years later it happened that the younger brother of Empress Dowager Wang, Tian Sheng, who was only an official at the time, was arrested in Chang'an. Zhang Tang did everything in his power to get Tian Sheng freed and, after his efforts proved successful and Tian Sheng had been released from prison and enfeoffed as marquis of Zhouyang, Tian Sheng became fast friends with Zhang Tang and introduced him to all his acquaintances among the nobility.

Zhang Tang served in the office of the prefect of the capital, acting as aide to Ning Cheng, who held the post of prefect at that time. Ning Cheng, recognizing Zhang Tang's honesty and impartiality, recommended him for a post in one of the higher ministries. On the basis of this recommendation he was promoted to the position of commandant of Mouling and was put in charge of the construction work there.[6]

When Tian Sheng's older brother Tian Fen, the marquis of Wuan, became chancellor, he selected Zhang Tang to act as his secretary. From time to time he praised Zhang Tang to the emperor, who appointed Zhang Tang to assist the imperial secretary and take over most of the latter's duties. He was responsible for investigating the charges of sorcery brought against Empress Chen and having her deposed, and he worked to root out and bring to justice all the members of her clique. The emperor, impressed by his ability, gradually promoted him until he made him a palace counsellor and put him to work with Zhao Yu drawing up a number of new statutes. Zhang Tang did his best to make the laws more severe and prevent the government officials from abusing their positions.

Later, Zhao Yu was transferred to the post of military commander of the capital and then was appointed privy treasurer, while Zhang Tang was made commandant of justice. The two men were close friends, Zhang Tang treating Zhao Yu like an older brother.

Zhao Yu was a very parsimonious and arrogant sort of person. From the time he first became an official he never once entertained any guests at his lodgings. Though the other high officials would sometimes go to call on him, he never returned their calls. He did everything he could to prevent his friends and acquaintances from coming to him with requests and sought to act wholly on his own without any advice from others. If he saw that someone was breaking the law, he would have him arrested at once, but he did not extend his investigations or attempt to ferret out the secret faults of his subordinates.

---

[6]The construction work was the building of Emperor Wu's mausoleum at Mouling, but since Sima Qian is writing during the reign of Emperor Wu, he avoids direct mention of the gloomy nature of the work.

Zhang Tang, on the other hand, was a very deceitful person who knew how to make use of his wisdom to get the better of others. When he was still a petty clerk he tried his hand at making a profit and was secretly friendly with Tian Jia, Yu Wengshu, and other wealthy merchants of Chang'an. Later, when he had risen to one of the nine highest ministerial posts in the government, he attracted some of the most eminent gentlemen in the empire to his side and, though he secretly disliked them, he made a pretence of admiring them.

The emperor at this time showed a great fondness for literature and learning, and Zhang Tang decided that when he was passing judgement in important cases it would be well to back up his decision with references to the Classics. He therefore asked some of the students and court erudites who were familiar with the *Book of Documents* and the *Spring and Autumn Annals* to act as his secretaries in the office of the commandant of justice and help in deciding on doubtful points of law. When he was presenting memorials to the throne concerning difficult cases, he would always inform the emperor beforehand of all the facts of the case. When the emperor had indicated what he thought was the right decision, Zhang Tang would then make a careful record of the emperor's decision and write it down among the statutes of the commandant of justice's office so that it could be used as a precedent in future cases and would make clear to all the wisdom of the ruler.

If the emperor happened to criticize his judgement in some case, he would accept the blame himself and apologize, claiming that he recognized the superior wisdom of the emperor's viewpoint. Then he would invariably mention the name of some worthy man among his aides or secretaries and say, "So-and-so expressed exactly the same opinion as Your Majesty, but I refused to listen to his advice and so I have committed this stupid blunder!" In such cases the emperor would always pardon him. At other times, when the emperor happened to praise him for some judgement, he would say, "I had nothing to do with preparing this memorial. It was drawn up by So-and-so" (mentioning the name of the one of his aides or secretaries). This was the way he worked to advance the officials in his office and make known their good points, at the same time covering up their faults.

In prosecuting cases, if he knew that the emperor was anxious to see the accused man condemned, he would turn the case over to his harshest and cruellest secretaries, but if he knew the emperor wanted the man pardoned, he would turn it over to secretaries who were more lenient and fair-minded. If he was dealing with a member of some rich and powerful family, he would invariably find a way to twist the law around and prove the man's guilt, but if it was someone from a poor and insignificant family, he would say to the emperor, "Although, according to the letter of the law, the man is guilty, I trust that Your Majesty will consider the matter in a generous light." As a result, many of the men whose cases Zhang Tang handled were pardoned.

After Zhang Tang became a high official he was very careful about his conduct.[7] He would entertain guests, dine and drink with his old friends, and look out for their sons and brothers who had become officials or their poor relations with extreme generosity. When it came to paying calls on others, he was not deterred by the hottest or the coldest weather. Thus, although he was severe in legal matters, suspicious and by no means impartial, he managed in this way to win fame and praise. Many of the sternest officials who acted as claws and teeth for him were students of the Classics who were studying under the erudites, and the chancellor Gongsun Hong, himself a scholar, often praised his virtues.

Later, when Zhang Tang investigated the charges that the kings of Huainan, Hengshan, and Jiangdu were plotting revolt, he succeeded in ferreting out all the facts of the case. The emperor wished to pardon Zhuang Zhu[8] and Wu Bei, who were implicated in the case, but Zhang Tang objected, saying, "Wu Bei took the lead in planning the revolt, and Zhuang Zhu was one of your most trusted ministers, coming and going in the palace and carrying out your missions, and yet he engaged in secret doings with one of the feudal lords. If men such as these are not executed, there will be no way to control the officials hereafter!" As a result, the emperor approved the death sentence which Zhang Tang had recommended.

There were many instances like this in which Zhang Tang, in the course of his prosecutions, brought about the downfall of high officials and won merit for himself. Thus he continued to enjoy greater and greater honour and trust and was finally transferred to the post of imperial secretary.

It was at this time that the Hunye king and his followers surrendered to the

---

[7] As opposed to his earlier days, when he associated with merchants and tried to make a profit, conduct which was considered highly degrading for an official.

[8] Zhuang Zhu has appeared earlier in the accounts of Southern and Eastern Yue as the emperor's envoy to those regions. His surname is sometimes written Yan instead of Zhuang. He later became a palace counsellor and enjoyed great favour with the emperor. He was very friendly with Liu An, the king of Huainan, and was therefore implicated when Liu An was accused of plotting revolt.

Han, and the government was busy raising large armies and sending them to attack the Xiongnu. The region east of the mountains was suffering from floods and droughts, and the poor and destitute were wandering from place to place, depending entirely upon the government for aid and sustenance, until the resources of the government were exhausted. Zhang Tang, acting on the suggestion of the emperor, proposed the minting of white metal coins and five-*shu* cash, and arranged for the government to take complete control of the salt and iron industries, removing them from the hands of the rich merchants and large-scale traders. He also drew up a law making it possible to confiscate the wealth of anyone attempting to evade the *suan* tax on his possessions and used it to bring about the ruin of the powerful families and great landowners, twisting the letter of the law around, devising clever ways to convict others, and patching up loopholes in the statutes. Whenever Zhang Tang would appear at court with some proposal and would begin to discuss the government's fiscal policy, the emperor would listen until sundown in rapt attention, forgetting even to take time out for meals. The chancellor soon became no more than a figurehead, all the affairs of the empire being decided by Zhang Tang.

But the common people continued to be restless and dissatisfied with their lot, and before the measures taken by the government to remedy the situation had had a chance to do any good, corrupt officials began utilizing them to snatch illegal gain. To prevent this, Zhang Tang made the punishments for violation of the law even more severe. Eventually everyone, from the highest officials down to the common people, was pointing an accusing finger at Zhang Tang.

Once, when Zhang Tang was ill, the emperor went in person to his bedside to see how he was: such was the respect and favour that Zhang Tang enjoyed.

When envoys from the Xiongnu came to court with requests for a peace alliance, the ministers deliberated their proposal in the presence of the emperor. One of the erudites named Di Shan suggested that it would be best to conclude a peace alliance and, when the emperor asked him to state his reasons, he replied, "Weapons are the instruments of ill fortune; they cannot be lightly resorted to time and again! Emperor Gaozu wanted to attack the Xiongnu, but after the extreme difficulties he encountered at Pingcheng he finally abandoned the idea and concluded a peace alliance. Thus during the reigns of Emperor Hui and Empress Dowager Lü the empire enjoyed peace and security. When Emperor Wen came to the throne he tried again to deal with the Xiongnu by force and the northern border was once more thrown into turmoil and forced to suffer the hardships of warfare. In the time of Emperor Jing, when the kings of Wu and

Chu and the other states raised the Revolt of the Seven Kingdoms, Emperor Jing spent several anxious and fearful months hurrying back and forth between his own palace and that of the empress dowager and planning how to deal with the situation, and once the revolt had finally been put down, Emperor Jing never again mentioned the subject of warfare. Thus under him the empire enjoyed wealth and plenty. Now, since Your Majesty has again called out the armies to attack the Xiongnu, the resources of China have become more and more depleted and the people on the border are troubled by severe poverty and hardship. In view of this situation, I believe that it would be better to conclude a peace alliance."

The emperor then asked Zhang Tang what he thought of this statement, and Zhang Tang answered, "This man is only a stupid Confucianist. He knows nothing about such matters!"

"It is quite true that my loyalty is the loyalty of the stupid," replied Di Shan. "But the loyalty of the imperial secretary Zhang Tang is deceitful and meretricious! Look how he prosecuted the kings of Huainan and Jiangdu, applying the law with the utmost severity and forcing the kings into a position of guilt, bringing about estrangement between the ruler and his own blood relations and filling the other feudal lords with anxiety! This is quite enough to convince me that Zhang Tang's so-called loyalty is meretricious!"

The emperor's face flushed and he said, "Master Di, if I made you the governor of a province do you think you could keep the barbarian wretches from plundering the region?"

"No, I could not," replied Di Shan.

"Suppose I made you the magistrate of a district?"

"No," Di Shan replied again.

"Or the commander of a guard post on the border?"

Di Shan realized that he could not argue his way out of the situation and that if he did not say yes he would be handed over to the law officials for trial. So he replied, "In that case I could do it."

The emperor then sent Di Shan to take command of one of the guard posts on the border. A month or so after he arrived there the Xiongnu raided the post, cut off Di Shan's head, and withdrew. After this the other officials were all too terrified to say a word.

Among Zhang Tang's friends was a certain Tian Jia who, although a merchant, was a man of worth and upright in conduct. When Zhang Tang was still a petty official, he carried on various money dealings with Tian Jia, but after he became a high minister Tian Jia scolded Zhang Tang about his behaviour and warned him of his faults in the manner of a truly virtuous man.

Zhang Tang's downfall occurred seven years after he assumed the post of imperial secretary and came about in the following way. There was a man from Hedong named Li Wen who had once had a falling out with Zhang Tang. Later he became an assistant in the office of the imperial secretary, but he continued to bear a fierce grudge against Zhang Tang and from time to time, whenever he was able to discover some point in the documents handled by the office that would reflect to Zhang Tang's discredit, he saw that it was made known and that Zhang Tang was given no opportunity to escape responsibility. One of Zhang Tiang's favourite secretaries, a man named Lu Yeju, knew that Zhang Tang was worried about the situation and therefore got someone to submit an anonymous emergency report to the emperor accusing Li Wen of disaffection and evil-doing. The case was referred to Zhang Tang, who conducted an investigation and ordered Li Wen's execution. Zhang Tang knew quite well that Lu Yeju had engineered the move to relieve him from worry, but when the emperor asked Zhang Tang, "Who do you suppose it was that first brought the charges of disaffection against Li Wen?" Zhang Tang pretended to be completely at a loss and replied, "I suppose it must have been some old acquaintance of Li Wen's who had a grudge against him."

Some time after this Lu Yeju fell ill and was put to bed in the home of a friend in his neighbourhood. Zhang Tang went in person to see how he was and even massaged his legs for him.

The kingdom of Zhao was the site of an important smelting industry, and the king of Zhao on several occasions had brought suit against the iron officials of the central government for the way they were running the industry, but Zhang Tang had always dismissed the complaints. The king of Zhao then began to look around for evidence of some secret doings of Zhang Tang that he could use as a weapon against him. In addition, Lu Yeju had in the past once had occasion to draw up charges against the king of Zhao, and the king hated him as well. The king therefore submitted a memorial to the throne accusing both Zhang Tang and Lu Yeju and charging that Zhang Tang, although a high minister, had visited his secretary Lu Yeju, when the latter was ill and had even gone so far as to massage Lu's legs for him. There were grounds, he suggested, for suspecting that the two were plotting some major crime. The case was referred to the commandant of justice of investigation.

Lu Yeju meanwhile died of his illness, but the investigations implicated his younger brother, who was arrested and imprisoned in the office of the grain selector.⁹ Zhang Tang had occasion to cross-examine some other prisoner in the grain selector's office and at that time he saw Lu Yeju's brother but, hoping to find some way to help him secretly, he deliberately pretended not to recognize him. The brother, not realizing this, was deeply resentful and got someone to send a memorial to the throne accusing Zhang Tang and Lu Yeju of conspiring together to bring false charges of disaffection against Li Wen. The case was referred to Jian Xuan who, being on bad terms with Zhang Tang, was only too happy to have this opportunity to conduct a thorough investigation.

Before Jian Xuan had had a chance to submit the results of his investigation to the emperor, however, it was discovered that someone had broken into the funerary park of Emperor Wen and dug up and stolen the offerings of money that had been buried in the mausoleum. When the chancellor Qing Di arrived at court, he and Zhang Tang agreed that, as the two highest ministers, they should both present their apologies to the emperor for the crime. After the two men appeared before the emperor, however, Zhang Tang indicated that, since it was the duty of the chancellor to make seasonal inspections of the funerary parks, it was proper for the chancellor alone to make the apologies for the crime. As he himself had nothing to do with such affairs, there was no reason for him to apologize, he said. The chancellor accordingly submitted his apologies and the emperor referred the case to Zhang Tang for investigation. Zhang Tang then set about trying to prove that the chancellor had deliberately failed to report the theft, until the chancellor became concerned about his own safety. The chancellor's three chief secretaries, Zhu Maichen, Wang Chao, and Bian Tong, all hated Zhang Tang and began looking about for ways to trip him up.

The chief secretary, Zhu Maichen was a native of Kuaiji. He was recommended to the emperor by Zhuang Zhu because of his knowledge of the *Spring and Autumn Annals*; he and Zhuang Zhu, who were both from the region of Chu and were versed in the *Elegies of Chu*,¹⁰ enjoyed great favour with the emperor, serving in the palace and taking part in government affairs as palace counsellors. At this time Zhang Tang was still only a petty clerk and used to get down on his knees before Zhu Maichen and the others and take orders from them. Later, when Zhang Tang became commandant of justice and was put in charge of

---

⁹Zhang Tang had managed to fill all the regular jails to capacity, and it became necessary to use the office of the grain selector to house the overflow.

¹⁰The collection of poems by the Chu poet Qu Yuan and his disciples and imitators.

investigating the king of Huainan and his fellow conspirators, he brought about the downfall of Zhuang Zhu, and from that time on Zhu Maichen hated Zhang Tang intensely. When Zhang Tang became imperial secretary, Zhu Maichen, who was governor of Kuaiji at the time, was made master of titles chief commandant, ranking among the nine highest ministers of the government. A few years later he was tried for some offence and removed from his post and made a chief secretary. Whenever he had occasion to visit Zhang Tang, the latter would receive him perched on a couch, treating Zhu Maichen like a petty clerk and refusing to show him any respect. Zhu Maichen, being a true man of Chu, burned with indignation and was constantly looking for some way to bring about Zhang Tang's death.

The second of the chancellor's three chief secretaries was Wang Chao, a native of Qi who reached the post of right prefect of the capital because of his knowledge of legal matters. The third was Bian Tong, a stubborn and violent-tempered man who studied the strategies of the Warring States period and twice served as prime minister of Ji'nan. Thus all three of these men had previously held higher posts than Zhang Tang but had later lost them and become chief secretaries. As a result they were forced to bow and scrape before Zhang Tang who, knowing that they had formerly been highly honoured, never lost an opportunity to humiliate them in his frequent dealings with the chancellor's office.

The three of them plotted together and said to the chancellor, "Originally Zhang Tang promised to apologize with you, but later he betrayed his promise. Now he is trying to impeach you for what happened at the grave of Emperor Wen. It is obvious that he simply wants to get you out of the way so that he himself can replace you as chancellor. But we know all about his secret dealings!" Then they sent law officers to arrest Tian Xin and others of Zhang Tang's merchant friends, and got them to give evidence against Zhang Tang. "Whenever Zhang Tang was about to present some proposal to the emperor," Tian Xin stated, "he would let me know about it beforehand. In that way I was able to buy up whatever goods would be affected by the proposal and hoard them until the price had gone up. Then I would split the profits with Zhang Tang." Tian Xin also revealed other corrupt practices of Zhang Tang, all of which were reported to the emperor. The emperor said to Zhang Tang, "Whenever I do something, the merchants always seem to find out about it beforehand and start busily buying up the articles that will be affected. It would almost appear as though someone were deliberately informing them of my plans!"

Zhang Tang made no admission of guilt but instead pretended to be completely taken aback and exclaimed, "Why yes, that must be what is happening!"

Meanwhile Jian Xuan submitted his report to the emperor on Zhang Tang's involvements with Lu Yeju and the other charges which he had investigated. The emperor finally became convinced that Zhang Tang was guilty of deceit and had been cheating him before his very eyes. He dispatched eight envoys with a list of charges to confront Zhang Tang. Zhang Tang denied all of them and refused to make any admission of guilt, whereupon the emperor sent Zhao Yu to press the charges once more. When Zhao Yu appeared, he began to berate Zhang Tang, saying, "After all the men you have tried and condemned to execution along with their families, don't you even realize what your own position is now? Every charge that people have brought against you is backed up by evidence! The emperor would hate to have to send you to prison. Instead he hopes that you will settle things for yourself! What do you expect to gain by denying the charges?"

Zhang Tang then wrote a letter of apology, saying, "I, though a man of no merit whatsoever, rose from the position of a brush-and-scraper clerk and, through Your Majesty's generosity, became one of the three highest ministers in the government. Though I have failed in my duties, it is the three chief secretaries of the chancellor who have plotted to bring about my ruin." Then he committed suicide (116 BC).

After his death it was found that he had no more than 500 pieces of gold in his home, all of which he had received as salary or gifts from the emperor; outside of this he left no estate whatsoever. His brothers and sons wanted to give him a lavish burial, but his mother objected. "Although Tang was one of the highest ministers of the emperor, he got a name for corruption and evil and had to kill himself. Why give *him* a lavish burial?" So in the end they carried his coffin to the graveyard in an oxcart and buried him with only an inner coffin and no outer one. When the emperor heard of the incident he remarked, "If she weren't that kind of mother she could never have borne that kind of son!"

The emperor then had charges brought against all three of the chief secretaries and executed them; the chancellor Qing Di committed suicide. Tian Xin was pardoned and released. The emperor felt sorry for what had happened to Zhang Tang and promoted his son Zhang Anshi to a higher post in the government.

Zhao Yu had once been deprived of his post but was later appointed as commandant of justice. Earlier in his career Zhou Yafu had refused to trust him, saying that he was much too intent upon harming others and applying the law with severity; later, when Zhao Yu became privy treasurer and ranked with the nine highest ministers of the government, he did indeed become one of the harshest of the officials. In his old age, however, as the number of criminal cases continued to increase and the other officials all worked to apply the laws with the greatest possible sternness, Zhao Yu became more lenient in his prosecutions and won a reputation for fairness. Later, when men like Wang Wenshu appeared on the scene, they were much harsher than Zhao Yu. In his old age he was transferred to the post of prime minister of Yan, which he held for several years until he became senile and, committing some blunder, was forced to retire to private life. Some ten or more years after Zhang Tang's suicide Zhao Yu died of old age in his own home.

YI ZONG

Yi Zong was a native of Hedong. When he was young he and a friend named Zhang Cigong became highwaymen and formed a band of thieves. His older sister Yi Xu had won favour with Empress Dowager Wang because of her knowledge of medicine, and one day the empress dowager asked her if she had any brothers who might be appointed to posts in the government. "I have a younger brother," she replied, "but he is worthless and could never be appointed." The empress dowager nevertheless reported her words to the emperor, who made her brother Yi Zong a palace attendant and appointed him as magistrate of one of the districts in Shangdang Province. He governed with great determination and little leniency, and no one in the district was behind time in paying taxes. Having won an outstanding record there, he was transferred to the post of magistrate of Changling and Chang'an. He applied the laws with honesty and directness and made no exceptions even for the emperor's in-laws. When he arrested and tried Zhong, the son of Lady Xiucheng, Empress Dowager Wang's granddaughter, the emperor concluded that he was a man of ability and transferred him to the post of chief commandant of Henei. When he reached Henei he succeeded in wiping out the powerful Rong family that lived in that province, and the people of Henei were soon too frightened even to pick up objects that had been dropped in the road.

Zhang Cigong was also appointed a palace attendant and, being a brave and reckless man, joined the army and won merit by daring to fight his way deep into the enemy lines. He was enfeoffed as marquis of Antou.

Ning Cheng was at this time living in retirement and the emperor wanted to make him the governor of a province, but the imperial secretary Gongsun Hong said, "When I was still a petty official and living east of the mountains, Ning Cheng was serving as chief commandant of Ji'nan. He ruled the inhabitants like a wolf driving a flock of sheep — it would never do to let him govern the people of a province!"

The emperor instead appointed Ning Cheng as chief commandant of the Hangu Pass. After he had been in this post for a year or so, the officials from the provinces and kingdoms east of the Pass who had had occasion to go in or out of the Pass used to say to each other, "Better to face a nursing tigress than the wrath of Ning Cheng!"

Later, Yi Zong was transferred to the post of governor of Nanyang. He had heard that Ning Cheng had retired and was living at his home, which was in Nanyang, but when he reached the Pass he found that Ning Cheng had very politely come to greet him and escort him on his way. Yi Zong, however, treated the matter very lightly and did not deign to return the courtesy. When he got to Nanyang he proceeded to bring charges against the Ning family and had their houses completely destroyed. Even Ning Cheng himself was convicted of some offence. The members of the Kong, Bao, and other powerful families all fled from the province, and the rest of the officials and people of Nanyang went around on tiptoe for fear of breaking some law. Zhu Qiang of Pingshi and Du Zhou of Duyan served under Yi Zong, acting as his teeth and claws in applying the law, and were later transferred and made secretaries in the office of the commandant of justice.

The armies had from time to time marched out of Dingxiang Province to attack the Xiongnu, and the officials and people of that province had been thrown into turmoil by their presence. The emperor therefore transferred Yi Zong to the post of governor of Dingxiang. When he reached the province he made a surprise visit to the jail, seized over 200 prisoners accused of major and minor crimes, along with another 200 or so of their friends and relatives who had slipped into the jail to visit them, and had the entire group arrested and tried at once. "These men were plotting to free prisoners who deserved to die!" he announced, indicating the friends and relatives of the prisoners, and in one day passed sentence on the entire group of over 400 and had them all executed. Though the season was warm enough, the entire province shivered and trembled, and the more cunning and rascally among the people hurried forward to make themselves useful to the officials.

At this time Zhao Yu and Zhang Tang had advanced to the highest posts in the government through their severe application of the law, but their ways were mild compared with Yi Zong's and at least had a legal basis. Yi Zong governed like a hawk spreading its wings and swooping down upon its prey.

Sometime later, when the five-*shu* and white metal coins were put into circulation, the people resorted to all sorts of evil practices to make a profit, those living in the capital being among the worst offenders. The emperor therefore appointed Yi Zong as right prefect of the capital and Wang Wenshu as military commander of the capital. Wang Wenshu was one of the harshest officials. If he did not inform Yi Zong in advance of what he was going to do, Yi Zong would invariably use his influence to wreck Wang Wenshu's plans and turn his successes into failures. Between them they executed an extraordinary number of people, but the effect of such measures was only temporary, and the offenders continued to increase until it became impossible to deal with them all. At this time the posts of imperial inquisitor were set up, the officials spent all their time arresting people and cutting off heads, and men like Yan Feng were appointed to office because of their severity. Yi Zong was scrupulously honest and in this point resembled Zhi Du.

It was at this time that the emperor was taken ill while visiting Cauldron Lake and was forced to remain there for some time. After he had recovered, he made a sudden trip to the Palace of Sweet Springs and on the way he noticed that the road was in bad repair. "Did Yi Zong think I would never have occasion to use this road again?" he remarked angrily, and seemed to be very upset by the incident.

When winter came, Yang Ke was put in charge of hearing accusations against men who had failed to report their possessions for the property tax. Yi Zong believed that this procedure would throw the people into turmoil, and he therefore sent out his officials to arrest Yang Ke's agents. When the emperor heard of this, he ordered Du Shi to investigate the case. Yi Zong was convicted of disobeying an imperial edict and impeding the business of the government and was executed and his corpse exposed in the market place. This happened a year before Zhang Tang's death.

WANG WENSHU

Wang Wenshu was a native of Yangling. In his youth he robbed graves and committed similar evil deeds, but later he was given a trial post as village head in one of the districts. Though he was removed from this position several times, he finally managed to become an official and was made a secretary in the office of the commandant of justice, handling criminal affairs under Zhang Tang. He was transferred to the office of the imperial secretary and put in charge of suppressing robbers and bandits, in which capacity he had occasion to execute an extraordinary number of men. Sometime later, he was transferred to the post of chief commandant of Guangping. There he selected some ten or more daring men from the powerful families of the province whom he believed worthy to be employed as his officials and had them act as teeth and claws for him. Meanwhile he ferreted out all of their secret crimes, but overlooked what he had found and put them in charge of capturing the bandits in the region. So long as they did as he wished and brought in the bandits he wanted captured, he did not press charges against them, even though they might be guilty of 100 crimes. But if they allowed any of the bandits to escape, then he would utilize the information he had gathered to prosecute them and would not rest until he had wiped out their whole families. As a result of this policy, none of the bandits in the region of Qi and Zhao dared come near Guangping, and the province gained a reputation for being so strictly governed that people would not even pick up objects that had been dropped in the road.

The emperor, hearing of this, transferred Wang Wenshu to the post of governor of Henei. Wang Wenshu had already learned during his stay in Guangping who all the powerful and lawless families of Henei were. When he reached his new post in the ninth month, he got together fifty privately owned horses from the province and had them disposed at the various post stations between Henei and the capital for later use. In appointing his officials he followed the same strategy that he had used in Guangping and had soon arrested all the powerful and crafty men in the province. By the time they had been investigated and tried, over 1,000 families were implicated in their guilt. He then sent a letter to the throne asking that the major offenders be executed along with the members of their families, the lesser offenders put to death, and all their estates confiscated by the government to compensate for the illegal gains which they had gotten in the past. He forwarded the letter by means of the post horses he had stationed along the way, and in no more than two or three days an answer came back from the emperor approving his proposal. He proceeded to carry out the sentence at once, and the blood flowed for miles around. The whole province was astounded at the supernatural speed with which his proposal had been carried to the capital and approved, and by the time the twelfth month ended no one in the province dared speak a word against him. People no longer ventured out of their houses at night and there was not a single bandit left to set the dogs in the fields to barking. The few offenders who had managed to escape arrest and had fled to neighbouring provinces and kingdoms found themselves pursued even there.

When the beginning of spring came Wang Wenshu stamped his foot and sighed, "Ah! If only I could make the winter last one more month I could finish my work to satisfaction!"[11] Such was his fondness for slaughter and demonstrations of power and his lack of love for others. When the emperor heard of this he concluded that Wang Wenshu was a man of ability and transferred him to the post of military commander of the capital.

He proceeded the same way in this post as he had in Henei, summoning all of the most notoriously cruel and cunning officials to aid him in his work, such as Yang Jie and Ma Wu of Henei, and Yang Gong and Cheng Xin from within the Pass. At this time Yi Zong was acting as prefect of the capital, and Wang Wenshu, who was rather afraid of Yi Zong, did not dare to do everything he would have liked to do. Later, when Yi Zong was executed and Zhang Tang fell from power, Wang Wenshu was transferred to the post of commandant of justice and Yin Qi replaced him as military commander of the capital.

Yin Qi was a native of Shiping in Dong Province. From the position of a brush-and-scraper clerk he gradually advanced until he had become a secretary in the office of Zhang Tang, the imperial secretary. Zhang Tang often praised him for his integrity and fearlessness and put him in charge of suppressing bandits. When it came to ordering executions, Yin Qi did not make exceptions even for the emperor's in-laws. He was transferred to the post of chief commandant of the area within the Pass, where his reputation for sternness surpassed that of Ning Cheng. The emperor, concluding that he was a man of ability, made him military commander of the capital, and the officials and people under him were driven to even greater exhaustion and destitution.

Yin Qi was a boorish man with little refinement or learning. Under his administration the powerful and evil officials all went into hiding, while the good officials were unable to carry out his policies, so that things were continually going wrong in his office and he was even convicted of some fault. With this, the emperor transferred Wang Wenshu back to the post of military commander of the capital. It was at this time that Yang Pu won the post of master

---

[11] Because capital punishments could not be carried out in the spring months.

of titles chief commandant because of his harshness and severity.

Yang Pu was a native of Yiyang. By purchasing the military rank of *qianfu* he managed to become an official and was recommended for his ability by the governor of Henan. He advanced to a post in the office of the imperial secretary and was put in charge of suppressing bandits in the region east of the Pass, where he carried out his duties in the fashion of Yin Qi, swooping down upon his victims with the fierceness of a hawk. He continued to advance gradually until he became master of titles chief commandant and ranked among the nine highest officials. The emperor considered him a man of ability and, when the kingdom of Southern Yue rebelled, appointed him as General of Towered Ships and sent him to attack the rebels. He won merit in this campaign and was enfeoffed as marquis of Liang. When he was sent on another campaign, this time to Chaoxian (Korea), he was arrested by his fellow commander Xun Zhi and was reduced to the rank of commoner. He died some time later of illness.

As has been stated above, Wang Wenshu was once more appointed to the post of military commander of the capital after the failure of Yin Qi. Wang Wenshu was a man of little refinement, and when he appeared in court he appeared rather stupid and confused and could never express himself clearly. When he reached the post of military commander of the capital, however, he seemed to find his element and set about suppressing thieves and bandits with great enthusiasm. Since he was a native of the area, he was thoroughly familiar with the customs of the people in the region within the Pass and knew all the powerful and evil officials. The latter for their part did all they could to assist him in carrying out his policies and kept a close watch for thieves, bandits, and young men of bad character. He put out boxes in which people could deposit accusations and reports of crimes, for which the accusers would receive a reward, and set up chiefs in the villages and rural communities to watch for and arrest bandits.

Wang Wenshu was very much of a toady, playing up to people who had power and treating like so many slaves those who did not. In the case of really powerful families, although they had committed a mountain of crimes he would never bother them, but if he were dealing with people who had no real power, he would invariably impose upon them and insult them, even though they might be in-laws of the emperor himself. He would twist the law around in clever ways and bring about the ruin of all sorts of petty rogues in order to intimidate the more powerful families and show them what he could do if he wanted to. This was the way he carried out his duties as military commander of the capital.

Under his administration knaves and evil-doers were subjected to the most thorough investigation; most of them were beaten to a pulp in prison, and none was ever known to have refuted the charges brought against him and got out of prison alive. The officials who acted as his teeth and claws were no better than tigers with hats on. In this way he forced all the lesser rogues in the area under his jurisdiction to their knees, while the more powerful ones went around singing his praises and commending the way he governed. During the several years of his administration many of the officials under him were able to utilize his authority to accumulate fortunes.

Later, he was sent to take part in the campaign against the kingdom of Eastern Yue, which had rebelled, and on his return the report he made did not entirely meet with the emperor's approval. He was accused of some trifling fault, tried, and dismissed from the post of military commander of the capital.

Just at this time the emperor was planning to construct the Terrace that Reaches to Heaven, but he had not been able to get together enough workmen. Wang Wenshu then asked to be allowed to round up all the men under the jurisdiction of the military commander of the capital who should have been conscripted for service earlier but who had managed to evade their duty, and was able in this way to get together a force of 20,000 or 30,000 men. The emperor was delighted and appointed him to the post of privy treasurer; later he transferred him to that of right prefect of the capital. Wang Wenshu continued to carry out his duties in the same way as before, doing little to prevent evil and corruption, and was accused of some fault and removed from office. Later he was restored to office as right military commander, carrying out the same duties which he had earlier as military commander of the capital. He continued to behave as before.

A year or so later preparations were begun to send an army against Dayuan (Ferghana) and an imperial edict was issued summoning various powerful officials to take service in the campaign. Wang Wenshu contrived to hide one of his subordinates named Hua Cheng from the conscription. Shortly afterwards, someone sent in a report of disloyalty, accusing Wang of having accepted bribes from the regular members of his cavalry force in exchange for military exemption, and of other corrupt doings. Wang and his three sets of relatives were sentenced to execution; he himself committed suicide. At the same time, Wang's two younger brothers, along with their wives' families, were accused of some other crime and sentenced to execution. The superintendent of the imperial household Xu Ziwei remarked, "Alas! In ancient times men were condemned to die along with their three sets of relatives, but Wang Wenshu's crime was so great, it seems, that five sets of relatives had to be executed at one time!"[12] After Wang's death it was found that the fortunes of his family were equal in value to some 1,000 pieces of gold.

A few years later Yin Qi died of illness while holding the post of chief commandant of Huaiyang. He left behind him an estate of less than fifty pieces of gold. He had been responsible for the execution of a very large number of people in Huaiyang, and when he died the families which bore grudges against him planned to seize his corpse and burn it. The members of his own family were obliged to conceal the corpse and flee with it to his old home before they could bury it.

From the time when Wang Wenshu demonstrated the way to rule by harshness, all the governors and chief commandants of the provinces, the feudal lords and 2,000 picul officials who wanted to rule effectively began to imitate his ways. The lower officials and people more and more came to regard law-breaking as a trifling matter, and the number of thieves and bandits continued to increase until there were men like Mei Mian and Bai Zheng in Nanyang, Yin Zhong and Du Shao in Chu, Xu Bo in Qi, and Jian Lu and Fan Sheng in the region of Yan and Zhao. The more powerful of these gathered bands numbering several thousand men, assumed any title they pleased, attacked cities, seized the weapons from the arsenals, freed the convicts, bound and humiliated the governors and chief commandants of the provinces, killed the 2,000 picul officials, and circulated proclamations through the districts demanding that they be supplied with food. The lesser ones formed robber bands of a few hundred men, plundering the villages and hamlets in numbers too great to be counted.

The emperor first tried appointing the aides of the imperial secretary and chief secretaries of the chancellor to remedy the situation, but when they failed to achieve any success, he sent out Fan Kun (one of the lords under the superintendent of the imperial household), the military commanders of the capital, and men such as Zhang De, who had formerly been very high officials,

---

[12] The three sets of relatives are the families of the father, mother, and wife of the condemned man. In Wang Wenshu's case two more families, those of his two younger brothers, were executed at the same time.

dressed in brocade robes and bearing the imperial credentials and the tiger seals, to call out the troops and attack the bandits. They began cutting off heads in great numbers, sometimes as many as 10,000 or more at one time, and when they started arresting people for aiding and giving supplies of food to the bandits, the number of persons involved swelled at times to several thousand, the inhabitants of several provinces being implicated in one investigation.

After a few years of this most of the leaders of the robber bands had been caught and the others had scattered and fled into hiding. It was not long, however, before they began to gather again in the mountain and river fastnesses and to form new bands here and there. At a loss to know how to deal with them, the government promulgated the so-called concealment law, which stated: "If bandits arise and their presence is not reported, or if the full number are not arrested after their presence has been reported, everyone responsible, from the 2,000 picul officials down to the lowest clerks, will be executed."

After this the minor officials, terrified of punishment, did not dare to report the presence of bandits, even though they were aware of it, for fear that they would not be able to capture them all and that the investigations would involve them with the provincial office. The provincial offices for their part were only too anxious to have the lower officials remain silent. As a result, the number of bandits began gradually to increase again, but both the higher and lower officials conspired to conceal the fact and sent in false reports to the central government in order to save themselves from involvement with the law.

JIAN XUAN

Jian Xuan was a native of Yang. Having won a reputation for impartiality as a district secretary, he was promoted to serve in the provincial office of Hedong. General Wei Qing employed him to purchase horses for him in Hedong and, observing that he was very fair in carrying out his duties, recommended him to the emperor. Jian Xuan was summoned to the capital and made an aide in the imperial stables, where he fulfilled his duties with great competence. He was gradually advanced to the post of secretary and then of aide to the imperial secretary. He was in charge of the prosecution of Zhufu Yan and, later, of the conspirators involved in the king of Huainan's plans for revolt. He paid strict attention to the letter of the law and applied it with great severity, bringing about the death of a very large number of people, and at the same time achieved a reputation for his decisiveness in settling doubtful cases. He was occasionally dismissed from office, but was always reappointed, and served some twenty years as a secretary and aide under the imperial secretary.

When Wang Wenshu was dismissed from the post of military commander of the capital, Jian Xuan was appointed left prefect of the capital. He attended to every detail in the area under his jurisdiction down to the very grain and salt consumed; all matters, great and small passed through his hands. He even doled out the supplies to the various district offices in person in order to prevent the district magistrates and their aides from drawing and handling supplies in any way they wished. He maintained order by applying the law with the utmost severity, and during his several years in office every affair in the province, down to the most trifling, was perfectly arranged. However, only a man like Jian Xuan could have personally attended to every matter, from the smallest to the largest, in this way. It would be difficult to expect 'such behaviour from all officials.

Later he was removed from his post and appointed supervisor of the right district of the capital. He bore a grudge against one of his subordinate officials named Cheng Xin, who subsequently fled and hid in the Shanglin Park. Jian Xuan ordered the district magistrate of Mei to have Cheng Xin sought out and killed, and when the magistrate's guards located him and shot at him, some of their arrows struck the gate of the emperor's garden in the park. Jian Xuan was charged with the responsibility for the incident and was handed over to the law officials for trial. He was convicted of high treason and was sentenced to die along with the members of his family, but he anticipated the sentence by taking his own life. After this Du Zhou came to power.

DU ZHOU

Du Zhou was a native of Duyan in Nanyang. While Yi Zong was acting as governor of Nanyang, he employed Du Zhou as one of his subordinates. Later, Du Zhou was promoted to secretary in the office of the commandant of justice and served under Zhang Tang. Zhang Tang frequently commended him to the emperor for his impartiality, and in time he was appointed to the office of the imperial secretary and put in charge of investigating the losses of men, animals, and supplies that were taking place in the border regions. He was responsible for condemning a very large number of persons to execution. His proposals always won the approval of the emperor, and he enjoyed the same degree of confidence that Jian Xuan did. He and Jian Xuan took turns serving as aides to the imperial secretary for over ten years, and Du Zhou imitated Jian Xuan's ways, though Du Zhou had a much more grave and sedate bearing. On the surface Du Zhou appeared to be tolerant, but at heart he had a severity that cut to the bone.

When Jian Xuan was appointed left prefect of the capital, Du Zhou was made commandant of justice. He carried out the duties of this office in much the same way that Zhang Tang had, and in addition he was very skilful at divining the ruler's wishes. If the emperor wanted to get rid of someone, Du Zhou would proceed to find some way to trap the victim; if the emperor wanted someone let free, Du Zhou would keep the person bound in prison for an indefinite period awaiting further instructions, meanwhile doing all he could to make it seem that the person had been unjustly accused.

Once one of his guests chided him about this, saying, "You are supposed to be the dispenser of justice for the Son of Heaven, and yet you pay no attention to the statute books, but simply decide cases in any way that will accord with the wishes of the ruler. Do you really think that is the way a law official should be?"

"And where, may I ask, did the statute books come from in the first place?" replied Du Zhou. "Whatever the earlier rulers thought was right they wrote down in the books and made into laws, and whatever the later rulers thought was right they added as new clauses and stipulations. Anything that suits the present age is right. Why bother with the laws of former times?"

After Du Zhou became commandant of justice the flood of cases referred to his office by imperial command grew larger and larger. The number of officials of the 2,000 picul class in prison, counting old and new arrests, never fell below 100 or more men. All cases involving the provincial officials, as well as those of the high ministries in the capital, were referred to the commandant of justice, who handled over 1,000 of them a year. In important cases, several hundred men would be arrested or called in to act as witnesses, and even in less important cases the number was twenty or thirty. Men living anywhere from several hundred *li* to several thousand *li* away were summoned to the capital for investigation. When a case was being tried, the prison officials would confront the accused with a list of charges, and if he refused to acknowledge his guilt they would beat him until they had forced a confession. For this reason anyone who heard that he was to be arrested would flee into hiding. Although several amnesties might have been issued in the meantime, men were held in prison for indefinite periods of time and not released. In other cases men who had been in hiding for over ten years were accused when they were found and were almost always tried for immoral conduct or some even more serious charge. In time, the commandant of justice and the other law officials of the capital had succeeded in arresting 60,000 or 70,000 persons on imperial order, while the officials found legal grounds for bringing charges against another 100,000 or more.

Later Du Zhou was dismissed from the post of commandant of justice and then reappointed as military commander of the capital.[13] He worked to rid the area of thieves, and was responsible for the arrest and prosecution of Sang Hongyang and the brothers of Empress Wei, whom he prosecuted with great severity. The emperor admired him for his untiring efforts and impartiality and promoted him to the post of imperial secretary. His two sons became governors of the provinces of Henei and Henan on either side of the Yellow River and governed with even greater harshness and cruelty than Wang Wenshu or the rest.

When Du Zhou was first summoned to serve as a secretary in the office of the commandant of justice, he owned only one horse, and even that was maimed. But by the time he had worked in the government for a number of years and had advanced until he ranked among the three highest ministers, his sons and grandsons all held high offices and the wealth of his family ran to several hundred million cash.

The Grand Historian remarks: These ten men, from Zhi Du to Du Zhou, all won fame for their harshness. Nevertheless, Zhi Du had a certain stubborn frankness and strove to decide between right and wrong in order to provide a basis for justice in the empire. Zhang Tang knew how to be either stern or mild depending upon the will of the ruler, but his decisions on what was fitting and what was not were often of benefit to the nation. Zhao Yu stuck to the letter of

---

[13] According to *Han shu* 19B, Du Zhou was relieved of his duties as commandant of justice and made military commander of the capital in the second year of *tianhan* (99 BC). This was the same year that Sima Qian, having aroused Emperor Wu's anger by speaking in defence of General Li Ling, was sent to prison and condemned to suffer castration. It is quite possible, therefore, that Sima Qian's case was handled by Du Zhou, or at least by the officials trained under Du Zhou. Sima Qian's description of prison methods used at this time may accordingly be based upon personal experience. Certainly, from Sima Qian's letter to Ren An describing his experience in prison it is obvious that he too was beaten and cowed by the prison officials into acknowledging guilt. See the translation of the letter in *Ssu-ma Ch'ien: Grand Historian of China*, p. 62.

the law and was careful to be fair, but Du Zhou simply flattered the whims of the ruler and believed that gravity consisted in saying little. From the time of Zhang Tang's death on, the net of the law was drawn tighter and tighter, and harsh penalties became increasingly frequent, so that the work of the government officials was gradually hampered and brought to a standstill. The high ministers went about their duties meekly and compliantly, and gave no thought to reforming defects in government policy. Indeed, they were so busy staying out of trouble that they had no time to think of anything but laws and regulations.

Yet among these ten men, those who were honest may serve as an example of conduct, and those who were corrupt may serve as a warning. These men, by their schemes and strategies, their teaching and leadership, worked to prevent evil and block the path of crime. All were men of strong character, combining in themselves both military and civil ability. And although they were known for their cruelty and harshness, it was a reputation that went well with their duties. But when it comes to men like Feng Dang, the governor of Shu, who violently oppressed the people; Li Zhen of Guanghan who tore people limb from limb for his own pleasure; Mi Pu of Dong Province who sawed people's heads off; Luo Bi of Tianshui who bludgeoned people into making confessions; Chu Guang of Hedong who executed people indiscriminately; Wu Ji of the capital and Yin Zhou of Fengyi who ruled like vipers or hawks; or Yan Feng of Shuiheng who beat people to death unless they bribed him for their release — why bother to describe all of them? Why bother to describe all of them?

SHI JI 124: THE BIOGRAPHIES OF
THE WANDERING KNIGHTS[1]

Saving others in distress, helping those who cannot help themselves — is this not what a benevolent man does? Never betraying a trust, never going back on one's word — this is the conduct of a righteous man. Thus I made "The Biographies of the Wandering Knights".

Han Fei Zi has remarked: "The Confucians with their learning pervert the laws; the knights with their contentiousness violate the prohibitions."[2] Thus he condemns both groups.

Yet the Confucian scholars have often been praised by the world. Some of them, by their knowledge of statesmanship, succeeded in becoming prime ministers and high officials and acted as aides to the rulers of the time. Their achievements are fully recorded in the annals of the Zhou states, and there is therefore no reason to discuss them here. Others, however, such as Confucius' disciples Ji Ci and Yuan Xian, were simple commoners living in the village lanes. They studied books and cherished independence of action and the virtues

---

[1] The word "knight" here should not be understood as designating any particular formal rank in society. It is used rather to suggest the kind of honourable and self-sacrificing conduct which characterized this group of men at their best. Such self-appointed "bosses" or protectors of others no doubt served a very useful purpose in the chaotic society of the late Zhou and early Han. With the restoration of peace and stability, however, they often became a nuisance and the Han government took strict measures to suppress them. Sima Qian has been severely criticized by later Chinese writers for praising the knights and according them a place in his history. As a historian, however, he could hardly have ignored their existence entirely, while his own bitter experiences at Emperor Wu's court undoubtedly encouraged his admiration for men who "hasten to the side of those who are in trouble". Writers of the Chinese communist regime have praised Sima Qian for his recognition of the knights, but this is because they regard them as "heroes of the people" who fought against the oppression of the feudalistic system.

[2] *Han Fei Zi, zhuan* 19, "Wudu".

of the superior man; in their righteousness they refused to compromise with their age, and their age in turn merely laughed at them. Therefore they lived all their lives in barren hovels with vine-woven doors, wearing rough clothes, eating coarse food and scarcely enough of that. Yet, though it is over 400 years since they died, their disciples have never tired of writing about them.

As for the wandering knights, though their actions may not conform to perfect righteousness, yet they are always true to their word. What they undertake they invariably fulfil; what they have promised they invariably carry out. Without thinking of themselves they hasten to the side of those who are in trouble, whether it means survival or destruction, life or death. Yet they never boast of their accomplishments but rather consider it a disgrace to brag of what they have done for others. So there is much about them which is worthy of admiration, particularly when trouble is something that comes to almost everyone some time.

The Grand Historian remarks: In ancient times Emperor Shun was caught in a burning granary and trapped in a well; Yi Yin was obliged to carry tripods and sacrificial stands; Fu Yue served as a convict labourer among the cliffs of Fu; Lü Shang was reduced to selling food at the Ji Ford; Guan Zhong was bound with fetters and handcuffs; Baili Xi tended cattle; Confucius was threatened at Kuang, and between Chen and Cai he grew pale from hunger. All of these are what scholars call men of benevolence and followers of the Way. If even they encountered such misfortunes, how much more so must men of only ordinary character who are trying to make their way in a discordant and degenerate age? Surely the troubles *they* meet with will be too numerous to recount!

Ignorant people have a saying, "Why bother to understand benevolence and righteousness? Whoever does you some good must be a virtuous man!" Bo Yi hated the Zhou dynasty and chose to starve on Shouyang Mountain rather than serve under it, but Kings Wen and Wu did not give up their thrones on that account. Zhi and Qiao were cruel and lawless bandits, yet their own followers never tired of singing their praises. From this we can see that "he who steals a fishhook gets his head chopped off, but he who steals a state becomes a great lord, and when one is a great lord, he automatically acquires benevolence and righteousness."[3] These are no empty words!

---

[3] *Zhuang Zi, zhuan* 4, "Quque".

Men who stick fast to their doctrines and observe every minute principle of duty, though it means spending all their lives alone in the world, can hardly be discussed in the same breath with those who lower the tone of their discourse to suit the vulgar, bob along with the current of the times, and thereby acquire a glorious name. Yet among the knights of the common people there are men who are fair in their dealings and true to their promises, who will risk death for others without a thought to their own safety, and who are praised for their righteousness a thousand miles around. So they have their good points, too; they do not simply strive to get ahead at any price. Therefore when people find themselves in trouble they turn to these men for help and entrust their lives to them. Is it not just this sort of men that people mean when they talk about the "worthy" and the "eminent"? As a matter of fact, if we speak in terms of actual authority and power and the effect which their actions had *upon their own times,* the knights of the hamlets and villages so far surpass men like Ji Ci and Yuan Xian that there is hardly any basis for comparison. And this is true mainly because their achievements were immediately apparent to everyone and because they were faithful to their word. How then can we say that the righteousness of these knights and retainers is insignificant?

It is no longer possible to discover anything about the knights of the common people in ancient times. In more recent ages there were men like Yan Ling and the princes of Mengchang, Chunshen, Pingyuan, and Xinling.[4] All of these men, because they were related to the ruling families of the time and could rely upon their wealth as landowners and high officials, were able to summon worthy men from all over the empire to be their retainers and thus achieve fame among the feudal lords. This is not to say that they themselves were not worthy men. But it is more like the case of a man "who shouts downwind. The sound of his voice is not necessarily increased in strength";[5] it is the force of the wind that bears it along.

Yet there were others, knights of the lanes and byways, who, though they had no such advantages, were so upright in conduct and careful of their honour that their reputation was known all over the empire and there was no one who

---

[4] Yan Ling was a prince of Wu in the sixth century BC. The other four men, often referred to as the Four Heroes, were princes of Qi, Chu, Zhao and Wei respectively, and lived in the third century BC. All were famous for their ability to attract large bands of retainers to their service.

[5] *Xun Zi, zhuan* I, "Quanxue".

did not praise them as worthy men. This is not quite so easy to do. Nevertheless, the Confucians and Mohists have brushed them all aside and failed to make any mention of them in their writings. As a result, the names of the knights of the common people who lived before the Qin have vanished like smoke and can no longer be known. I find this very regrettable indeed!

From what I myself have been able to learn, after the founding of the Han there were men like Zhu Jia, Tian Zhong, Wang Gong, Ju Meng, and Guo Xie who, although they sometimes ran afoul of the law in their day, were in their personal relations scrupulously honest and humble. Such qualities are surely worthy of praise. Their reputations were not founded on air and it was not without reason that men gathered about them.

On the other hand, when it comes to those who band together in cliques and powerful family groups, pooling their wealth and making the poor serve them, arrogantly and cruelly oppressing the weak and helpless, giving free rein to their own desires and treating people any way they please — such men the wandering knights despise even as others do. I am grieved that so many people of my day do not take the trouble to examine the intentions of the knights, but foolishly consider Zhu Jia, Guo Xie, and the others to be in the same class as these cruel and arrogant men, and so ridicule both groups.

ZHU JIA

Zhu Jia of Lu was a contemporary of Emperor Gaozu, but while most of the men of Lu were teachers of Confucianism, Zhu Jia won fame as a knight. He sheltered and concealed hundreds of eminent men in his house, thus saving them from their enemies, while the ordinary men among his followers were too numerous to mention. Yet all his life he never boasted of his abilities nor bragged of the favours he had done for others. On the contrary, his only fear was that the people he had once aided might come to see him and try to repay him. In helping men who were in need, he considered first those who were poor and humble. He and the members of his family had little money, they wore no fine clothes, their food was simple, and their carriage nothing more than an oxcart. He spent all his time hastening to the side of others who were in trouble, considering their well being more important than his own. Once he concealed General Ji Bu, who was fleeing from the anger of Emperor Gaozu, but later, when Ji Bu became honoured at the Han court, Zhu Jia never made any attempt to see him again. Among the people living east of the Pass there were none who did not stretch forth their necks, longing to become friends with Zhu Jia.

Tian Zhong of Chu won a reputation as a knight and loved swordsmanship. He looked up to Zhu Jia like a father and considered that he himself could never equal Zhu Jia's deeds.

JU MENG

After Tian Zhong died, there was Ju Meng of Luoyang. The men of the old region of Zhou rely mostly on commerce for their livelihood, but Ju Meng won a name among the feudal lords by his daring and chivalrous deeds.

When the kings of Wu and Chu began their revolt, Zhou Yafu, the marquis of Tiao, was made grand commandant of the Han armies and hastened by relay carriage east to Henan, where he met Ju Meng. He was delighted and said, "Wu and Chu have embarked on a very serious undertaking, but since they have not sought your services, I am sure they will not be able to accomplish anything!" By this he meant that, at a time when the whole empire was in turmoil, the support of Ju Meng was worth more to him than the conquest of one of the rebel kingdoms. Ju Meng's conduct was much like that of Zhu Jia except that he was fond of dice and other amusements of young people. Yet when his mother died, people came from great distances to attend the funeral, their carriages numbering as many as 1,000. When Ju Meng himself died, the wealth of his family did not amount to more than ten catties of gold.

There was also a man of Fuli named Wang Meng who won fame as a knight in the region between the Yangtze and Huai rivers. At this time the Xian family of Ji'nan and Zhou Yong of Chen were both noted for their great power and influence. When Emperor Jing heard of this, he sent an envoy to execute all the members of their group. After this, various members of the Bai clan of Dai, as well as Han Wubi of Liang, Xue Kuang of Yangdi, and Han Ru of Jia came to prominence.

GUO XIE

Guo Xie, whose polite name was Guo Wengbo, was a native of Zhi. He was a grandson on his mother's side of the famous physiognomist Xu Fu, who was skilled at reading people's faces. Guo Xie's father was executed in the time of Emperor Wen because of his activities as a knight.

Guo Xie was short in stature and very quick-tempered; he did not drink wine. In his youth he was sullen, vindictive, and quick to anger when crossed in his will, and this led him to kill a great many people. In addition, he would take it upon himself to avenge the wrongs of his friends and conceal men who were fleeing from the law. He was constantly engaged in some kind of evil, robbing or assaulting people, while it would be impossible to say how many times he was guilty of counterfeiting money or looting graves. He met with extraordinary luck, however, and no matter what difficulties he found himself in, he always managed to escape or was pardoned by a general amnesty.

When he grew older, he had a change of heart and became much more upright in his conduct, rewarding hatred with virtue, giving generously and expecting little in return. In spite of this, he took more and more delight in daring and chivalrous actions. Whenever he had saved someone's life, he would never boast of his achievements. At heart he was still as ill-tempered as ever, however, and his meanness would often flare forth in a sudden angry look. The young men of the time emulated his actions and would often take it upon themselves to avenge his wrongs without telling him.

The son of Guo Xie's elder sister, relying upon Xie's power and position, was once drinking with a man and tried to make him drink up all the wine. Though the man protested that it was more than he could do, Xie's nephew threatened him and forced him to drain the cup. In anger the man drew his sword, stabbed and killed the nephew, and ran away.

Xie's sister was furious. "For all my brother's so-called sense of duty," she exclaimed, "he allows his own nephew to be murdered and won't even go after the culprit!" Then she threw her son's corpse into the street and refused to bury it, hoping to shame Xie into action.

Guo Xie sent men to discover where the murderer was hiding and the latter, fearful of the consequences, returned of his own accord and reported to Xie exactly what had happened. "You were quite right to kill my nephew," said Xie. "He was at fault!" Then he let the murderer go and, laying the blame for the incident entirely on his nephew, took the corpse away and buried it. When men heard of this, they all admired Xie's righteousness and flocked about him in increasing numbers.

Whenever Guo Xie came or went, people were careful to get out of his way. Once, however, there was a man who, instead of moving aside, merely sat sprawled by the road and stared at Xie. Xie sent someone to ask the man's name.

Xie's retainers wanted to kill the man on the spot, but Xie told them, "If I am not respected in the village where I live, it must be that my virtue is insufficient to command respect. What fault has this man committed?" Then he sent secret instructions to the military officials of the district, saying, "This man is very important to me. Whenever his turn comes for military service, see that he is let off!"

As a result, the man was let off from military service every time his turn came, and the officials made no attempt to look for him. The man was baffled by this and asked the reason, whereupon he discovered that Xie had instructed that he be excused. The man then went to Xie and, baring his arms, humbly apologized for his former disrespect. When the young men of the district heard of this, they admired Xie's conduct even more.

In Luoyang there were two men who were carrying on a feud and, although ten or more of the worthy and eminent residents of the city had tried to act as mediators between them, they refused to listen to talk of a settlement. Someone came to ask Guo Xie to help in the matter and he went at night to visit the hostile families, who finally gave in and agreed to listen to Xie's arguments. Then he told them, "I have heard that the gentlemen of Luoyang have attempted to act as mediators, but that you have refused to listen to any of them. Now, fortunately, you have consented to pay attention to me. However, I would certainly not want it to appear that I came here from another district and tried to steal authority from the virtuous men of your own city!" He therefore went away the same night so that people would not know of his visit, telling the feuding families, "Pay no attention to my advice for a while and wait until I have gone. Then let the eminent men of Luoyang act as your mediators and do as they say!"

Guo Xie was very respectful in his behaviour and would never venture to ride in a carriage when entering the office of his district. He would often journey to neighbouring provinces or kingdoms in answer to some request for aid. In such cases, if he thought he could accomplish what had been asked of him, he would undertake to do so, but if he thought the request was impossible, he would go to pains to explain the reasons to the satisfaction of the other party, and only then would he consent to accept food and wine. As a result, people regarded him with great awe and respect and vied with each other in offering him their services. Every night ten or more carriages would arrive at his gate bearing young men of the town or members of the eminent families of neighbouring districts who had come begging to be allowed to take some of Xie's guests and retainers into their own homes.

When the order went out for powerful and wealthy families in the provinces to be moved to the city of Mouling, Guo Xie's family was exempted, since his wealth did not come up to the specified amount.[6] He was so well known, however, that the officials were afraid they would get into trouble if they did not order him to move. General Wei Qing spoke to the emperor on his behalf, explaining that Guo Xie's wealth was not sufficient to require him to move. But the emperor replied, "If this commoner has enough influence to get you to speak for him, general, he cannot be so very poor!" So in the end Guo Xie's family was ordered to move, and the people who came to see him off presented him with over 10,000,000 cash as a farewell gift.

The man who was responsible for originally recommending Guo Xie for transportation to Mouling was a district official named Yang, the son of Yang Jizhu of Zhi. In retaliation for this, the son of Guo Xie's elder brother cut off the head of the Yang official, and as a result the Yang and the Guo families became bitter enemies.

After Guo Xie entered the Pass, the worthy and eminent men within the Pass, both those who had known him before and those who had not, soon learned of his reputation and vied with each other in making friends with him.[7]

Some time after this, Yang Jizhu, the father of the official who had recommended that Xie be moved to Mouling, was murdered. The Yang family sent a letter of protest to the throne, but someone murdered the bearer of the letter outside the gate of the imperial palace. When the emperor learned of this, he sent out the law officials to arrest Guo Xie. Xie fled and, leaving his mother and the other members of his family at Xiayang, escaped to Linjin.

Ji Shaogong, who had charge of the pass at Linjin, had never known Guo Xie and therefore, when Xie assumed a false name and asked to be allowed to go through the pass, Ji Shaogong gave him permission. From there Xie turned and entered the region of Taiyuan. Whenever Xie stopped anywhere in his flight, he would make his destination known to his host, so that as a result the law officials were able to trail him without difficulty. When his trail led to Ji

---

[6]Emperor Wu had established his mausoleum at Mouling, and in 127 BC he ordered that rich and powerful families (those whose wealth exceeded 3,000,000 cash) be moved there from other parts of the empire. The purpose of this was to populate the town and at the same time to break the power of the big provincial families and settle them near the capital where they could be more easily watched.

[7]The thirteen characters which follow in the text do not belong here and have been omitted in the translation.

Shaogong, however, Ji Shaogong committed suicide to keep from having to give any information.

After some time, Guo Xie was captured, and a thorough investigation made of all his crimes. It was found, however, that all the murders he had committed had taken place before the last amnesty.

There was a certain Confucian scholar from Zhi who was sitting with the imperial envoys at Guo Xie's investigation. When one of Xie's retainers praised Xie, the Confucian scholar remarked, "Guo Xie does nothing but commit crimes and break the law! How can anyone call him a worthy man?" The retainer happened to overhear his words and later killed the Confucian scholar and cut out his tongue. The law officials tried to lay the blame on Xie, though as a matter of fact he did not know who had committed the murder. The murderer disappeared, and in the end no one ever found out who he was.

The officials finally submitted a report to the throne declaring that Xie was innocent of the charges brought against him, but the imperial secretary Gongsun Hong objected, saying, "Xie, although a commoner, has taken the authority of the government into his own hands in his activities as a knight, killing anyone who gave him so much as a cross look. Though he did not know the man who murdered the Confucian scholar, his guilt is greater than if he had done the crime himself. He should be condemned as a treasonable and unprincipled criminal!" In the end Guo Xie and all the members of his family were executed.

After this there were a great many men who acted as knights, but they were an arrogant lot and hardly worth mentioning. In the area within the Pass there was Fan Zhongzi of Chang'an, Zhao Wangsun of Huaili, Gao Gongzi of Changling, Guo Gongzhong of Xihe, Lu Gongru of Taiyuan, Ni Changqing of Linhuai, and Tian Junru of Dongyang, but although they acted as knights, they were rather timid and retiring and had the manners of gentlemen. Others such as the Yao family of the northern region, the various members of the Du family of the west, Chou Jing of the southern region, Zhao Tuoyu Gongzi of the east, and Zhao Tiao of Nanyang, were no more than robbers and brigands of the lowest sort and certainly do not deserve to be treated here. To do so would only be an insult to former men such as Zhu Jia.

The Grand Historian remarks: I have seen Guo Xie, and I can report that in looks and bearing he hardly measured up to the average man, while nothing he said was worth remembering. Yet throughout the empire both worthy men and base men, those who knew him and those who did not, all admire his reputation and whenever they talk about the knights, they always cite his name. There is a common saying "The real looks of a man lie in his reputation, for that will never die!" Alas, that he met with such an end!

SHI JI 125: THE BIOGRAPHIES OF
THE EMPERORS' MALE FAVOURITES

Those who served the ruler and succeeded in delighting his ears and eyes, those who caught their lord's fancy and won his favour and intimacy, did so not only through the power of lust and love; each had certain abilities in which he excelled. Thus I made "The Biographies of the Emperors' Male Favourites".

The proverb says, "No amount of toiling in the fields can compare to a spell of good weather; no amount of faithful service can compare to being liked by your superiors." This is no idle saying. Yet it is not women alone who can use their looks to attract the eyes of the ruler; courtiers and eunuchs can play at that game as well. Many were the men of ancient times who gained favour in this way.

When the Han arose, Emperor Gaozu, for all his coarseness and blunt manners, was won by the charms of a young boy named Ji, and Emperor Hui had a boy favourite named Hong. Neither Ji nor Hong had any particular talent or ability; both won prominence simply by their looks and graces. Day and night they were by the ruler's side, and all the high ministers were obliged to apply to them when they wished to speak to the emperor. As a result all the palace attendants at the court of Emperor Hui took to wearing caps with gaudy feathers and sashes of seashells and to painting their faces, transforming themselves into a veritable host of Jis and Hongs. Both young men were ordered to move from their native places and to take up residence at Anling, where Emperor Hui had his mausoleum.

The gentlemen who enjoyed favour in the palace under Emperor Wen included a courtier named Deng Tong and the eunuchs Zhao Tan and Beigong Bozi. Beigong Bozi was a worthy and affectionate man, while Zhao Tan attracted the emperor's attention by his skill in observing the stars and exhalations in the sky; both of them customarily rode about in the same carriage with Emperor Wen. Deng Tong does not seem to have had any special talent.

Deng Tong was a native of Nan'an in the province of Shu. Because he knew how to pole a boat he was made a yellow-capped boatman in the grounds of the imperial palace.

Once Emperor Wen dreamed that he was trying to climb to Heaven but could not seem to make his way up. Just then a yellow-capped boatman boosted him from behind and he was able to reach Heaven. When the emperor turned around to look at the man, he noticed that the seam of the boatman's robe was split in the back just below the sash.

After the emperor awoke, he went to the Terrace of Lapping Water, which stood in the middle of the Azure Lake, and began to search furtively for the man who had boosted him up in his dream. There he saw Deng Tong, who happened to have a tear in the back of his robe exactly like that of the man in the dream. The emperor summoned him and asked his name, and when he learned that the man's family name was Deng (ascend) and his personal name Tong (reach), the emperor was overjoyed. From this time on, the emperor bestowed ever-increasing favour and honour upon Deng Tong.

Deng Tong for his part behaved with great honesty and circumspection in his new position. He cared nothing about mingling with people outside the palace and, though the emperor granted him holidays to return to his home, he was always reluctant to leave. As a result, the emperor showered him with gifts until his fortunes mounted to tens of billions of cash and he had been promoted to the post of superior lord. The emperor from time to time even paid visits to Deng Tong's home to amuse himself there.

Deng Tong, however, had no other talent than this of entertaining the emperor and was never able to do anything to advance others at court. Instead he bent all his efforts toward maintaining his own position and ingratiating himself with the emperor.

Once the emperor summoned a man who was skilled at physiognomizing and asked him to examine Deng Tong's face. "This man will become poor and die of starvation," the physiognomist announced. "But *I* am the one who has made him rich!" exclaimed the emperor. "How could he ever become poor?" With this, he presented Deng Tong with the rights to a range of copper-bearing mountains in Yandao in Shu Province and allowed him to mint copper coins for himself until the so-called Deng family cash were circulating all over the empire. Such was the wealth which Deng Tong acquired.

Once Emperor Wen was troubled by a tumour, and Deng Tong made it his duty to keep it sucked clean of infection. The emperor was feeling depressed by his illness and, apropos of nothing in particular, asked Deng Tong, "In all the empire, who do you think loves me most?"

"Surely no one loves Your Majesty more than the heir apparent!" replied Deng Tong.

Later, when the heir apparent came to inquire how his father was, the emperor made him suck the tumour. The heir apparent managed to suck it clean, but it was obvious from his expression that he found the task distasteful. Afterward, when he learned that Deng Tong had been in the habit of sucking the tumour for the emperor, he was secretly filled with shame. From this time on he bore a grudge against Deng Tong.

After Emperor Wen passed away and the heir apparent, Emperor Jing, came to the throne, Deng Tong retired from court and returned to his home. He had not been there any time, however, when someone reported to the throne that he was guilty of smuggling cash which he had minted across the border to the barbarians. He was handed over to the law officials for investigation and it was found that the evidence for the most part supported the charges. In the end he was condemned and all of his fortune was confiscated by the government. Even so, it was claimed that his wealth was insufficient to cover the damages and that he still owed the government several hundred million more cash. Emperor Jing's older sister, the Elder Princess, presented Deng Tong with a gift of money, but the officials immediately seized this as well, until Deng Tong was not left with so much as a pin to hold his cap on. After this the Elder Princess provided him with food and clothing in the form of a loan so that it could not be confiscated. In the end Deng Tong did not have a single copper cash to call his own, and died as a dependent in someone else's home.

Emperor Jing did not have any particular favourites among the officials at his court. There was one man, a chief of palace attendants named Zhou Wenren, who enjoyed rather more favour than ordinary men, but even so it was nothing very extraordinary. Among the favourites of the present emperor were the courtier Hann Yan, the great grandson of Xin, the king of Hann, and the eunuch Li Yannian.

Hann Yan was an illegitimate grandson of Hann Tuidang, the marquis of Gonggao. When the present emperor was still king of Jiaodong, he and Yan studied writing together and the two grew very fond of each other. Later, after the emperor was appointed heir apparent, he became more and more friendly with Yan. Yan was skilful at riding and archery and was also very good at ingratiating himself with the emperor. He was well versed in the fighting techniques of the barbarians and therefore, after the emperor came to the throne and began making plans to open attacks on the Xiongnu, he treated Yan with even greater respect and honour. Yan had soon advanced to the rank of superior lord and received as many gifts from the ruler as Deng Tong had in his days of honour.

At this time Yan was constantly by the emperor's side, both day and night. Once the emperor's younger brother Liu Fei, the king of Jiangdu, who had come to court to pay his respects, received permission from the emperor to accompany him on a hunt in the Shanglin Park. The order had already been given to clear the roads for the imperial carriage, but the emperor was not yet ready to depart, and so he sent Yan ahead in one of the attendant carriages, accompanied by fifty or 100 riders, to gallop through the park and observe the game. The king of Jiangdu, seeing the party approaching in the distance, supposed it was the emperor and ordered his own attendants off the road while he himself knelt down by the side of the road to greet the emperor. Yan, however, raced by without even noticing him, and after he had passed, when the king of Jiangdu realized his error, he was enraged and went to the empress dowager in tears. "I beg to return the kingdom which has been granted to me and become a bodyguard in the palace," he said. "Perhaps then I may be accorded as much honour as Hann Yan!" From this time on the empress dowager bore a grudge against Yan.

Because he attended the emperor, Hann Yan was allowed to come and go in the women's quarters of the palace and did not have to observe the customary prohibitions against entering them. Some time later, it was reported to the empress dowager that Yan had had an illicit affair with one of the women there. She was furious and immediately sent a messenger ordering him to take his life. Although the emperor attempted to make apologies for him, he was able to do nothing to change the order, and in the end Yan was forced to die. His younger brother Hann Yue, the marquis of Andao, also managed to win great favour with the emperor.

Li Yannian was a native of Zhongshan. His mother and father, as well as he and his brothers and sisters, were all originally singers. Li Yannian, having been convicted of some crime and condemned to castration, was made a keeper of the dogs in the palace. Later, the princess of Pingyang recommended his younger sister Lady Li to the emperor because of her skill in dancing. When the emperor saw her, he took a liking to her and had her installed in the women's quarters of the palace, at the same time summoning Li Yannian to an audience and appointing him to a higher post.

Li Yannian was a good singer and knew how to compose new tunes. At this time the emperor wanted some hymns set to music and arranged with string accompaniment to be used in the sacrifices to Heaven and Earth which he had initiated. Li Yannian accepted the task and performed it to the emperor's satisfaction, composing melodies and string accompaniments for the new words that had been written. Meanwhile his sister, Lady Li, bore the emperor a son.

Li Yannian by this time wore the seals of a 2,000 picul official and bore the title of "Harmonizer of Tunes". Day and night he was by the emperor's side and his honour and favour equalled that which Hann Yan had formerly enjoyed.

When some years had passed, his younger brother Li Ji began carrying on an affair with one of the palace ladies and becoming more and more arrogant and careless in his behaviour.[1] After the death of Lady Li, the emperor's affection for the Li brothers waned, and he ended by having them arrested and executed.

From this time on, the courtiers who enjoyed special favour with the emperor were for the most part members of the families related to the emperor by marriage, but none of them are worth discussing here. Wei Qing and Huo Qubing, who were in-laws of the emperor, also won great honour and favour, but in their case their advancement was due primarily to their talents and abilities.

The Grand Historian remarks: How violent are the seasons of love and hatred! By observing the fate of Mi Zixia, we can guess what will happen to favourites of later times. "Even the future a hundred ages hence may be foretold!"[2]

---

[1] Following the reading in *Han shu* 93. The *Shi ji* text reads as though Li Yannian himself were carrying on the affair, which would hardly be likely.

[2] The last sentence is a quotation from the *Analects* II, 23. The story of Mi Zixia is related by Han Fei Zi and is quoted in Han Fei Zi's biography in *Shi ji* 63. As it is told there, Mi Zixia was much loved by the lord of Wei in ancient times. Once when Mi Zixia heard that his mother was ill, he forged an order from the ruler and went to visit her in the royal carriage of Wei, though he knew that the penalty for such an action was amputation of the feet. The lord of Wei, however, simply praised the young man for his filial piety. Another time Mi Zixia was strolling in an orchard with the ruler and, biting into a peach and finding it tasty, he offered the remainder to his lord. "How deep is your love for me!" exclaimed the lord of Wei. "You forget your own appetite and think only of me!" Later, however, Mi Zixia's looks faded, and the ruler ceased to care for him and found some excuse to condemn him to punishment. "After all," said the lord of Wei, "he once stole my carriage, and another time he gave me a half-eaten peach to eat!"

SHI JI 127: THE BIOGRAPHIES OF THE DIVINERS OF LUCKY DAYS

The customs of the diviners of lucky days differ in the regions of Qi, Chu, Qin, and Zhao. In order to present a systematic survey of their general methods, I made "The Biographies of the Diviners of Lucky Days".[1]

From ancient times the rulers who have received the mandate and become kings always seem to have consulted the tortoise shells or the milfoil stalks in order to determine the will of Heaven. The custom was certainly much in use during the Zhou dynasty, and we have evidence that it was continued under the Qin. When the king of Dai, who became Emperor Wen, was considering whether or not to journey to the capital to take the throne, he left the decision up to the diviner. The office of court grand diviner originated at the beginning of the Han dynasty.

Sima Jizhu[2] was a native of Chu who practised divination in the eastern market of Chang'an. Once Song Zhong, a palace counsellor under Emperor Wen, and the erudite Jia Yi, their bath and hair washing days having fallen on the same day, left the palace together to return to their homes. As they proceeded on their way they began discussing the *Book of Changes*, which they regarded as the embodiment of the wisdom of the ancient kings and sages and the key to an understanding of all human affairs, debating its meaning, quoting passages from the Classic, and gazing at each other and sighing.

"I have heard it said," remarked Jia Yi, "that the sages of antiquity, if they

---

[1] This chapter has long been eyed with suspicion. Though Sima Qian says in his summary that he has discussed the diviners of Qi, Chu, Qin, and Zhao, the chapter contains only one account concerning a diviner from Chu, supplemented by notes (not translated here) which were added to the chapter by Chu Shaosun some years after Sima Qian's death. For these reasons many critics have maintained that Sima Qian never got around to writing the chapter he had planned, and that what we have today is from another hand. Regardless of its authorship or reliability as history, it is a fine piece of writing done in the vivid, novelistic style typical of early Chinese philosophical literature.

[2] His personal name, Jizhu, may be interpreted to mean "Master of the Seasons".

did not hold positions at court, were invariably to be found among the ranks of diviners and doctors. Now I am already acquainted with all the high ministers and court officials and I know what they are like. Let us try searching among the diviners and see what sort of men we can find."

The two men then got into a carriage and drove to the market, where they strolled among the diviners' stalls. It had just begun to rain and there were few people in the street. Sima Jizhu was sitting at leisure, attended by three or four of his students, expounding to them the way of heaven and earth, the movements of the sun and moon, and the origin of the good and bad influences of the *yin* and *yang*.

Song Zhong and Jia Yi bowed twice before him and requested an interview. Sima Jizhu examined their appearance and, deciding that they looked like intelligent men, greeted them and ordered his students to spread mats for them to sit down. After the two had taken their seats, he repeated his earlier discussion, explaining the cycles of heaven and earth and the movements of the sun, moon, stars, and constellations, distinguishing the uses of benevolence and righteousness, and describing the signs of good and evil fortune. He spoke at considerable length, and nothing he said was contrary to reason.

Song Zhong and Jia Yi were struck with wonder and, realizing that he was no ordinary man, they tightened the strings of their hats, arranged their robes, and sat up straight on their mats, saying, "We have observed your appearance, master, and listened to your words and, limited as our experience in the world may be, we have never met anyone like you before! Why, may we ask, do you live in a humble place like this and pursue such a disreputable occupation?"

Sima Jizhu clasped his belly and gave an enormous laugh. "From looking at you two gentlemen," he said, "I supposed you must know something about the arts of the Way. But now what stupid things you say! What a barbarous manner of speech! Just what occupation, may I ask, do you consider worthy and what kind of person do you look up to? What do you mean by calling one of your elders humble and disreputable?"

"The world looks up to men who occupy high posts and receive generous stipends," replied the two courtiers, "and therefore men of worth and talent are to be found in such positions. But your present position is certainly quite different, and so we spoke of it as lowly. The words of a diviner cannot be trusted, the value of his actions cannot be verified, and he gets his living by unjust means. Therefore we said that your occupation was disreputable. It is the custom of the world to despise and make light of diviners. People all say, 'Oh, the diviners — all they do is talk exaggerated and imposing nonsense to play on people's feelings, make absurdly glorious predictions about people's fates to delight them, invent stories about disasters to fill their hearts with fear, and babble lies about the spirits to get all their money away from them, demanding generous rewards so they can line their own pockets!' Such actions we consider disgraceful, and therefore we spoke of your occupation as disreputable."

"Gentlemen, make yourselves comfortable and listen a while," said Sima Jizhu. "Do you see that little boy there with his hair not yet bound up? When the sun and the moon are shining, he goes out for a walk, but when they are not shining he stays home. But if you were to ask him about the eclipses or the lucky and unlucky seasons of the sun and moon, he could not explain the reasons for them. In the same way, those who can distinguish clearly between worthy and unworthy men are few indeed.

"It is the way of a worthy man to follow what is right and speak out against what he believes to be wrong, but if after admonishing the ruler three times he finds that he is not being heeded, then he will retire from office. When he praises others he has no reward in mind, and when he hates others it is not because of personal grudges; his only concern is what will benefit the nation and profit the mass of people. Therefore, if he is not fitted for a particular post, he will not occupy it, and if he feels that his stipend is greater than he deserves, he will not accept it. He will refuse to respect men who do wrong, no matter how eminent they may be; he will not humble himself before corrupt men, no matter how high their position. He does not rejoice if he is appointed to a post, nor has he any regrets if he must leave it. As long as he himself is not at fault, he will feel no shame no matter what disgraces are heaped upon him.

"But what *you* have called worthy men — they are the ones who ought to be ashamed! Bowing and scraping, they appear before the ruler; fawning and flattering, they speak their piece. Banding together for greater power, leading each other on with promises of profit, they flock together into cliques to drive out honest men. Seeking position and fame, living off the public funds, they devote themselves to private advantage, pervert the ruler's laws, and prey upon the farmers. Using their offices to terrorize others, taking advantage of the power of the law, they seek by every violent and unlawful means to win gain. They are in fact no different from a bunch of bandits who swoop down upon men with drawn swords!

"When they are first put in office for a trial period, they exaggerate their influence with clever deceits and build an imposing facade of achievement with false reports in order to deceive the ruler. They pride themselves upon their high positions and refuse to let worthy men have a try in office. In enumerating their achievements they puff up truth with falsehood, make something out of nothing, and convert little into much, seeking to increase their power and better their positions. While they dash about the countryside feasting and drinking, accompanied by ladies in waiting and singing boys, they disregard the welfare of their parents, break the laws, oppress the people, and waste the resources of the ruling house. They rob without depending upon spears and bows, plunder without resorting to bowstrings and blades. Though they swindle their parents, they go unpunished; though they assassinate their lords, they are not struck down. How can you look up to such men and call them worthy and talented?

"When bandits appear, such officials are powerless to put them down; though the barbarian tribes are disobedient, they cannot control them. Evil arises and they are incapable of stopping it; corruption and disorder appear among the lower officials and they cannot stamp them out. They are unable to restore harmony to the four seasons, helpless to take proper measures when the harvests are poor. If they are indeed talented and worthy and yet fail to do these things, then they are guilty of disloyalty. And if they are occupying their posts without having any talent or worth, profiting from the ruler's stipends and blocking the way for really worthy men, then they are simply thieves of high office. Recommending others only because of their influence, being polite to men because of their wealth — this is simply hypocrisy. Have you not seen such owls and kites soaring side by side with the phoenixes?[3] Have you not seen the orchid and the spikenard cast out on the broad plain, while the common artemisia flourishes in groves? It is you and your like who cause the truly worthy gentlemen to retire into obscurity!

"It is the business of the gentleman to be 'a transmitter and not a maker'.[4] Now the diviner invariably takes heaven and earth as his pattern and the four seasons as his model. Conforming to benevolence and righteousness, he divides the milfoil stalks and determines the hexagram, revolves the divining instrument and calculates the correct formula. Only then does he venture to discuss what is profitable and unprofitable in heaven and earth or to predict the success or failure of undertakings.

---

[3] The owls and kites are metaphors for evil men, the phoenix a metaphor for the man of true worth.

[4] A reference to Confucius' description of himself in *Analects* VII, I.

"In ancient times, when the former kings managed the affairs of the state, they invariably consulted the tortoise or the milfoil stalks and observed the sun and moon before undertaking the charge of Heaven. Only after determining the correct hour and day did they come and go. When a child is born to a family, the father divines to see whether its future will be lucky or unlucky before deciding whether to rear it. Ever since Fu Xi devised the eight trigrams and King Wen of the Zhou expanded them with the 384 explanations of the lines, the world has been well ordered. Goujian, the king of Yue, by imitating the eight trigrams of King Wen, was able to defeat his enemies and become one of the dictators of China. In view of all this, what fault can you find with the arts of divination?

"Moreover, when the diviner sets to work, he first sweeps a place and spreads his mat, straightens his hat and arranges his sash, and only then does he begin to discuss business. So the diviner has a sense of propriety. As a result of his words, offerings are made to the gods and spirits, loyal ministers serve their lords, filial sons look after their parents, and affectionate fathers take care of their sons. These are the virtues the diviner confers. And for all these benefits he is paid with twenty or thirty or a hundred cash!

"As a result of his instructions the sick are sometimes made well, those in mortal danger are saved from death, and those in distress are freed from their worries. Undertakings are brought to a successful conclusion, sons and daughters are happily married off, and people live to a ripe old age. Are such virtues as these worth no more than a handful of coins? This is what Lao Zi meant when he said, 'The man of superior virtue does not appear to have any virtue; therefore he keeps his virtue.'[5] Now if the diviner confers such great benefits as these and receives such a small recompense, is he any different from the man Lao Zi is describing?

"Zhuang Zi has said, 'At home the gentleman does not worry about cold and hunger; abroad he has no fear of being robbed. If he is in a superior position he commands respect; if in an inferior one he suffers no harm. This is the way of the gentleman.'[6] Now the diviner in pursuing his profession does not need to gather together a lot of equipment, nor does he require a storehouse to keep his goods. When he travels he does not have to have baggage carts to move the tools of his trade; he may carry them on his back and they are not heavy. He puts them

---

[5] Lao Zi, *Daode jing* 34.

[6] No such passage is found in the present text of the *Zhuang zi*.

down any place and is ready to start; he uses them as often as he likes and they never give out. Bearing in his hands such inexhaustible tools, travelling the endless reaches of the world — even Zhuang Zi's gentleman could do no better than this! Why then do you tell me that divination is worthless?

"Heaven sags in the northwest, and therefore the stars and constellations move in that direction; earth slumps in the southeast, and so the waters all flow there to form the lake which is the sea. The moment the sun reaches the meridian, it begins to move on; as soon as the moon is full, it starts to wane. The way of the ancient kings sometimes flourishes in the world and sometimes is lost. You attack the diviners and demand that everything they say must be true, but are you yourselves not deluded in thinking so?

"Surely, gentlemen, you have observed the rhetoricians and orators. All their plans and schemes are simply the products of their own minds. But if they merely blurted out their own ideas they could never capture the imagination of the ruler. Therefore they always begin their speeches by discussing the kings of antiquity and open their orations with a description of ancient times. In setting forth their schemes and plans they make up elaborate tales about the successes of the former kings or tell about their failures, in order to move the ruler to admiration or fear and thereby achieve their objective. When it comes to talking exaggerated and imposing nonsense, as you put it, no one can match them. Yet if one wishes to strengthen the state, insure the success of the ruler, and fulfil his duty as a loyal minister, he must resort to such means or his words will never be heeded.

"It is the diviner's job to guide people who are confused and to teach the ignorant. And when one is dealing with confused and ignorant people, how can one make them understand in a word or two? Therefore the diviner does not hesitate to speak at length.

"The fleet-footed stallion cannot be harnessed with the worn-out nag; the phoenix does not fly with the flocks of little sparrows. No more so, therefore, does the worthy man stand side by side with the unworthy. Hence the true gentleman hides away in a lowly position in order to avoid the crowd, retires in order to sever his relations with other men, and reveals only a glimmer of his true virtue so as to escape the envy of the masses. In this way he makes clear the heavenly nature of men, assists the governors, and nourishes the governed. He achieves great merit and profit, but does not seek for high position or praise. Men like you with your gaping and gabbling, what do you know about the way of the superior man?"

Song Zhong and Jia Yi sat listening in bewildered amazement. Their heads swam and the colour drained from their faces; their mouths fell open and they could not answer a word. Finally they straightened their robes and, rising from their mats, bowed twice and took their leave. They wandered down the street in a daze, and when they emerged from the gate of the market place they could barely pull themselves up into their carriage. Leaning upon the carriage bar, their heads hanging low, they could not seem to recover their spirits.

Three days later Song Zhong met Jia Yi outside the gate of the palace. Drawing him aside where they could speak without being overheard, he sighed and said, "The greater one's understanding of the Way, the more security he enjoys; but the greater one's power, the more danger threatens him. When a man enjoys such great power and influence as you and I, the day of his downfall cannot be far off! The diviner, even if he makes a false prediction, does not have his wages taken away from him. But if those who lay plans for the ruler make a mistake, there is no place where they can hide. In this respect we and Sima Jizhu are as far apart as the hat that brushes heaven and the shoes that tread the earth. This is what Lao Zi meant when he said, 'The nameless is the source of all creatures.'[7] Heaven and earth are broad, and the things of creation varied and manifold. At times safe, at times in peril, no one knows where to abide! How can you and I hope to imitate men like Sima Jizhu? The longer he lives the greater safety he enjoys. Even Zhuang Zi's gentleman could do no better."

Some time later Song Zhong was sent as envoy to the Xiongnu. He returned to the capital without having carried out his mission, however, and was condemned to execution. Jia Yi was appointed tutor to King Huai of Liang, but when the king one day fell from his horse and was killed, Jia Yi refused to eat, and died of shame and remorse. So these two men, by striving only for the glory of the world, ended by destroying themselves.

The Grand Historian remarks: The reason I have not said anything here about the diviners of ancient times is that very little material can be found on them in the old books. In the case of Sima Jizhu I have been able to gather enough information to write this account.

---

[7] Lao Tzu, *Daode jing* I. What Lao Zi actually said was, "The nameless is the source of heaven and earth." By "nameless", needless to say, he meant the indescribable Tao, not unknown men like Sima Jizhu living in humble obscurity, though this is the way Song Zhong and Jia Yi choose to interpret the passage.

SHI JI 129: THE BIOGRAPHIES OF
THE MONEY-MAKERS[1]

Though only commoners with no special ranks or titles, they were able, without interfering with the government or hindering the activities of the people, to increase their wealth by making the right moves at the right time. Wise men will find something to learn from them. Thus I made "The Biographies of the Money-makers".

Lao Zi has said that under the ideal form of government, "though states exist side by side, so close that they can hear the crowing of each other's cocks and the barking of each other's dogs, the people of each state will savour their own food, admire their own clothing, be content with their own customs, and delight in their own occupations, and will grow old and die without ever wandering abroad."[2] Yet if one were to try to apply this type of government, striving to drag the present age back to the conditions of primitive times and to stop up the eyes and ears of the people, it is doubtful that one would have much chance of success!

The Grand Historian remarks: I know nothing about the times of Shen Nong and before but, judging by what is recorded in the *Odes* and *Documents*, from the age of Emperor Shun and the Xia dynasty down to the present, ears and eyes have always longed for the ultimate in beautiful sounds and forms, mouths have desired to taste the best in grass-fed and grain-fed animals, bodies have delighted in ease and comfort, and hearts have swelled with pride at the glories of power and ability. So long have these habits been allowed to permeate the lives of the people that, though one were to go from door to door preaching the subtle

---

[1] The title of the chapter, *huozhi*, literally "wealth increasing", is taken from Confucius' remark about his disciple Zigong (discussed in this chapter): "Ce (Zigong) does not acquiesce in his fate and his wealth increases" (*Analects* XI, 17). The chapter, containing as it does a great many technical terms and details of the economic life of the Han, is one of the most difficult in the *Shi ji*, and commentators differ on numerous points of interpretation.

[2] Lao Zi, *Daode jing* 80.

arguments of the Taoists, he could never succeed in changing them. Therefore the highest type of ruler accepts the nature of the people, the next best leads the people to what is beneficial, the next gives them moral instruction, the next forces them to be orderly, and the very worst kind enters into competition with them.[3]

The region west of the mountains is rich in timber, bamboo, paper mulberry, hemp, oxtails for banner tassels, jade and other precious stones. That east of the mountains abounds in fish, salt, lacquer, silk, singers, and beautiful women. The area south of the Yangtze produces camphor wood, catalpa, ginger, cinnamon, gold, tin, lead ore, cinnabar, rhinoceros horns, tortoise shell, pearls of various shapes, and elephant tusks and hides, while that north of Longmen and Jieshi is rich in horses, cattle, sheep, felt, furs, tendons, and horns. Mountains from which copper and iron can be extracted are found scattered here and there over thousands of miles of the empire, like chessmen on a board. In general, these are the products of the empire. All of them are commodities coveted by the people of China, who according to their various customs use them for their bedding, clothing, food, and drink, fashioning from them the goods needed to supply the living and bury the dead.

Society obviously must have farmers before it can eat; foresters, fishermen, miners, etc., before it can make use of natural resources; craftsmen before it can have manufactured goods; and merchants before they can be distributed. But once these exist, what need is there for government directives, mobilizations of labour, or periodic assemblies? Each man has only to be left to utilize his own abilities and exert his strength to obtain what he wishes. Thus, when a commodity is very cheap, it invites a rise in price; when it is very expensive, it invites a reduction. When each person works away at his own occupation and delights in his own business then, like water flowing downward, goods will naturally flow forth ceaselessly day and night without having been summoned, and the people will produce commodities without having been asked. Does this not tally with reason? Is it not a natural result?

The *Book of Zhou* says, "If the farmers do not produce, there will be a shortage of food; if the artisans do not produce, there will be a shortage of

---

[3] A reference to Emperor Wu's economic policies, which put the government officials into competition with the people for profit. This whole chapter must be read in the light of the historian's earlier description of economic measures and conditions in "The Treatise on the Balanced Standard".

manufactured goods; if the merchants do not produce, then the three precious things will not circulate; if the foresters, fishermen, miners, etc., do not produce, there will be a shortage of wealth, and if there is a shortage of wealth the resources of the mountains and lakes cannot be exploited.[4] These four classes are the source of the people's clothing and food. When the source is large, there will be plenty for everyone, but when the source is small, there will be scarcity. On the one hand, the state will be enriched, and on the other, powerful families will be enriched. Poverty and wealth are not the sort of things that are arbitrarily handed to men or taken away: the clever have a surplus; the stupid never have enough.

At the beginning of the Zhou dynasty, when the Grand Duke Wang was enfeoffed with Yingqiu in the state of Qi, where the land was damp and brackish and the inhabitants few, he encouraged the women workers, developed the craft industries to the highest degree, and opened up a trade in fish and salt. As a result, men and goods were reeled into the state like skeins of thread; they converged upon it like spokes about a hub. Soon Qi was supplying caps and sashes, clothes and shoes to the whole empire, and the lords of the area between the sea and Mt. Tai adjusted their sleeves and journeyed to its court to pay their respects.

Later, the power of the state of Qi fell into decline, but Master Guan Zhong restored it to prosperity by establishing the nine bureaus for controlling the flow of money. As a result Duke Huan of Qi (685-643 BC) was able to become a dictator; nine times he called together the other feudal lords for conferences and set the empire to rights again. Moreover, Guan Zhong himself, though only a court minister, owned the mansion called the Three Returnings,[5] and his wealth exceeded that of the lord of a great feudal kingdom. Thus the state of Qi remained rich and powerful through the reigns of Wei and Xuan (378-323 BC).

Therefore it is said, "Only when the granaries are full can people appreciate rites and obligations; only when they have enough food and clothing do they think about glory and disgrace."[6] Rites are born of plenty and are abandoned in

---

[4] No such quotation is found in the section of the *Book of Documents* devoted to the Zhou dynasty or in the *Yizhou shu*. The "three precious things" are usually identified as the products of the other three classes, i.e., agricultural products, manufactured goods, and the products of mountains, lakes, etc.

[5] On the "Three Returnings" see the biography of the Marquis of Pingjin, p. 190, note 1.

[6] The quotation is found in the opening paragraph of the *Guan zi*, a text which purports to represent the sayings and theories of Guan Zhong.

hen superior men become rich, they delight in practising virtue;
minded men are rich, they long only to exercise their power. As
vell in the deepest pools and wild beasts congregate in the most
ains, so benevolence and righteousness attach themselves to a
man of wealth. So long as a rich man wields power, he may win greater and
greater eminence, but once his power is gone, his guests and retainers will all
desert him and take no more delight in his company. This is even more the case
among barbarians.

The proverb says, "The young man with a thousand catties of gold does not
meet death in the market place."[7] This is no idle saying. So it is said,

> Jostling and joyous,
> The whole world comes after profit;
> Racing and rioting,
> After profit the whole world goes!

If even the king of a land of 1,000 chariots, the lord of 10,000 households,
or the master of 100 dwellings must worry about poverty, how much more so
the common peasant whose name is enroled in the tax collector's list?

In former times when King Goujian of Yue (496-465 BC) was surrounded
on Mt. Kuaiji by the armies of the state of Wu and was in great difficulty, he
followed the advice of Fan Li and Jiran. Jiran said, "If you know there is going
to be a battle, you must make preparations beforehand, and for ordinary use you
must know what goods are needed in each season. When you understand these
two necessities clearly, then you can perceive how all kinds of goods should be
disposed. When Jupiter is in the western portion of the sky, which is dominated
by the element metal, there will be good harvests; when it is in the northern
portion dominated by water, there will be destruction by floods; when it is in
the eastern portion dominated by wood, there will be famine; and when in the
southern portion dominated by fire, there will be drought. When there is a
drought, that is the time to start laying away a stock of boats; and when there is

---

[7]Commentators generally take this to mean that a son of a wealthy family has enough
moral training to avoid breaking the law and thus incurring execution in the market place.
Obviously, however, it may also be interpreted more cynically to mean that money can buy
one's way out of any difficulties.

a flood, that is the time to start buying up carts. This is the principle behind use of goods.

"Every six years there will be a good harvest, every six years there will be a drought, and every twelve years there will be one great famine. If grain is sold as low as twenty cash a picul, then the farmers will suffer, but if it goes as high as ninety cash, then those in secondary occupations will suffer. If the merchants and others in secondary occupations suffer, then they will produce no goods, while if the farmers suffer they will cease to clear their fields. If, however, the price does not go over eighty cash nor fall below thirty, then both farmers and those in secondary occupations will benefit. If the price of grain is kept level and goods are fairly distributed, then there will be no shortages in the customs barriers and markets. This is the way to govern a country.

"The principle of storing goods is to try to get commodities which can be preserved for a long time without damage or depreciation[8] and can be easily exchanged for other things. Do not store up commodities that are likely to rot or spoil, and do not hoard expensive articles. If you study the surpluses and shortages of the market, you can judge how much a commodity will be worth. When an article has become extremely expensive, it will surely fall in price, and when it has become extremely cheap, then the price will begin to rise. Dispose of expensive goods as though they were so much filth and dirt; buy up cheap goods as though they were pearls and jade. Wealth and currency should be allowed to flow as freely as water!"

King Goujian followed this advice for the next ten years until the state of Yue became rich and he was able to give generous gifts to his fighting men. As a result, his soldiers were willing to rush into the face of the arrows and stones of the enemy as though they were thirsty men going to drink their fill; in the end King Goujian took his revenge upon the powerful forces of Wu, demonstrated his military might to the other states of China, and came to be known as one of the Five Hegemons.

Fan Li, having helped to wipe out the shame of Yue's defeat at Kuaiji, sighed and said, "Of Jiran's seven strategies, Yue made use of five and achieved its desires. They have already been put into practice in the state. Now I would like to try using them for my own family."

---

[8] Following the reading in the *Suoyin* and *Zhengyi* commentaries.

Then he got into a little boat and sailed down the Yangtze and through the lakes. He changed his family name and personal name and visited Qi, where he was known as Chiyi Zipi, the "Adaptable Old Wine-skin". Later he went to Tao, where he was called Lord Zhu. He observed that Tao, located in the middle of the empire, with feudal lords passing back and forth in all directions, was a centre for the exchange of goods. He therefore established his business there, storing away goods, looking for a profitable time to sell, and not making demands upon others. (Thus one who is good at running a business must know how to select men and take advantage of the times.) In the course of nineteen years Fan Li, or Lord Zhu, as he was now called, three times accumulated fortunes of 1,000 catties of gold, and twice he gave them away among his poor friends and distant relations. This is what is meant by a rich man who delights in practising virtue. Later, when he became old and frail, he turned over his affairs to his sons and grandsons, who carried on and improved the business until the family fortune had reached 100,000,000 cash. Therefore, when people speak of rich men they always mention Tao Zhugong, Lord Zhu of Tao.

Zigong, after studying with Confucius, retired and held office in the state of Wey. By buying up, storing, and selling various goods in the region of Cao and Lu, he managed to become the richest among Confucius' seventy disciples. While Yuan Xian, another of the Master's disciples, could not get even enough chaff and husks to satisfy his hunger, and lived hidden away in a tiny lane, Zigong rode about with a team of four horses attended by a mounted retinue, bearing gifts of bundles of silk to be presented to the feudal lords, and whatever state he visited the ruler never failed to descend into the courtyard and greet him as an equal. It was due to Zigong's efforts that Confucius' fame was spread over the empire. Is this not what we mean when we say that a man who wields power may win greater and greater eminence?

Bai Gui was a native of Zhou. During the time of Marquis Wen of Wei (403-387 BC), Li Ke stressed full utilization of the powers of the land, but Bai Gui delighted in watching for opportunities presented by the changes of the times.

What others throw away, I take;
What others take, I give away,

he said. "When the year is good and the harvest plentiful, I buy up grain and sell silk and lacquer; when cocoons are on the market, I buy up raw silk and sell

grain. When the reverse marker of Jupiter is in the sign *mao*, the harvest will
be good, but the following year the crops will do much worse. When it reaches
the sign *wu*, there will be a drought, but the next year will be fine. When it
reaches the sign *you*, there will be good harvests, followed the next year by a
falling off. When it reaches the sign *zi*, there will be a great drought. The next
year will be fine and later there will be floods. Thus the cycle revolves again to
the sign *mao*."

By observing these laws, he was able to approximately double his stores of
grain each year. When he wanted to increase his money supply, he bought cheap
grain, and when he wanted to increase his stock, he bought up high-grade grain.
He ate and drank the simplest fare, controlled his appetites and desires, economized on clothing, and shared the same hardships as his servants and slaves,
and when he saw a good opportunity, he pounced on it like a fierce animal or a
bird of prey. "As you see," he said, "I manage my business affairs in the same
way that the statesmen Yi Yin and Lü Shang planned their policies, the military
experts Sun Zi and Wu Zi deployed their troops, and the Legalist philosopher
Shang Yang carried out his laws. Therefore, if a man does not have wisdom
enough to change with the times, courage enough to make decisions, benevolence enough to know how to give and take, and strength enough to stand his
ground, though he may wish to learn my methods, I will never teach them to
him!"

Hence, when the world talks of managing a business it acknowledges Bai
Gui as the ancestor of the art. Bai Gui tried out his theories in practice, and his
experiments proved successful. He knew what he was talking about.

Yi Dun rose to prominence by producing salt in ponds, while Guo Zong of
Handan made a business of smelting iron, and their wealth equalled that of the
ruler of a kingdom.

---

9. Since Jupiter takes approximately twelve years to complete one cycle of the heavens,
the years of the cycle were designated by the twelve signs that marked the division of the
horizon, depending upon which portion of the sky Jupiter was in. But because Jupiter appeared
to revolve counterclockwise through the sky, and the order of the twelve signs ran clockwise,
an imaginary marker, called *suiyin* or *taiyin*, was postulated, which revolved in the opposite
direction from Jupiter. As this works out, when the reverse marker was in *mao* (east), Jupiter
was in *zi* (north); when the marker was in *wu* (south), Jupiter was in *you* (west); when the
marker was in *you* (west), Jupiter was in *wu* (south); and when the marker was in *zi* (north),
Jupiter was in *mao* (east). Hence Bai Gui is saying that when Jupiter is in the north or south,
there will be good harvests; when it is in the west there will be drought; and when it is in the
east there will be a great drought. The reader may compare this with Jiran's laws above.

Wuzhi Luo raised domestic animals, and when he had a large number, he sold them and bought rare silks and other articles which he secretly sent as gifts to the king of the Rong barbarians. The king of the Rong repaid him ten times the original cost and sent him domestic animals until Wuzhi Luo had so many herds of horses and cattle he could only estimate their number roughly by the valleyful. The First Emperor of the Qin ordered that Wuzhi Luo be granted the same honours as a feudal lord and allowed him to join the ministers in seasonal audiences at court.

There was also the case of a widow named Qing of the region of Ba and Shu. Her ancestors got possession of some cinnabar caves and were able to monopolize the profits from them for several generations until they had acquired an inestimable amount of wealth. Qing, although only a widow, was able to carry on the business and used her wealth to buy protection for herself so that others could not mistreat or impose upon her. The First Emperor of the Qin, considering her a virtuous woman, treated her as a guest and built the Nühuaiqing Terrace in her honour.

Wuzhi Luo was a simple country man who looked after herds, while Qing was only a widow living far off in the provinces, and yet both were treated with as much respect as though they had been the lords of a state of 10,000 chariots, and their fame spread all over the world. Was this not because of their wealth?

After the Han rose to power, the barriers and bridges were opened and the restrictions on the use of the resources of mountains and lakes were relaxed. As a result, the rich traders and great merchants travelled all around the empire distributing their wares to every corner so that everyone could buy what he wanted. At the same time the powerful families of the great provincial clans and former feudal lords were moved to the capital.

The area within the Pass,[10] from the Qian and Yong rivers east to the Yellow River and Mt. Hua, is a region of rich and fertile fields stretching 1,000 *li*. Judging from the tribute exacted by Emperor Shun and the rulers of the Xia dynasty, these were already at that time considered to be among the finest fields. Later the ancestor of the house of Zhou, Gongliu, made his home in Bin in the region; his descendants Dawang and Wangji lived in the area called Qi, King

---

[10] In the following description of the various geographical areas of the empire and the customs of the people in each, there are no indications of tense and it is not certain whether Sima Qian is talking about the customs of older times or those of his own day. I have in most cases translated as though he meant the latter.

Wen built the city of Feng; and King Wu ruled from Hao. Therefore the people of the region still retain traces of the customs they learned under these ancient rulers. They are fond of agriculture, raise the five grains, take good care of their fields, and regard it as a serious matter to do wrong.

Later, Dukes Wen and Mu[11] of Qin (765-621 BC) fixed the capital of their state at Yong, which was on the main route for goods being brought out of both Long and Shu and was a centre for merchants. Dukes Xian and Xiao (384-338 BC) moved the Qin capital to the city of Yue. The city of Yue drove back the Rong and Di barbarians in the north and in the east opened up communication with the states that had been created out of the former state of Jin. It too was a centre for great merchants. Kings Wu and Zhao (310-251 BC) made their capital at Xianyang, and it was this site that the Han took over and used for its own capital, Chang'an. People poured in from all parts of the empire to congregate in the towns established at the imperial tombs around Chang'an, converging on the capital like the spokes of a wheel. The land area is small and the population numerous, and therefore the people have become more and more sophisticated and crafty and have turned to secondary occupations such as trade to make their living.

South of this region are the provinces of Ba and Shu, which also contain rich fields and produce large quantities of gardenias for making dye, ginger, cinnabar, copper, iron, and bamboo and wooden implements. In the south these provinces control the regions of Dian and Po, the latter noted for its young slaves. Nearby on the west are the regions of Qiong and Zuo, the latter famous for its horses and oxtails. Though the area is hemmed in on all four sides by natural barriers, there are plank roadways built along the sides of the mountains for 1,000 *li* so that there is no place that cannot be reached. All these roads are squeezed together into one in the narrow defile running between the Bao and Ye rivers. By means of such roads, areas which have a surplus may exchange their goods for the things which they lack.

North of the capital area are the provinces of Tianshui, Longxi, Beidi, and Shang, whose customs are the same as those of the area within the Pass. To the west there are profits to be gained among the Qiang barbarians, while to the north are the herds of the Rong and Di barbarians, which are one of the riches of the empire. Nevertheless, the region is mountainous and inaccessible and the

---

[11] Omitting the name of Duke Xiao, which erroneously appears between Wen and Mu in present texts.

only route out of it is that which leads to the capital.

Thus the region within the Pass occupies about a third of the area of the empire. The inhabitants represent only three tenths of the total population, but they possess six tenths of the wealth of the nation.

In ancient times the men of the state of Emperor Yao made their capital in Hedong, those of the Yin dynasty established their capital in Henei, and those of the Zhou dynasty in Henan. These three regions stand like the legs of a tripod in the centre of the empire and were used as the sites of their capitals by the successive dynasties, each of which lasted for several hundred or even 1,000 years. The region is narrow and constricted and the population large. Since the capitals of the various dynasties served as gathering places for the feudal lords, the people are very thrifty and experienced in the ways of the world.

Yang and Pingyang[12] in Hedong have customarily traded with the area of Qin and the Di barbarians in the west and with Zhong and Dai in the north. Zhong and Dai are situated north of the old city of Shi. They border the lands of the Xiongnu and are frequently raided by the barbarians. The inhabitants are proud and stubborn, high-spirited and fond of feats of daring and evil, and do not engage in agriculture or trade. Because the region is so close to the territory of the northern barbarians, armies have frequently been sent there, and when supplies were transported to them from the central states, the people were often able to profit from the surplus. The inhabitants have mingled with the barbarians, and their customs are by no means uniform. From the time before the state of Jin was divided into three parts they were already a source of trouble because of their violent temperament. King Wuling of Zhao (325-299 BC) did much to encourage this trait, and the inhabitants today still retain the ways they developed when they were under the rule of Zhao. The merchants of Yang and Pingyang roam through the region and obtain whatever goods they want.

Wen and Zhi in Henei have customarily traded with Shangdang in the west and Zhao and Zhongshan in the north. The soil in Zhongshan is barren and the population large. Even today at Sandy Hill are to be found the descendants of the people who took part in the decadent revels of Emperor Zhou, the last ruler of the Yin dynasty, who had his summer palace there. The people are of an impetuous nature and are always looking for some cunning and clever way to make a living. The men gather together to play games, sing sad songs, and lament. When they really put their minds to business, they go out in bands to

---

[12] Omitting the place name Chen, which does not seem to belong here.

rob and kill, and in their spare time they loot graves, think up ways to flatter and deceive others or, dressing up in beautiful array, become singers and actors. The women play upon the large lute and trip about in dancing slippers, visiting the homes of the noble and rich to sell their favours or becoming concubines in the palaces of the feudal lords all over the empire.

Handan, situated between the Zhang and Yellow rivers, is a city of major importance. In the north it has communications with Yan and Zhuo, and on the south with the regions of the old states of Zheng and Wey. The customs of Zheng and Wey are similar to those of Zhao except that, since they are located nearer to Liang and Lu, the people are somewhat more sedate and take pride in virtuous conduct. The inhabitants of Yewang were moved there from their city on the Pu River when the latter was taken over by the state of Qin (207 BC). They are high-spirited and given to feats of daring, traits which mark them as former subjects of the state of Wey.

Yan, situated between the Gulf of Bohai and Jieshi, is also a major city. The region of Yan communicates with Qi and Zhao in the south, borders the lands of the Xiongnu in the northeast, and extends as far as Shanggu and Liaodong, a distant and remote area, sparsely populated and often subject to barbarian raids. On the whole the customs are similar to those of Zhao and Dai, but the people are as fierce as hawks and exercise little forethought. The region is rich in fish, salt, jujubes, and chestnuts. On the north it adjoins the Wuhuan and Fuyu tribes and on the east it controls the profits derived from trade with the Huimo, Chaoxian (Korean), and Zhenpan peoples.

Luoyang in the region of Henan trades with Qi and Lu to the east and with Liang and Chu to the south.

The region south of Mt. Tai is the former state of Lu and that north of the mountain is Qi. Qi is bounded by mountains and sea, a fertile area stretching 1,000 *li*, suitable for growing mulberry and hemp. The population is large and produces beautifully patterned silks and other textiles, fish, and salt. Linzi, the capital, situated between the sea and Mt. Tai, is a city of major importance. The people are by nature generous and easy-going, of considerable intelligence, and fond of debate. They are very attached to the land and dislike turmoil and uprising. They are timid in group warfare but brave in single combat, which accounts for the large number of highway robbers among them. On the whole, however, they have the ways of a great nation. All the five classes of people (scholars, farmers, travelling merchants, artisans, and resident traders) are to be found among them.

Zou and Lu border the Zhu and Si rivers and still retain the ways which they learned when they were ruled by the duke of Zhou. They are fond of Confucian learning and proficient in matters of ritual, which makes them very punctilious. Mulberries and hemp are grown to some extent, but no resources are to be gained from forests or lakes. Land is scarce and the population numerous, so that the people are very frugal; they are much afraid of committing crimes and give a wide berth to evil. In later days, however, as the state has declined, they have become very fond of trade and are even more assiduous than the men of Zhou in pursuing profit.

East of the Hong Canal and north of the Mang and Dang mountains as far as the marsh of Juye is the region of the old states of Liang and Song. Tao and Suiyang are the most important cities in the area. In ancient times Emperor Yao built his pleasure palace at Chengyang, Emperor Shun fished in the Lei Marsh, and King Tang settled in Bo, so that the people still retain traces of the customs they learned from these former sage rulers. They are grave in demeanour, devoted to agricultural pursuits, and include a large number of true gentlemen. Though there are no riches to be gained from the mountains and rivers, the people are willing to put up with poor clothing and food and even manage to store up a surplus.

The regions of Yue and Chu are divided into three areas which differ in their customs. From the Huai River north to Pei, Chen, Runan, and Nan provinces is the area of western Chu. The people are very volatile and quickly give vent to their anger. The land is barren and there is little surplus to be stored up. Jiangling occupies the site of Ying, the old capital of the state of Chu. To the west it communicates with Wu and Ba and in the east draws upon the resources of the Yunmeng lakes. Chen is situated on what used to be the border between Chu and the old empire of the Xia dynasty and carries on a trade in fish and salt. The population therefore includes a large number of merchants. The people of the districts of Xu, Tong, and Qulü are honest and strict and pride themselves on keeping their promises.

From the city of Pengcheng east to Donghai, Wu, and Guangling is the region of eastern Chu. The customs are similar to those of Xu and Tong. From the districts of Qu and Zeng on north, however, the customs are similar to those of Qi, while from the Zhe and Yangtze rivers on south, they resemble those of Yue. Helu, the ancient king of the state of Wu (725-702 BC), the lord of Chunshen (third century BC), and Liu Pi, the king of Wu in Han times, all did their best to attract wandering scholars and protégés to the city of Wu. The city enjoys the rich salt resources derived from the sea in the east, copper from the Zhang Mountains, and the benefits from the three mouths of the Yangtze and the Five Lakes nearby, and is the most important city in the area east of the Yangtze.

Hengshan, Jiujiang, Jiangnan, Yuzhang, and Changsha make up the region of southern Chu. The customs of the people are generally similar to those of western Chu. Shouchun, which the Chu kings used as their capital after they moved from Ying, is the most important city in the area. The district of Hefei receives goods transported down both the Huai River in the north and the Yangtze in the south and is a centre for the shipping of hides, dried fish, and lumber. The customs of the people have become mixed with those of the Min and Yue tribes. Thus the men of southern Chu are fond of fancy phrases and clever at talking, but what they say can seldom be trusted. Jiangnan, the area just south of the Yangtze, is low and damp, and even hardy young men die early there. It produces large quantities of bamboo and timber. Yuzhang produces gold and Changsha produces lead ore, but the quantity is so small that, though it exists, it seldom repays the cost of extraction.

From the Nine Peaks and Cangwu south to Daner the customs are in general similar to those of Jiangnan, though with a large admixture of the customs of the Yang and Yue people. Panyu is the most important city in the area, being a centre for pearls, rhinoceros horn, tortoise shell, fruit, and cloth.

Yingchuan and Nanyang were the home of the people of the ancient Xia dynasty. The Xia people valued loyalty and simplicity in government, and the influence of the Xia kings is still to be seen in the ways of the inhabitants of the region, who are warmhearted and sincere. In the latter days of the Qin dynasty the government moved large numbers of lawbreakers to the region of Nanyang. Nanyang communicates on the west with the area within the Pass through the Wu Pass, and with Hanzhong through the Xun Pass, and from the east and south it receives goods by way of the Han, Yangtze, and Huai rivers. Yuan is the most important city in the region. The customs are rather heterogeneous; the people are fond of business and there are many merchants among them. The local bosses in the area work in cooperation with their counterparts in Yingchuan. Even today people refer to the inhabitants of the entire region as "men of Xia".

Various products are rare in one part of the empire and plentiful in another part. For example, it is the custom of the people east of the mountains to use salt extracted from the sea, while those west of the mountains use rock salt. There are also places in Lingnan in the far south and in the deserts of the far north which have long produced salt. In general, the same is true of other products as well.

To sum up, the region of Chu and Yue is broad and sparsely populated, and the people live on rice and fish soups. They burn off the fields and flood them to kill the weeds, and are able to gather all the fruit, berries, and uni-valve and bi-valve shellfish they want without waiting for merchants to come around selling them. Since the land is so rich in edible products, there is no fear of famine, and therefore the people are content to live along from day to day; they do not lay away stores of goods, and many of them are poor. As a result, in the region south of the Yangtze and Huai rivers no one ever freezes or starves to death, but on the other hand there are no very wealthy families.

The region north of the Zhe and Si rivers is suitable for growing the five types of grain, mulberries, and hemp, and for raising the six kinds of domestic animals.[13] Land is scarce and the population dense, and the area often suffers from floods and drought. The people therefore take good care to lay away stores of food. Hence in the regions of Qin, Xia, Liang, and Lu agriculture is favoured and the peasants are held in esteem. The same is true of Hedong, Henei and Henan, as well as Yuan and Chen, though in these regions the people also engage in trade. The people of Qi and Zhao with their intelligence and cleverness are always on the lookout for a chance to make a profit. Those of Yan and Dai gain their living from their fields and herds of domestic animals, and also raise silkworms.

Judging from all that has been said above, when wise men lay their profound plans in palace chambers or deliberate in audience halls, guard their honour and die for their principles, or when gentlemen retire to dwell in mountain caves and establish a reputation for purity of conduct, what is their ultimate objective? Their objective is simply wealth. So the honest official after years of service attains riches, and the honest merchant in the end becomes wealthy.

The desire for wealth does not need to be taught; it is an integral part of all human nature. Hence, when young men in the army attack cities and scale walls, break through the enemy lines and drive back the foe, cut down the opposing generals and seize their pennants, advance beneath a rain of arrows and stones, and do not turn aside before the horrors of fire and boiling water, it is because they are spurred on by the prospect of rich rewards. Again, when the youths of the lanes and alleys attack passers-by or murder them and hide their bodies,

---

[13] Horses, cattle, pigs, goats, dogs, and chickens. Dogs were raised to be eaten.

threaten others and commit evil deeds, dig up graves and coin counterfeit money, form gangs to bully others, lend each other a hand in avenging wrongs, and think up secret ways to blackmail people or drive them from the neighbourhood, paying no heed to the laws and prohibitions, but rushing headlong to the place of execution, it is in fact all because of the lure of money. In like manner, when the women of Zhao and the maidens of Zheng paint their faces and play upon the large lute, flutter their long sleeves and trip about in pointed slippers, invite with their eyes and beckon with their hearts, considering it no distance at all to travel 1,000 miles to meet a patron, not caring whether he is old or young, it is because they are after riches. When idle young noblemen ornament their caps and swords and go about with a retinue of carriages and horsemen, it is simply to show off their wealth. Those who go out to shoot birds with stringed arrows, to fish or to hunt, heedless of dawn or nightfall, braving frost and snow, galloping around the animal pits or into ravines without shying from the dangers of wild beasts, do so because they are greedy for the taste of fresh game. The reason that those who indulge in gambling, horse racing, cock fighting, and dog racing turn red in the face, shouting boasts to one another, and invariably quarrel over the victory is that they consider it a very serious matter to lose their wagers. Doctors, magicians, and all those who live by their arts are willing to burn up their spirits and exhaust their talents only because they value the fees they will receive. When officials in the government juggle with phrases and twist the letter of the law, carve fake seals and forge documents, heedless of the mutilating punishments of the knife and saw that await them if they are discovered, it is because they are drowned in bribes and gifts. And when farmers, craftsmen, traders, and merchants lay away stores and work to expand their capital, we may be sure that it is because they are seeking wealth and hope to increase their goods. Thus men apply all their knowledge and use all their abilities simply in accumulating money. They never have any strength left over to consider the question of giving some of it away.

The proverb says, "You don't go 100 miles to peddle firewood; you don't go 1,000 miles to deal in grain. If you are going to be in a place for one year, then seed it with grain. If you are going to be there ten years, plant trees. And if you are going to be there 100 years, provide for the future by means of virtue." Virtue here means being good to people. Now there are men who receive no ranks or emoluments from the government and who have no revenue from titles or fiefs, and yet they enjoy just as much ease as those who have all these; they may be called the "untitled nobility". A lord who possesses a fief lives off the

{ Virtue

taxes. Each year he is allowed to collect 200 cash from each household, so that the lord of 1,000 households has an income of 200,000 cash. But out of this he has to pay the expenses of his spring and autumn visits to the court and pay for various gifts and presentations. Common people such as farmers, craftsmen, travelling traders, and merchants on the whole may expect a profit of 2,000 cash a year on a capital investment of 10,000. So if a family has a capital investment of 1,000,000 cash, their income will likewise be 200,000. Out of this they must pay the cost of commutation of labour and military services, as well as property and poll taxes, but with the rest they may buy whatever fine food and clothing they desire.

Thus it is said that those who own pasture lands producing fifty horses a year, or 100 head of cattle, or 500 sheep, or 500 marshland swine; those who own reservoirs stocked with 1,000 piculs of fish or mountain lands containing 1,000 logs of timber; those who have 1,000 jujube trees in Anyi, or 1,000 chestnut trees in Yan or Qin, or 1,000 citrus trees in Shu, Han, or Jiangling, or 1,000 catalpas north of the Huai River or south of Changshan in the region of the Yellow and Qi rivers; those who own 1,000 *mu* of lacquer trees in Chen or Xia, 1,000 *mu* of mulberries or hemp in Qi or Lu, or 1,000 *mu* of bamboo along the Wei River; those who own farmlands in the suburbs of some famous capital or large city which produce one *zhong*[14] of grain per *mu*, or those who own 1,000 *mu* of gardenias or madder for dyes, or 1,000 beds of ginger or leeks — all these may live just as well as a marquis enfeoffed with 1,000 households. Commodities such as these are in fact the sources of considerable wealth. Their owners need not visit the market place or travel about to other cities but may simply sit at home and wait for the money to come in. They may live with all the dignity of retired gentlemen and still enjoy an income.

At the other extreme, when it comes to those impoverished men with aged parents and wives and children too weak or young to help them out, who have nothing to offer their ancestors at the seasonal sacrifices, who must depend upon the gifts and contributions of the community for their food and clothing and are unable to provide for themselves — if men such as these, reduced to such straits,

---

[14] One *zhong* is equal to ten *hu*, or about five and a half U.S. bushels. One *mu* at this time was probably about 0.114 acres. The units used in this list are often obscure, and commentators disagree on their interpretation. Throughout the chapter I have followed the interpretations given by Professor Miyazaki Ichisada in his article, in Japanese, "A Price-list in the Biographies of Millionaires in the *Shi ji*", *Miscellanea Kiotensia* (Kyoto University, 1956), pp. 451-74.

still fail to feel any shame or embarrassment, then they hardly deserve to be called human. Therefore, when men have no wealth at all, they live by their brawn; when they have a little, they struggle to get ahead by their brains; and when they already have plenty of money, they look for an opportunity for a good investment. This in general is the way things work.

When it comes to making a living, the wise man will look around for some way to gain an income that does not involve any personal danger. Hence the best kind of wealth is that which is based upon agriculture, the next best is that which is derived from secondary occupations, and the worst of all is that which is acquired by evil means. But if a man is not a gentleman of unusual character who has deliberately sought retirement from the world, and if he grows old in poverty and lowliness and still insists upon talking about his "benevolence and righteousness", he ought to be thoroughly ashamed of himself.

As for the ordinary lot of tax-paying commoners, if they are confronted by someone whose wealth is ten times their own, they will behave with humility; if by someone whose wealth is 100 times their own, they will cringe with fear; if by someone whose wealth is 1,000 times their own, they will undertake to work for him; and if by someone whose wealth is 10,000 times their own, they will become his servants. This is the principle of things.

It is said, "If a man is trying to work his way up from poverty to riches, then farming is not as good as handicrafts, and handicrafts are not as good as trade; embroidering lovely patterns at home is not as good as lounging about the market gate." This means that the secondary occupations are the best source of wealth for a poor man.

Anyone who in the market towns or great cities manages in the course of a year to sell the following items: 1,000 brewings of liquor; 1,000 jars of pickles and sauces; 1,000 jars of syrups; 1,000 slaughtered cattle, sheep, and swine; 1,000 *zhong* of grain; 1,000 cartloads or 1,000 boat-lengths of firewood and stubble for fuel; 1,000 logs of timber; 10,000 bamboo poles; 100 horse carriages; 1,000 two-wheeled ox carts; 1,000 lacquered wooden vessels; brass utensils weighing 30,000 catties; 1,000 piculs of plain wooden vessels, iron vessels, or gardenia and madder dyes; 200 horses; 500 cattle; 2,000 sheep or swine; 100 male or female slaves; 1,000 catties of tendons, horns, or cinnabar; 30,000 catties of silken fabric, raw silk, or other fine fabrics; 1,000 rolls of embroidered or patterned silk; 1,000 piculs of fabrics made of vegetable fiber or raw or tanned hides; 1,000 pecks of lacquer; 1,000 jars of leaven or salted bean relish; 1,000 catties of globefish or mullet; 1,000 piculs of dried fish; 30,000 catties of salted fish; 3,000 piculs of jujubes or chestnuts; 1,000 skins of fox or sable; 1,000 piculs of lamb or sheep skins; 1,000 felt mats; or 1,000 *zhong* of fruits or vegetables — such a man may live as well as the master of an estate of 1,000 chariots. The same applies for anyone who has 1,000 strings of cash (i.e., 1,000,000 cash) to lend out on interest. Such loans are made through a money-lender, but a greedy merchant who is too anxious for a quick return will only manage to revolve his working capital three times while a less avaricious merchant has revolved his five times. These are the principal ways of making money. There are various other occupations which bring in less than twenty percent profit, but they are not what I would call sources of wealth.

Now I should like to describe briefly the ways in which some of the worthy men of the present age, working within an area of 1,000 miles, have managed to acquire wealth, so that later generations may see how they did it and select what may be of benefit to themselves.

The ancestors of the Zhuo family of Shu were natives of Zhao who made a fortune by smelting iron. When the Qin armies overthrew the state of Zhao, the family was ordered to move to another part of the empire for resettlement. Having been taken captive and plundered of all their wealth and servants, the husband and wife were left to make the move alone, pushing their belongings in a cart. All of the other captives who were forced to move and who had a little wealth left vied with each other in bribing the officials to send them to some nearby location, and they were therefore allowed to settle in Jiameng. But Mr. Zhuo said, "This region is too narrow and barren. I have heard that at the foot of Mt. Min there are fertile plains full of edible tubers so that one may live all his life without suffering from famine. The people there are clever at commerce and make their living by trade." He therefore asked to be sent to a distant region, and was ordered to move to Linqiong. He was overjoyed, and when he got there and found a mountain which yielded iron ore, he began smelting ore and laying other plans to accumulate wealth until soon he dominated the trade among the people of Dian and Shu. He grew so rich that he owned 1,000 young slaves, and the pleasures he indulged in among his fields and lakes and on his bird and animal hunts were like those of a great lord.

Cheng Zheng, like Mr Zhuo, was one of those taken captive east of the mountains by the Qin armies and forced to resettle in the far west. He too engaged in the smelting industry and carried on trade with the barbarians who wear their hair in the mallet-shaped fashion. His wealth equalled that of Mr Zhuo, and the two of them lived in Linqiong.

The ancestors of the Kong family of Yuan were men of Liang who made their living by smelting iron. When Qin overthrew the state of Liang, the Kong family was moved to Nanyang, where they began smelting iron with bellows on a large scale and laying out ponds and fields. Soon they were riding about in carriages with a mounted retinue and visiting the feudal lords, and from these contacts they were able to earn large profits in trade. They also won a reputation for handing out lavish gifts in the manner of noblemen of leisure, but at the same time the profits they derived from their business were surprisingly large — far larger, in fact, then those derived by more cautious and tightfisted merchants — and the family fortune eventually reached several thousand catties of gold. Therefore the traders of Nanyang all imitated the Kong family's lordly and openhanded ways.

Lu people are customarily cautious and miserly, but the Bing family of Cao were particularly so. They started out by smelting iron and in time accumulated a fortune of 100,000,000 cash. All the members of the family from the father and elder brothers down to the sons and grandsons, however, made a promise that they would

> Never look down without picking up something useful;
> Never look up without grabbing something of value.

They travelled about to all the provinces and kingdoms, selling goods on credit, lending money and trading. It was because of their influence that so many people in Zou and Lu abandoned scholarship and turned to the pursuit of profit.

The people of Qi generally despise slaves, but Diao Xian alone valued them and appreciated their worth. Most men worry in particular about slaves who are too cunning and clever, but Diao Xian gladly acquired all he could of this kind and put them to work for him, sending them out to make a profit peddling fish and salt. Though he travelled about in a carriage with a mounted retinue and consorted with governors of provinces and prime ministers of kingdoms, he came to rely more and more upon his slaves, and in the end managed by their labour to acquire a fortune of 20,000,000 or 30,000,000 cash. Hence the saying, "Is it better to have a title in the government or to work for Diao Xian?" which means that he made it possible for his best slaves to enrich themselves while at the same time he utilized their abilities to the fullest.

The people of the old state of Zhou have always been very close in money matters, but Shi Shi was an extreme example. With a couple of hundred cartloads of goods he travelled around to the various provinces and kingdoms peddling his wares; there was absolutely no place he did not go. The city of Luoyang is situated right in the middle of the old states of Qi, Qin, Chu, and Zhao, and even the poor people of the town study to become apprentices to the rich families, boasting to each other about how long they have been in trade and how they have several times passed by their old homes but were too busy to go in the gate. By making use of men like this in his business, Shi Shi was finally able to accumulate a fortune of 70,000,000 cash.

The ancestor of the Ren family of Xuanqu was an official in charge of the granary at Dudao. When the Qin dynasty was overthrown and the leaders of the revolt were all scrambling for gold and jewels, Mr Ren quietly dug a hole and stored away the grain that had been in his charge. Later, when the armies of Chu and Han were stalemated at Xingyang and the people were unable to plough their fields and plant their crops, the price of grain rose to 10,000 cash a picul, and all the gold and jewels of the great leaders soon found their way into the hands of Mr Ren. This was the start of the Ren family fortune. But while other rich people were outdoing each other in luxurious living, the Ren family lived very frugally and devoted all their energies to farming and animal raising. And while most people try to buy the cheapest fields and pasture lands, the Ren family bought up only those that were really valuable and of good quality. Thus the family remained wealthy for several generations. Mr Ren made all the members of the family promise that they would not eat or wear anything that was not produced from their own fields or herds, and that none of them would dare to drink wine or eat meat until their public services had been completed. Because of this rule they became the leaders of the community and, while continuing to be wealthy, enjoyed the respect of the ruler.

When the frontier was expanded and the border regions opened, only Qiao Tao took advantage of the opportunity, acquiring resources calculated at 1,000 horses, twice that number of cattle, 10,000 sheep, and 10,000 *zhong* of grain.

When Wu, Chu, and the other kingdoms, seven in all, raised their revolt in the time of Emperor Jing, the feudal lords in Chang'an made preparations to join the imperial armies in putting down the rebellion and began looking around for ways to borrow money to provide for the expedition. The moneylenders, considering that the fiefs and kingdoms of the feudal lords were all located east of the mountains and that the fate of that region was still a matter of grave doubt, were unwilling to lend them any money. Only one man, a Mr Wuyan, consented to lend them 1,000 catties of gold at an interest of ten times the amount of the loan. By the end of three months the states of Wu and Chu had been brought under control, and within the year Mr Wuyan received his tenfold interest. As a result he became one of the richest men in the area within the Pass.

Most of the rich merchants and big traders of the area within the Pass belonged to the Tian family, such as Tian Se and Tian Lan. In addition, the Li family of Weijia and the Du families of Anling and Du also had fortunes amounting to 100,000,000 cash.

These, then, are examples of outstanding and unusually wealthy men. None of them enjoyed any titles or fiefs, gifts, or salaries from the government, nor did they play tricks with the law or commit any crimes to acquire their fortunes. They simply guessed what course conditions were going to take and acted accordingly, kept a sharp eye out for the opportunities of the times, and so were able to capture a fat profit. They gained their wealth in the secondary occupations and held on to it by investing in agriculture; they seized hold of it in times of crisis and maintained it in times of stability. There was a special aptness in the way they adapted to the times, and therefore their stories are worth relating. In addition, there are many other men who exerted themselves at farming, animal raising, crafts, lumbering, merchandising, and trade and seized the opportunities of the moment to make a fortune, the greatest of them dominating a whole province, the next greatest dominating a district, and the smallest dominating a village, but they are too numerous to be described here.

Thrift and hard work are without doubt the proper way to gain a livelihood. And yet it will be found that rich men have invariably employed some unusual scheme or method to get to the top. Ploughing the fields is a rather crude way to make a living, and yet Qin Yang did so well at it that he became the richest man in his province. Robbing graves is a criminal offence, but Tian Shu got his start by doing it. Gambling is a wicked pastime, but Huan Fa used it to acquire a fortune. Most fine young men would despise the thought of travelling around peddling goods, yet Yong Lecheng got rich that way. Many people would consider trading in fats a disgraceful line of business, but Yong Bo made 1,000 catties of gold at it. Vending syrups is a petty occupation, but the Zhang family acquired 10,000,000 cash that way. It takes little skill to sharpen knives, but because the Zhi family didn't mind doing it, they could eat the best of everything. Dealing in dried sheep stomachs seems like an insignificant enough trade, but thanks to it the Zhuo family went around with a mounted retinue. The calling of a horse doctor is a rather ignominious profession, but it enabled Zhang Li to own a house so large that he had to strike a bell to summon the servants. All of these men got where they did because of their devotion and singleness of purpose.

From this we may see that there is no fixed road to wealth, and money has no permanent master. It finds its way to the man of ability like the spokes of a wheel converging upon the hub, and from the hands of the worthless it falls like shattered tiles. A family with 1,000 catties of gold may stand side by side with the lord of a city; the man with 100,000,000 cash may enjoy the pleasures of a king. Rich men such as these deserve to be called the "untitled nobility", do they not?

FINDING LIST OF CHAPTERS OF THE *SHI JI*

Basic Annals (*SJ* 1-12)

SJ 1-6	Omitted
SJ 7	Vol. I, Part II
SJ 8	Vol. I, Part III
SJ 9	Vol. I, Part VII
SJ 10	Vol. I, Part VII
SJ 11	Vol. I, Part VII
SJ 12	Vol. I, Part VII

Chronological Tables, Introductions (*SJ* 13-22)

SJ 13-15	Omitted
SJ 16	Vol. I, Part III
SJ 17	Vol. I, Part X
SJ 18	Vol. I, Part X
SJ 19	Vol. I, Part X
SJ 20	Vol. II, Part II
SJ 21-22	Omitted

Treatises (*SJ* 23-30)

SJ 23-27	Omitted
SJ 28	Vol. II, Part I
SJ 29	Vol. II, Part I
SJ 30	Vol. II, Part I

Hereditary Houses (*SJ* 31-60)

SJ 31-47	Omitted
SJ 48	Vol. I, Part I
SJ 49	Vol. I, Part VIII
SJ 50	Vol. I, Part IX
SJ 51	Vol. I, Part IX
SJ 52	Vol. I, Part IX
SJ 53	Vol. I, Part IV
SJ 54	Vol. I, Part IX
SJ 55	Vol. I, Part IV
SJ 56	Vol. I, Part IV
SJ 57	Vol. I, Part IX
SJ 58	Vol. I, Part IX
SJ 59	Vol. I, Part IX
SJ 60	Omitted

Biographies and Accounts of Foreign Peoples (*SJ* 61-130)

SJ 61-83	Omitted
SJ 84	Vol. I, Part XI
SJ 85-88	Omitted
SJ 89	Vol. I, Part V
SJ 90	Vol. I, Part V
SJ 91	Vol. I, Part V
SJ 92	Vol. I, Part V
SJ 93	Vol. I, Part V
SJ 94	Vol. I, Part V
SJ 95	Vol. I, Part VI
SJ 96	Vol. I, Part VI
SJ 97	Vol. I, Part VI
SJ 98	Vol. I, Part VI
SJ 99	Vol. I, Part VI
SJ 100	Vol. I, Part VI
SJ 101	Vol. I, Part XI
SJ 102	Vol. I, Part XI
SJ 103	Vol. I, Part XI
SJ 104	Vol. I, Part XI
SJ 105	Omitted
SJ 106	Vol. I, Part X
SJ 107	Vol. II, Part II
SJ 108	Vol. II, Part II
SJ 109	Vol. II, Part II
SJ 110	Vol. II, Part II
SJ 111	Vol. II, Part II
SJ 112	Vol. II, Part II

SJ 113	Vol. II, Part II	*SJ* 122	Vol. II, Part IV
SJ 114	Vol. II, Part II	*SJ* 123	Vol. II, Part II
SJ 115	Vol. II, Part II	*SJ* 124	Vol. II, Part IV
SJ 116	Vol. II, Part II	*SJ* 125	Vol. II, Part IV
SJ 117	Vol. II, Part II	*SJ* 126	Omitted
SJ 118	Vol. II, Part III	*SJ* 127	Vol. II, Part IV
SJ 119	Vol. II, Part IV	*SJ* 128	Omitted
SJ 120	Vol. II, Part II	*SJ* 129	Vol. II, Part IV
SJ 121	Vol. II, Part IV	*SJ* 130	Omitted

INDEX

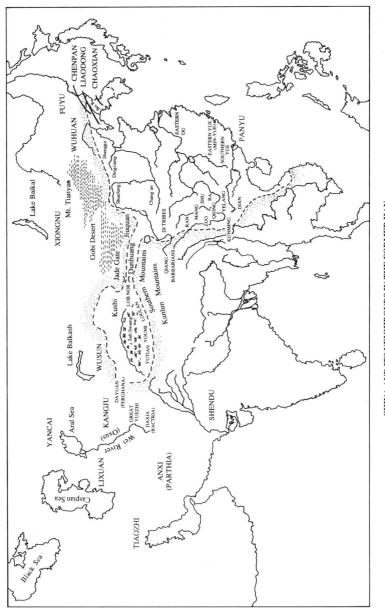

CHINA AND ITS NEIGHBOURS IN THE FORMER HAN

Based on Yanai Watari, *Tōyō dokushi chizu* (Tokyo, Fuzambō, 1931), map 7. The dotted line indicates the extent of Han power under Emperor Wu. Names of countries and bodies of water not mentioned by Sima Qian and therefore probably unknown to him do not appear on this map. There is some doubt as to which part of India was meant by the Chinese name "Shendu".